Melodious Guile ᨠ

Melodious Guile

FICTIVE PATTERN IN POETIC LANGUAGE

John Hollander

YALE UNIVERSITY PRESS

NEW HAVEN AND LONDON

Designed by Nancy Ovedovitz and set in Galliard type by
Brevis Press, Bethany, Connecticut. Printed in the United
States of America by Murray Printing Co., Westford,
Massachusetts.

Library of Congress Cataloging-in-Publication Data

Hollander, John.
Melodious guile : fictive pattern in poetic language / John
Hollander.
   p.   cm.
"Some of these essays originally appeared, often in different
form, in other places"—Pref.
   Bibliography: p.
   Includes index.
   ISBN 0–300–04293–0 (alk. paper)
   1. English poetry—History and criticism.   2. English
language—Versification.   3. Poetics.   I. Title.
PR508.V45H59   1988
821'.009—dc19   *AAX3935*   88–10080
                                          CIP

The paper in this book meets the guidelines for permanence
and durability of the Committee on Production Guidelines
for Book Longevity of the Council on Library Resources.

10   9   8   7   6   5   4   3   2   1

For J. D. McClatchy and Alfred Corn

Contents 🙐

Preface 🙠

In my earlier *Vision and Resonance* I found it helpful to arrange some observations on several aspects of poetic form with respect to the figures of music and picture. Notwithstanding the range of problems this helped me to consider, after a decade it seemed to me that I had been treating poetic pattern—whether of deep or surface structure—variously as a kind of incantation or charm for summoning up the spirit of fiction, or as a frame or loom on which its fabrication is executed. The fictive character of form itself had remained unexamined, and in the following essays I try to delineate that character. This time my implements are rhetorical. In writing of how variously poems tell ancillary but crucial tales about their own formal elements—tales about what they mean, of what is to be made of, as well as with, them—I shall argue that poems trope their own schemes, allegorize their own arrangements. Because I move directly into this matter in the opening essay, there is no need for further preliminaries here.

I should add only this: Many of the observations and modes of framing them in these pages arose, in nothing like expository form, in poems of my own written long before the essays in question. The latter now seem to me at moments to have been written to explain, to myself as well as to others, what I had been up to in the poems all along. I have therefore taken the unusual step of reprinting a few of them in an appendix, with brief glosses on their role in the genesis of this book.

A number of acknowledgments are in order. My greatest debts are to Angus Fletcher, who read the whole manuscript of this book and made some crucial suggestions, and to David Bromwich and Richard Poirier, who went over portions of it in considerable detail and with devoted and responsible attention. Richard Strier and the seminar in literary theory at the University of Chicago submitted some of these pages to profound interrogation, in which they were joined by Stanley Cavell, to whom my debt over the years has been immeasurable. The graduate students in my seminar in poetics at

Yale a few years ago helped me to formulate a number of important questions. For particular suggestions, discussion, and comment I am delightedly beholden to Eleanor Cook, Susan Edmonds, Harry Frankfort, Kenneth Gross, Karen Hanson, Nicholas Howe, Herbert Marks, Edward Mendelson, Ronald Paulson, Roger Poole, Joan Richardson, Pamela Schirmeister, Heinrich von Staden, and James Thorne. Ellen Graham's patience and encouragement were invaluable, as always. I owe a particular debt to Lawrence Kenney for his careful and most intelligent copy-editing. John Watkins prepared the index, with skill and dispatch.

Some of these essays originally appeared, often in different form, in other places. Chapters 2, 3, and 4 were first given as the Glasgow lectures at Washington and Lee University in the spring of 1983 and were published in *Shenandoah* 34.3 later that year. A shorter version of chapter 7 appeared in *Lyric Poetry: Beyond New Criticism,* ed. Chaviva Hošek and Patricia Parker (Ithaca, 1985). Chapter 8 was included in *Cannibals, Witches and Divorce,* ed. Marjorie L. Garber (Baltimore, 1986). Chapter 9 first came out in *On Poetry and Poetics,* ed. Richard Waswo (Swiss Papers in English Language and Literature 2, Tübingen, 1965), and chapter 10 in *The Linguistics of Writing,* ed. Nigel Fabb, Derek Attridge, et al. (Manchester, 1987). Chapter 12, although hitherto unpublished, contains a few pages from some remarks on Stanley Cavell that appeared in *Critical Inquiry.* Chapter 11, also unpublished, was expanded and rewritten from some remarks made at one of the Lionel Trilling Seminars at Columbia University. In all cases, I am grateful to the editors and publishers for allowing me to reprint.

I should also like to thank Random House and Edward Mendelson, as well as Faber and Faber, Ltd., for permission to reprint "'O, where are you going?' said reader to rider" from W. H. Auden's *Collected Poems* © 1976. Harper and Row and William Collins Sons and Co. allowed me to reprint a passage from Lee M. Capel's translation of Kierkegaard's *The Concept of Irony.* For my own poetry quoted in the Appendix, I acknowledge permission from Atheneum Publishers to reprint "Examples," from *Tales Told of the Fathers* (New York, 1975) and "Refrains" from *Powers of Thirteen* (New York, 1983); and from the Johns Hopkins University Press for "Others Who Have Lived in This Room" from *In Time and Place* (Baltimore, 1986).

Finally, I should like to thank the Rockefeller Foundation's Bellagio Study and Conference Center for a stay at Villa Serbelloni which enabled me to complete this book.

Woodbridge, Connecticut
November 1987

1 🙼

Turnings and Fashionings

That the matter of poetry is metaphor and not pattern will underlie the
concerns and guide the explorations of this book. But that the energies of
patterning are necessary to poetic representations is undeniable. Poets,
straight-talking in purportedly nonpoetic discourse about poetry, can often
misrepresent the connections between necessary (but insufficient) condition—the matter of verse—and ultimate concern—the matter of fiction.
And yet what they say about this parabolically in their poetry itself continually illuminates the relation of those two kinds of disturbance in the flow
of more usual discourse. These are the patterns made by curious and ordinarily irrelevant arrangements—of words, sublexical and suprasegmental
linguistic sounds, syntactic schemes, and graphic elements, on the one hand,
and twistings or turnings of sense and reference of words and utterances on
the other. The sixteenth-century English rhetorician Abraham Fraunce, following a tradition descending from Aristotle and Quintilian, distinguished
between "Tropes, or turnings" and "Figures, or fashionings."[1] It has been
more common in English to use the word *metaphor* generally to apply to all
sorts of semantic turnings. Thus Robert Frost in "The Constant Symbol"
asserts that poetry "is metaphor, saying one thing and meaning another,
saying one thing in terms of another, the pleasure of ulteriority." Frost implicitly distinguishes between good writing with metaphors occurring in it
and writing that is metaphorical writing per se: not literal writing, bills of
lading, legal briefs, letters home, news or feature stories, propagandas of
the multitudes of faiths, investigations into the nature of beauty or evil, or
into the behavior of doves or certain gases or the distribution of primes, or
proofs of the existence of God, but writing *as if*—as if any of those or indeed
anything.

   To use the word *metaphor* to cover all tropes or turnings has become
conventional following Aristotle, who stipulates that he will use the term

2 Turnings and Fashionings

collectively[2] (a later rhetorician might have added *synecdochically*) for what we now distinguish as metaphor, metonymy, synecdoche, irony, etc. This has been particularly the case in English; modern Continental rhetoric has tended to follow Quintilian in using the general term *trope* to cover the range of whatever figures the varying taxonomies of different rhetoricians would distinguish. I shall do so in these pages.

Frost's use of the last word, "ulteriority," however, raises another question. It is almost self-descriptive. As a strong Latinist, Frost felt the force of *ultus*—like the Greek *meta*, in its sense of *beyond*, transcendentally as well as spatially—inhering in *ulterior*. As a strong Miltonist, he played upon the modern connotations of *underhandedness*, of less than candid argumentation, with regard to its extended and most common sense: "going beyond what is openly said or shown, and esp. what is proper" (*Webster's New Collegiate Dictionary*). If "lying beyond the immediate point" has sunk, in common parlance, to "lying *below* it" (as frequently chained to dubiety in the commonest phrases, *ulterior purpose* or *ulterior motive*), the Miltonic sort of poet will make restitution for this fall by his or her own metaphor—in this case, by saying "beyond" in terms of "covert," by insisting on the prelapsarian meaning lurking in the fallen one.

There is something ulterior (in both senses) in the poet's use of the word in both senses. One might even call it a kind of guile. This is just the word used by the young William Butler Yeats in talking of how the mere expressions of supposedly actual feeling must become trope in poetry, here figured as a speaking seashell, "Rewording in melodious guile / Thy fretful words a little while."[3] The guiles of poetry are many and many-layered. But before the matter of their melodiousness is gone into, some more should be said about poetic fiction, and even poetry's fictions about fictiveness, whether one calls all this up in the name of Frost's "ulteriority" or Thoreau's "extravagance" or even in the transcendence which Coleridge stipulated of "symbol" as opposed to "allegory," and thus, he felt, of true poetry. (This stipulation was nicely cut by Angus Fletcher in the full title of his ever-fruitful *Allegory: The Theory of a Symbolic Mode*.) Sir Philip Sidney's often-quoted remark to the effect that poets don't *affirm* anything and therefore can't be said to lie is certainly cleverer and sounder than the positivists' extending to felonious fictions a contingent parole as "emotive language." From Sidney to Northrop Frye it has represented a good position from which to stand and deflect misdirected observations about poetry and truth. But Robert Browning's query, in *The Ring and the Book*, directed toward his own taletelling, invokes "Poetry—make believe / And the white lies it sounds like,"[4] and the question of to what degree the poet sometimes may be said to lie is implicitly raised. "White lies" are literally lies, though their badness is contingent; what "sounds like" them may be only metaphorical lying. But let us consider this for a bit.

G. C. Lichtenberg expressed in an aphorism the wish "that there might be a language in which it would be impossible to tell a falsehood, or where at least every lapse from the truth would be a lapse in grammar." I shall be arguing that poetic language is a little like this, although it might perhaps be indifferent to poets qua poets if ordinary, nonliterary discourse were indeed its own Pinocchio's nose. A modern philosopher might observe that if one couldn't get away with lying in it, it wouldn't be language. Browning's poetry that sounds like white lies raises another question about lying. According to the *New Catholic Encyclopedia,* church tradition distinguished between *mendacium iocosum*—the lie of fiction and amusement—and *mendacium officiosum*—the lie intended to gain some good or protect someone against harm. (Nonwhite lies, *mendacia perniciosa,* involve venial sin, unless their harmful effects, for example, scandal, make it mortal.) For poetry, iocosum *is* officiosum, even if the darker issues of the last, bad sort of lying are not raised. His Noble Lie aside, Plato (*Republic* 382b) has Socrates observe that the mere lie in words is a subsequent image of the *true* lie (*hōs alēthōs pseudos*) in the soul, and not entirely an unmixed falsehood. Bacon in "Of Truth" draws an analogous distinction: "It is not the lie that passes through the mind but the lie that sinketh in and settleth in it that doth the hurt," but here again, the "lie" means the falsehood that has been mistaken by the hearer for truth and not the utterance of same nor the act of so uttering. Philosophical interests in lying would engage these in such questions as whether or not an intention to deceive is a necessary component of a lie (Augustine maintaining this, Aquinas and Scotus apparently not) or whether a lie is (*a*) somehow wish-fulfilling, as in a lying boast of wealth or achievement, or (*b*) quite the opposite, as in, "No, I can't lend you the money because I'm short of cash," when the speaker is in no such want, *nor would want to be.* Lies to oneself, if they may indeed logically be said to exist,[5] could be of sort (*a*), Lying as Wish, or of sort (*b*), Lying against Shame, although whether lying to oneself can be said literally to be lying at all, or is some kind of trope of lying, is a question not to be resolved here. Another such is whether, if it were indeed lying, lying to oneself constituted *mendacium perniciosum* or not, and if so, of venial or mortal import. Certainly the lie we all appear to be telling and believing at once, the constant lie that death is not always with us, engages some kind of mortal question. And a vital one.

Poetic fictions may "sound like" white lies, and they may indeed involve some kinds of authorial and responsive modes of lying to oneself. It is tempting to employ a medieval and early Renaissance figurative term for tropes and schemes—the *colors* of rhetoric—and say that poetry is neither white lies nor transparent, literal lies but colored lies. The sixteenth-century rhetorician George Puttenham does indeed discuss lies and tropes when he talks of *Allegoria* as the figure of "false semblant, or dissimulation":

> And ye shall know that we may dissemble, I meane speake otherwise than we thinke, in earnest aswell as in sport, under covert and darke termes, and in learned and apparent speaches, in short sentences, and by longe ambage and circumstance of wordes, and finally aswell when we lye as when we tell truth. To be short every speach wrested from his owne naturall signification to another not altogether so naturall is a kinde of dissimulation, because the wordes beare contrary countenance to th'intent.[6]

From the standpoint of poetry, a literal, mundane lie of whatever quality or magnitude represents a failure of the imagination. For poetry, cleaving to the literal can be a terrible entrapment: William Carlos Williams, one of the best of modern poets to exhibit total imaginative blindness outside of his poems themselves, once remarked with regard to Nathanael West's magnificent *Miss Lonelyhearts* that the letters in it *must* be authentic. He could think of nothing better to say of them.[7] What the imagination might observe about actual letters written to authentic newspaper columns is that they *must* have been written by a cheap satirist. For poetry knows all too well how, the more sincere a literal expression of self (of feelings, beliefs, etc.) or a telling of one's own story, the more conventionalized and the more copied from a tattered paradigm it will be. Sincere self-expression is rather like vast paperback publication truly believing itself to be *samizdat*.

The masterpiece of modern criticism which connects lies with tropes is Oscar Wilde's *The Decay of Lying*. It propounds the outrageous doctrine that art invents nature, that representations create what to ignorant appearance are their originals—indeed, that the literal is a sleazy copy of the figurative and that factual truths are merely the ruined residues of living lies, or fictions. *The Importance of Being Earnest,* written soon after, provides a parabolic instance of this. Jack Worthing's fictive alter ego Ernest—the product of a set of lies of social convenience, although deeper than that which creates his friend Algernon's notional friend Bunbury—grows into reality in a complex plot, closer to *Oedipus Tyrannus* in its quest for origins, infantile mix-ups, and riddles of identity than one might suppose. The lie enables a comedy to play itself out, the marriages to occur, the puzzles to be worked through. It becomes, in fact, a redeeming and effective fiction. Only at the very end is it crowned with what is by then the mere badge of factuality: it turns out that Jack had indeed, unwittingly, been Ernest all along, had been in earnest when he sought to be most deceptive. The play is a great ancillary example to the essay's guile about the nature of fictional guile. In both of them, as in Nietzsche's not-quite-so-hilarious essay "On Truth and Lie in an Ultra-Moral Sense," the unfelt sway of trope is energetically acknowledged.

Only poetry has no such resources, nor could or would employ them. Its strength lies rather in its insistence on its own figurativeness, even if it does thereby claim a "truth" of its own. The root sense of *true* is "faithful," "loyal," and, poetry would insist, the idea of being *true to* something having general power over other meanings. The modern logical uses of *true* as a value of propositions—as "true-to-the-meanings-of-its-words" (analytic truth) or "true-to-what-is-the-case" (synthetic truth, or only the latter if the dualism is held to be untenable) are both mere instances of the matter of fidelity. So is that other sense of *consistency* (or "true-to-one's-nature-or-structure"), and likewise *essential, typical,* or *authentic* ("true-to-one's-essence, type form, etc."). Yet poetry's claim to the true truth is never argued logically or linguistically but rather in tropes of its own. "Tell the truth but tell it slant"—Emily Dickinson's famous formulation is most guileful in its "but" which encodes a strange sort of "because": a stronger claim than what looks at first like an agreeably hedged one. It is with the nature of the slanting—where, when, in and through what planes and axes, at what angles?—that poetic criticism must be concerned.

But poetry is a musical faker rather than a prosaic liar, and it is to the melodious nature of its guile that we must now turn. There are good grounds for guarding critical thought against the guiles of the very figure of melody here. One need not have shared the late Paul de Man's distaste for the metaphor of voice to agree that, at least as far as musical analogies for linguistic structures are concerned, the concept of euphony leads to interpretive error.[8] The figurative music of poetic language has often in the past been associated with a notion of "form" as opposed to something like "content" (Emerson, as will be seen, makes an analogous distinction between "meter"—here used to mean more than merely that—and "argument"). But these notions cast weak light on poetry, all the more since, once the distinction has been drawn, the point will immediately be made that poetry involves "form as content," or, for formalists like Roman Jakobson, "code as message."

Certainly the word *form* itself has been fraught with ambiguity for a long time: Erich Auerbach distinguishes between two senses of it that go back into Latinity, mere outward form, or empty *figura* (which he relates to the Greek *schēma*), and the *forma* which partakes of structure (related to *morphē*)—is one's form, as it were, one's silhouette or one's skeleton?[9] If "form" is popularly taken to be a kind of mold (or "form") into which content is poured, then one should have to say that no true poetry is "formal" in that sense. Content, being whatever form isn't, is even more unhelpfully problematic. Similarly, opposing "sound" and "sense" or "music" and "meaning" employs metaphors of the sort de Man found so rebarbative, for poetry is writing, not just songs. Texts have all sorts of inscriptional modes—being read right-left or left-right or *boustrophedon,* read from roll or codex, inscribed in "lines" of verse in various stichometric patterns or strophes, following various written or printed conventions: elements of *format,* as we would call it, are as available for patterning as those of speech-sound. Just as writing represents phonology, then, the figure of poetic "music" represents written language representing (in another system of *mimesis*) linguistic, nonmusical sound. Justus George Lawler, in his remarkable *Celestial Pantomime,* draws a hieroglyphic rather than a musical analogy when he puts so succinctly what much analytic poetics wants to work out in detail: "Poetic structure is, at the least, a kind of pictogram of poetic statement."[10] If by "poetic statement" is meant not "the statements poems make" but the slant statement, the ulterior statement, the extravagant statement of poetry, then the remark becomes even more pointed.

It is here that the rhetorician's "figures or fashionings" must be considered, although throughout this book I shall use the more usual term *scheme* to cover all those patternings of elements of language—phonological, lexical, syntactic, more broadly grammatical, and even metalinguistic (for example, orderings of nouns and adjectives in lines of verse)—which carry no meanings per se. (These as opposed, say, to interrogative word order and sentence pitch or the shift of stress between the words "per*mit*" and "*per*mit" that signifies a verb/noun difference.) Scheme results from the operations of what Jakobson called the "organized violence" that poetry performs upon the normal sound structures of a language (but its reorganizations are not confined to phonology). Instances of scheme obvious to readers of English poetry would be: various modes of versification, of inscribing language in lines with pathological spacings and unjustified right-hand margins, whether or not these would correspond to phonological patterns of stressed and/or unstressed syllables, etc.; various arrangements of rhyme, assonance, alliteration; of syntactic variation, of repetition and refrain, and so forth. Tropes or turnings can reside in a small utensil—a verb that predicates something fictional of a subject—or occupy a whole household of complex parable; so to with schemes, which can seem tiny atoms of pattern or great, complex polymers of formal structure—sonnet, irregular ode, song-form, idiosyncratic versifications, etc. Schemes alienate poetic language from other more frequent modes of discourse, but they are not inherently poetical: *A self-descriptive instance, clear and terse? / —These lines, not poetry, but merely verse.* Or: *Words arranged in chiasm are only arranged words*: no fable inheres in the very *abba* pattern of crossing.

It is possible to think of scheme not as a mold of form into which meaning is poured, but rather as a sort of crucible in which trope is cooked and which then is itself consumed in the cooking. Poets' ex cathedra stories about scheme range over deliberate, joking, or unconsciously framed evasions in the matter of how concern with pattern will conjure up the imaginative powers that create trope, denying this, puzzlingly asserting it, or whatever. One of the kinds of ulterior story told in their poems, however, will represent the relation of scheme and trope better than their own critical discourse could do. (An exemplary consideration of this is Stephen Cushman's fine study of how in one poet's practice fictions about language are more powerful and ring more true in every sense than in the errors and evasions of his critical writing about it.)[11]

One problem in dealing with the relation of scheme and trope, of pattern and metaphor, arises from a question of scale. Robert Frost can allegorize the whole notion of writing accentual-syllabic verse in an overarching sweep:

> Every single poem written regular is a symbol small or great of the way the will has to pitch into commitments deeper and deeper to a rounded conclusion and then be judged for whether any original intention it had has been strongly spent or weakly lost. . . . Strongly spent is synonymous with kept.[12]

On the other hand, great poetry is full of momentary tropes arising from local schemes. Modern criticism has often discussed such instances as matters of "sound and sense," or in terms of the way poetic language seems to "enact what it is saying." Samuel Johnson, confining his analytic observations to the narrow agenda of English couplets, called such occasions those of "representative versification." A general bias today against translating *mimesis* by "imitation" will cause Johnson's phrase to be preferred over, say, "imitative form." Alexander Pope's celebrated examples of the way in which "the sound must seem an echo to the sense"[13] argue implicitly that the devices they are brandishing will always be at work in good poetry and counterproductive (like lies producing wrong grammar) in bad. The ulterior burden of these lines is sung by the fact that in all the "good" examples (for example, "When Ajax strives, some Rock's vast weight to throw, / The Line too labours, and the Words move slow") the story being "echoed" is Homeric or Virgilian; the "bad" ones ("Though oft the ear the open vowels tire") tell only the story of their own ineptitude. But their critical paradigm has been perhaps only until recently the basis for teaching poetics in colleges, and for some of its residual appreciation.

The analysis of moments of representative versification, which can easily get lost in mazes of its own metaphor of "sound," can nonetheless pinpoint crucial moments of figuration. Those times when poetry is being most essentially (instead of merely startlingly) like itself are frequently the most deviously guileful. The guile seems to be merely "melodious," but it is in fact mucking about with the truth about our lives. To return to Pope's examples for a moment: "When Ajax strives, some Rock's vast weight to throw, / The Line too labours, and the Words move slow": We may easily observe that "some Rock's vast weight," although metrically resolved as iambs (because of our normal phrase-stress), momentarily *sounds like* two spondees, and that the second of these, "vast weight," engages the figurative use of "weight" for "syllabic stress" in seventeenth- and eighteenth-century prosodic terminology as well as for weight of meaning. The story compacted into few words here is that "even as extra weighted syllables can make the end of a line more of a burden for the heroic iambic paradigm to handle—and you can feel that happening right now—so did the heroic Ajax struggle with the rock in book 12 of the *Iliad* and so moved Homer's words. But the "Rock's vast weight" is made even "heavier" by the consonantal cluster, *ro[ck's v]ast,* itself repeating more mutedly an earlier *Aja[x str]ives,* which the reader's mouth must momentarily strive to articulate. The explicit Ajax and personified "line," on the one hand, and, on the other, the implicit but unmentioned reader (more like the absent *Ajax,* epistemologically closer to the present *line*), and the characters of the stressed-syllable-and-iambic-pattern story—all of these enter into a little ballet of analogy that is over in an instant. The ballet might have many titles, such as (1) the obvious one that the poet claims for it: *How Sound Echoes Sense*; (2) *How Great Poets Like Pope and Homer Can Turn a Reader into an Ajax for a Moment*; or (3) *How Form Frames Content (and if you ask do I mean by "frame" basic skeletal structure or rather that kind of mere clothing that paintings require on their edges to set them off properly, the answer is "Yes")*. Yet there are other such rubrics, all making further parables about what seemed a clearly glossed parable to begin with and making the poem's figure of "echo" sound like a conjurer's evasion.

Similarly with Keats's shivering bunny in *The Eve of St. Agnes*:

> St. Agnes Eve—ah, bitter chill it was!
> The owl for all his feathers was a-cold;
> The hare limped trembling through the frozen grass . . .

Here, the awkward consonantal cluster is not coped with agonistically by the reader but rather suffered, undergone; it is not just the clustering, but that, for the moment, *li[mped tr]embling* (with the near-rhyme *imped/emb* to make both limping and trembling seem more inherent in each other) tells a different tale from that of exertion. But in both cases, the "strives" and the "limped" are verbs of working through, and in both cases, the writing and the reader are caught up in the trope. Yet a larger moral envelops the others suggested in the rubrics for the Popean couplet: *Meaning, committed to a smoothness and regularity of a certain kind and for certain reasons (convention itself? language itself?), must make its way through phonological adversities.* This is an allegorical quest and can occur in a single line or phrase as well as in a whole romance, in an instant when a bit of scheme becomes opaque, calling attention to itself and asking, like a person, to be understood. The reader is told: *You're one of us. We have to do our logoanalytic work together.* The mode of transference and countertransference are one.

The subtle interruption of a larger schematic pattern is itself a common scheme, although undiagnosed and unnamed by the doctors of rhetoric. John Dryden, in an elegy for his young and none-too-accomplished poet friend John Oldham, averred that "wit will shine / Through the harsh cadence of a rugged line," but Pope, following him, turned the implicit "nevertheless" here into a case of "because" (in the same passage from *An Essay on Criticism* quoted above): "But when loud surges lash the sounding shore, / The *hoarse, rough Verse* should like the *torrent* roar." The effusive speaker of Browning's youthful *Pauline,* his poetic confidence flagging, vows, "So, I will sing as fast as fancies come; / Rudely, the verse being as the mood it paints," brandishing his Popean abilities, using the "fast as fancies" alliterative-assonant connection to emphasize an accentual regularity in order to set off the loosely conversational, flagging iambic movement in the following, "representative" line. There, the *rudely/mood* rhyme also occurs on the only two unambiguously accented syllables; its hasty story sounds like the white lie that this *mood* is *rude,* that accentual agitation is rough or rude, and moody rather than reasonable.

On the other hand, Tennyson (in "Lancelot and Elaine") makes one scheme of alliterations set up at the same time a trope and a pattern of schematic expectation whose defeat frames a new trope in the following line: "First as in fear, step after step, she stole / Down the long tower stairs, hesitating." The alliteration of "first as in fear," with its alliteratively marked stress pattern of [' ˙ ˙ '], signals nothing at all. But following it, and echoing the [' ˙ ˙ '] and the earlier alliteration, the "step after step, she stole" reinforces it with a story of phonemes walking downstairs: /st/ *after* /st/ she /st/ -*ole*. This movement, because /e/–/ow/ ("step" to "stole") suggests a lowering (in both acoustic and articulatory domains), is confirmed with the weakly enjambed "Down" that follows (*yes, she'd been walking downstairs as we'd felt*). But then the disruption of the [' ˙ ˙ '] "foot"-steps marks a slowing, and the two trochees [' ˙ ' ˙] of "hesitating" at the end—like the so-called *scazon* (limping) iambic line of Greek verse that terminated in a spondee—speak in a larger parable of motion. Stepwise movement, regularly if individually paced, dissolves into indeterminate, pause-ridden rest. Elaine, the reader, and the verse-scheme are all related through the allegory of scanning.

Sudden schematic fashionings are of all sorts. James Thomson, writing of migrating birds in his *Autumn,* asks

> Who can recount what transmigrations there
> Are annual made? what nations come and go?
> And how the living clouds on clouds arise?
> Infinite wings! till all the plume-dark air
> And white resounding shore are one wild cry . . .   [866–70]

The sight-hearing analogy is mapped onto the sky-shore relation in these lines, with sound seeming to envelop sight. And yet it is the "arise" of the birds' "clouds" that helps set up the prominence of the /ay/ phoneme of "white," "wild" and "cry" (occasional rhymes in blank verse are ad hoc schemes, sometimes transparent, sometimes framing a trope). But the phonological pattern of the last line makes the alliterating "one wild" and the assonant "wild cry" (the "wild" resounding from the previous "white") contend dubiously for spondaic prominence for an instant, until they fold up into the [$'\,'\,'$] accented package of "one wild cry." Sound and sight, braided together in written language, make a fable of how, in a sublime moment, sight will yield to sound. "White," charmed by melodious guile, becomes the "wild" of the honking of the geese (or whatever).

A beautiful quatrain of Emily Brontë's conjoins two such schemes:

> I'll walk where my own nature would be leading—
>   It vexes me to choose another guide—
> Where the grey flocks in ferny glens are feeding,
>   Where the wild wind blows on the mountainside.   ["Stanzas," ll. 13–16]

The regularity of the first two lines, maintaining the movement of the preceding quatrain ("I'll walk, but not in old heroic traces, / And not in paths of high morality") gives way to another sort of motion in the last two. Her "own nature" (in two senses of the word—her character and the rural landscape she has possessed herself of) has led the speaker to climb above the level of straight paths, and the more varied and discontinuous activities of climbing, pausing, and looking about her are figured in the kinds of rhythmic disruption in the lines of verse. The chiastic "*g*rey *f*locks in *f*erny *g*lens" is quietly undercut by the parallel clustering of /r/ and /l/, and, with the first alliterative "feeding," makes a schematic stopping-place, almost a bit of picturesque inscriptional landscape. The echoingly spondaic movement of "wild wind blows" roughens the rhythm differently. The monosyllables in the first of these are huddled together, in the second buffeted. In neither case do they walk as the previous lines do, briskly up the foothills of feeling.

Schemes of repetition are ubiquitous and various in poetry. The lyrical scheme of refrain, in which a repeated element insists upon the importance of its own reoccurrence (instead of, say, the endless repetitions of formulae, in formulaic places, in Homer), will be investigated in a subsequent chapter. I would note here that there are a host of nonce repetitive schemes, used in many ways. Anaphora can be used, for example, to unify disparate utterances in an ad hoc canon (for example, Christopher Smart's *Jubilate Agno* or dozens of Whitman's forms). Tennyson makes nonce repetition signal general stillness, linking acoustical silence and motionlessness, in "Oenone," where

> The grasshopper is silent in the grass.
> The lizard with his shadow on the stone
> Rests like a shadow, and the winds are dead.

The first line is far more effective and parabolic in its linguistic analysis than the fashionably invoked "red wheel- / barrow" and "rain- / water" of William Carlos Williams, about which he makes such guileless claims. The grass-hopper loses his *hop* morpheme in the grass to which he returns in a cyclical chiasm, as if he were *just—oh, well—grass* after all. The lizard-and-shadow rests like a shadow; and even though there is a shade here of another sense of "shadow" (an image generally, any trace of an absent substance) the return to "shadow" suggests that even the narrational, describing mind is now motionless, that in this high, Greek sunlight even simile cannot bestir it-self—"*x-y* like—oh, well—*y*." Analogously, in "The Lotus-Eaters," the re-peated "afternoon" and repeated "land," instead of another word to rhyme with its occurrence two lines back—"In the afternoon they came unto a land / In which it seemed always afternoon"—herald a coming lassitude and abandon, as if the description itself were like a whiff of the narcotic world that will claim the mariners.

Such momentary tropes set up by the use of various schemes will be looked at in detail later in this book. One taxonomic question, though, should be raised here. Some devices seem to sit on a shadowy boundary between trope and scheme—simile, for one. In most ordinary discourse, one likens, say, A to B without qualification. But in such cases one is always prepared to defend the act of comparison: "A is like B" "How? (or Why?)" "Oh, because they both are marked by X." The whole proposition "A is like B in that both are Xed" will be either true or false (A may not really have an X, etc.). The syntactically simpler, elliptical "A is like B," raising the questions of how or why, but neither answering nor acknowledging that they have been or could be asked, is another matter. Consider an epic simile of the implicit form "B. Let me tell you about B. Have you ever noticed how A does X, Y, and Z whenever O occurs? Well, that's what B was like." This is still a scheme of comparison only, and a frame for a brief expository narrative. It is when epic simile grows complex—even in Homer, and cer-tainly in Virgil, let alone Spenser and Milton—and when A and B are related in some way unavowed by the explicit grounds of the comparison, that there is an ulteriority. When such an unstated relation, C, lights up something in the background, the scheme of "A is like B" gets colored in with trope. The ellipsis, or even what we might want or not to call the suppression, of the unstated ground of comparison results in a figuration.

Poetry's guile is often most strongly at work not when hidden in silence, but in the midst of its noisiest music, drummed up by words at their most opaque. Lies depend upon the transparency of their language and shun the clouded and problematic; they want to be taken in only one sense (and perhaps when caught out, will lie about a cloudiness which is clearly not there). The guile of lies is to keep silent about what is wrong with their truth-telling. That of poems and other fictions is to bruit it about, as if the issue of truth were irrelevant, or else making such patently outrageous claims to truth as to preclude being taken seriously in that regard. Other major fictive systems retain their power over human assent by different means. Most notoriously, the Law deploys its metaphors by force of arms: In the U.S.A., Act X will be called a crime in the language of State A, but, performed identically a few feet away across a conventional boundary, it will not be a crime in State B. In the institutionalized fiction called State A's Criminal Code the metaphoric quality of *Act X as Crime AX* is denied, and the criminality held literally true, with no less transparency than the reiteration of a lie. But in any case, a refusal to subscribe to the fiction, an unwillingness to suspend disbelief, will nonetheless net the reader a jail term. It is as if State A and its Criminal Code were a different kind of human condition—like a state of sin or a state of being—from State B.

Theology, which poetry would also regard as a failed poem, has employed various combinations of the arm of the law and a net of hopes, fears, and unconcern for the truth to enforce its claims to literalness. And when one theology proclaims another to be metaphorical merely—even if (as with St. Paul on the letter and the spirit of the Law, or the Reformation on the Institution of the Church) the conceptual language insists that the literal is not the *true*—bloodshed results.

Another such case might be the scheme of oxymoron; but here, irony seems always present, and a further matter of a metalanguage about literalness and figurativeness which arises in the reading of oxymorons complicates the picture even more. Consider the oxymoron's general form $[a + non\text{-}a]$ (or $[a + anti\text{-}a]$—Shakespeare's "thou, the master-mistress of my passion" or Shirley's "See where the victor-victim bleeds" or Catullus's "Odi et amo"). Contrary to one's first puzzled feeling that $[a + non\text{-}a]$ is merely self-contradictory and can't make sense, the understanding arises that $[a]$ or $[non\text{-}a]$ or both must indeed be figurative. But if *"a"* stands for figurative *a,* then the statement $["a" + non\text{-}a]$ or $[a + "non\text{-}a"]$ or, indeed, the ultimate $["a" + "non\text{-}a"]$ will make a good deal of sense: the victor can be his own victim if the battle is a suicide, for example, and "victor" and "victim" don't mean winner and loser of a two-player, zero-sum game. The *Book of Common Prayer*'s "In the midst of life we are in death" depends upon both the "in's" being problematic, not literally spatial in either case but particularly figurative at "in death," which means "mortal, doomed surely to die." Nevertheless, the memento mori, by the very strength of its tropes of location, is a reminder of our constant suppression of its truth: "While living we're always going to die and act as if we weren't." In short, oxymoron is the essential scheme, almost reflecting a logical notation, of poetic paradox. And poetic paradox (unlike logical paradox which, if purely so, yields self-contradiction and consequent meaninglessness) always depends upon the solution of the puzzle by taking *a* or *non-a* or both, figuratively. Paradox might indeed be added to the list of four master tropes variously listed and expounded by Vico and Kenneth Burke, with expansions by Harold Bloom. Oxymoron would then be a characteristic scheme, ancillary, but impregnated with it.

One of poetry's major guiles, and one which will be explored in these pages, is of another sort, the question of which was raised with prophetic applicability by Schlegel:

> There is a kind of poetry whose essence lies in the relation between ideal and real, and which therefore, by analogy to philosophical jargon, should be called transcendental poetry. It begins as satire in the absolute difference of ideal and real, hovers in between as elegy, and ends as idyll with the absolute identity of the two. But just as we wouldn't think much of an uncritical transcendental philosophy that doesn't represent the producer along with the product and contain at the same time within the system of transcendental thoughts a description of transcendental thinking: so too this sort of poetry should unite the transcendental raw materials and preliminaries of a theory of poetic creativity—often met with in modern poets—with the artistic reflection and beautiful self-mirroring that is present in Pindar, in the lyric fragments of the Greeks, in the classical elegy, and, among the moderns, in Goethe. In all its descriptions, this poetry should describe itself, and always be simultaneously poetry and the poetry of poetry.[14]

All that I should want to add is that (*a*) all modern poetry—at least, that in English from Sidney to Spenser on—partakes of this transcendence and (*b*) a closely guarded poetic secret peers out of the last clause. Like Emily Dickinson's sly "*but* [tell it slant]," the casual "simultaneously poetry and the poetry of poetry" hides a more powerful assertion—not "and" but "*because.*" The notion that self-reflexiveness operates in despite of representation is widespread. Poetry that is "of" (about, representative of, devoted to) itself cannot be about something else, whether called "reality," "the world," "life," or whatever. A recently departed academic fad disseminated the reciprocal folly of denying that there could exist Schlegel's elliptically named "poetry," but only "the poetry of poetry." The mirror of nature, in this view, can only reflect itself. Modern poetry, at least that from the 1580s on, has had to contend with both of these modes of blindness. In the way it turns "descriptions" (as Schlegel terms them) of itself into allegories about what lies beyond it, it rejects the cloven fiction of what Harold Bloom has recently called "facticity"—blindness to trope—and deconstructive unsight—blindness to reference.

Poetry is neither a transparent window nor a pair of mirrors facing each other in an empty room. It is rather like a part-transparent, part-clouded, part-reflecting glass, variously stained and colored. Our modern trope of "mirroring" for "representing" has no doubt been affected by the vast amount of plate glass in our lives: the larger the view, the more irrelevant mirrored image we must read through to encompass it. But on the other hand, it affords more remarkable images we possess and live with, of the distant mountain, say, shadowed by a glimpse of our gazing faces less palpable to the eye than the object of their gaze. The Renaissance hemispherical mirror—Spenser's "world of glasse"—and the shadowy, mercury-backed planar glasses with which one saw *per speculum in aenigmate* ("darkly," in the KJV of St. Paul) provide the grounds for older allegories of representation. Modernity's figure is necessarily more complex, and reflections on transparency are not so easily to be separated.

Nor are representation and expression. M. H. Abrams's celebrated study of how neoclassical mimetic theories gave way to romantic expressive ones invoked the tropes of mirror and of lamp. Socrates, in Xenophon's too-little-known *Symposium,* anticipates Abrams in his use of the figures, but in a markedly different way. The tropes arise in a story. At one point in the banquet, after a dispute and loud voices of general disagreement, Socrates observes that, since all want to talk at once, all should rather sing at once, and starts singing:

> When he had done they brought a potter's wheel for a dancing-girl to spin herself around on. [Socrates disapproves of this, saying that it would be] "much more agreeable to see her in a natural easy posture than putting her handsome body into an unnatural agitation merely to imitate the motion of a wheel. Neither is it so rare to meet with surprising and wonderful sights, for here is one before our eyes, if you please to take notice of it. Why does that lamp, whose flame is pure and bright, give all the light to the room when that looking-glass gives none at all, and yet represents distinctly all objects on its surface?"[15]

The mirror-and-lamp is adduced casually, as if a "mere" example of something more worthy of intelligent attention than the trick of weak mimesis. And yet the example is ulterior in a poetical way. I shall discuss just that question of philosophical exemplification in a final chapter, but here shall point to the manner in which illuminating and reflecting are pointed out to be reciprocal tasks; the matter of mimesis has itself to be considered in a more figurative way, and the mirror-lamp pair, a mutually supplemental dyad, propounds a more instructive parable.

And so it does for us. Poetry's mirror-lamp is of a peculiar modern sort, as if it were a strange sort of electromagnetic object which needed to oscillate internally before being able to emit beams of reflective light, as if it had to mirror its own activity before being able to deal with what was outside it. The avowal of fictiveness by poetry (instead of, as I have suggested, the interdiction of the very thought of it by law or theology) generates light, transparency, color, and reflectiveness at once. Modernity finds puzzles of infinite regress, of recursion and self-reference, endlessly fascinating, but they are a maze in which the imagination gets lost. But the true center of such a maze is in fact the way out of it. Novalis's "We are close to waking when we dream of dreaming" [*Athenaeums Fragmente* 288] is itself close to the point of poetic self-description: poetry gets to be the poetry of life by successfully becoming first the poetry of poetry. And yet, knowing this about itself, it seeks by guile to hide this enigmatic condition from public gaze. Poetry's own theory of fiction is a book of reflections on transparency.

Poems talk to, and of, themselves, not to evade discourse about the rest of the world, then, but to enable it. Unsure ever as to whether its own language constitutes its body or its soul, it will nonetheless discourse of that language, in it, and by means of it, knowing that its parts of speech, perhaps its own bodily parts, are parts of a world. Its patterns of language, its fashionings of scheme, frame its tropes, one of its ways of saying—its way of sounding and sounding like—working with and on the other—its way of meaning.

It would be misleading, I think, to concentrate on too-literal instances of this, for example, metaphors which, for Paul Ricoeur, retain tinges of literal sense. These may indeed be at work in one species of wit. For instance, in a passage subtly ridiculing the French incapacity for apprehending the sublime (which Kant also noted) Laurence Sterne (in *A Sentimental Journey*) observes of someone's hyperbolic use in conversation of the example of the ocean when that of a pail of water would do, "No doubt, the ocean fills the mind with vast ideas." Here the trope of "filling the mind" (as water a container) works wittily in the use of the oceanic example when it could not in, for example, "No doubt, the night sky fills the mind with vast ideas." The ocean example fills the cliche of "filling the mind" with the living water of trope for a moment. This bit of wit that awakens a sleeping trope from its bed of literal usage is an atom of poetry: We say, "The Yankees threw away their lead in the ninth inning," and the figuration of "throwing away" an advantage or a possession is so minimal that we call it an extension and catalogue it among those of the literal. But, "Their relief pitcher threw away his lead" suddenly doubles the core literal sense with its extension and makes "throwing away" as "unnecessarily losing" more figurative by contrast. Or more obviously (and perhaps less pointedly), "He threw the game away with a wild pitch," where we might want to say that literal and figurative senses of "throw away" were being heavily punned on. This sort of thing works for one-liners, and sometimes for profound ones—the joke in *A Sentimental Journey* is about the failure of the French imagination, told with (and about) unwitting figurativeness. Similarly, the wonderfully ambiguous dash of ellipsis at the very end of that book. In reaching across (by way, he assures the reader, only of asseveration) to a lady in an adjacent bed (they have been forced by circumstances to share a room), he finds that her maid, awakened, had slipped into the narrow space between their beds, "so that when I stretch'd out my hand, I caught hold of the Fille de Chambre's——" If the maid's possessive case refers to her hand, the dash is simply standing in for a full stop, or a semicolon: the worst it might cancel is a subsequent clause. But if the dash is one of suppression, rather than perhaps inadvertent fragmentation (as if "the MS breaks off here"), then it is to be surmised that the name of the particular target of opportunity on the maid's body is being canceled. The joke here is being played on and with some of the various uses of that ubiquitous bit of eighteenth-century punctuation, but it is about sex, reticence, candor, and the entropy of suppression toward an erotic direction. Compared with these witty moves, the baseball joke is a rhetorician's example, and not about anything else.

And yet jokes can get out of hand. Ambrose Bierce, in one of those remarkable moments in *The Devil's Dictionary* when his comedian's scheme of the mock-definition becomes something else, defines *symbol* in a ringing way:

> SYMBOL, *n*. Something that is supposed to typify or stand for something else. Many symbols are mere "survivals"—things which having no longer any utility continue to exist because we have inherited the tendency to make them; as funereal urns carved on memorial monuments. They were once real urns holding the ashes of the dead. We cannot stop making them, but we can give them a name that conceals our helplessness.

Making symbols, poems, symbolic pots conceals our helplessness in the face of literal death as unsymbolic urns conceal the ashes (metamorphosed synecdoches of body, troped bones) of the dead. The carved, symbolic urns are not even solid, let alone hollow, let alone capable of literally concealing anything, even their own figurativeness. This is a poet's sort of "example," overloaded in its applicability, like one of the troped similes mentioned earlier. It makes us take the sentence containing "conceals" at its word.

But too narrow a rhetorical interpretation of the notion of literal and figurative interpenetrating will not begin to exhaust the hoard of strategies by which poetic guile, so often pretending to be merely melodious, will insinuate itself into truth. In the course of this book I examine a broader range of them, and, in general, the question of how poetry makes trope not merely with, but out of, its schemes, large and small. In brief, verse manifests schemes, but only poetry can trope them. "Representative versification," in Johnson's phrase, is always there in poetry, as part of its relevant texture, but representative representation occurs as well, not to distract discourse from its matter, but the better to focus it.

Three books that share some of my concerns here should be mentioned. Justus George Lawler's *Celestial Pantomime,* quoted from earlier, finds transcendental scheme in a magnificent variety of places in English and American poetry, pointing out familiar patterns as well as unnamed and unnoticed ones, such as augmenting and diminishing syllabic sequence in a given pattern of syntax (examples from Keats being—crescendo—"The grass, the thicket and the fruit-tree wild," where, as I would put it, the story being told is of growing and expanding growth, and—diminuendo—"The weariness, the fever and the fret," or a story of dying).[16] It is a profound and original work, although its theory of transcendence is not mine. Equally profound and original is Fred N. Robinson's study of the scheme of appositive structure in *Beowulf*.[17] Although it employs a concept of *style* which I do not engage, it seems to me in effect to be exploring a scheme which had previously seemed transparent and empty—an effect of syntactic habit, almost—showing its poetic function in, and for, the whole poem, and finally demonstrating how the expanded trope of that scheme plays an important role for a whole culture's sense of itself and its history. It is an exemplary investigation of an ulteriority hitherto unsuspected. Finally, Lee Charles Edelman's recent book on Hart Crane finds three schemes to be ubiquitous and emblematic in his poetry, both in their formal and metaphorical operations.[18] For a writer like Crane, who continually tropes linguistic term and rhetorical terminology in his poems, this is a fascinating matter. Edelman's work is exemplary, I think, in avoiding some of the injuries wrought by poststructuralist brandishing of rhetoricians' plowshares.

This book starts out with the question of the guiles of melodiousness. In subsequent chapters I explore a number of such occurrences, sometimes putting moments in poems under a rhetorical microscope, sometimes standing back in order to see a larger pattern. In three connected discussions, I consider poetry's figurations of the patterns of questions, answers, and commands. In an analysis of some sonnets on the sonnet, I look at an exemplary complex scheme, its history, its awareness of and tropes of itself, in a context of poetic parables of work, freedom, love, and death. Following this, a variety of smaller instances of troped schemes are taken up, and, after that, an extended consideration of one scheme of repetition and recurrence, the lyrical refrain, with an extended discussion of one great poet's figurative name for a famous refrain of his own. Another chapter explores one instance of a poet's favored scheme of verse, and how the primal scene of its occurrence in his work coincides strangely with that of a significant trope. Elsewhere, poetry's visionary linguistics—fictive theories of language that seem to lie implicit in certain local instances of pattern and trope—is glanced at. A slant look at the notion of fictional "character" and some reflections on the scheme of exemplification as opposed to parabolic trope, with its significance in the contention between poetry and philosophy, constitute the two final essays.

2 ☙

Questions of Poetry

Who has never asked a rhetorical question?

I must confess that, in opening up this matter in so blatantly self-descriptive a sentence, I was only following my great precursor in the study of figurative language, the Roman rhetorician Quintilian: "Quid enim tam commune," he asks at the beginning of his discussion of rhetorical questions (*Institutio Oratoria* 9.2.6) (What is more common), "quam interrogare vel percentari?" (than to ask or inquire?) We might go on, as Quintilian does, to try to distinguish between asking and interrogating (he suggests that one word implies a desire to know something, the other, a desire to prove something). Certainly we ask questions, even in the most casual and, we would argue, unrhetorical of contexts, with no desire to elicit any information. "Could you please bear with me for a moment before I start discussing poems?"—the very construction "Could you . . . ?" or "Would you . . . ?" or "Will you . . . ?" is understood as not being literal, but rather a very reticent figure of speech for commanding. "Could you bear with me . . . ?" means, "Bear with me," and yet the nonliteral use of the grammar of interrogation is one that we scarcely want to notice. Even less literal is a colloquial figure for this figurative use of "could you . . . ?"—when the nurse says, "Do you want to roll up your sleeve, please?" the last word of the utterance indicates that we would be joking, however mildly, to answer, "Not particularly." And yet, "Do you want to . . . ?" sounds as if it were asking for more interesting and more detailed information than, "Could you . . . ?"[1]

The fact is that we generally think of rhetorical questions as being those, like my opening one or, more particularly, Quintilian's (even in English translation it sounds like Latin prose), which occur in what was public discourse in antiquity or in formal writing in our own time. And yet even in the most direct and intimate discourse, asking can slip over into interrogation when a question becomes rhetorical. Thus: "Who were you in bed with last night, Sally?", when asked by a husband or lover with some interest in knowing, is a literal question (and even if the asker knows the answer already, he is still asking thereby another true question: "What will she say? Will she lie? and how?"). But with a rhetorical shift occasioned, as so often in English and so significantly for our poetry, by a shift of word stress, the question becomes something else: "Who were you in bed with *last* night, Sally?" is no longer a quest for information, but an instance of Quintilian's "desire to prove something" (arguendi gratia videtur adhiberi). In this instance, what purported to be the direct, honest answer (such as, "It was Juan; no, Juan was Thursday night. It was Pierre") would be a deliberate, nasty mistaking of intention, misprision in the highest degree. The question itself would have had the same relation to a request for information as a sarcasm to a declarative statement it purportedly framed.

But we might take our example one step further. Suppose that the same jealous (and zealous, for the words are etymologically almost twins) questioner were to ask something like this: "And who was it you were in bed with last night, Sally? Who let his hands linger impassioned for a moment at X, moved them slowly over to Y and Z while whispering all the while of A and B, then crept above you and did Alpha and then you did Beta and on to Omega?" In this case, we should say that the impulse to prove something had given literal way to another mode of figuration; whether it should turn out to be the impulse to tell a story, to create a character in a fiction (the "who" who did all these things), to intone a catalogue, to sing a kind of song, or whatever, which lay behind it, this mode of figuration would make the mere rhetorical questioning of the simple nonquery into something almost literal in *its* rhetorical innocence.

It is with the relation of the third of these questions—the long, drawn out routine—to the second that I should like to introduce the question of poetic, rather than rhetorical, questioning. Lest that very routine seem excessive and unpoetical, let me immediately cite a text which is extremely not so:

What slender youth bedewed with liquid odours
Courts thee on roses in some pleasant cave,
    Pyrrha? for whom bindst thou
    In wreaths thy golden hair,
Plain in thy neatness? O how oft shall he
On faith and changèd gods complain, and seas
    Rough with black winds and storms
    Unwonted shall admire
Who now enjoys thee credulous, all gold;
Who always vacant, always amiable
    Hopes thee; of flattering gales

> Unmindful. Hapless they
> To whom thou untried seemst fair. Me in my vowed
> Picture the sacred wall declares t'have hung
>   My dank and dropping weeds
>   To the stern god of sea.[2]

This, as many will recognize, is Horace, translated by Milton at what I take to be an early age (although some scholars do not) for the very good reason that there was some version of Pyrrha in his own life, not about whom he wished to complain, but whose relation to him he wanted at any rate to mythologize in the way of Horace to his own Miss Bad News, or whoever. The image of the ex-voto at the end of the poem, the offering of the poet's wet clothes hung up in the shrine of Neptune to thank the god for saving him from being shipwrecked in the sea of Pyrrha's voracity, makes the speaker's stance no less ambiguous; and though Milton's "courts thee" will hardly do for the force of the verb that Horace uses, "urget" (it has the urgent sense of "press," "push," "force"), there is no weakening in the representation of the youth's rude awakening to the storms of the golden girl's face when she turns nasty. He who is enjoying her "credulous, all gold" (for "te fruitur credulus aurea"), who fondly thinks her to be not only golden-haired but gold through and through, will be sadly deceived when she darkens. The slender youth who hopes that she will be always empty of other attachments, who is ignorant of the tricky winds (in the Latin, "Nescius aurea / fallacis," the deceiving gales of her temper deceptively half-punning—"aurea / aurae"—on the true gold she is only plated—or plaited—with)—who is he but the poet himself projected? "Miseri, quibus / intentata nites" (Miserable he for whom, untried yet, you glitter) becomes Milton, at least in Milton's remarkable, radically experimental, as far as prosody is concerned, translation which is really a kind of repossession of the original. Milton's own erotic fascination with beautiful hair, regardless of some Pyrrha of his own, has moved him into a figurative relation with the Horatian speaker, and perhaps far closer than that speaker to the slender youth invoked in the far from merely rhetorical question.[3]

Horace makes marvellous poetic use of figurative questioning. He can go so far in the direction he takes with Pyrrha's next victim that he composes a poem entirely in such questions. Ode 8 of book 1 frames these in a familiar pattern of taunting: "Lydia, tell me, in the name of all the gods, why you are rushing to ruin Sybaris with love . . . ?" but then goes on to pile question upon question: "Why is he afraid of the Tiber? Why doesn't he wrestle or throw the javelin any more?" Finally there comes the loaded question, the long one which itself unrolls an unpleasant simile: "Why does he skulk like Achilles, when Troy's tearful destruction neared, [hiding among the women] for fear that a man's clothing would drag him on to death and destruction?" Here, the pattern gives way to something more complex: we are invited to observe that in the comparison to Achilles, young Sybaris is not manifestly being hidden—as Achilles was by his mother—behind skirts to avoid death, but that this ridiculous parody of the heroic tale is indeed the bottom line. In a sense, the more innocently rhetorical questions have led up to the more profoundly poetic one.

On the other hand, Horace can suddenly interject a pair of questions whose answers must be supplied in order that their very interjection make any sense at all. In Ode 3 of book 2, the poet gives his friend Dellius Epicurean counsel (I quote here James Michie's beautiful English version):

> Maintain an unmoved poise in adversity;
> Likewise in luck one free of extravagant
>   Joy. Bear in mind my admonition,
>   Dellius. Whether you pass a lifetime
>
> Prostrate with gloom, or whether you celebrate
> Feast-days with choice old brands of Falernian
>   Stretched out in some green, unfrequented
>   Meadow, remember your death is certain.⁴

But here Horace asks, "Why do the pine so tall and the white poplar love to associate their branches in welcoming shade? Why does the hurrying water work to bustle in the winding stream?" The answer is, "For us, lying out on that grass in the previous stanza—all for us, so let us drink now, while we can . . . and so forth." The question of to what end the pleasant scene can exist might seem, following the certainty of death, to demand a negative answer ("It doesn't make any at all; no—to no end, like our own lives, unless you mean to the end of death"). The reader is turned interpreter here, for the answer might go either way, and only the opening of the next strophe will correct any wrong reading:

> Come, bid them bring wine, perfume and beautiful
> Rose-blooms that die too swiftly. . .

But it is the suppression of the overt answer which gives the questions their tactful poignancy; we have only to look at a cruder, rhetorical power play by Milton's Comus, attempting to seduce the virgin Lady by a fallacious argument from design:

> Wherefore did Nature pour her bounties forth
> With such a full and unwithdrawing hand,
> Covering the earth with odors, fruits and flocks,
> Thronging the seas with spawn innumerable,
> But all to please and sate the curious taste?   [ll. 710–14]

This slams its answer home with some of the same obtuseness with which it perverts Epicureanism. Comus is a magician and a rhetorician, but he is

no poet. And yet only a great poet could have made him so seriously unpoetical.

I want to postpone until the next chapter the question of how poems
answer their own questions, save to observe briefly that even the most dead-
eningly answered rhetorical questions may have more to them than they
immediately reveal. I suppose that nothing could represent a textbook case
of the rhetorical, rather than the poetical, question more clearly than the
opening of Catullus's first poem, the preface to his whole book: "To whom
do I give my smart new little book, polished with dry pumice-stone? To
you, Cornelius, for you used to think well of my trifles long ago." But is
this really so cut-and-dried a matter of, say, overhearing the poet talking to
himself—internalizing the empty formula "Which one shall we . . . ?" "Why,
X!"—or even playing with it, as when we introduce a child to rhetorical
questioning by making a game out of it? I ask this rhetorically because I'm
not sure: what kind of very crucial question would it be for a poet to ask
about presentation, dedication, ascription of love and authority? The rhetoricity of the question suggests that it was to be—*everyone* knew it was to
be—Cornelius Nepos all along; and yet, as the poem continues, another
matter unfolds, one which points up the choice more sharply: "[for you
used to think well of my trifles long ago] when you alone in Italy were bold
enough to undertake a history of the whole world, in three learned and, by
Jupiter, laboriously written volumes. So have this little book for your own,
for whatever it's worth, and may it, O my virgin patroness, outlast more
than a century." It is clear that Cornelius Nepos as historian of the *aevum,*
the whole age of the world, rather than merely as admirer of earlier *nugae,*
or little poems, is the dedicatee. And it is clear that the modest bid for
eternity that is purportedly being made at the end is no modest one at all.
The scope of Cornelius's history is slyly being filched by the little book of
love poems, witty scurrilities, epyllia, and so forth which make up Catullus's
book. "Cui dono lepidum nevum libellum?" is not really, then, "Cui
dono?"—"to whom shall I give this book?"—but rather "with what in
mind? What kind of claim or statement of intention is going to be boot-
legged into this apparently merely fond and self-effacing protocol?" It is
only the annotation of a secondary dependent clause that reveals what the
question was really about. But more of the nature of answers like this later
on.

Opening questions in poetry can carry considerable figurative weight. At
the very least, they may presuppose not the usual empty answer (for example, "Yes" or "No" or "Nobody" or "Everybody" or the like), but rather
some hedged response, like "You may well ask! There are great problems
implicit in putting it that way. Let's see what they are." (Despite its expository format, this is far from being a philosophical move.) At best, the
opening question may implicitly be making inquiry within a group of poems

with which the one just commencing is to be associated. I think of Shakespeare's sonnets in this way: of 154 sonnets, 30, or over 20 percent, commence with a question; moreover, out of a total of 88 questions asked in the sonnets, over 34 percent are initial ones. Whether apparently innocently formulaic ("Shall I compare thee to a summer's day?" would be merely a rhetorical question doing the work of a rubric—for example, "this poem works out a fair weather–fair temperament conceit: here goes . . .") or far more complex, the questioning mode is central to their very dramatic mode of discourse. An occasional opening question with very high stakes riding on the answer can be quite startling, as with Sonnet 53: "What is your substance, whereof are you made, / That millions of strange shadows on you tend?" Here the matter is not only that of Platonist vocabulary, of "shadow" or appearance vs. "substance" or formal reality, coming up against ordinary usage, in which the particular would be substantial, and the immutable idea or form a mere conceptual shadow.[5] The poet is asking of one of his central fictions (the young man) what he, as fiction, is made up of, why he must entail so much else in the way of fictions; it is a question which comes close to breaking the frame of the whole poem, and if ever a moment of philosophical quibble should generate such a dance at the edge of doubt (the *aporia* of the rhetoricians), surely this one is most appropriate.

A rhetorical analysis of the questions in Shakespeare's sonnets could occupy a vast amount of scrutiny. I shall only observe here that the 30 percent of them which commence with questions should be contrasted with the analogous figures for Petrarch (only 6 out of 328 sonnets in the *Rime Sparsi,* or less than 2 percent); for Samuel Daniel, the sonnets of whose *Delia* are in some ways rhetorically closest to Shakespeare's (none out of 50); for Sidney's *Astrophel and Stella* (5 out of 108, or 4 percent); or for Spenser's *Amoretti* (11 out of 89, or slightly over 12 percent). It is clearly the Shakespearean sonnet, then, which deploys the interrogative opening, and it is surprising that it is Spenser's sonnets, which are by tradition the least "dramatic" of all these cycles, which begin to approach Shakespeare's in their querying openings.[6]

But I shall proceed to a sonnet written the year after the quarto volume of Shakespeare's sonnets was published in 1609. A young man of seventeen, soon after he had arrived at Cambridge, writes a letter to his mother in which he piously declares his intention not to write love poetry. He encloses two sonnets, in which he declares his "resolution to be that my poor abilities in poetry shall be all and ever consecrated to God's glory."

Here is the first of them. It is all, *all,* questions:

My God, where is that ancient heat towards Thee
  Wherewith whole shoals of martyrs once did burn,
  Besides their other flames? Doth poetry

> Wear Venus' livery? only serve her turn?
> Why are not sonnets made of Thee, and lays
>   Upon Thine altar burnt? Cannot Thy love
> Heighten a spirit to sound out Thy praise
>   As well as any she? Cannot Thy Dove
>
> Outstrip their Cupid easily in flight?
>   Or, since Thy ways are deep and still the same,
>   Will not a verse run smooth that bears Thy name?
> Why doth that fire, which by Thy power and might
>   Each breast does feel, no braver fuel choose
>   Than that which one day worms may chance refuse?

The opening question—"Where has it gone, that religious version of erotic passion which is itself called a metaphorical fire in all of the love poetry since Sappho?"—seems only half-aware of what it is indeed asking. Any question of this "Where is it now?" sort—touching on what medievalists call the topos of *ubi sunt,* which we shall consider shortly—calls for the usual rhetorical answer: "Nowhere. Not any more." But the next question, "Doth poetry / Wear Venus' livery? only serve her turn?" is tougher; the very figure of fire with which the poem starts is half-borrowed from Venus's livery (indeed, even the literal flames of martyrdom had been in hock to her in some of Donne's poems with which the young poet in question was well acquainted). It is also, this fire-trope, an emanation of something more personal and immediately occasional: the young man in question—it was George Herbert—wrote to his mother as follows: "I fear the heat of my late ague hath dried up those springs by which, scholars say, the Muses use to take up their habitation. However, I need not their help to reprove the vanity of these many love poems that are daily writ and consecrated to Venus." The heat of the fever from which he has recently recovered—and so he dutifully reports to his mother—dries up the figurative counterparts in the poet of those fountains, Hippocrene and Castalia, sacred to the Muses. This figurative fire works its way through the sonnet and emerges astonishingly at the end. "Doth poetry / Wear Venus' livery?" Well, yes and no; most poets' work does, and the young Herbert wants his own not to. But he would be struggling with Venus's livery all his poetic life, propounding a one-sided dialogue with God which strove to divest itself of just the rhetorical garments it nonetheless needed to don. He would also never stop asking questions in poems, asking questions *of* those same poems, asking questions about his very mode of interrogation. The 1610 sonnet might be considered a kind of formal experiment—like the sonnet from *The Temple* later on called "Prayer," which is all predicates, the copular verb being understood throughout, the subject being the word of the title, and the last and closing predicate, indeed, being grammatically self-descriptive for the whole poem: "something understood." But it is also a case of poetic, rather than rhetorical, self-questioning, and each of the answers could and perhaps should be a book. Some of these books would be literary and cultural history, but some would have to be philosophically speculative. The last one is almost helpless in its unanswerableness, and even to consider it a rhetorical question is to limit its scope. From an almost formulaic "Why" question at the beginning, through a group of "yes-no" questions introduced by "can't" and "won't," and a fairly explainable "Why," the poem comes down to a "Why" of a thunderingly ineffable sort. The question of why human bodies have to embody human life and thereby human devotion is not merely a masked grammatical optative, an "Oh, that this were not so," but a more searching one.[7]

Questions that occur in poems that talk directly to themselves or to God or back to the poet writing them touch on deep and sometimes dark matters, and on realms of what can or cannot be said, or be borne to be said. Literary texts do indeed propound questions of staggering import, even though they may seem to be casually rhetorical, opening up a matter for future discourse. The locus classicus of this may be the opening sentence of Francis Bacon's essay "Of Truth."

"What is truth?" asked jesting Pilate and did not stay for an answer. As Bacon puts it, this is one of the classics of rhetorical questioning, in that its greater strength, or point (ever the obvious alternative: "Who knows what truth really is?") is palpable. But what is a question like that anyway? The general form of even the literal question, "What is X?" cannot have a single correct answer, unless we are playing by tournament rules, which would have specified in advance what sort of answer would be appropriate. The question seems to request an essence of an entity, or the definition of a word, or a distinguishing feature of something. Yet in any unique milieu, the distinguishing feature will be different (in the dark, say, or in terror, in lust, in a purple light, from behind, in plan, in elevation). And the essence, as Plato reminds us ad nauseam, is never to be grasped by what in us distinguishes among features anyway. The assertion, then, that any of the candidates for a distinguishing feature is canonical, is an interpretive and possibly a poetic act.[8]

"What *is* truth?"—an apparently street-wise response might be, "It depends on what you mean by 'truth,'" but a more philosophically handy one might be, "It depends on what you mean by 'what is . . . ?'" These are matters for the logic of questioning, for the laying-down of whatever ground rules by which the tournament of certainty is going to be playing games that can be clearly won or lost. The rhetoric of questioning is a different matter. But here I mean to invoke not the rhetoric of the classical law court or forum, the taxonomic analysis of linguistic persuasion which would enable us to convict X or honor Y, but rather the troped, internalized rhetoric of poetry. Classical rhetoric became in the Renaissance a metaphor for what it had originally been, a theory of poetry instead of a manual of oratorical power. In poetic rhetoric, *we are convinced by tropes of logos, pathos, and ethos—of meaning, feeling, and authority—masquerading as one another,* not to vote against Catiline, say, but to grant rightness to a fiction or an interpretation, to confer on it, if only momentarily, the truth of scripture—not a matter of illusion, but of belief. In this sense, Plato was right: poetry, the better it is, is more and more of a philosophical disaster, although for different reasons than he might have given. For poetry can never be quite logically serious in the way in which it asks questions. It always means, as we have already begun to see, at best something else by the question it is asking. Its very mode of interrogation is itself a trope.

In the case of the famous opening of Bacon's essay "Of Truth," the question is an invitation to himself and a reader to essay, to try, a walk about what we would today—with some philosophical confusion—call a subject (to remove that confusion, we should probably have to call it an object). Bacon does not call his essay "About Truth," although that preposition is the one we use, and almost think with, in considering the notion of content, or "subject matter." The Greek preposition *peri* (around), the Latin *de* (of), German *um* (around, about), but also *über* (over), all suggest different stances of the writing with respect to the subject. In any case, the question "What is X?" is frequently a poetic invocation, an opening chant like the imperative "Sing, Muse . . ." (which we will consider later on), a clearing of the discursive way for a consideration of X, for being about X. Bacon triumphantly displaces the question onto the proverbial remark of Pilate (who not only jests, but who washes his hands of the matter of truth as well as, according to Matthew, the figurative trace of blood). This allows him to plunge into a trial or essay of a certain kind of free-ranging seriousness in writing, a true seriousness called forth by nothing save authorial will and, in Bacon's case, Montaigne and his embodiment of that will for English seventeenth-century prose.

Bacon is as much poet as philosopher, and certainly his citation of Pilate's question is poetic to the degree that there is some fruitful enigma in his raising of it. There are certainly philosophical questions—indeed, philosophy however we may define it starts with, or perhaps even in, questioning. But it is questioning in one of a number of kinds of logical good faith. Philosophical questions start where matters of accessible fact, as we know, give way, but they are pursued with the intention of literally answering them. "Is there anything I can be absolutely certain of?" "Why is there anything at all, rather than just nothing?" "Is there any manifestation of art or nature which everyone who is to be taken seriously ought to admire purely for itself?" "How can I know whether machines really think?" "How ought the word 'ought' be used in statements about human actions?" "What really is there, and what is only fairy tales told by philosophers' mistakes?" These

have all been (and some still are) philosophical questions; and even if philosophizing may lead to abandoning the question, or to choosing to ask
another, quite openly, in its place, the literal integrity of the question is
always presumed and honored. Sometimes abandoned philosophical questions, like used-up scientific models, become poetic matters (as, too, from
the seventeenth century on, tools, objects, texts, even institutions abandoned by adults entered the world of childhood as plaything). Consider,
for example, the overall rhetorical point of asking, today, "Where did everything start from?" "What was there before there was anything else?" (or St.
Augustine's) "What is time?" These can be seen as requests for poetry, as
openings for some kind of fiction or parable that will answer a weird version
of what such questions mean, just as they can lead to bad writing by cos-
mologists. On the other hand, with respect to either of these, the question
"What could such a question mean?" is still a request for philosophy, and
not for poetry.

Perhaps there should be noted here the matter of questioning in the realm
of Socratic irony. Are Socrates' questions merely rhetorical or poetic? Is he,
as a Shakespearean or modern dramatic character, in quest not so much of
a right or good answer but merely an immediately useful one? Does he seek
to discover, or merely uncover, truth through dialectic? Does the writer
Plato thereby question himself? Perhaps the incessant return of Socrates'
questioning, its basic structural quality, gives it a schematic rather than a
more deeply figurative role. All of these problems are intensified in the
dialogue of the modern drama and novel. William Blake's Idiot Questioner
represents a satirical view of Socratic questioning, among other things.
Identified with the inimical Spectre within every man, he is

> the idiot Questioner who is always questioning,
> But never capable of answering; who sits with a sly grin
> Silent plotting when to question, like a thief in a cave;
> Who publishes doubt and calls it knowledge; whose Science is Despair,
> Whose pretence to knowledge is Envy, whose whole Science is
> To destroy the wisdom of ages to gratify ravenous Envy.[9]

It is perhaps to the moral and philosophical credit of a greater kind of
questioner even than Nietzsche that we can think of Wittgenstein recogniz-
ing this figure and being able to raise the further question of what sort of
image of himself it might possibly be.

And yet some of the questions we have seen arise in poems seem to be
philosophical ones that have gone off, like soured milk, or are being played
with, instead of being used appropriately, or whatever. "How *could* anything
originate out of its opposite? For example, truth out of error? or the Will
to Truth out of the will to deception?" asks Nietzsche in the mock-tones of
what he takes to be bad philosophy. A few lines earlier, in the opening

paragraph of *Beyond Good and Evil,* Nietzsche explores the no-man's-land between philosophical and poetic questioning, wandering off, I should have to claim, into undisputed territory at the very end:

> Granted that we want the truth: *why not rather* untruth? And uncertainty? Even ignorance? The problem of the value of truth presented itself before us—or was it we who presented ourselves before the problem? Which of us is the Oedipus here? Which the Sphinx? It would seem to be a rendezvous of questions and notes of interrogation.[10]

I wonder whether that rendezvous is not taking place on certain pages of the *Philosophical Investigations,* thereby disputing the territory once more. And then I should perhaps have to ask, about the role of Wittgenstein's continual rhetoric of questioning, not "What does Wittgenstein in the *Investigations* mean by his questions?" but "What does he do with them?" And that might be an invitation to rhetorical analysis, to literary criticism, as much as to philosophizing. But the questions, whatever is done with them, are always to be taken literally, even if the very act of "taking literally" certain matters that are difficult to handle becomes part of the reason for asking the questions in the first place.[11]

And yet Nietzsche's rendezvous of literal and figurative questioning remains, after all, in the semifurtive world of *alibi* (literally, "elsewhere"), in that peculiar displacement of question, of not wanting a right answer, which poetry is always so variously enacting. Or rather, of wanting some answer that would be somehow better than a literally correct one. Harold Bloom, in some observations on Wallace Stevens's "Le Monocle de Mon Oncle," distinguishes between the effects of two adjacent questions in the poem by calling the first one, "Alas, have all the barbers died in vain / That not one curl in nature has survived?", a rhetorical question, specifying an implicit assent.[12] The second one, immediately following it in the poem, begins with an understood "Then yet . . .": "Why, without pity on these studious ghosts / Do you come dripping in your hair from sleep?" Bloom correctly distinguishes it as "open." But "why" is always more open, somehow, than "how," unless the latter is used purely rhetorically, that is, as part of a "how can it be that . . . ?" question flourished to insist on an impossibility. The most poetic answer possible for the first rhetorical question would be, "Well, yes and no"; the second would, in any case, require a complex fiction to answer it (indeed, whether it had been literally or figuratively asked of an already established fiction).

A modern rhetorician whose theory is purely classical nonetheless maintains that "by inducing the audience to make the appropriate response, the rhetorical question can often be more effective as a persuasive device than a direct assertion would be."[13]

But actual readers of poems, putative, fictional readers of poems projected by the texts themselves, poets as readers of their own poems by which their words come back to them with "a certain alienated majesty" (as Emerson put it) are not strictly speaking audiences, but rather tropes of audiences, and the very question of what is "appropriate response" is always being called into poetic question. This is obviously true of questioning one's own self; certainly there is something very figurative, as I observed earlier, about Wittgenstein's continuing internalization of Socratic questioning, and whatever audience overhears us asking, say, "Isn't this a rhetorical question?" or even "Isn't this rhetorical question I'm now asking self-descriptive?" is not simply being persuaded to produce the appropriate response.

Renaissance rhetoricians think more as poets do. George Puttenham, in *The Arte of English Poesie,* makes the classical point cited above, but by the very example it employs (the first of several) opens up the mode of questioning. "There is a kinde of figurative speach when we aske many questions and looke for none answere, speaking indeed by interrogation, which we might as well say by affirmation. This figure I call the *Questioner* or inquisitive, as When *Medea* excusing her great crueltie used in the murder of her owne children which she had by Jason, said:

Was I able to make them I praie you tell,
And am I not able to marre them all aswell?"[14]

But, of course, Jason made the children too, and it is in the very begging of that question that Medea's becomes ironic and self-deconstructing, as it were. "Begging the question," or the logicians' *petitio principii,* is a matter of assuming that some principle was assumed in the begging—in the case just mentioned, that principle would be the parthenogenesis of the children. Seldom is a simple logical error a poetic device, but in a complex enough rhetorical situation, it can very well be. In any event, the begged question tends to generate what we should usually classify as dramatic irony, in which a speaker is clearly perceived by an audience—or a reader, or some figure of audience—not to understand the meaning of the question he or she has just asked. Dramatic irony exists at a more exalted poetic height than do hyperbole and sarcasm, whose inflations and reversals of the literal themselves lie perilously close to being mere variants of principal meanings. But it remains a trope closer to persuasive, oratorical rhetoric than to the more open modes of poetic question.

At this point I should say a word about exemplary questions, about questions which, we are told, some sage asked of himself with the implication that we all ought to do likewise. The remarkable sequence of three questions asked, according to Talmudic tradition,[15] of himself by Rabbi Hillel in the first century B.C. has a powerful build to it; the first enacts a straightforward critique of a religiosity which would deny the dignity of the self, the second undercuts a complacent misconstruction of the meaning of the first, and the third moves beyond the dialectic of self and other into ethical immediacy: "If I am not for myself, who will be for me? If I am only for myself, what am I? If not now, when?" It will also be observed that the questions move toward greater rhetorical openness: "Who will be for me?"—"Nobody; but if *you* are, anyone can and will be." "What am I?"—"Well, the only debate could be about whether you were slightly less than, or merely at the bottom of being, human. In any event, you wouldn't be too much." Then the last one closes up again: "When?" "Well, never." And yet the openness of the suppressed part, the action not named which must be performed now or never, is staggering. We are left with a host of other questions, continually asking themselves in our memory, and the mandate of the sage's anecdote is to keep faith with our own sagacity.

Rabbi Hillel's implied generations upon generations of students make up one kind of figurative audience; Medea's listeners are, by being theatrical listeners, only obliquely her "audience" in the rhetoricians' sense; the figurative voice in poems which asks questions, perhaps of some sort of reader, perhaps of itself, moves further and further away from a literal presence who speaks by interrogation. In a drama or novel, scenes of interrogation are controlled by some relation of authority and power maintained between questioner and questioned. That this relation may itself evolve or reveal itself to any of the parties or audience in the course of the interrogation is no matter. But in lyrical or meditative poems, the nature of the text's authority is always in some sort of flux. The deep scepticism concerning the authority of all poetic voices for a postbiblical and post-Homeric reader is jolted somewhat, if not chastened, by being asked questions, instead of being urged to believe that some fiction "was so," or to pay a particular kind of poetic attention to what will follow, etc. (I shall address that urging, the whole rhetorical mode of imperative and command in which poems so often speak, in chapter 4.) But in a late—which is to say, a critical—age, a questioning voice seems to hold more authority than a propounding one. It is in this condition of thoughtful readership—the one we think of as being modern in that, for example, doubt seems to be a necessary and authenticating way station on the road to faith—that the poetic question hits home. It is in this way that the poem, rather than the orator, can better persuade by interrogation.

A very special and, rhetorically speaking, most interesting case of authority in the questioning voice is that of questions asked between men and God. They must seem at first glance to be plagued by dramatic irony. The "Eli, Eli lama sabachtani?" of Jesus on the cross [Matthew 27:37] (My God, my God, why hast thou forsaken me?) has, of course, to be treated as a unique case of unwitting self-questioning or whatever interpersonal interrogation within the Trinity might be. Even so, the answer would involve a strange reconstruing of the question itself. What appears to be begged is the forsaking; the answer would be that if the cross and the soldiers all suddenly disappeared in a whirlwind, the real forsaking would be there. This is just what Samson comes to understand before the end of *Samson Agonistes,* that the divine scenario written for him required a series of failures as ascending rungs on a moral ladder, and quite literally so as preparations for a subsequent total act. This is what Emerson enigmatically proclaims when he insists, in *Nature,* that "Nature's dice are always loaded; that in her heaps and rubbish are concealed sure and useful results." So that the "Eli" of Jesus's question would have to answer, according to the state of theological dogma at the moment, "In fact, I [or "we"] haven't forsaken you at all."

Nowhere does the power of poetic questioning seem stronger than in the Hebrew Bible. Although my concerns are with mostly lyric, rather than epical or dramatic poetry, the paradigmatic character of scriptural questioning is inescapable. We tend to think of Cain's response, in Genesis 4:9, to God's question, "Where is Abel thy brother?"—the infamous "Am I my brother's keeper?"—as the First Rhetorical Question. It does indeed occur under fascinating conditions, as an evasion of an answer to a literal interrogation (for only under later rabbinic and Augustinian tradition would Yahweh's absolute omniscience force one to consider the "Where is Abel?" as a rhetorical question). We might think of this first instance as being stained with the stuff of evasion, of a kind of lying, that the subsequent meditative tradition of answering a question by asking another would both always seek to escape and have to contend with. In fact, the First Rhetorical Question is Yahweh's. In KJV (Genesis 4:7), God asks Cain, before the murder of Abel, ["Why art thou wroth? and why is thy countenance fallen?"] "If thou doest well, shalt thou not be accepted?" (Actually, there is a problem in interpreting the Hebrew text at this point, and perhaps the only questions are the ones about why Cain is so grumpy.) But it is clear that God's initial rhetorical questions are those of a teacher, at least in the Greek Septuagint text and the KJV, and in those instances—which affect our vernacular poetic tradition far more strongly than the Hebrew text does—he has opened the door to the same mode of questioning in his sullen, recalcitrant and failed pupil, Cain. And God's own next rhetorical question, "What hast thou done?" becomes one we shall all ask.

Clearly paradigmatic is what Sir Thomas Browne called "that poetical taunt of Isaiah," asked by the prophet, in a particular taunting way of the king of Babylon (identified as: "Lucifer, son of the morning" in KJV) as he is brought down into hell: "They that see thee shall narrowly look upon thee, and consider thee, saying, Is this the man that made the earth to tremble, that did shake kingdoms; That made the world as a wilderness, and destroyed the cities thereof; that opened not the house of his prisoners?" (Isaiah 14:16–17). "Is this the man that made the earth to tremble?" The answer, "Yes, in fact, it is; but O, how fallen, how changed!" is assigned here to half of the fictional crowd of witnesses, the other half of whom are supposed to be asking the question. It is not Isaiah's rhetorical question— he is beyond asking it—but the taunt consists in his establishment of the scene of its being asked another famous later question blossoming from the paradigm of this one in Isaiah is, of course, that of Marlowe's Faustus to Helen: "Was this the face that launched a thousand ships / And burned the topless towers of Ilium?" Just as it echoes the pentameter cadence it hears in the KJV's "Is this the man that made the earth to tremble?", it resonates with the noise of cities falling as well.[16]

The veritable avalanche of rhetorical questions in the book of Job could lead us to spend many pages on the taxonomy of their forms; from the pointed questionings of proverb literature in Hebrew through the range of presumptuous interrogations put by the three comforters, through Elihu's more finely and deeply pointed questions aimed at Job's knowledge, as well as those whose answer is simply, "God. And you know it," it is almost as if the available array of human interrogations were being exhausted. They all lead up to the questioning of the voice from the whirlwind, in chapters 38– 41, those terrible queries which mark the limits of all inquisitorial modes. Through that Voice's relentless questioning, the whole realm of nature is violently represented, the momentarily horrifying but ultimately consoling contingency of human will and groundings of human knowledge canonically revealed. Thenceforth, any human interrogator subjecting another human to such a barrage can only be some form of terrorist; any human soul en- visioning its own position as a central point of weakness in the vastness of creation can only be some form of madman.

And so indeed with the echoer of God's questions in Job, the sublimely deluded questioner of Blake's "The Tyger," who addresses an unbroken string of questions to a creature whose awesomeness seems to a reader to emanate not from his discernible form, but from the world of terror formed by the kinds of questions, and the spirit in which they are asked. As one critic has put it, "The poem's speaker, though a man of considerable imag- ination (quite possibly a poet like William Cowper), is at work terrifying himself with a monster of his own creation." We must remember, in reading this poem from *Songs of Experience,* to consider two important contextual elements: First, there are the child's questions of the Lamb in the comple- mentary, prior *Songs of Innocence* volume, in which the child asks the creature who is a trope for its own creator, "Little lamb, who made thee? / Dost thou know who made thee?" and answers its own question in the following stanza. Second, there is the inescapable fact of the illustration, always in Blake at work in an interpretive give-and-take with the text it does so much more than "illustrate" in some synecdochical, narrative sense. The tiger is represented as a sort of pussycat, and the object of the questions is no more a ferocious presence of our own experiences or imaginings than the questioner himself is Blake. With these in mind, let us return for a moment to that famous string of rhetorical questions:

Tyger, Tyger, burning bright,
In the forests of the night;
What immortal hand or eye,
Could frame thy fearful symmetry?

In what distant deeps or skies
Burnt the fire of thine eyes!
On what wings dare he aspire?
What the hand dare seize the fire?

And what is fearful about the mitigating symmetry of a ferocious beast? And what have stars or submarine antitheses to them to do with even feral cats' eyes? And what do the wings of Icarus, son of the fabulous artificer who made them and type of youthful, thoughtless daring, have to do with tiger-makers? And what has the generous—at least for humanity—hand of Prometheus who grabbed fire (and thereby all technology) from Olympus have to do with this? And, please, what is being dared? What are the stakes? What is instructively infuriating about the speaker of this dramatic monologue is how many poetic questions he virtually forces us to ask: like all madmen with whom we have intimately to deal, he tends to enlist us actively, as well as passively, in what used to be called his "paranoid pseudo-community." And he keeps on going:

And what shoulder, & what art,
Could twist the sinews of thy heart?
And when thy heart began to beat,
What dread hand? & what dread feet?

When the heart begins to beat, even the speaker's syntax becomes somewhat paratactic (and although Blake seems to have some second thoughts about this, correcting the line by hand in a late copy to "What dread hand forged [or formed] thy dread feet," the earlier version seems expressively stronger). This continues, the terror beginning to infuse even the tools employed by all those dread members:

What the hammer? what the chain?
In what furnace was thy brain?
What the anvil? what dread grasp,
Dare its deadly terrors clasp?

When the stars threw down their spears
And water'd heaven with their tears:
Did he smile his work to see?
Did he who made the Lamb make thee?

The submission of the rebel angels is hardly evidence of the kind of work accomplished in hexameral creation, is it? And why shouldn't the agnufacturer frame, in a different frame of mind, a tiger? Doesn't William Blake frame both lamb- and tiger-inquiry? That this chain of questions must come to an end in the pungent juxtaposition of the last two is confirmed by the return of the opening stanza, both as a device of conventional lyric closure (ballads, etc.) and as a horrible hint that a new chain of mad questions will continue, but in a more intense mode, for the repetition incorporates the obsessive verb "dare" to which its own opening query has given rise:

> Tyger, Tyger burning bright,
> In the forests of the night:
> What immortal hand or eye
> Dare frame thy fearful symmetry?

A general concern for poetic questioning would want to dwell for a moment on the relation of text and picture here, but not with respect to the way in which the image is a clue to the tonal and rhetorical framing of the song. Rather it is more a matter of the questioning of pictures by texts generally. The kind of poem which might be called *ekphrastic,* which addresses a particular visual image in order to give a reading of it, has frequent recourse to the interrogative mode. Pictures, according to a Renaissance formula adapted from antiquity, being mute poems, poetry itself is required to give voice to them; a tradition starting with the prose *ekphrases* of the Hellenistic writer Philostratus ends up with the modern ekphrastic poem, such as Rilke's famous sonnet to an archaic torso of Apollo in the Louvre or W. H. Auden's "Musée des Beaux Arts." Philostratus himself starts out one of his descriptions—in this case, of a putative painting of a young man playing the *aulos,* or oboe (usually mistranslated as "flute," but no matter) by asking, "For whom are you playing, Olympus? and what need is there of music in a desert place?"[17] But of course, the painting cannot answer, and the only answer to this poetic (rather than more literal or oratorical) sort of rhetorical question must be given to the text itself. When we get to complex, modern ekphrastic poems, addressed not to emblems or images, but to particular paintings by particular artists, the matter of questioning becomes correspondingly more complex. Dante Gabriel Rossetti's great sonnet on the *Madonna of the Rocks* of Leonardo da Vinci constitutes a brilliant interpretation of the powerfully puzzling landscape in that painting showing the Madonna, the infant Jesus and the child St. John, and the angel Gabriel, in a dark prospect. He addresses his opening ekphrastic question (and the word in Greek means "to speak out") to the Virgin, but with regard to the landscape and its meaning:

> Mother, is this the darkness of the end,
>   The Shadow of Death? and is that outer sea
>   Infinite, imminent Eternity?

And does the death-pang by man's seed sustained
In time's each instant cause thy face to bend
   Its silent prayer upon the Son, while He
   Blesses the dead with His hand silently
To His long day which hours no more offend?

So ends the octave of the sonnet. But the painting cannot answer, nor can its usual surrogates, art historians, literary iconographers, or whoever. The poem will have to answer—in a mode we shall explore more fully later on—its own question about how an image of the childhood of Christ can be a picture of Death. A normal introductory answer would be something like, "Mother of grace, the questions are difficult." The sestet of Rossetti's sonnet plunges instead right into the significant features of the landscape, particularly the narrow pass between the rocks, the river reaching out into wider water, the common trope of a narrow passage as both birth canal and passage out of life into death:

Mother of grace, the pass is difficult,
   Keen as these rocks, and the bewildered souls
     Throng it like echoes, blindly shuddering through . . .

In another sonnet of Rossetti's, this time for Botticelli's *Primavera*, the questioning goes so far as to turn upon itself. In the octave of the sonnet, Rossetti asks what we may all reasonably ask of the painting, namely, "What is going on here?" The painted allegorical poem of spring, with the three graces in their famous significant choreographic pattern, the wind gods, the goddess Flora, Hermes on the left margin, whether stirring up clouds of incomprehensibility or clearing them away so that spring may occur and meaning shine forth plain, no one can know—what is the structure of its unfolding fable? And so Rossetti interrogates the painting:

What masque of what old wind-withered New Year
   Honours this Lady? Flora, wanton-eyed
   For birth, and with all flowrets prankt and pied:
Aurora, Zephyrus, with mutual cheer
Of clasp and kiss: the Graces circling near,
   Neath bower-linked arch of white arms glorified:
   And with those feathered feet which hovering glide
O'er Spring's brief bloom, Hermes the harbinger.

So far, so good: Rossetti has simply read the painting by enumerating its personages; and yet he hasn't really told us what the masque, what the evolving allegory, really adds up to. In the sestet, he returns, as in the sonnet on the Leonardo painting, to the circularity of life, to the matter of deaths and entrances, births and exits. And then, once more, he will return to questioning:

> Birth-bare, not death-bare yet, the young stems stand
>> This Lady's temple-columns: o'er her head
>> Love wings his shaft. What mystery here is read
> Of homage or of hope? . . .

And finally, he breaks off into a rhetorical questioning of the grounds of his own questions, of the figurativeness of *ekphrasis* itself:

> But how command
> Dead Springs to answer? And how question here
> These summers of that wind-withered New Year?

A final poetic question like this one makes for a strange sort of closure for a short poem. One thinks of Keats's "Fled is that music. Do I wake or sleep?" at the end of the Nightingale Ode; of Shelley's "If winter comes, can spring be far behind?" as the bottom line, as it were, of the West Wind Ode. Yeats's famous sonnet "Leda and the Swan" is really an ekphrastic poem in its own way, employing probing questions of the sort that Walter Pater might:

> How can those terrified vague fingers push
> The feathered glory from her loosening thighs?
> And how can body, laid in that white rush
> But feel the strange heart beating where it lies?

—he asks of the scene he has invoked, of the virgin being raped by the god-as-swan. And thus he ends the poem, in an early draft of it, with the question of whether, at the violent moment in which the Trojan War and the tragic cycle of the House of Atreus are being ushered in, and in which an ignorant girl is being raped by a swan, that girl is vouchsafed any vision at all of what was happening, or what the consequences might be:

> Being so caught up,
> Did nothing pass before her in the air?

But Yeats eventually rewrote this into the famous closing question,

> Did she put on his knowledge with his power
> Before the indifferent beak could let her drop?

—which begs, as Yvor Winters pointed out, the question of how she put on his power, if at all. Still, the question has, by virtue of its very *petitio principii,* a certain power of openness (which, say, the question addressed to the reader about pistol-brandishing Maud Gonne, his beauty-turned-revolutionist, "Was there no second Troy for her to burn?", lacks). Perhaps I should quote the entire final stanza of "Among School Children":

> Labour is blossoming or dancing where
> The body is not bruised to pleasure soul,

> Nor beauty born out of its own despair
> Nor blear-eyed wisdom out of midnight oil.
> O chestnut tree, great rooted blossomer,
> Are you the leaf, the blossom or the bole?

—a question rhetorical to the degree that it specifies an answer, but poetic to the degree that what is specified is the response that the question is unanswerable, that the truth of the tree is not to be cloven into two fictions. But the final question, the celebrated conclusion of the poem, poses another problem:

> O body swayed to music, O brightening glance,
> How can we know the dancer from the dance?

Here, the further, more radical appositive paraphrase of the first question moves to a different level of conceptual organization.[18] It is not merely that the second question implies, "—*Or*, if you prefer another figure of conceptual inadequacy in dealing with Process, try this one: How can we distinguish between dancer and the dance itself, the movement, the whirl of veil or skirt, etc.?" For the confusion of act and agent is reflected in an ambiguous sense of the phrase "know from." It not only can mean "distinguish between," as the usual and obvious construing of the question suggests; it can also mean "infer from," "know by means or evidence of." And whereas the first meaning of the phrase depends upon an epistemological priority of actual, present dancer over derived entity of action, or dance (*dancing* is present, but less thing- or personlike than the *dancer*), here this is momentarily reversed. The dance gets priority, and the same hopelessness framed by the rhetorical question about not being able to distinguish between the two ends up by celebrating the contingency of what had been thought to be the more prominent and substantial member of the pair. If the question might be said (although I should prefer not to talk this way) to deconstruct itself, it does so in a most resonant way.[19]

Concluding questions in poems are often final questions in another sense. The great refrain of François Villon's "Ballade of Dead Ladies" (as it is usually called in English)—"Mais ou sont les neiges d'antan?" (But where are the snows of yester-year? in Rossetti's translation)—concludes each stanza, and the poem itself as a question which interprets the preceding ones. "Where are X, and Y, and Z, who was always so this way and that? Where are A and B and C? *But where are the snows of yesteryear?*"[20] The rhetorical question averts response from the literal answer—"Dead. All dead, as we all will be sooner than we wish"—to the poignant metaphor of the mortality not of human bodies, but of total personal presences. For lives and bodies, as Scripture, Homer, Virgil, Dante, and others tells us, are like leaves and grass, decaying into the ground, which will generate new leaves and fresh grass. But snow melts away into dampness, into air, and gives visible rise to no new snow.[21]

Villon's famous lines are an instance of a conventional motif of questioning that seems to pervade medieval literature. The widely known formula identified as the *ubi sunt* device—the "where are they now?" asked of particular dead persons—presents interesting rhetorical problems of questioning. It is not expected to elicit a chorus of responses such as the "Dead. All dead" just mentioned; rather, perhaps, its effect is to remind the reader not only of all of our deaths, but of all our usual suppression of our consciousness of it. The question expects, even demands, a knowing silence. Educated people of an older generation may perhaps know the formula best from the Latin lyric of an eighteenth-century German students' song (itself based on a thirteenth-century text), the "Gaudeamus Igitur." "Let us rejoice, then, while we're young," it begins; "after joyful youth, after troublesome old age, the earth will have us." Then comes the second stanza:

> Ubi sunt, qui ante nos
> In mundo fuere?

[Where are those who were before us in this world?]

The student song, full of learning, snaps back its answer: "Go up to heaven, go down to hell, if you want to see them," in effect half mocking the formula by returning a literal, rather than a figurative, answer.

Not so literal is the response given in one of the most famous ubi sunt passages of all, the one from the Old English lament of "The Wanderer." I quote in translation:

> Where has the horse gone? where has the man gone? where has the treasure-giver gone? Where have the banqueting seats gone? where the hall-joys? Alas, the bright cup! Alas, the mailed warrior! Alas, the princes' glory! How that time has departed, has darkened under night's helmet as if it had never been . . .

It is not only that an exclamation ("Alas!" etc.) is given in answer, but that the individual synecdoches for a whole age, for a whole condition of culture, are reintegrated in an avowal of the loss of a whole time.

The origins of the ubi sunt questions are biblical, and because I shall want to refer to the device subsequently, I want to dwell momentarily on an interesting feature of those origins.[22] A passage in Isaiah (33:18) addresses the righteous: "Thine eyes shall see the king in his beauty: they shall behold the land which is very far off. / Thine heart shall meditate terror. Where is the scribe? where is the receiver? where is he that counted the towers?" The implication seems to be that along with present vision will come remembered fears, the memory of asking, "Where are the scribes, counsellors, chroniclers, census-takers (so the Greek translation construes it), counters

of treasure?" But the sense hovers between that of "Where have they all
gone?" and the quite different "Where were they when we needed them?"
It is the last sense which St. Paul picks up when he echoes this passage in
1 Corinthians 20: "Where is the wise? where is the scribe? where is the
disputer of this world? hath not God made foolish the wisdom of this
world?"—And where is their philosophy? And what is it good for? It is not
the dead who are invoked as such; it is only the supersession of their *sophia,*
their worldly wisdom, by the word from the cross, says Paul, which renders
them obsolete, defunct. Another precursor of the medieval motif is in the
apocryphal book of Baruch (3:16–19) and accompanies its catalogue with
the appropriately moralizing answer, making it clear that the speaker is sat-
isfied with the lesson he can teach. Formally, it establishes the pattern, yet
tonally it is far from the medieval lamenter who implicitly numbers himself
and his audience among the items in the catalogue of "Where are they?"'s:

> Where are the princes of the heathen become, and such
> as ruled the beasts upon the earth;
> They that had their pastime with the fowls of the air,
> and they that hoarded the silver and gold, wherein men
> trust, and made no end of their getting?
> For they that wrought in silver, and were so careful,
> and whose works are unsearchable.
> They are vanished and gone down to the grave, and others
> are come up in their steads.

But perhaps the most direct paradigm for the later medieval passages of
ubi sunt lament is provided by Isidore of Seville (*Synonyma de lamentatione
animae peccatoris* [P.L. 83, col. 825f.]): "Brief is the joy of this earth, mean
the glory of this world. . . . Say where are the kings? where the princes?
where the emperors? where the possessions of the rich? where the power of
the world? where the wealth of the earth? gone like a shadow, even as a
dream dissolves." More and more, though, in later literature the ubi sunt
question, whose answer can only be "Dead," receives poetic answers or
evasions of answers, which try to ignore death or face it figuratively and
obliquely. The exceptions to this are such devotional poems as the anonymous thirteenth-century lyric "in contempt of the world" (as the topos is
called). It starts out with a beautifully turned ubi sunt catalogue:

> Where beth they, before us weren,
> Houndes ladden and havekes beren,
> And hadden feld and wode?
> The riche levedies in hoere bour,
> That wereden gold in hoere tressour,
> With hoere brighte rode?[23]

(But these questions are all answered in eight subsequent stanzas of emphatic preaching.) And yet more and more, the dead in question become lost objects of desire, as with Villon's ladies, and eventually dead poets, as in Dunbar's famous "Lament for the Makers," with its explicit confession reiterated in refrain: "Timor mortis conturbat me" (The fear of death confounds me).

Finally, coming a century after the conventional use of the ubi sunt motif had waned, Spenser seems almost to be asking, "Where now is that old 'ubi sunt'?" The occasion, at the opening of canto 4, book 3 of *The Faerie Queene,* is the praise of Britomart for her military prowess:

> Where is the Antique glory now become,
>   That whilome wont in women to appeare?
> Where be the braue atchieuements does by some?
> Where be the battels, where the shield and speare,
> And all the conquests, which them high did reare,
>   That matter made for famous Poets verse,
>   And boastfull men so oft abasht to heare?
>   Bene they all dead, and laid in dolefull herse?
> Or doen they onely sleepe, and shall againe reuerse?

This stanza, with its final and highly characteristic Spenserian near-pun on the senses of "return" and "re-verse," "make poems again," is on the brink of allegorizing its own mode of questioning the nature of the absence of textual personages and events.

Questions whose answers point toward finality, and questions about death itself, frame their own kind of unanswerability. Thus when the great romantic Italian poet Ugo Foscolo asks, in his meditation "De Sepolcri" (*On Tombs*), "All'ombra de cipressi e dentro l'urne / confortate di pianto e forse il sonno / della morte men duro?" (In the shade of cypresses and inside urns / comforted by weeping is the sleep / of death perhaps less hard?) What kind of question is that? And how does the poem make us think about it, and remember it? And what does it mean that a poem leaves something hanging in a final question? And is questioning one's own questioning always self-destructive? May it not be more serious to leave a major question one has oneself propounded unanswered?

3 ❧

Poetic Answers

I ended the last chapter on poetic questioning with a string of questions. Toward the beginning of it I cited George Herbert's sonnet about not writing love poetry, one which began with a sort of ubi sunt lament for the possibility of seriously erotic verse. It's perhaps appropriate at the beginning of this discussion of the ways in which literary texts answer poetically to cite Herbert's own answer to some of the questions he asks, an answer given in a second sonnet, written as a companion to the first one. All of the first poem's questions about ardor, about heat that is not erotic, are answered by appeal to divine heat of another sort, and that applies directly to the young poet's own concerns about writing:

> Sure Lord, there is enough in thee to dry
>   Oceans of ink; for, as the Deluge did
>   Cover the Earth, so does thy Majesty:
> Each Cloud distills thy praise, and doth forbid
> Poets to turn it to another use.
>   Roses and Lilies speak thee; and to make
>   A pair of cheeks of them is thy abuse.
> Why should I Women's eyes for Crystal take?

And so he ends his octave on another questioning note. But it will be apparent that his answer has by no means been a direct, or even a literal one. He has, rather, taken up the metaphor of heat, of fire, from the stock of erotic tropes of the tradition of love poetry in which he is refusing to write. God does not answer Herbert directly.

And yet how are we to consider the indirect, oblique, evasive ways in which poems purport to give answers to their own questions? There is no such standard concept as the "rhetorical answer" to appeal to; and indeed, we will find that there is something figurative about all mock, or "as if," answering.

We have seen how merely rhetorical questions may specify their answers with a crudity which makes it hard to call that sort of specifying implicit. And we have seen how poetry, rather than oratory, asks questions of itself, questions of another sort which can only be answered, if at all, in figurative ways.

But there are rhetorical answers, as well as rhetorical interrogatives, although they usually occur along with those questions. The rhetoricians variously called this scheme of explicitly answering one's own question *apocrisis* or *hypophora*; Puttenham in the 1580s spoke of it as *antipophora* or the figure of Response, suggesting that its rhetorical strategy was to anticipate "such matter as our adversarie might object and then to answere it our selves" and by so doing to "unfurnish and prevent him of such helpe as he would otherwise have used for himselfe."[1] But rhetoric in general becomes poetry, as we observed previously, through an internalization, or other kind of figurative replacement of "our adversarie"; and so antipophora can be redirected inwardly and move a step closer toward poetic trope. Consider a famous example, that of Falstaff on the matter of honor: He starts out by using a rhetorical question to mock his own statement of a formula: "Well, 'tis no matter, honor pricks me on. Yea, but how if honor pricke me off when I come on? how then?" Then the questioning moves into another mode:

> Can honor set to a leg? No. Or an arm? No. Or take away the grief of a wound? No. Honor hath no skill in surgery then? No. What is honor? A word. What is in that word honor? What is that word honor? Air. (A trim reckoning!) Who hath it? He that died a' Wednesday. Doth he feel it? No. Doth he hear it? No. 'Tis insensible then? Yea, to the dead. But will't not live with the living? No. Why? Detraction will not suffer it. Therefore I'll none of it, honor is a mere scutcheon.
>
> [*Henry IV*, pt. 1, act 5, sc. 1]

"And so ends," Falstaff avers, "my catechism," and indeed, the poetic consequences of internalized catechism involve, particularly for the sixteenth century, reason's usurping ecclesiastical authority to put itself through its own paces. What Falstaff is doing, as any introductory course in careful reading will seek to show, is first to carry on with the original reification of honor as a spur or goad, then pretend that it was a full personification (honor as a knight or warrior), reveal its personal inadequacies, and then shift ground to the battlefield of deconstructive nihilism ("honor's only a word, a puff of air"), which is always shaky in its own way (after all, we can follow "What's honor?" with the answering question, "What's *what*?"— it's the same puff of air).[2]

But Falstaff's catechistic routine is still rhetorical, although complicatedly so. So is, but even more complicatedly so, the question-and-answer structure of the "Ithaca" episode of Ulysses. (Here the problem of whether the reader is being (*a*) allowed to overhear the book's own Falstaffian catechism of itself or (*b*) "unfurnished or prevented" in asking questions, and mocked by the minute particulars of those questions, about the most problematic work of fiction since perhaps *Don Quixote,* will not admit to easy solution.) A less rhetorical and more poetical type of answered question might be exemplified by a brief, intense exchange from one of the sources of our lyric poetry. Moreover, it is about a problematic aspect of erotic lyric poetry itself. Consider Catullus's famous couplet

> Odi et amo. quare id faciam, fortasse requiris.
> nescio, sed fieri sentio et excrucior.

> [I hate and love. Why do I do it? perhaps you ask.
> I don't know; but I feel it and I'm tortured.]

The poem propounds what looks like an oxymoronic paradox, and then refuses to gloss or resolve it (by showing, in the ordinary way of interpretation, that either or both of the apparently mutually contradictory terms is meant figuratively). But from the point of view of poetic answering, it is the word *fortasse* ("perhaps") which is most complex, for it hedges the usual orator's bet which frames the rhetorical question with "you ask" by an acknowledgment of just that rhetoricity (nonliteralness). Catullus's way of answering the possible question is to say that he doesn't know the answer, but that he suffers from the erotic torment which, when put into ordinary language, results in something so extraordinary—poetic paradox—that it provokes questioning about what it could mean. Here, the poetic answer makes a point about poetic language and feeling.

Apocrises abound in literature, and often the force of figurative catechism, or some other form of ritual questioning, lends them more than oratorical force. Christina Rossetti's "Up-Hill," a wonderful little allegory of life's journey, unfolds in full catechistic language, although it is never determined who the two speakers are:

> Does the road wind up-hill all the way?
>   Yes, to the very end.
> Will the day's journey take the whole long day?
>   From morn to night, my friend.

> But is there for the night a resting-place?
>   A roof for when the slow dark hours begin.
> May not the darkness hide it from my face?
>   You cannot miss that inn.

Perhaps only at this point in the answering of questions do we begin to perceive that the matter may be an allegorical one, and that such archaic figures as that of darkness hiding an inn from one's face may indeed imply their own reversal, that the darkness is no ordinary one, and that we all hide our faces from it. The poem concludes with a grim avowal of the unlimited capacities of the grave:

> Shall I meet other wayfarers at night?
>   Those who have gone before.
> Then must I knock, or call when just in sight?
>   They will not keep you standing at the door.
>
> Shall I find comfort, travel-sore and weak?
>   Of labour you shall find the sum.
> Will there be beds for me and all who seek?
>   Yea, beds for all who come.

—a conclusion which will give consolation only to a Christian reader who can fully take the "inn" of death as resting-place on an even longer journey. Rossetti's poem stops short of belonging to that genre of poetic dialogue called by scholars amoebean, and usually associated with pastoral, in which there is an overt or implied contest of poetic skill between the two voices. But neither are the two voices fully incorporated in the tone of one speaker, probing its own discourse.

Even when the paradigm of catechism is absent from the background of a particular literary apocrisis, there will often be something to replace it. In the constant answering of self-posed questions in Yiddish proverbial humor, as in the monologues of Sholom Aleichem's Tevye, there is an undercurrent of Talmudic or midrashic questioning, the interpreter's eternal prelude to a rereading of a text: "How can we show that X in this verse really means Y? Well . . ." This is a kind of meditative parallel to the formulaic *démandes d'amour* or *questione d'amore* of medieval literature, the invitation to a debate, originally on matters of courtly love, eventually, by the time of Chaucer's Franklin, who asks at the end of his tale which was the most "fre," or generous, the nobleman or the bourgeois in his story, becoming announced agenda for discussion of manners and morals generally. And yet the particular debunking tone of Falstaff's colloquy with what he knows much better than pervades much of this sort of apocrisis, with the text of the quotidian providing tragic-comic relief from the sanctity of scripture.

The rhetorical scheme of answering one question with (if not actually by) another one can simply constitute a move in a conversational game—however high the stakes—or a parry and counterthrust in a bout of that exchange of line for line called stichomythia in drama from Aeschylus through Tom Stoppard's grand revision of it in the game of questions in *Rosencrantz and Guildenstern Are Dead*. When there is only monologue, however, the two voices become aspects of one, and thereby figurative at yet one more remove.[3] This can occur in a formal dramatic monologue, such as Browning's

"Soliloquy of the Spanish Cloister," where the embittered speaker, full of hatred for Brother Lawrence, the mindless, garrulous gardener, talks to himself, asking the other's questions and answering them. When he actually imitates this hated other, the nastiest answer is itself a question:

> Not a plenteous cork-crop: scarcely
>   Dare we hope oak-galls, I doubt:
> What's the Latin name for "parsley"?
> What's the Greek name for Swine's Snout?

This is the mocking interrogative reply, in a manner we all recognize.

In Thel's Motto (*The Book of Thel*), Blake has a second question half-answering, half being genuinely appositive to, a first one:

> Does the Eagle know what is in the pit?
> Or wilt thou go ask the Mole?
> Can Wisdom be put in a Silver Rod
> Or Love in a Golden Bowl?

The transformations of the rod and the bowl from their allegorical role in Ecclesiastes 12 : 6 are as complex here as the relation of the interrogations. But other uses of this scheme may be far from ironic. Those which return a question about the nature of the original query range from the merely metalinguistic to the philosophical. The literal request for clarification might be put at one end of a spectrum—a question asked about any utterance, indicative, interrogative, or imperative. But the famous reported deathbed words of Gertrude Stein, "What is the answer?" followed somewhat later by perhaps answering, "What is the question?" are another matter. (Is there a chance that Stein's sentence was poorly transcribed, and that she stated [not asked] in fact " 'What?' is the question"?—as if perhaps to disagree with Hamlet's designation of *the* existential question, the central matter, as "To be or not to be?") One might fill in the silence separating the two questions with explicit discourse, thus claiming that the silence had concealed anything from a mere "On the other hand—" to a Wittgensteinian sentence or two. The second question seems, in the context of the official anecdote, to float between internalized and analytic meditation.[4] In one of Heinrich Heine's *Lazarus* poems, the one beginning "Lass die heilgen Parabolen," the old questions of theodicy are rehearsed: Whose fault is injustice? is God perhaps not so almighty? or is all this his fault?—Ach! that would be contemptible. But in the last stanza, the implicit ironic recognition that to ask such sorts of question is to invent the wheel is accompanied by a sense that the very matter of such questioning is as old a story as well, but that, in the end, all this has nothing to do with the case:

> Also fragen wir beständig,
> Bis man uns einer Handvoll

Erde endlich stopft die Mäuler—
Aber ist das eine Antwort?

[So we keep asking / until someone finally / stops up our mouths with a handful of earth / —but is that an answer?]

Questioning one's own question seems more figurative than self-catechism, the *ratiocinatio* of classical rhetoric. It is one way of avowing the peculiar nature of answering oneself, which, like lying to oneself, partakes of problems of fiction rather than merely of logic. Consider the opening— along with its title, so typically functioning as the poem's initial line—of Marianne Moore's "What Are Years?" It puts a question in the title, asks a purportedly appositive pair of others, responds with a far-from-literally answering statement, and then continues with a remarkable, long, periodic question that comes to definitive rest only in the second stanza:

> What is our innocence,
> what is our guilt? All are
>   naked, none is safe. And whence
> is courage: the unanswered question,
> the resolute doubt,—
> dumbly calling, deafly listening—that
> in misfortune, even death,
>   encourages others
>   and in its defeat, stirs
>
> the soul to be strong?

Most interestingly, this last question glosses "courage" as an "unanswered question" and a "resolute doubt," calling attention to the poem's own evasions of direct answer. The scheme of question-for-question generally is certainly a mode of evasion.

But poetry has other ways of withdrawing from the consequences of a direct answer to a question it has just posed. "Dear, dead women, with such hair, too—" muses the speaker of Browning's "A Toccata of Galuppi's," thinking of the dust and ashes to which eighteenth-century Venetian life had fallen—"What's become of all the gold, / Used to hang and brush their bosoms? I feel chilly, and grown old." Even as he hears himself asking a version of that good old ubi sunt question considered in chapter 2, the tripping meter of his discourse provides a nonanswer like Catullus's, but more elliptical. Not "I don't know precisely what's become of it but the question makes me shiver with the fear of death," but instead following the paradigm of refusing to philosophize because of another, more powerful claim on one's attention. (Thus, A: "Is there anything you can be absolutely certain of? B: Go away, I don't feel so good.")

A lyrical poem can go so far as to specify such a refusal, as Keats does so frequently. "Where are the songs of spring? Aye, where are they? / Think not of them, thou hast thy music too—" So, in the third stanza of "To Autumn," the visual imagery of the previous parts of the poem begins to darken to the rising undersong of the music of oncoming evening and death. Keats's earlier rhetorical question, which actually calls up a full personification, asks, "Who hath not seen thee oft amid thy store?" Its implication is not that everyone has seen Autumn personified, but that she is ubiquitous amid her store of harvest and, by poetic implication, her store of tropes, of emblematically pictorial attributes. But the second question is of a different order. "Where are the songs of spring?"—no sooner are those words out when an echo of what they might mean troubles the hearing. Keats hears his own query just as Browning's Venetian narrator did, as a version of the ubi sunt complaint. We all know well that the songs of spring have died on the summer air that we prefer to think of as killing nothing which had preceded it, but only fulfilling. "Aye, where are they?" is the revisionary metaquestion, the one which acknowledges this repressed meaning and treats the first question as one asked of itself. "Think not of them, thou hast thy music too" is a brave attempt to divert attention from the realization that the songs catalogued in the stanza will all turn out to be dirges, even for their own brief musical periods. They implicitly answer the ubi sunt questions "Where are they? Where we're headed now?" Keats turns aside—turns his persona and his reader aside—from the question with a strange shudder, not merely of dread, but of dread half-warming into erotic excitement.

A celebrated early-sixteenth-century anonymous song avows the rhetorical quality of its own opening question by responding to it, not in an indicative sentence, but in a burst of longing:

Westron wynd when wilt thou blow,
The smale rain down can rain?
Christ, if my love were in my arms
And I in my bed againe.

("Small," incidentally, means "thin" here—it is spring showers, rather than autumnal downpours, that are being invoked.) The tropes of loosening, relieving, refreshing, and renewing—not to speak of a natural cyclic return, an elemental homing—that connect seasonal fulfillment and gratified desire are strengthened by the manifest disjunction, whereas in the last two lines, on the other hand, the concentricity of bed–speaker's arms–lover's body is pointed up by the syntax.

More subtle is the half-answer, half-nonanswer which Wallace Stevens gives himself in "Le Monocle de Mon Oncle," that remarkable series of meditations on middle-aged sexuality. The poem starts with a response to what has clearly just been a sexual refusal—"two words that kill," whether, as Harold Bloom has suggested,[5] "No, no" or perhaps the more chilling, low-domestic "Not tonight":

"Mother of heaven, regina of the clouds,
O sceptre of the sun, crown of the moon,
There is not nothing, no, no, never nothing,
Like the clashed edges of two words that kill."
And so I mocked her in magnificent measure.

The poem itself has so far propounded a "magnificent measure" of high dudgeon in blank verse and then revoked it. But now come a pair of rhymed lines that successively question and appear not to answer: ["And so I mocked her in magnificent measure."] "Or was it that I mocked myself alone? / I wish that I might be a thinking stone." A reasonable answer might have been, "No. I was mocking myself as well, myself as mocker, even as I mocked her"; but the speaker turns away in a kind of disgust at the meditative consequences of pursuing this sort of analysis. The question taken this way means, "Or was I mocking only myself, merely mocking myself?" But the magnificent measure of the high, inverted word order leaves "alone" in a terminal, resonant position in the line—rather like the resonant "forlorn" in Keats's Nightingale Ode—and just before the question is to be answered, another ghostly reading presents itself. "Or was it that I was mocking my own aloneness, solitude, or loneliness or whatever?" is this second question. And perhaps it is the last straw. The heavily rhyming line which follows underscores the word "alone" and appears totally to break off the thread of discourse as absolutely as anacoluthon might. "Or was it that I mocked myself alone? / I wish that I might be a thinking stone."— This does not, of course, mean a stone to think on, or at, or of, or with, not a *think*ing-stone. English poetic rhythm always leads us to parse as well as to scan, and the cadence at the rhyming line-end requires that we say "thinking stone," with a somewhat greater degree of stress on the last word, and thus implicitly contrasting it with something else—a "thinking X" (some monosyllabic noun). But what could this be? The available one is Pascal's epithet for man, a "thinking reed" being the biblical epitome of what bends in the wind, what moans as the wind bends it. (Classically, it is the reed into which the nymph Syrinx was transformed just before Pan could rape her, and through whose hollow core the longing sigh of the god for his sexual object-loss initiates a whole mode of the music of absence. Also, a clump of reeds sounding in the wind would always, as Ovid tells us, speak of how Midas had donkey-ears beneath his cap, a punishment for choosing the erotic music of Pan over that of Apollo.)

There may be many echoes here of "The Love Song of J. Alfred Prufrock," with its own strings of overwhelming questions throughout, so many of them leading up to "I should have been a pair of ragged claws / Scuttling across the floor of silent seas," which the line about the thinking stone may be recalling. Certainly the erotic tone is a revision of Eliot's.

Stevens's line must then be heard as saying, "I don't want to be a thinking reed, but a thinking *stone*—better strong, hard, smooth silence than weak, windy expression." It is a remarkable sort of answer, after all. This kind of allusive complexity presents some of the aspects of a riddle of one sort hiding under one of another. Here, the half-answering line was a puzzling non sequitur until we listened to it as the poet himself did. The most poetic riddles frequently employ one mode of puzzlement to hide the fact that another is going on. And frequently, the answer to a riddle destroys the wondrous fiction that the puzzle, or the puzzling question, brings into being.

"What walks on four legs, two legs, three legs—you know when?" The answer transforms the *Unheimlich,* the uncanny, chimerical monster with a nastily indeterminate number of legs, into what is merely a clear picture of ourselves. The answer, "Mankind," is literal, not a trope. And of course it is terrifying, in part because we see that the next stage must be "On no legs at all. Flat on its back six feet under. And that's it." So that unanswered puzzle questions, unsolved riddles, not only preserve wonderful fictions, but remain benign. Their answers, as Freud demonstrated, frequently point to a malignant state of affairs. The poetics of riddle is a fascinating subject, not to be explored further here. It is not unrelated to the rhetoric of jokes, in which a punch line, like the answer to a riddle, utterly explodes and destroys the whole fictional apparatus, the narrative, the anecdotal frame-work, the trap set for the reader's or listener's habits of thought and belief, of the earlier part of the joke. I shall only comment here upon a pair of poetic riddles, not totally unrelated in their mode of questioning, which provide answers in a somewhat riddling fashion.

The first of these is called, very conveniently for the purpose of citation here, "The Question Answered." It is an epigram of William Blake's. It is puzzling in that it starts out with a literal question and answer, not poetic nor even rhetorical, but merely put into a rhymed couplet: "What is it men in women do require? / The lineaments of gratified desire."—In other words, a bit of proverbial counterwisdom, antithetical to all sorts of eigh-teenth-century notions, whether conventionally pious (for example, "What do men want from women? Chastity, obedience, attentiveness, domesticity, etc.") or else its rakish antithesis, "Some spirited resistance to penetration, the abandon to feelings that said penetration alone could elicit." Blake's answer underlies the cloven fiction of these two sorts of chaste and unchaste submission.

But this is only half his poem. It continues with an additional question: "What is it women do in men require?" And here, once again, a trap is set for conventional folklore about the relations between the sexes.[6] We expect an answer here which will redound to the detriment of women, or which will enforce their subordination—something like "What is it women do in men require? Gifts of fine clothes, and jewels that shine like fire."[7] For Blake, uncritical and degraded pseudo-wisdom could chuckle as its dogmas were petted once again, and its intellectual torpor allowed to sleep on undisturbed. But what, in fact, is the answer here? Let me cite the whole quatrain now:

> What is it men in women do require?
> The lineaments of gratified desire.
> What is it women do in men require?
> The lineaments of gratified desire.

The trap is sprung on the blockhead in all of us: "Men and women need the same thing, you fool—the conviction that each sex has been able to give pleasure to the other!" But then the deeper, hidden riddle emerges: To what question does the title of the poem, "The Question Answered," refer? Here are two supposedly antithetical questions, perhaps flung at each other in a rage by a more subtle Zeus and Hera. Yet they have the same answer, which leads us to conclude that they may be different forms of the same question. There is, indeed, only one such question about humankind. It is not a question about the war between men and women, which is imaginative failure. The question that has been answered turns out to be, after all, rather like Gertrude Stein's "What is the question?"—a question about how the question should really be put.[8]

A very Blakean answer which somehow deconstructs the choice between alternatives offered by its question occurs in a little poem of Yeats which, because of its brevity, nastiness and, for some, blasphemy, has been generally overlooked. "A Stick of Incense" was first published in 1939, and goes as follows:

> Whence did all that fury come?
> From empty tomb or virgin womb?
> Saint Joseph thought the world would melt
> But liked the way his finger smelt.

The question is a mythopoeic one, asking not history, but rather interpretation, to locate the mythological source of the energies of the whole Christian era either in the mystery of the virgin birth or of the resurrection. The "or" of the second line, that is, seems disjunctive (Latin *aut* rather than *vel*), and the concluding couplet, given by way of answer, is most puzzling. The whole poem is like a riddle whose title itself provides only a riddling clue: is the stick of incense a figure for the finger, redolent of female body in an obscene joke about Mary's husband? And would this, then, disqualify the "virgin womb" alternative? The solution lies, of course, in the fact of there being *two* Saint Josephs, the other being Joseph of Arimathea, who obtained the body of Jesus and gave it proper burial. A quite literal stick of incense would apply to this part of the story. The two Josephs are connected by a trope of cyclical topology, even as the womb and the tomb are connected by more than their rhyme in English. Their relation was the subject of perfectly orthodox, if baroque, Christian epigram, for example, Richard Crashaw's "Upon Our Saviour's Tomb wherein Never man Was Laid":

How Life and Death in Thee
  Agree!
Thou had'st a virgin wombe
  And Tombe.
A *Joseph* did betroth
  Them both.

In a Latin epigram on the same subject, Crashaw explicitly remarks on the circularity of the story—"How well the end loves its beginning! How elegantly the virgin wedding bed goes with the virgin tomb (where no one has lain)!" In Yeats's lines, however, it is the relation between the two Saint Josephs in their roles as attendant, somewhat peripheral personages in the Christ story which is elicited. They both live in a natural world. And yet they both "thought the world would melt," they both put on some of the knowledge and the power of the events at which they attended. But they are both ultimately self-absorbed, and if their minds do not move upon silence like those of Caesar, Helen of Troy, or Michelangelo, caught in private moments in another of Yeats's poems, their senses do indeed dwell momently on the aroma of their own involvement with the physical part of the epic of transcendence. And in their full figural relation, they remove all meditative weight from the posed alternatives of the opening question, and underlie the matter of "all that fury," or the subsequent course of Christianity itself—the institutional energies of two thousand years, the perjured, murderous, bloody history of religion. Whence all that fury? Tomb? Womb? But they are the same thing. *After all* (and this is the phrase connecting question and strange answer), neither of the Saint Josephs lost touch with mere pleasure—no fury *there*—and they were in on the beginning and the end. And so the question remains unanswered literally, but has been revealed as having been inappropriate all along, after all.

There are other riddles about the nature of questions which can be revealed as one sort of riddle and then solved by means of the same answering process. Catechistic questions and answers abound, for example, in folk poetry, as in "Lord Randall" or in the inquisition over the death of Cock Robin or in the matter of "The Cutty Wren":

Oh, where are you going, says Milder to Malder,
Oh, I cannot tell, says Festel to Fose,

We're going to the woods, says John the Red Nose.
We're going to the woods, says John the Red Rose.

Oh, what will you do there, says Milder to Malder,
Oh, I cannot tell, says Festel to Fose,
We'll shoot the Cutty Wren, says John the Red Nose.
We'll shoot the Cutty Wren, says John the Red Nose.

But in W. H. Auden's epilogue to *The Orators,* based on the foregoing nursery rhyme, we have a different problem. The poem quotes a series of half-accusatory questions all asked by someone whose relation to the person questioned is mysteriously figured in the twisted echoing of their epithets:

"O where are you going?" said reader to rider,
"That valley is fatal when furnaces burn,
Yonder's the midden whose odours will madden,
That gap is the grave where the tall return."

"O do you imagine," said fearer to farer,
"That dusk will delay your path to the pass,
Your diligent looking discover the lacking
Your footsteps feel from granite to grass?"

"O what was that bird," said horror to hearer,
"Did you see that shape in the twisted trees?
Behind you swiftly the figure comes softly,
The spot on your skin is a shocking disease."

The idiot, repressive questioner and the youthful adventurer differ as do the front and back vowel sounds that distinguish their alliterating names; in the last stanza, we are given the answers, and the singular pronoun in the final line suggests that there was only one adventurer being attacked by a hail of questions which may even, in fact, have come from internalized, superegolike entities within him. If he and they differ by result of their vowels, their alliteration yokes them in more than a question-and-answer relation:

"Out of this house"—said rider to reader.
"Yours never will"—said farer to fearer,
"They're looking for you"—said hearer to horror,
As he left them there, as he left them there.

George Herbert is a poet who, as we have seen, asks meditative questions of himself to which the very literal answer "God knows" frequently replaces the hyperbolic use of that phrase, colloquially, to provide the empty rhetorical answer (as a trope of "No one"). When his poems do indeed answer their own questions, the circumstances are usually special, and the conditions of answering, unique. The long list of reproaches which constitute the poem called "The Sacrifice" rehearses the details of the story of Christ's

Passion in stanzas of rhyming triplets ending in each case with the querying refrain, itself adapted from the *Lamentations,* "Was ever grief like mine?" If it were not Christ himself who, in the poem, narrates the events, the questions might tend to diminish in strength and become more and more rhetorical ones. But here, the poem's governing trope maintains, is the unique case in which it is not maudlin, blasphemous, or obscene to say, "No. Never," as it might be in any case of human suffering. The poem's particular art, however, involves two different occasions on which the refrain provides the answer, rather than the question. The first, at the end of the fifty-fourth stanza, is dramatically placed so as to serve an additional rhetorical purpose, that of concluding an anacoluthon which is in itself a veritable cry of pain. I quote it with the preceding stanza:

Such sorrow as, if sinful man could feel,
Or feel his part, he would not care to kneel,
Till all were melted, though he were all steel:
        Was ever grief &c.
But, *O my God, my God!* why leav'st thou me,
The Son in whom thou dost delight to be?
My God, my God———
        Never was grief like mine.

The answered refrain completes the broken pentameter, and at the same time turns away from the overwhelming emotion of the breaking syntax like an evasive answer turning away from its question. Finally, at the end of the poem, the sixty-fourth stanza concludes, once more, with the answer to the question; but in this case, the speaker, Christ, does not give the answer which he, uniquely, might be entitled to give. Rather, it is given to the voice of human acknowledgment of the truth of its assertion:

But now, I die; now all is finished.
My woe, man's weal: and now I bow my head.
Only let others say, when I am dead,
        Never was grief like mine.

Here, at the end, the answer is in indirect discourse, and the very sacrificial gesture of wanting all men to realize that this was, indeed, to be the paradigm of all human suffering, the intense synecdoche of it that, as an instance, is greater than the whole class it typifies.

This device can be seen as an interesting mirror image of the deflected answering of, in this case, taunting questions, of "The Quip." Here, Herbert answers the world and his cohorts with the refrain line in each of four encounters, for example,

First, Beauty crept into a rose,
Which when I plucked not, Sir, said she,

> Tell me, I pray, Whose hands are those?
> *But thou shalt answer, Lord, for me.*

What remains displaced, throughout these encounters, is *how* God will answer and what he will say. Only at the end of the poem do we learn both
the answer and something problematic about it:

> Yet when the hour of thy design
> To answer these fine things shall come,
> Speak not at large; say, I am thine:
> And then they have their answer home.

God will say for the poet "I am thine" and also, given the ambiguity of the
grammar which allows the ellipsis of "that," will say that he is the poet's
(with the direction of discourse reversed). He will therefore have answered
for the speaker in the other sense of having been accountable for him, and
the ambiguous grammar of the original phrase in the refrain emerges: *Thou
shalt answer their jeering rhetorical questions, and thereby be responsible for me.*
And after all, as A. D. Nuttall reminds us, it is hesitating Herbert who
answers "for" God, who must write the direct-indirect discourse of what
God says.[9] The quip of the title is more than a quibble on who belongs to
whom, and it powerfully casts into disrepute the interrogative power of
rhetorical questioning.

It does seem, then, that if there is something wrong with, something
funny about, poetic questioning, there is something even more wrong with
a poetic answer. One simple case to be considered is undue digressiveness,
an answer that gets out of hand, as it were. An early and significant instance
is Pindar's second Olympian ode, commemorating the victory of one
Thērōn of Akragas in a chariot race in 476 B.C. Significantly, the poet starts
out addressing his own poems—

> Lord of the lyre, odes,
> which god, what hero, what man shall we acclaim?

—and immediately answers his own question in a way so as to suggest the
inevitability and, indeed, even the almost scriptural authority of his choice:
Zeus (who, he says, is lord of Pisa, a city near Olympia, standing here for
the Olympic festival itself); Hērakles, who established the festival from the
spoils of war; and Thērōn, the winner, the pillar of his city. Pindar then
moves on to deal with the founding of Akragas and with the myth of the
Islands of the Blessed, and he takes time out to denounce rival poets (possibly Simonides and Bacchylides) as ravens who chatter vainly against Zeus's
eagle (great poets are seldom generous—they cannot afford to be—with
bad ones). The ode concludes with observations of how praise is stamped
on by envy, always eager to obscure the deeds of good men, and, finally, a
return at the end to another, final question: "For sands are numberless, and

who could enumerate the joys this man has given to others?" The poet leaves this unanswered; but in the light of his opening, "Whom should I write about now?" the implicit answer is surely not the expected "No one" but the alternative "I, Pindar."

The most authentic form of poetic praise is never unmixed with self-congratulation, not for the person of the particular poet but for the poetic language itself which carries the utterance beyond what in ordinary speech would have to answer to the question of sincerity. Horace, praising Augustus in the twelfth ode of his first book, recalls Pindar's opening questions, cleverly transferring the decision about whom to praise from the "We" of the poem and the poet to Clio, the muse of history: "Quem virum aut heroa lyra vel acri / tibia sumis celebrare, Clio? / quem deum?" (What man or hero do you take, Clio, to celebrate on the lyre or bright-toned flute? What god?) The lyre and flute also come from Pindar, incidentally, from the third Olympian ode, also in praise of Thērōn, which starts out by reminding the listeners that it is itself the product of a shining new style and that it will proceed to mingle the sounds of wind instrument, string, and sung words. But Horace continues the line of questioning with a sequence of queries which are purportedly appositive to the first one, paraphrases of it, but which actually shift attention from the matter of who it is who will be celebrated onto the implicit praise of poetic praise itself:

> Whose name shall the playful echo make resound on
> the shady slopes of Helicon or on Pindus' top or on
> cool Haemus, whence in confusion the trees followed
> after tuneful Orpheus, who by the skill his mother
> had imparted stayed with the swift courses of the streams and
> rushing winds; persuasive, too, with his melodious lyre to draw
> the listening oaks in his train?[10]

Consider the rhetorical strategy of this: it's a bit like saying, "Now, children, which of you is to get the prize, which is a batch of cookies that I spent all morning baking, first creaming my sugar and butter, and then taking my . . ." (but we need not continue). In this instance, we should say that there was something wrong with the suggestion that the prize-giver's question was an expression of doubt about whom to confer the cookies upon. So with Horace's opening: Helicon, the home of the muses in Boeotia, Pindus, their site in Thessaly, Haemus, in Thrace, and the allusion to Orpheus all call attention to the history not of heroism, but of poetry. The answer to this pair of opening questions is to be deferred through the course of Horace's poem; what immediately follows is one of those half-answering questions: "What should I sing before the customary praises of Jove the Father, who rules sea and land and sky with its changing seasons?" But then Pallas Athena comes in for praise, Diana, Apollo, Hercules, Castor and Pollux, and then a line of Romans starting with Romulus and ending with Augustus, the order man-hero-god of the opening question being reversed in the answer. Ultimately, the reader is carried back to an implied, unstated line of descent of another sort—the Muses, Orpheus, and Horace. Pindar, the immediate ancestor, is present in the poem by allusion and quotation, and in a sense the whole ode is an answer to his.

The fate of Pindar's questioning, though, rests not with Horace, but in a poetic milieu of early Anglo-American modernism in which the query, and indeed its very sound, has become as a tinkling symbol. Ezra Pound's Hugh Selwyn Mauberley, in one of his better moments, hears the line which Pound once cited as an instance of what he called "Pindar's big rhetorical drum" echoing ironically in the tawdry modern air:

O bright Apollo,
τίν' ἄνδϱα, τίν' ἤϱωα, τινα θεόν,
What god, man or hero
Shall I place a tin wreath upon!

Inverting Pindar's order (and Horace's differing one) in both his Greek and English versions of the question, Pound puns on the Greek interrogative particle itself ("tin")—the very sound of that sort of poetic questioning has become tinny for him. But it was Pound's reduction of such matters to those of rhetoric and style which was so generally characteristic of his poetic failings.

This is another kind of poetic answering. A poem treats an earlier one as if it posed a question, and answers it, interprets it, glosses it, revises it in poetry's own way of saying, "In other words. . . ." In these terms, the whole history of poetry may be said to constitute a chain of answers to the first texts—Homer and Genesis—which themselves become questions for successive generations of answerers. These answers which occur between poems and earlier, questioning ones are of a different sort from those which occur between parts of the same poem, but they may be related by the ways in which they trope, or make nonliteral, the rhetoric of answering. Horace's opening questions answer, in this sense, Pindar's opening and closing ones. Intertextual answer can often be the minute matter of a single word or scheme taken up by another writer and used significantly, particularly with respect to its original use. When Robert Frost, in the wonderful sonnet of one sentence called "The Silken Tent," elaborates his comparison of a particular woman's life to a tent in a field, speaks of being "loosely bound / By countless silken ties of love and thought," the "silken ties" answer to those with which poetic speech links lovers in the scene from Keats's "I Stood Tip-Toe" cited earlier: ". . . the soft numbers in that moment spoken / Made silken ties that never may be broken." Noticing this sends the reader back into Frost's poem again in a new wonder. "For truth has such a face and

such a mien," writes Dryden in the first part of *The Hind and the Panther,*
"As to be lov'd needs only to be seen." He is suggesting in this allegory of
the Roman Church in England that if the hind had not run by so quickly
its beauty (allegorically, the truth of the Church) would have smitten the
hunters, who could then never have shot it. Alexander Pope, in a context of
moral discourse about how black and white, vice and virtue, usually blend
into gray, answers Dryden's white hind with moral blackness in a direct
inversion of value in the famous lines "Vice is a monster of such frightful
mien, / As, to be hated, needs but to be seen." Indeed, reading this as an
answer to Dryden would make us want to stress the implicit contrastive
words, "Vice" (as opposed to "truth") and "hated" (as opposed to "lov'd").

One might go on at great length to consider the multitude of such local
instances which the history of poetry provides, but I shall turn to a few
larger cases of poetic answer in this general sense of the ways in which poems
answer each other. Whether or not a prior poem has actually asked a question, a later one will assume that it has, and answer what it insists on interpreting as having been a figurative query. In a little book on the poetic
use of half-avowed, or half-suppressed, allusion,[11] I called the poetic device
of revising a word or phrase or trope from a precursor text "The Figure of
Echo." But to call poetic echoes of the sort I have just exemplified "answers,"
itself begs an interesting question. Ovid's nymph in the story (*Metamorphoses*
3) of Echo and Narcissus returns the final syllable of whatever is stated or
asked or commanded *as if all discourse were interrogations, and as if each
question contained, in its final syllable, its own answer.* Sometimes, indeed, an
actual question is mockingly answered. Ovid's splendid deployment of the
device, or scheme, of echoing is nicely caught by his seventeenth-century
translator, George Sandys, in such a moment, when Narcissus is pursuing
the nymph, who has not yet—after his death from longing for his own
image—withered away into a mere voice: "The Boy, from his companions
parted, said; / Is any nigh? I, Eccho answer made"—punning on the "aye"
of assent and the first person singular pronoun.

But in any case, such echoes as those of the voices of nature in caves and
mountains and halls and domes are usually mocking ones, in both senses of
that word. Echoes imitate, and make game of, original voices. No writer
before the twentieth century has so keenly perceived the relation between
the ironic voice of echoing and the mockeries of poetic derivativeness as
Kierkegaard, in a remarkable journal entry of 1837:

> Each time I wish to say something there is another who says it at the very
> same moment. It is as though I *thought double,* and my other self continually
> stole a march on me; or while I am standing and speaking everyone thinks it
> is another, so I can rightly ask the question which the bookseller Soldin put
> to his wife: Rebecca, is that I who am talking? I will flee out of the world
> (not to a cloister—I have strength in me yet) in order to find myself (every

other driveller says the same), no, in order to forget myself. Nor shall I go where some jabbering brook plods across a field. I don't know if this verse is by some poet, but I could wish *an inflexible irony* would compel some senti-mental poet to write it, yet *in such a way that he himself all the while read something else.* Or Echo, yes Echo, thou great master of irony! You who parody in yourself the highest and deepest on earth: the Word which created the world, since you merely give the contour not the fullness. Yes Echo, *avenge* all the sentimental twaddle that conceals itself in wood and meadow, in church and theatre, and which now and then detaches itself and drowns out every-thing for me. When in the woods I don't hear the trees conversing of old legends. No, *to me* they whisper all the drivel they have so long been witness to, and ask me in God's name to cut them down so as to be set free from all the nonsense of these nature enthusiasts. Oh, if all these drivel-heads sat on one throat, I would know with Caligula what I had to do. I see you are already afraid I might end on the scaffold. No, you see, there is where the drivel-head (I mean that which comprises all the particulars) would have me; yet you forget that it does no harm in the world. Yes, Echo, you whom I once heard chastise a nature lover when he exclaimed: 'Hear yonder, the lonesome flute tones of a lovelorn nightingale' [*Nattergal*]—and you answered: 'Mad' [*gal*]. Yes, *avenge, avenge yourself—you are the man!*[12]

But Kierkegaard's favorite trope aside, there are other figures than irony which are enacted by poems echoing prior ones. What I have elsewhere called the metaleptic role of echoic allusion in poems[13] we can see here as another aspect of poetic answer. One text answers a prior one as if that prior one had posed a question. And yet, for the reader, it is the earlier poem which sends back echoes to the voice of the later one, echoes that resound from the cave of memory and remembered poetry.

The poem ascribed to Shakespeare (and, I feel, indeed his) called *A Lover's Complaint* is an exercise in a familiar genre of the 1590s. It starts out with an open avowal of its own generic derivativeness by invoking the trope of echo:

From off a hill whose concave womb reworded
A plaintful story from a sist'ring vale,
My spirits t'attend this double voice accorded,
And down I laid to list the sad-tuned tale.

"Reworded" is a strange word here. That a human song will be affirmatively echoed by the landscape is a trope as old as Virgil or Theocritus. But here, the poet, listening to the "double voice" of a more than twice-told tale, "sod-tun'd" (in the sense of being intoned by the earth), is in the position of being a reworder himself, a belated narrator. And the metaphor of echo-ing in the Shakespearean poem is troped again beyond or after these lines, when the young William Butler Yeats rewords *its* word, in the course of rewording an image from Keats, in his "The Song of the Happy Shepherd"

(1889). The poem that commences "The woods of Arcady are dead / And over is their antique joy" is obsessed with its speaker's inability to be even what we call now a second-generation English romantic poet. It urges, in some lines invoked at the beginning of this book, that the reader

> Go gather by the humming sea
> Some twisted, echo-harbouring shell,
> And to its lips thy story tell,
> And they thy comforters will be,
> Rewording in melodious guile
> Thy fretful words a little while,
> Till they shall singing fade in ruth
> And die a pearly brotherhood;
> For words alone are certain good:
> Sing, then, for this is also sooth.

The seashell's ear is its mouth; it hears with its organ of discourse, the way a new poem speaks its rewordings with the same organ of writing by which it hears earlier poems. This is one way of talking to oneself, of telling oneself one's own story, of asking and answering one's own questions. Echo answers even a statement by rewording its declarative grammar into an implicit interrogative that demands reply. We call out, "Hello!" but Echo feigns to hear this as "Hello?" and, as if helpfully rather than mockingly, answers in the affirmative which we, of course, have actually uttered. There is a sense in which Echo mistakes our declaration by calling it a question, and thereby calling it into question.

A particularly elegant instance of the echoic answering of one poem by another is one which also engages the matter of intratextual questions and answers previously discussed. A celebrated seventeenth-century poem by Thomas Carew uses the strategy of declining to answer an offstage rhetorical question in order to answer it poetically, and to call attention to how literary or conventional the issues raised by the question were to begin with. Its celebrated opening words, "Ask me no more," which return at the beginning of each stanza in the pattern known as *anaphora,* are usually given as the title (although Carew called it "Song"):

> Ask me no more where Jove bestows,
> When June is past, the fading rose;
> For in your beauty's orient deep
> These flowers, as in their causes, sleep.
>
> Ask me no more whither do stray
> The golden atoms of the day;
> For in pure love heaven did prepare
> Those powders to enrich your hair.
>
> Ask me no more whither doth haste
> The nightingale when May is past;

For in your sweet dividing throat
She winters and keeps warm her note.

Ask me no more where those stars light
That downwards fall in dead of night;
For in your eyes they sit, and there
Fixed become as in their sphere.

Ask me no more if east or west
The Phoenix builds her spicy nest;
For unto you at last she flies,
And in your fragrant bosom dies.

These stanzas embody not so much rhetorical questions as rhetorical imperatives. "Don't ask X or Y" is a little like "Don't think of purple umbrellas" in its precise way of being counterproductive, and the questions smuggled into the caution not to ask them are a counterpart to answers smuggled into questions obviously demanding them. Each stanza's question is manifestly about the fate of some short-lived flash of beautiful phenomenon—rose, bits of sunlight, nightingale's song, falling stars, and, finally, the Phoenix. Aside from being transient, however, these phenomena are all cyclical and will return again, and the various aspects of the beauty of the lady being addressed in the poem will each be seen to harbor one of them during its term of absence. The "causes" in the first stanza are the four Aristotelian causes or sources of any entity, the material (what it's made of), the efficient (who or what made it), the formal (what makes it *it* rather than something else), and the final (what it's for). To say that the roses "sleep" in the lady's beauty the way they do in their causes is very wittily to define a sort of implicitness, conceptually authoritative, which makes the lady herself the stuff of, the authoress, the idea defining and the ultimate purpose of each of the bits of beauty. She is not merely a storehouse, but a place of creation and recreation. The forestalled questions, "Don't ask where *this* has gone" are deflected for the purported reason that "Everybody knows that. . . ." And yet the purported questioner and the idealized personage of the poem are the same, and the questions asked are both new and old ones. No poem in the Petrarchan tradition has indeed asked those questions about the transient beauties; rather the ubi sunt? would specify the answer, "Dead. All dead. Gone. Like all of us soon."[14]

On the other hand, all these beauties are cliches of Petrarchan poetry and, in its mythology, serve as synecdoches of the lady's more general beauty. The rosy cheeks, sunny golden hair, naturally musical voice, starry eyes, and fragrant, nestlike bosom where flaming passion spends itself and erotically dies are all part of the stock in trade of the verse of Carew's age and its precursor. The poem is acutely aware of how much it is about literary conventions, and the turn of wit which says "falling stars, which literally vanish, endure always in the metaphor of starry-eyedness" and so forth is far more potent than the mere naive retailing of the cliches in a slightly new package. The very form of the imperative is an allusive one, in fact.[15] One of the most important poems of Horace for earlier seventeenth-century English poetry is the eleventh ode of book 1, the one which ends with the famous injunction to *carpe diem*—pluck the flower of the passing day before it dies (and all of us with it). But it opens with just such an injunction not to ask what happens to something soon over, in this case, our own lives: "Tu ne quaesieris—scire nefas—quem mihi, quem tibi, fine di dederint, Leuconöe . . ." (Ask not, Leuconöe [we can't know] what end the gods have ordained for me and you)—nor, Horace goes on, go to Babylonian astrology to try to find out. Better take what comes. . . .

When Carew comes to echo Horace's injunction not to ask, it is with a powerful repression of the irrevocability of death, which returns only with the last word of the poem. But the seventeenth-century poem is also conscious of responding to a whole intervening poetic convention, and it is almost as if the fictive lady purportedly doing the asking is not merely an ad hoc personage, as in many love poems, but an allegorized figure of the poetic convention itself. For a last time, the poem seems to suggest, the poet will cope with questions of this sort. His final answer is, "The body dies; the body's beauty lives," but only in the seminary of trope, from which phenomenal instances will, from time to time, be resurrected. Ultimately his poem maintains, despite its manifest rhetorical strategy, that love lives in love poetry, lives on in it.

Tennyson's celebrated lyric from *The Princess* echoes Carew's poem and, in complex ways, answers it. (Tennyson himself, in another lyric from the same work—"The Splendour Falls from Castle Walls"—invokes echoes as *answerers* of the bugles of romantic imagination.) What can be immediately observed is that Carew's anaphora is echoed, but also reechoed in that each stanza repeats it as a refrain. The poem is both lyric and dramatic monologue, however, and whereas Carew's blocked question is epistemological, in Tennyson it is specifically erotic, not a request for information, but one for compliance:

Ask me no more: the moon may draw the sea;
    The cloud may stoop from heaven and take the shape,
    With fold to fold, of mountain or of cape;
But O too fond, when have I answered thee?
        Ask me no more.

Ask me no more: what answer should I give?
    I love not hollow cheek or faded eye:
    Yet, O my friend, I will not have thee die!
Ask me no more, lest I should bid thee live;
        Ask me no more.

> Ask me no more: thy fate and mine are sealed;
>   I strove against the stream and all in vain;
>   Let the great river take me to the main.
> No more, dear love, for at a touch I yield;
>   Ask me no more.

This is a Victorian "answer" to the implicit question posed by Carew's poem. Not only is the lady now the speaker-singer of an aria which we can almost hear musically unfolding, rather than the mistress-muse addressee; more remarkably, the storehouse of late romantic erotic posturing has supplanted the treasury of Petrarchan devices. In the first stanza, it is made clear that an "answer" would entail an ultimate embrace, "fold to fold," the feminine cloud fitting itself to the male projections of land, after the opening figure of preliminary attraction, with the virgin Cynthia drawing on the admiring and enslaved ocean. In the second, the metaquestion about the answer is in itself ambiguous: what sort of answer? which of several within a sort? what answer ought I give? what answer would I give if I let you ask me a last time? The lady herself is unsure which of these she means, and her very question is both invitation and refusal. But her command has, by the end of that stanza, become impossible—she has herself put the man's predicament in posturing positions, making a matter of life and love one of life and death. The "hollow cheek and faded eye" are literary symptoms of pining, rather than of consumption by any ill worse than desire; the conclusion, "Don't ask me not to let you die," undoes itself in a turn of bad faith.[16]

In the final stanza, the refrain has not been modified syntactically, but the context of the question has totally shifted. "Ask me no more"—it's hardly necessary, she all but observes—and there is no need to ask any more. The moon has become a frail vessel in a proverbial current, and the masculine sea, invoked originally as part of an Elizabethan conceit (Raleigh's, in particular), now does the drawing and awaits the feminine arrival. The strongest rhetorical revision is effected by an implicit contrast with the word "touch" in the penultimate line, and we should read the final phrase *"Ask* me no more," as if to say, *"Ask* me no more—my answer could only be another strophe like this one, but touch me, and you have me." The echoed phrase, the allusive "answer" to Carew's, becomes a sort of "No" which, through reiteration in refrain as well as in anaphora, metamorphoses into the "Yes" which was always lurking inside it, not as a result of Circe's magic, but of that of poetry. The poem is also not one whit less about poetry than Carew's. In each case, the woman personifies a literary convention; in Tennyson's poem, set into a longer work which takes very seriously for a while some of the claim of Victorian feminism, she embodies a set of gestures and perhaps an ideology, rather than a cabinet of emblems. But in any case, the inversions of dramatic syntax, as it were, with the woman "answering" the man of the earlier poem, the eloquent poet-figure being the woman, the shift of conceptual ground from knowledge to feelings, the trivialization of the matter of death in the operatic language in Tennyson, all correspond to the inversions of syntax which in our language convert declaratives into interrogatives and vice versa.

My discussion has drifted into the perhaps inevitable matter of poetic and rhetorical imperatives. An injunction not to ask a question, as in the Tennyson and Carew poems, is a command nonetheless, and in the next chapter I shall explore the general terrain of imperatives that can't mean what they claim to, not through fault, but through trope. The question of answers in poetry has hardly been answered itself, but only raised. The Tennysonian answer about not answering is only one of many instances in Tennyson—as in Eliot (who pretended that this was not so) or Stevens—of echoic answering, answering which is figuratively so because no actual question has been asked. At one point, he presents us with an instance which almost begs to be used to conclude this discussion.

At the very beginning of *Maud,* the near-mad narrator speaks of the spot where the body of his father, possibly a suicide, was found, a "ghastly pit" that is nonetheless the type of all graves:

I hate the dreadful hollow behind the little wood,
Its lips in the field above are dabbled with blood-red heath,
The red-ribbed ledges drip with a silent horror of blood,
And Echo there, whatever is asked her, answers "Death."

There are all sorts of echoes in this passage, all sorts of answers. We cannot help but hear the terraced echoes in the words "lips—above—dabbled—blood-red—red-ribbed ledges drip," building up in density toward the end. But the bottom line, as it were, is the universal answer to all rhetorical questions about the nature of life. In the presence of the grave, there is only one serious answer, and, by giving it, Echo need not mock. But Tennyson's Echo here herself echoes an earlier one: In book 2 of *Paradise Lost,* the moment of the birth of Death as described by his mother, the monster Sin: "he my inbred enemy / Forth issu'd, brandishing his fatal Dart / Made to destroy," like a horrifying transmogrification of Eros. Sin goes on:

I fled, and cri'd out *Death*;
Hell trembl'd at the hideous Name, and sigh'd
From all her Caves, and back resounded *Death*.

This is an ultimate travesty of the pastoral trope, from Virgil on, of landscape echoing the name of the beloved as sung by the poet. Tennyson's Echo is, in this instance, more than a mere imitator, but no more than a mortifying deconstructor of the particularity of questions. And her dusty answer allows of no subsequent ones.

4 ❧

Poetic Imperatives

My previous essay concluded with the discussion of a grim, but inevitable poetic answer which was instanced in an echoing word. I had remarked in passing that echoes are always figurative answers, rather than literal ones. They don't answer questions which have actually been asked, but, like all allusive rejoinders, they treat statements or even imperatives as if they were questions. Poetic answers, then, were seen as tropes of answering, even as, in chapter 2, poetic questions were shown to be tropes of interrogation and inquiry far more figurative than so-called rhetorical questions are. I had even implied that rhetorical questions are really schemes, rather than tropes, even as sarcasm and hyperbole are almost on the verge of the literal, rather than over the edge of irony and metaphor. That is, the mere interrogative or responsive form is like a surface pattern (an alliterative or rhyme scheme, say) rather than like a use of such a pattern, a reasoning rhyme, say, or a figuration of alliteration. A poetic question or answer, on the other hand, is a metaphor of asking, or of responding. Instead of using the rhetoricians' extremely useful *scheme* and *trope,* I might have appealed to a distinction Coleridge draws between "form" and "shape," as he calls them. "Remember," he remarks in his essay "On Poesy or Art," "that there is a difference between form as proceedings, and shape as superinduced;—the latter is either the death or the imprisonment of the thing;—the former is its self-witnessing and self-effected sphere of agency." A poem sunk in mere rhetorical questions would be dead, or an automaton of the imagination, would it not? But a poem asking the kinds of only poetically answerable question of the sort I have been exploring would, and does indeed, live.

Bear with me, then, while I consider the form—in Coleridge's sense—rather than the mere shape, of poetic imperatives. Let us consider, too, the slightly less assertively enacting grammatical mode of what Latin grammars used to call the jussive, the "let it be that X . . ." construction I have just employed in this sentence. A Latin grammar of the mid-nineteenth century quoted in the *OED* distinguishes between them by saying that whereas the imperative commands, the jussive directs.[1] In either case, we are to be considering metaphoric commands and urgings, schemes of the imperative that are designed not literally to enact, but poetically to bring a fiction into being. To take a poetic command literally—that is, to treat it like a legal injunction or the binding command on the square of a board game: "GO DIRECTLY TO JAIL"—is trivially to misread the poetry. We cannot, of course, literally become the west wind addressed in Shelley's ode, and thus cannot, as idiotic literalists, attempt to comply with his injunction to "Be thou me, impetuous one!" (how would one do that, anyway?) nor even with the final advice to "Scatter, as from an unextinguished hearth /Ashes and sparks, my words among mankind!" even "by the incantation of this verse" (which is ambiguous about whether it specifies the wind's chanting or the verse's own incantatory powers). On the other hand, throughout the poem, we can and do absorb the spill, as it were, of the first three strophes' concluding imperatives, "Oh, hear!" We, as readers, hear, and not merely overhear, those elaborate predictions and specifications which in fact make up the earlier part of the ode. The command, addressed not to ourselves, which says, "O You over there, with your X and Y and Z, and your tendency to do A and B to C whenever you can, and your nasty mother M from whom you derive your vile habit of always doing D and your poor father F from whom you never learned to L . . . and so forth, O You, listen to me!" is, we might say, a crudely rhetorical command, from the point of view of the putative listener, who will have thrown something at the speaker or left the scene. He will do the opposite of listen. We, as oblique listeners, are also attending to a figurative command: what we are in fact made to listen to is a polemically moralizing description of the "You." All that material has been smuggled into any listener's hearing in the lining of the manifest subject of the imperative. As far as the grammar is concerned, the imperative is no different from "Listen, Mac . . . !" The difference is that the shape (as Coleridge would have called it here) of the imperative becomes a form of the creation and revelation of a new and rich notion of Mac-ness.

There is an easier opportunity to brutalize poetry by wringing its neck into literalness in a beautiful echo of Shelley's lines about scattering his words at the end of Hart Crane's elegy "Praise for an Urn": "Scatter these well-meant idioms / Into the smoky spring that fills / The suburbs, where they will be lost." No reasonable reader would take this as an injunction to him or her to take the page containing "Praise for an Urn"—or, indeed, the rest of Crane's book—tear it up into tiny bits, and fling them, however sacramentally, to the west wind, east wind, or whatever. And yet readers of all sorts do indeed take literally metaphoric uses of the word "I" in lyrics ("I" being indeed almost always a complex fictional character in poems).

But for a poem to be talking to an entity within itself is in a sense for it to be talking to the general question of itself, commanding itself rather than a reader. Wise poets are usually careful about their commands, whereas foolish ones (at any time in modern history, we might say, "That is, most poets writing today") write as if they expected to be taken literally. Perhaps that is one of the many reasons why one of the wisest of poets, Wallace Stevens, avoids Crane's openings to misconstruction in *his* version of one of Shelley's imperatives in the *Ode*. In section 6 of the second part of "Notes Toward a Supreme Fiction" the speaker calls out to the monotonies of all the poetical birdsong of the past, calls out to the wren, the jay, and the robin, "Bethou, bethou, bethou me in my glade." Not Shelley's "Hey, you, wind, become me, be me!" Rather, Stevens makes up a new verb, to "be-thou," an English equivalent of the French *tutoyer,* meaning here, "Address me as 'thou' as opposed to 'you'" (and thereby, perhaps, engage the other meaning of 'be me'). Shelley's extravagant imperative becomes a more guarded but, in the end, equally outrageous one.[2]

Wallace Stevens's imperatives are always fascinating from the point of view of a rhetorical analysis of what, in the fact, they really appear to be commanding. For example, the very opening of "Notes Toward a Supreme Fiction" addresses the reader as if he or she were a Greek youth, student not of Socrates but of poetry, whose name, in the first section, will come to sound like Apollo's name, "Phoebus," but who must reject the significance of that possible pun (for "Phoebus is dead, ephebe"). He is enjoined to come out of a late, literary version of Plato's cave and cope with a reality stripped of fancy, the first idea, the sun. "Begin, ephebe, by perceiving the idea / Of this invention, this invented world, / The inconceivable idea of the sun." "This invention" is the poetic process, the faculty of inventing, but even more, it is the poem itself. The powerful mode of imperative opening of a major long poem here audaciously harks back to the original imperative openings of the original long poems.[3]

And perhaps it is with these opening imperatives that we should have started, after all. The commands to the muses to "sing" the Iliad and the Odyssey which start out each of those poems are tropes of commands to the poems themselves to start up, to the singer to start singing. In the English versions in which we usually read Homer today, the imperative verb begins each poem: "Sing, goddess, the anger of Peleus' son Achilleus" (so Richmond Lattimore's *Iliad*) and "Sing in me, Muse, and through me tell the story / of that man skilled in all ways of contending" (Robert Fitzgerald's *Odyssey*). (Actually, the *Iliad*'s first word is "anger," and the *Odyssey*'s, "the man"—"Mēnin aede thea . . ." and "Andra moi ennepe, Mousa." Lucretius, near the opening of his great poem *On the Nature of Things,* makes explicit what the Homeric openings had troped under the command to the muse. After an opening twenty lines of invocation to *alma Venus,* the basic source of creative energy in his poem's vision of nature, he explains what a prior poet might have meant by "Tell, Muse . . ." (I quote from the translation of Rolfe Humphries):

> Since you alone control the way things are.
> Since without you no thing has ever come
> Into the radiant boundaries of light,
> Since without you nothing is ever glad,
> And nothing ever lovable, I need,
> I need you with me, goddess, in the poem
> I try to write here, on *The Way Things Are*.
> This book will be for Memmius, a man
> Your blessing has endowed with excellence
> All ways and always.[4]

—And only here, after invoking his friend and patron, does Lucretius finally produce his epic imperative:

> Therefore, all the more,
> Give to our book a radiance, a grace,
> Brightness and candor . . .

which is followed by other specific commands to bring peace to the world by seducing her lover Mars away from war so that he might write his great meditative work in a troubled time.[5] And only then does a command more literal—a sort of writerly imperative to a specific reader—order Memmius to pay the right sort of attention to what will turn out to be a difficult poem:

> For what ensues, my friend,
> Listen with ears attentive and a mind
> Cleared of anxiety; hear the reasoned truth
> And do not without understanding treat
> My gifts with scorn, my gifts, disposed for you
> With a loyal industry.

(True poets know how vain such an injunction almost always is. They are bound not to be listened to appropriately and bound to be misunderstood. As Schlegel reminded us, a classic text must never be entirely comprehensible. "But those who are cultivated and who cultivate themselves must always want to learn more from it."[6] Writers of versified journalism, which is mostly what is called poetry today, always expect quite correctly to be understood, which makes their work not worth studying.)

Virgil, also, resists Homer's initial epical command, deconstructing it as it were one stage further than Lucretius does. Instead of substituting a "Help me, O Muse, to write this difficult poem" for the "Write, Muse, this poem about thus and so" of Homer, Virgil makes no bones about what

"Sing, muse" has always meant. In addition, he acknowledges in the same breath the priority of Homer's two poems and announces his intention to write of both of their subjects—the "anger" of the *Iliad*'s opening word and the "man" of the *Odyssey*'s:

> Arms and the man I sing, who from the Trojan shore
> First came, exiled by fate, to Italy and to
> The coast of Lavinia . . .

Only in the eighth line does Virgil introduce his imperative, having made it clear beforehand that the singing—that is, the writing—is his and not tha· of a muse singing in, or through, him. "Musa, mihi causas memora, quo numine laeso," he begins (Muse, tell me the cause [for the Queen of Heaven's driving so fine a man to such hardship]). He desires unascertainable knowledge—that of divine intentions—and directs his poetic questions to the only appropriate source: "tantaene animis caelestibus irae?"—"Can heav'nly minds such high resentment show, / Or exercise their spite in human woe?" as Dryden gives it. (It will have been observed, I trust, that this is a poetic, and not a rhetorical question.) Although Virgil does not address his own work through his muse, urging the poem to start telling itself, he gathers strength from his very belatedness, from his Homeric background, so that if there were indeed to have been a "Sing, goddess" at the opening, she should have had to have been identified as a Muse of post-Homeric poetry. (Apollonius Rhodius, at the beginning of his Alexandrian cyclical poem of the Argonauts, had preceded Virgil and Lucretius both in his "Beginning with you, O Phoebus, I will recount . . ." but, more weakly than Virgil, avoids Homeric allusion and implicit acknowledgment. Hesiod assigns the *Works and Days* to the Pierian Muses. The *Theogony,* on the other hand, starts out with a most complex invocation to the Heliconian Muses, whose role as *source* is more interestingly figured than in all other epic. It seems to me to prefigure the Miltonic and Spenserian complexities.)

Ovid, at the beginning of his *Metamorphoses,* slyly introduces the imperative after an initial Virgilian indicative: "I am in mind to tell of bodies changed into new forms. You gods, who have worked these changes, breathe on my undertaking, and lead my songs, unbroken, from the world's beginning until our day." The seventeenth-century English translation of these lines by George Sandys (lines which were very probably written in Virginia in the first decade of the century) puts the matter of divine help rather neatly:

> Of bodies chang'd to various forms I sing;
> Assist, you Gods (from whom these changes spring).
> And from the world's first fabrick to these times,
> Deduce my never-discontinued rhymes.

One final classical imperative, hardly as familiar as the Homeric and Virgilian ones, nevertheless provides an important paradigm for the language
in which poetry urges itself to do all that it can really do in the world,
namely, truly to generate itself. Theocritus's second idyll, written in the third
century B.C., is a dramatic monologue of a girl who is working a spell with
a kind of magic wheel to bring her lover home to her. Her only actual
incantation—most of what she says is narration or description—is the command to her wheel itself, in the first part of the poem. It is in a line which
keeps returning as one of the earliest refrains in our literature: "Magical
whirligig, fetch to my house my unfaithful beloved" (Daryl Hine's fine version). Halfway through the poem another refrain displaces it, and here the
imperative is directed to the goddess Artemis: "Holy and reverend Moon-
goddess, show me my love, where it came from." But the girl's imperatives
of knowledge and power are directed beyond her own utterance—she
doesn't sing, for example, "Wheel, *become* magical." Yet in the first idyll,
Theocritus initiates a far more resonant type of imperative refrain. The
poem commences with a dialogue between Thyrsis and a goatherd who asks
him to sing a song he had sung on another occasion and offers him the gift
of a carved cup. Thyrsis begins his song with a line which returns throughout as a refrain: "Start up the pastoral music, dear Muses, begin the performance." It comes back every few lines, until, toward the middle of the
poem, it shifts its form to "Muses, continue the pastoral music, on with the
performance." (In the Greek, the lines are more delicately varied: "archete
boukolaikas Moisai philai archet'aoidas" changing to "archete boukolaikas
Moisai palin archet'aoidas"—the "dear" Muses becomes "back, again"
Muses.) It is as if different sorts of poetic energy and skill were required to
initiate a poem and to keep it going; similarly, the last four occurrences of
the refrain invoke, as it were, the Muses of closure: "Muses, come finish the
pastoral music, conclude the performance" (this time, with a greater alter-
ation of the words in Greek). The poet talks to himself and to that part of
himself, in particular, which is in the process of becoming his poem, by
talking the only language which poems understand, the language of tropes,
of fictions. There is an overtone of spell, perhaps, here as well: what if
Thyrsis had said to his song, "Watch out, now. Remember about build;
you've just been writing about how a character in this poem remains silent
in his amorous suffering; soon you're going to have him deliver a long
rebuke to Aphrodite. Better remember that the refrain has become a fairly
boring drone by now, and isn't really marking time out usefully for the
hearer any more. Better change the refrain to allow the poem to shift gears.
There. That's it"? Very simply, this would have wrecked the poem, refrains,
remainder, and all. But the varied instructions to the Muses of writing do
indeed effect just that shift of gears.

Theocritus does not actually invent a new set of Muses for each invocation nor does he mythographically interpret, as medieval and Renaissance poetry would do, the individually named muses as having different roles, presiding over different musico-poetic genres. Renaissance verse romance, as we shall see in a moment, adopted a number of such strategies. The immediate tradition established by the refrains in Theocritus involves other lyrical imperative refrains. Catullus's three Fates, singing over their spindles at the marriage of Peleus and Thetis in his poem number 64, prophesy the birth of Achilles. They start out addressing the bridegroom, Peleus, asking him to "accept the true oracle which on this bright day the Sisters reveal to you." But then, in midline, another imperative is prepared, another "you" addressed: "But you, run, drawing on the woof-threads which fates follow, run, you spindles" (sed vos quae fata sequuntur / currite ducente subtegmina, currite, fusi). It is that last line which becomes the refrain of the whole song—"Run on, drawing the woof-threads which fates follow, run on, you spindles." Their imperative echoes both of Theocritus's two idylls in asking the spindles to spin out human destiny even as Catullus's language is spinning out the poem, even as their singing is spinning out the song contained in it: their *fusi,* spindles, are a combination of the Muses and the girl's jinxing magic wheel. The most complex and triumphant summation of this tradition of imperative refrain, perhaps, is in the great returning line of Spenser's "Prothalamion"—"Sweete Thames, runne softly, till I end my song." In a late poem shadowed with losses and failed hopes for poetry and its relation to power, the poet commands the river—the one he has made into a trope for the course of English poetry and poetic truth—neither to inspire, amplify, or become his poem, but rather to modulate its volume to provide an accompaniment to his clear but somewhat weakened voice.[7]

Chaucer remembers Ovid's and Virgil's combinations of assertions of authorial power and requests for supplementary aid when, at the opening of the proem to the first book of *Troilus and Criseyde,* after stating his purpose, he enlists as his muse one of the Furies of antiquity: "Thesiphone, thou help me for t'endite / These woeful vers that weepen as I write." But by the time of the proem to his second book of the same poem, Chaucer switches muses: "O Lady mine, that callèd art Cleo, / Thou be my speed fro this forth, and my muse, / To rime well this book till I have do." The Muse of history now must needs light his poem's way. At the beginning of book 3, Chaucer devotes six stanzas to the praise and in supplication of Venus but concludes his proem by calling up the powers of Calliope, the Muse of epic. At the beginning of book 4, all three Furies are commanded as muses; at the beginning of book 5, the three fates are invoked but not commanded. These mutations of presiding muse mythologize what had been implicit in Theocritus's three refrains. But Spenser, brooding over the significance of Chaucer's modulations, himself invokes the aid of a pentad of figures in the proem to book 1 of *The Faerie Queene:* "Helpe then, O holy

Virgin, chiefe of nine / Thy weaker Novice to perform thy will," he begins, carefully refraining from naming the head muse (convention elevates none of these), and, more particularly, leaving it open as to whether he has Clio or Calliope, the truth of history or the power of fiction, in mind as president spirit. The Cupid, Venus, and Mars are commanded to come and be of help in generating the poem. Finally, command having totally weakened into supplication and prayer, Spenser calls up the true earthly muse of his great poem, troping this political power in metaphors of heaven. If the previous four have been more traditionally invoked in Virgilian and Chaucerian ways, Queen Elizabeth is asked to do something beyond all these:

> And with them eke, O Goddesse heavenly bright,
>   Mirrour of grace and Majestie divine,
>   Great Lady of the greatest Isle, whose light
>   Like Phoebus lampe throughout the world doth shine,
>   Shed thy faire beames into my feeble eyne,
>   And raise my thoughts too humble and too vile,
> To think of that true glorious type of thine,
>   The argument of mine afflicted stile:
> The which to heare, vouchsafe, O dearest dred a-while.

In short, while the queen herself is *asked* to give political, financial, and moral support to the poet who is her subject, the fiction of her is *told* to give originality to the poem which is inventing that fiction. Here again, the poet commands his own poetry to produce itself.

It is no wonder that Milton, as conscious of Spenser before him as Spenser is of Chaucer, should embed his epic—perhaps we should say his postepic—imperative in such a dense tangle of allusion and qualification as he does in the opening lines of *Paradise Lost*. "Sing, Heavenly Muse, the tale of Adam's fall / Of how it fell that death devours us all"—these straightforward couplets, oblique enough (with their half-submerged play on an original devouring of an apple) to be poetic in the mid-seventeenth century, might have done for a less original poem. But look at Milton's opening; every term is nested in glosses and interpretations, the radical blank verse does far more teaching about expectation and consciousness, about the figurative and the literal (by means of its enjambments) than even Alexander Pope's rhyming could. And as for the command to the Muse, it not only goes Spenser's ambiguity in invoking an unspecified "chiefe of nine" one better, but its deferred naming of the Muse Urania until the middle of the poem is accompanied by detailed flight-plans and instruction to the Muse on how and where the aid is to be applied. Let me quote the whole of the opening invocation:

> Of Man's first Disobedience, and the Fruit
> Of that Forbidden Tree, whose mortal taste

Brought Death into the World, and all our woe,
With loss of *Eden,* till one greater Man
Restore us, and regain the blissful Seat,
Sing Heav'nly Muse, that on the secret top
Of *Oreb,* or of *Sinai,* didst inspire
That Shepherd, who first taught the chosen Seed,
In the Beginning how the Heav'ns and Earth
Rose out of *Chaos* or if *Sion* Hill
Delight thee more, and *Siloa's* Brook that flow'd
Fast by the Oracle of God; I thence
Invoke thy aid to my advent'rous Song,
That with no middle flight intends to soar
Above the'*Aonian* Mount, while it pursues
Things unattempted yet in Prose or Rhyme.
And chiefly Thou, O Spirit, that dost prefer
Before all Temples th'upright heart and pure,
Instruct me, for Thou know'st; Thou from the first
Was present, and with mighty wings outspread
Dove-like sat brooding on the vast Abyss
And mad'st it pregnant: what in me is dark
Illumine, what is low raise and support;
That to the highth of this great Argument
I may assert eternal Providence
And justify the ways of God to men.   [1–26]

—and here Milton is off into his subject, the relation of the literal fall, from Heaven to the bottom of everything, of Satan and his failed revolutionary contingent to the figurative "fall" of humanity, from perfection into nature. The spirit invoked is hardly the Greek muse of astronomy, nor some tutelary genius of biblical poetry, but the spirit of Originality itself. This is then a muse so far beyond any allegory or any theology, so far beyond ordinary fictive presence that it has been totally internalized. More than any poet before him, Milton is commanding poetry to guide him. And by "poetry" is meant a notion much more complex than, say, Dante's Virgil and what he stands for: there has been so much more history, and so many more issues, and so many more false or bad poetries. It is no wonder—even as it is wonderful—that Milton must take such a long running jump over the eternal hurdle of the obvious.

Indeed, after Milton, no major poem could ever again straightforwardly or even deviously command the muse to sing, save satirically. Pope's "Books and the man I sing . . ." signals the opening of *The Dunciad,* and its subsequent imperative, "Say, goddess," is part of a literary joke, even though the joke is as profound and the moral stakes as high as possible. One can hardly imagine *The Prelude* starting out with something like "Blow, gentle breeze, upon me, stir within / A correspondent, mild creative breeze / To sing through me the subject of myself?" Indeed, the modern poem (by which I mean, I suppose, the romantic one) must hedge its assertive, self-authorizing commands even more than Milton does. Literal command addressed to a fiction would be poetic child's play. Wordsworth starts out by asking questions, questions of some of the sorts we considered earlier: "In starting out on this poetic walk through the countryside that can be, at this stage of things, the only authentic heroic quest, the only true poetic journey, where shall I go? What, in these other words, am I to write about that would be some graver subject than those of all the literature that versifiers continue to write?" Wordsworth's questions are those of a hiker:

> What dwelling shall receive me? in what vale
> Shall be my harbour? underneath what grove
> Shall I take up my home? and what sweet stream
> Shall with its murmurs lull to my rest? . . .

Where, he asks, is he to find his poetic home. The "sweet stream" cannot be officially connected to Spenser's "sweet Thames," and yet there is some underground link.[8] And only after wandering on through 260 lines of meditative essay does the poem wander into the space of its own subject with a rhetorical question of a different sort from the "What shall I be about?" which the poem asked itself previously. Musing on what in him prevents him from writing poetry about some topic or some sweet theme (and it seems shocking that professors of literature still talk about "themes" of modern poetry), Wordsworth voices his bafflement. Then he asks in high rhetorical fashion about that bafflement:

> Was it for this
> That one, the fairest of all rivers, loved
> To blend his murmurs with my nurse's song,
> And, from his alder shades and rocky falls,
> And from his fords and shallows, sent a voice
> Which flowed along my dreams?

The river Derwent remembered has become his Thames, his initial musical theme or motive. His memory and his imagination have been commanded to sing without an actual imperative ever having been uttered.[9]

The epical opening of the untitled poem in Walt Whitman's 1855 *Leaves of Grass* which came successively to be titled "Poem of Walt Whitman, an American," "Walt Whitman," and, finally, "Song of Myself" mixes what appears to be a violently literal indicative of purpose with a most peculiarly guarded version of an imperative, directed—as if this were a simple, literal matter—to the reader: "I celebrate myself ["and sing myself" he later added, remembering Homer] / And what I assume you shall assume, / For every atom belonging to me as good belongs to you." "You shall assume"?—is that a threat, we must ask, or a promise? a prediction? In any event, a disguised command, starting that most problematic poem out with the most outrageous trope of talking to itself—through a fiction called "you," the American Reader—I know of. The figurative gap between a direct command to a poetic audience and the internalized dialectic of Whitman's poem is staggering. The famous opening of *Beowulf* is no more figurative than the text of a performance ever is, "Hwaet wē Gār-Dena in geār-dagum" (Lo! we spear-Danes in days of yore) commences with a literal command to an audience to pay attention: the modern word "Lo!" derives from something like "Look, man . . ." and the injunction is to shut up and listen now. (Modern "Look! . . ." means "Listen and heed!") Compared with all of the epic and romantic imperatives I have been citing, it is politically effective; and it is poetically most uninteresting, in that, among other things, new fictions of origination are being established.

Remember, then, the poetic imperative which opens "Notes Toward a Supreme Fiction" and which I quoted before:

> Begin, ephebe, by perceiving the idea
> Of this invention, this invented world,
> The inconceivable idea of the sun . . .

Perhaps in light of the figurative imperatives which literally start up the poetic machinery of previous supreme fictions, we can understand the point of the initiation of the later one whose strength, rather than whose weakness, comes in avowing the "notes toward"-ness of late greatness, the asymptotic approach of imaginative figuration to the name and the claim of reality. The imperative "Begin" is not addressed to a complex revision of Whitman's "you" alone, but to "Notes" itself; the "ephebe" is the young great poem, still in its opening phase of candidacy, still in its first of three canticles (the one insisting that "it must be abstract," which is to say, invented). It is modernity's supreme instance of great poetry talking to itself in that double way of speech by which we *hear* it addressing a putative, if fictional, hearer, while its commanding of itself is only overheard.

I must skip over, for want of time, a whole range of implicit commands, including that most fascinating instance of the inevitably surefire one of the punch line of a joke, with its implicit but suppressed imperative "Laugh! Here! Now!" I characterized the effect of imperatives like "Attention!" in literary texts as political, in that their authority seems, for the moment, to be part of nature. Certainly there is a deep sense in which being told a joke is partaking of a situation which is, linguistically speaking, quite totalitarian. If you are listening to my joke, I am going to *make* you laugh: this is tyranny. Yet we willingly and lovingly submit to this tyranny, with its sharp physical effects (consider the violence of laughter, the explosive metaphor of cough and sneeze and sexual ejaculation that can make us weep and collapse). Poems are as jokelike as they are dreamlike, and while Freud instigated the modern study of the rhetoric of closure in 1900 with what is still one of the greatest pieces of literary criticism of our century, the subject remains fascinatingly full of possibilities. It is only jokes—and in formal poetry, epigrams—which conclude with an implicit imperative in any way analogous to the opening ones of major poems. Commands along the way, unless they continue a mode of fictional address established at the outset, are rare. The reasons are obvious; even in a set of very literal lines like those that follow, the inserted command is given in, as it were, another language—certainly a metalanguage to that of the poem:

> Blake said a robin redbreast in a cage
> Enrages heaven, in (PLEASE TURN THE PAGE)
> A poem in four-beat couplets, terse and dense,
> And known as "Auguries of Innocence."

One significant mode of closing imperative is an explicit one. It can be considered a form of what the medieval French ballade called the *envoi*, the envoy or send-off. Often addressed to a dedicatee—certainly not ever the fallen or belated form of a muse—the formulaic form usually invokes some unnamed "Prince," as at the end of Villon's ballade with the questioning refrain which I considered in my first chapter: "Prince, don't ask this week where they [all the dead ladies] are, nor this year, or you'll end up with this refrain: 'Where are the snows of yesteryear?'" Dante's *ballate* and *canzone* address themselves, sometimes throughout, sometimes at the end (as, almost at random from the *Vita Nuova*, we find the conclusion, or *tornata*, commanding, "Pietosa mia canzone, or va piangendo"—"My piteous song, go your way weeping," he says and urges it to find the ladies to whom its sister poems have given joy). The remarkably explicit personification of the text, by the text, in the text, that we get in this tradition which moves from Dante through Petrarch to the Renaissance shows up interestingly in, for example, the *tornata*, the Italianate conclusion, of Spenser's great *Epithalamion*, the magnificent and complex ode he had written for his own wedding, whose intricacies and riches of figuration had to make do as a substitute for an entertainment, with musicians and dancers and perhaps scenery, actually performed. Spenser tells his long and remarkable original poem at—and in—its conclusion:

> Song, made in lieu of many ornaments
> With which my love should duly have bene dect,
> Which cutting off through hasty accidents,
> Ye would not stay your dew time to expect,
> But promist both to recompens,
> Be unto her a goodly ornament,
> And for short time an endless moniment.

Spenser wisely commands his poem not to do something, but to be something. Yet even so sophisticated a poetic theorist of representation as he can, in a youthful and experimental work, follow the tradition of medieval envoy. *The Shepheardes Calender* was published pseudonymously (under the name of Immerito, or Unworthy) when Spenser was about twenty-seven. It starts out with a set of dedicatory verses; but to whom?

TO HIS BOOKE

Goe, little booke: thy selfe present
As child whose parent is unkent,
To him that is the president
Of noblesse and of chevalree:
And if that Envie barke at thee,
As sure it will, for succoure flee
Under the shadow of his wing;
And asked, who thee forth did bring,
A shepheards swaine, saye, did thee sing,
All as his straying flocke he fedde:

The mixture of modesty and ambition here is of the kind that only comes with greatness. Even more remarkable is the way in which this send-off concludes:

But if that any aske thy name,
Say thou wert base begot with blame:
Forthy thereof thou takest shame.
And when thou art past jeopardee,
Come tell me what was said of mee:
And I will send more after thee.

That the young anonymous poet should ask his book to claim bastardy for itself is strange enough; that he should ask it to report back to him on the fame it has generated is even more so. The yapping dogs of envy—the very issue, indeed, of the poem's relation to its contemporaries and its noble forebears—however, comes from one of those principal forebears, Chaucer. Toward the end of the fifth book of *Troilus and Criseyde,* we hear the very words which Spenser echoes:

Go, litel book: go, litel mine tragedye,
Ther God thy maker yet, ere that he die,
So sende might to make in some comedye.
But litel book, no making thou n'envye,
But subjet be to alle poesye,
And kiss the steppes wher-as thou seest passe
Virgil, Ovid, Homer, Lucan and Stace.

The modest claims which Chaucer makes for his poem in its relation to authoritative tradition are typical of the rhetoric of authorial self-effacement which makes him claim that his book is derived from an author of his own invention, named Lollius. But for the young Spenser, Chaucer's steps are a more complex matter, and he acknowledges them once again at the very end of *The Shepheardes Calender.* After quite reasonably and most immodestly claiming that he has "made a Calender for every yeare, / That steele in strength, and time in durance, shall outweare," he takes back the formula from Chaucer, makes the "book" *his* book, specifically mentions (as Tityrus) Chaucer and another earlier English poet, Langland, and once again stakes out, by his metaphorical imperative, a place in poetic history:

> Goe, lyttle Calender! thou hast a free passeporte:
> Goe but a lowly gate emongste the meaner sorts:
> Dare not to match thy pype with Tityrus his style,
> Nor with the Pilgrim that the Ploughman playde awhyle:
> But followe them farre off, and their high steppes adore:
> The better please, the worse despise; I aske no more.

In the pastoral allegory of the eclogues of his foregoing book, "Tityrus" had meant both Virgil and Chaucer, and Spenser had indeed, in his poem, been daring to match his pipe with the styles of both of them. And he did not presume. And, of course, the little book did indeed go far.

Modern poetry could no more use the address to the text, the manifest command to the work to be poetic, than it could ever say, save in gleeful irony, like Byron, "Hail, Muse, etcetera." But Walt Whitman, at the age of seventy-two, prefaces his last poems in the book called *Good-bye My Fancy* with a sad, late envoy. The trope of "little book" is what he calls his yacht, the sailing of which had been a figure for the process of writing as far back as Ariosto and Spenser, and Horace before them. Specifically, this is Whitman's "eidolon yacht," the ship of image; his envoy is heartbreaking:

> Heave the anchor short!
> Raise main-sail and jib—steer forth,
> O little white-hull'd sloop, now speed on really deep waters,
> (I will not call it our concluding voyage,
> But outset and sure entrance to the truest, best, maturest;)

—But alas, the poetic voyage is both a final one and very far from the truest and best. The commands to a crew to heave anchor and set sail become the command to the sloop of his poetry itself which, as he concludes the envoy, inevitably becomes refigured as Walt Whitman *him*self:

> Depart, depart from solid earth—no more returning to these shores,
> Now on for aye our infinite free venture wending,
> Spurning all yet tried ports, seas, hawsers, densities, gravitation,
> Sail out for good, eidolon yacht of me!

Even as he says this, he is putting momentarily into the port of envoy. But the series of entities, "ports, seas, hawsers, densities, gravitation," is so ecstatic that his originality takes back in the next line what it had yielded in the preceding one.

It is Whitman's central trope to conflate the turning leaves of his book with the mortal grass-blades of his bodily life; and his return, in this late lyric, to the older metaphor of sea-voyage, whether of the ship of state from Horace, or the ship of self, from Petrarch, is not surprising.[10] A splendid version of Whitman's yacht is the "high ship" of Wallace Stevens's introductory poem to his second volume, *Ideas of Order.* Stevens had concluded his first book, *Harmonium,* with a strangely masked sort of envoy, a haunting, epigrammatic conjunction of question and command called "To the Roaring Wind": "What syllables are you seeking, / Vocalissimus, / In the distances of sleep? / Speak it," which functions as a misplaced epic opening, in its way. Written in 1917, it takes its place as the envoy to a book published six years later, and clearly addresses its Shelleyan inquiry to the wind of poetry to come. The poem means, "Well, what now?" and its imperative is no answer or evaded answer to the question, but an underlining of it. That poetry to come will be both preserver and destroyer of the imaginative machinery which has preceded it, and we may imagine Stevens, in putting his first book together, realizing the significance of his earlier epigram, giving it an interpretive reading as an envoy. But when he published his next volume in 1936, he wrote a combined introductory-valedictory to the book containing such poems as "The Idea of Order at Key West." Here he addresses the high ship of his writing which is his life. He is making her the muse of a new phase and avows this with an image of renewal from Shelley. Seldom in the whole tradition of self-addressed poetic imperatives do we get so clear a sense of the command being obeyed by the very language which frames it. I quote the first stanza entire of "Farewell to Florida":

> Go on, high ship, since now, upon the shore,
> The snake has left its skin upon the floor.
> Key West sank downward under massive clouds
> And silvers and greens spread over the sea. The moon
> Is at the mast-head and the past is dead.
> Her mind will never speak to me again.
> I am free. High above the mast the moon
> Rides clear of her mind and the waves make a refrain
> Of this: that the snake has shed its skin upon
> The floor. Go on through the darkness. The waves fly back.

The Florida that had proved such a natural hothouse of green metaphor and steamy mythology for Stevens right up through this book now is being cast off. Clothes which, when removed, could only leave us bare can, in another condition of our minds and bodies, leave us free of them. And so Stevens urges his boat onward, which is to say, northward. In the last stanza,

he avers that his "North is leafless and lies in a wintry slime / Both of men
and clouds, a slime of men in crowds," and then concludes:

> To be free again, to return to the violent mind
> That is their mind, these men, and that will bind
> Me round, carry me, misty deck, carry me
> To the cold, go on, high ship, go on, plunge on.

And on to the cold of his hardest and greatest poetry his ship will sail.
Originally Stevens had intended what is now the second poem of *Ideas of
Order* to serve as the starting one. It is called "Sailing after Lunch," and in
it he rejects a servitude to an element he calls the Romantic, "This heavy
historical sail / Through the mustiest blue of the lake." At the end of that
poem, he wishes

> To expunge all people and be a pupil
> Of the gorgeous wheel and so to give
> That slight transcendence to the dirty sail,
> By light, the way one feels, sharp white,
> And then rush brightly through the summer air.[11]

But in the end, Stevens supplants his mediative formula "It [with the an-
tecedent long buried and even lost earlier in the poem] It is to X and Y with
a Z . . ." with the powerful imperatives of "Farewell to Florida" and actually
takes the wheel, not particularly gorgeous as in the weathery yawl he had
been sailing after lunch, but the serious helm that will move him into the
next stage of life. He has transformed his trope of sailing by becoming his
own wind, as it were, and the boat of poetry, now with a larger keel, sails
deeper and more dangerous waters.

I have spent a good deal of time on poetic invocations and closures. They
represent clear instances of poetry's discourse with itself in that they talk
not to an audience or an active agent which might respond to the imperatives by clearly observable action. To this degree, they partake of prayer.
They also partake of spell, or magic, and thereby inherit the traditions of
both of Theocritus's refrains considered earlier. But there are two other
questions I should like to touch on at this point. The first might be introduced by quoting one of the most famous opening lines in our literature:
"Call me Ishmael." As an imperative, it is both the instantiation of an act
of naming, which the reader is to perform, and the cancellation of some other
one. The narrator of *Moby-Dick* does not say (1) "My name is Ishmael" or
(2) "My name is unimportant, but I am known as Ishmael in nautical cir-
cles." The reader is not asked, on the other hand, to bestow a name upon
him, but rather to know him by the name of the ancestor of all nomads,
whose name meant "God heard." The KJV usually uses the phrase "Call his
name [for example, Ishmael]" for a similar Hebrew construction, yet we

cannot but distinguish between naming and renaming, or calling. A nick-name, an epithet, a title, the name that results from a heroic renaming (often after a combat, as when Jacob wrestles someone beside a brook and was renamed Israel, or when, in another story, John Little fought with Robin Hood on a bridge over a brook and was renamed Little John)—all of these somehow cancel and reinterpret the earlier name. To have a name seems to its bearer to result from an act of nature; it is rather like having one's own body, with its own peculiarities and similarities. But taking a name is an-other matter, an act of the imagination, powerful, yet risky, in that the results can often be silly. Suppose, for example, that I decide to rename myself Hitler Hollander. When asked why, I reply that I saw the name in a book which I had only glanced at, that I knew this was a historical personage of some fame, and that I liked the alliteration and the fact that the short /i/ sound was more euphonious with my surname than the assonantal vowel of John. I will clearly have made an appalling fool of myself in the eyes of time, let alone in the eyes of those less ignorant than myself. For the poet, how-ever, all names are in some way or other as allusive as *Hitler*. It is not only, as Emerson observes (in "The Poet"), that "the poet is the Namer or Lan-guage-maker, naming things sometimes after their appearance, sometimes after their essence, and giving to every one its own name and not another's, thereby rejoicing the intellect, which delights in detachment or boundary." Troping, thereby, is the type of naming. But Emerson goes on to observe that "though the origin of most of our words is forgotten, each word was at first a stroke of genius, and obtained currency because for the moment it symbolized the world to the first speaker and to the hearer. (This is hardly an account of the origins of language; it is an account of the origins of poetry.) The etymologist finds the deadest word to have been once a brilliant picture. Language is fossil poetry." Even without being the kind of etymol-ogists that poets, true poets, so often are, we may all observe how true this is of names. *Hitler* was a crude example. *Ishmael* is more subtle; we have to go back to the biblical Ishmael, and then back to the interpretive reading of his name, which does not occur, as so often it does, in Genesis itself. I can name my son "after" an uncle or an admired public figure, say; but the irony will always be that the name is "after" so many others, in so many different senses, and that, poetically speaking, it is always "after" its ety-mology. Even the far-from-Emersonian Cicero remarks that the etymology of a proper name is among the attributes of a person bearing it (*De Inv.* 1.34).

I have written elsewhere about the poetics of naming, and much more remains to be said.[12] But at this late point in my discussion, and with the modes of grammar of poetic speech in mind, I want only to observe that most names are not bestowed in an imperative. Rather, the conventional form is a speech-act like "I baptize thee X"; X can, however, command,

"Call me Y," and the legitimacy of that "calling" depends partially upon there having been an X in the first place. The grammar of the imperative "Name me Y" is rather different: we are tempted to respond, "No. You'd best do *that* yourself." Parents, institutions acting *in loco parentis,* and people themselves have a right to name; that is, their optative mode of utterance, "Let this person be named X," has a potent creative power over the world. Even thereafter, that person is in fact X, and that is something which has become part of the world. For the early Wittgenstein, at least, an atom of reality has been created, an atom just as hard and even more durable than the gestated body of the person now named X. The poetic grammar of "Let it be that this person is named X" is fully creative of reality, and I wish to conclude these observations with a glance at the peculiar version of the imperative exemplified by "Let it be. . . ."

This grammatical mode is called in Latin the jussive, as I observed at the beginning of this chapter. In Greek, the equivalent is the optative mood. They are both instanced in the Primal Optative in our literature, a modulated but absolutely absolute, as it were, command which provided grounding for all others. It is the voicing of what was an epistemological, moral, metaphysical axiom: "Y'hi or"—"Fiat lux," "Let there be light!"—which in poetic terms might be interpreted as the axiomatic "Let there be meaning!" In the Hebrew original, the verb is not the imperative "Become!" (associated with the second person), and the great paradigm of the Latin jussive of the Vulgate's "Fiat lux!" and of the English remains at the heart of our poetic tradition. In Latin and English God does not say to the world, "Light up!" or even, "Light, start to exist!"; in the language of imperatives, one can only command that which already exists to act. To summon up non-existent entities and call upon them to assume being is magical logic as well as black magic.[13] In the original Hebrew of Genesis, there is a sense that the Creator in Genesis 1 is indeed addressing an imperative to a chaotic, preexistent *something,* however rabbinic Judaism may rule that whatever preexisted the divine command may not be considered or discussed. At any rate, this injunction has been successful in the Christian Old Testament's adoption of the optative mood for the imperative.

The stakes need not be so mighty and so ultimate. Among the early refrains that create templates for utterance in later poetry, the beautiful recurring line of the late Latin "Vigil of Venus," the "Pervigilium Veneris," is in a jussive of secular, erotic benediction: "Cras amet qui nunquam amavit, quiquam amavit cras amet"(Tomorrow may those make love who never have before, and may those who have make love tomorrow).[14] There is in the optative mood a sense of conjuring up, of bringing about things, which the more direct specifications of an imperative tend to demystify. The poetic optative is somewhere in among hope and prayer and contrivance; the imperative, in designating an understood subject, a specific "you" who is being called upon to act, limits the effect of the order (that is, suppose that the implied subject of "Sing, Muse . . ." is hoarse or unwilling or visiting some other poet that day or whatever?). But, "Let there be poetry, here, now," while certainly not self-descriptive, self-instigating, or self-fulfilling—after all, all that was there, then, was the expression of a wish—is certainly less contingent. Hence the jussive or optative of St. Jerome and the KJV.

This instigative or creative power of the optative mode of speech certainly underlies what Emerson makes of it in a moment in his essay called "The Transcendentalist" when he remarks that

> Our American literature and spiritual history are, we confess, in the optative mood; but whoso knows these seething brains, these admirable radicals, these unsocial worshippers, these talkers who talk the sun and moon away, will believe that this heresy cannot pass away without leaving its mark.

—which is to say that all this poetry of becoming must in time come to something. And in this sense, all poetry is itself in the optative mood. Like painting, which changes the world (not in the sense that an infantile Marxist would want it to, by prodding dormant spirits into violent acts, but by working epistemological changes), poetry changes the world *by*—not, pace the Marxist again, *rather than*—interpreting it. "X, be A" is addressed to X and contingent, as we have observed, on the power and willingness of X to do so. "Let X be A" invokes, without addressing, far more general powers.

Like a spell, you will say. Yes, like a spell or a curse, even, and I cannot terminate these remarks without a final word or two about curses and spells. Spells in poems can range from the demonic and frightening to the urbanely comic. For example, the famous termination of Coleridge's "Kubla Khan," distanced as it is from the narrator's voice in the poem by indirect discourse ("And all should cry, Beware! Beware! / His flashing eyes, his floating hair!"), eventually seems to turn its magical imperative upon the reader: "Weave a circle round him thrice, / And close your eyes with holy dread. . . ." On the other hand, a curse cast in verse can have just the opposite effect. Whereas in "Kubla Khan," the four-beat couplets seem themselves to be the natural language of spells in English, the loose, bouncing five-beat lines of the curse which follows serve somehow to domesticate the spirited fancy of the framing of the curse itself. Inventive cursing is poetic in its own right; the Yiddish language is adorned with long, epic curses and with ironically self-fulfilling ones, such as "You should drop dead on the most beautiful holiday," implying not only that the victim would then miss the event but, more subtly, that any day on which such a person died would immediately become a major festival thereby. Irish is equally rich in the rhetoric of curse, and the poem I quote from is James Stephens's "A Glass of Beer," in which a barmaid is denounced for not lending the speaker a glass of beer on credit.

Its third and final stanza is magnificent in both the inventiveness of the imprecation and the way in which the verse holds it in humor:

> If I asked her master he'd give me a cask a day;
> But she, with the beer at hand, not a gill would arrange!
> May she marry a ghost and bear him a kitten, and may
> The High King of Glory permit her to get the mange.

The grammar of our colloquial cursing is most interesting and complex, and on some other occasion I should like to consider the difference between imperatives like "Go to Hell" or "Be damned" and absolute expletives like "Shit!" or that grammatically most curious formation "Fuck you!" (probably modeled syntactically on the earlier "Damn you!," equally violent in its time, equally weakened later on). But save for the ways in which poetic imperatives and optatives are so frequently prayerlike or spell-like, the figurativeness of cursing in everyday life is of limited imaginative interest.

It is, ultimately, the powers by and with which poems address their own tropes and myths which somehow induce currents in the coils of the world. In the very words of Robinson Jeffers's phrase "Shine, perishing republic" there is a glimmer of some kind of light, and the republic lives on for at least another instant that it might not otherwise have had. And in the mighty conclusion of Hart Crane's proem "To Brooklyn Bridge," a literal object in American urban nature becomes an emblem of a more general condition of bridging, of connecting. And thus the self-fulfilling force of the final quatrain

> O sleepless as the river under thee,
> Vaulting the sea, the prairies' dreaming sod,
> Unto us lowliest sometime sweep, descend,
> And of the curveship lend a myth to God.

The vocative address of the "O"—earlier the bridge had been addressed as "O harp and altar, of the fury fused"—reminds us that the very grammar of invocation can establish an agent to whom imperatives are addressed. And ever since this was uttered, nature's god has been putting the borrowed myth of curveship to use.

All of these grammatical and rhetorical devices we have been considering—questions, answers, and commands—are in a sense aspects of one underlying trope, *Prosopopoeia,* as it is called in Greek, or personification, is usually thought of in its more limited role of turning abstractions into fictive persons (even as what we might call a figure of location might give us places—the forest of error—and reification things, like a web of deceit, which you have to remember as a spider web, invisible to a fly until he's caught in it, if the trope is to make sense, even as a cliché). But to address any object or place with an imperative is to personify it at another level of figuration. Poetry which does this is, after all, to be seen or heard as addressing a part of itself; Stevens's roaring wind becomes part of his poem when he addresses it as "Vocalissimus," the very most vocal, just as Shelley's west wind indeed became him—had become his poem—with the injunction to "Be thou me."

If in these discussions of grammar I have appeared to suggest that poems talk only to themselves and never to readers or, in another sense, "to" nature or "to" issues, it is only because I have been concerned with what is most genuinely poetical about them. But I hope it has also been clear that some of these features of poetry's discourse with itself have not been merely solipsistic, self-absorbed, or even narcissistic, but rather, parabolic. That is, these stories about being able to bring things about, these fictions of presence, these nonquestions and oblique answers, have all had morals which lie deep in our own experience. The notion that poetry is only about itself is as appalling to me as the notion that poetry is directly "about" life—that it is a kind of emotional journalism, trivially true to a kind of natural history of feelings. In their misunderstanding of true poetry, the journalist and the totalitarian sceptic, who affirms that nothing is about anything, deserve each other's company in a no-exit hell. Meanwhile, poetry, which has itself invented the punishments of such a hell, will go on talking to and with itself, about everything else, and the highest human attention will continue to overhear and to learn.

5 ❧

Garlands of Her Own:
Bondage, Work,
and Freedom

Poems, as we have seen, may be overheard talking to themselves. The question of how and when they talk *about* themselves is a much more problematic one. The matter of "about"-ness as a purely interpretive concept aside for the moment, recent literary theory has considered the question from a number of extreme viewpoints. Some of these rest in the bog of opacity: Since language can't refer to anything, poetry can't be "about" anything except itself. Or (a bit more subtly), since language can't refer without some looseness or slippage, it is the condition of poetry to manifest that characteristic looseness more than practical discourse; and in the end, the knots and uncouplings and bendings that accompany any rigid designation are always the point of any poetic text. Or, in other words, no matter what we may hear a poem say, we always *overhear* its talk about itself.

Other, antithetical views stand on the brink of transparency: Poetry is directly, or slightly indirectly, about major human concerns; it is those slight indirections which make it poetry, but which have nothing whatever to do with making it "true to" or "true of" what it represents. And if indirectness or mediation has any necessary function other than to charm the otherwise disloyal attention, it is only because seeing face-to-face would be blinding, and the engines of mirroring are there to preserve our fragile vision.

In the light of this other kind of thinking about representation, poems that are manifestly about poetry, about other poems, or, worst of all, about themselves as poems must seem extremely limited and trivial, either merely didactic or more generally part of the freemasonry of the bardic profession, and only incidentally amusing to nonmembers thereof. A poem "about" writing a poem or "about" a particular mode or device could seem at best to be a sort of witty or allusive shoptalk to which an outsider could unwittingly condescend. But there is more to it than that, just as there is more to the structural puzzles and exercises which writers set for themselves than the merely technical questions of what imaginative muscles, what technical skills, such exercises are designed to develop. It is not so much a matter of a dancer moving alone at the bar, his or her mind moving—as Yeats had it—"upon silence," but rather of the exercise turning into a piece of original choreography, drawing upon all the skills of design that its proposed aid to better execution had rendered momentarily moot.

This is perhaps once more to observe that whatever the "subject" of a poem may be presumed to be, the poem's relation to that "subject" (or, as I shall call it, its way of being about) is a trope of a normal expository about-ness. Poems and their subjects are much like poems and their occasions. From Pindar and Sappho to the present day, actual public occasions, like the winning of a chariot race, and putative private ones, like seeing someone you desire across a room, have unwittingly occasioned poetic fictions which transcend them. In Pindar's case, the victory ode calls subtle and complex attention to the victory of the ode-maker himself over the transience of the contest. And so with all occasional poetry, whether elegiac, ceremonial, or whatever. In the case of erotic lyric, the capacity of the subjective singer to supplement ordinary language's incapacity to express feelings itself becomes a new object of praise and longing. And so with the subsequent history of meditative lyric, erotic, religious, philosophical. And yet in both of these cases, the question of what the poem is about does not by any means come to rest in this reflexive allegory. As I shall suggest later on, poetry's hidden, or derived, agenda—its concern with itself—is itself figurative of something more general about life apart from art.

It will be instructive to start with the clear case of a poem that is "about" some aspect of itself, or its linguistic terrain, in a very direct way. Wordsworth's celebrated sonnet on the sonnet, a poem about its own form (rather than its own genre or tone or literary heritage), written in 1802, is usually considered to reflect his interest in the sonnet form deriving from Milton. The brevity of the scheme and the trope of confinement within a set of ruled contingencies are immediately at issue in the opening lines:

> Nuns fret not at their convent's narrow room;
> And hermits are contented with their cells;
> And students with their pensive citadels;
> Maids at the wheel, the weaver at his loom,
> Sit blithe and happy; bees that soar for bloom,
> High as the highest Peak of Furness-fells,
> Will murmur by the hour in foxglove bells:

In truth the prison, unto which we doom
Ourselves, no prison is: and hence for me,
In sundry moods, 'twas pastime to be bound
Within the sonnet's scanty plot of ground;
Pleased if some souls (for such there needs must be)
Who have felt the weight of too much liberty,
Should find brief solace there, as I have found.

But if the scantiness of the plot of ground seems to be the point of the
first three lines, "room" in line 1 is by no means synonymous with "cell."
The "narrow room" is that of the general, not the concrete, noun and means
"space," not "chamber." (In a letter written at about the same time as the
sonnet, Wordsworth commented on how Milton's sonnets manifest "an en-
ergetic and varied flow of sound crowding into narrow room more of the
combined effect of rhyme and blank verse than can be done by any other
kind of verse I know of." Here the ellipsis of the article before "narrow
room" is definitive.)[1] The syntax of "convent's narrow room" in the sonnet
could allow for either, but the singular number of the *room/loom* rhyming
pair as opposed to the plural *cells/citadels* makes the reading quite clear. In
Donne's famous formulation of the power of pointedness over grandeur
(and of texts over stones) "We'll build in sonnets pretty roomes; / As well a
well-wrought urne becomes / The greatest ashes, as half-acre tombes," the
"roomes" are chambers, built and decorated. (This is aside from the question of whether or not these lines generate their own conceit or depend
upon the newly borrowed Italian term *stanza* for both verse strophe and
the more general "chamber," "space," or "stopping place.")[2] But in any
case, Wordsworth's "convent's narrow room" involves darker matters than
Donne's "pretty roomes," no matter how much the modern ear tends to
picture the nuns as fretting at, and in, their cells, rather than, as Wordsworth
suggests, at the limitations of their whole conventual lives.

The start of the sonnet, then, generates this opening sequence: narrowed
general space—personal confinement in clearly defined structures (*cells*)—
fortresses that protect the scene of thought by, or with, something thoughtful about their structure and their walls (for so I read the ambiguous grammar of "pensive citadels"). But space then yields significance to its contents;
the scene of solitary work is refigured as the instruments that could be at
work within it. The sonnet is no longer a scanty plot of fourteen confining
lines into which one is locked, but a spinning wheel which twists matted,
fibrous stuff into thread, and a loom—almost as with fourteen warp-threads
already in place—within whose framing structure a fabric will be woven.

This effects a remarkable revision of the relation of phases of creativity
in writing specified by Renaissance rhetoric and invoked in the opening
sonnet of Sidney's *Astrophel and Stella: inventio, dispositio, elocutio.* Here they
are revised as two, that of the female spinners, who draw thread out of the

mess around the distaff, and that of the single male weaver, who uses the thread for (and loses its singularity in) a larger design. The imagination is thus seen at work *in* a sonnet's room, *on* a sonnet's wheel and loom. For a major poet of our own day, the scene and the means of creation are always inherent in the poem itself; as John Ashbery observes at the opening of "Tapestry" (which I have always felt to be a revision, among other things, of Wordsworth's sonnet),

> It is difficult to separate the tapestry
> From the room or loom which takes precedence over it
> For it must always be frontal and yet to one side . . .

We are reminded that in the very phrase "the work of art" there lurks a fruitful grammatical ambiguity. The verbal noun *work* is identical with the concrete term designating the product of working, so that the concrete product is designated by "the work of art," whereas the deed alone is meant in "work of charity" or "good works" generally. (Or, of Creation, "the work of six days," where "work" would be interchangeable with "labor," and the term implies the gerund rather than the product.) Hannah Arendt pointed out that there is no such analogous ambiguity with the word "labor"—I cannot ordinarily call my shoveled sidewalk a "labor," only the shoveling of it.[3]

Ashbery and Wordsworth both remind us, then, of how "work of art" can confuse the making with the thing made, the being-in-and-*at*-the-sonnet with the poem or the paradigm of the poem itself. And thus it must be obvious that the workers in this sonnet "sit blithe and happy" in no cold or fatuous suppression of the horrible lives of mill-workers. Wordsworth is invoking what John Locke called "the work of our hands" (and, by extension, minds), rather than "the labour of our bodies," and the glimpses of the makers, their minds moving upon silence, provide instances of the freedom that absorption in being at work provides.

In the next half-line the bees are strangely envisioned as being solitary workers rather than communal mill-workers (or Mandevillean entrepreneurs). They are troped as sublime high-fliers who delight in the low enclosures in which the sounds of their own working will resound. Indeed, the sonic pattern of these very lines generates an underscoring resonance. Thus the alliteration of *blithe/bees/bloom* is followed by the linking resonating assonance of the following line's *high/(highest)/peak*. That the name of the specific local hilltops west of Windermere does not rhyme or assonate with *bloom* underlines, also, the deferral of the semantic along the rhyme words we have followed so far: *room/cells/citadels/loom*. Only after *bloom/fells* do we return to a trope of enclosure and instrumentality, the *bells,* which are in their way both rooms and looms, full of the sound of work. Indeed, we are almost tempted to misread "murmer by the hour" as something like *murmur the hour away* or *by* (instead of *for hours at a time,* the "hours by hours" of meditative languor in Keats's "To Autumn"). The reflexive sound of true work does indeed consume time, as opposed to dismal, repetitive labor, which seems to aid time in its slow-chapped power to consume human life.

The bees soar high in the sublime freedom of, say, blank verse and yet delight in the more enclosed, rhyming rooms. Wordsworth's admiration of the Miltonic sonnet is well known to scholars, his praise of the way in which it overwhelmed the partitions of rhyming groups and of octave-sestet division (as opposed to the syllogistic mode of argument enacted by the Shakespearean, three-quatrain-and-couplet scheme). He distrusted epigrammatic closure and seemed in his own sonnets to be struggling to achieve the condition of blank verse, going so far as to point out to Crabb Robinson fourteen lines from *Paradise Lost* which he considered to be "a perfect sonnet without rhyme." The "Nuns fret not" poem works its rhymes, as we have seen, very carefully and significantly, but it also lets the thought "run over" (Wordsworth's own phrase) the octave-sestet boundary, actually by closing short of the eighth line. Parable and interpretation are thus locked into two equal-sized rooms of seven lines.

They are linked by the rhyme of *doom,* the only verb in its rhyming sequence; the rhymes of the following subsestet tell on their own a story of the discovery of freedom in restraint: *me/be/liberty; bound/ground/found.* It is this finding of solace (and from what? from the weight of the liberty? perhaps from the fear of something?) which in itself allows a kind of freedom that is not only the solace of the writer or of other writers but of readers as well. And although the last seven lines purport to point out a moral about *technē* (mere *ars poetica,* mere tradecraft), rather than a grander, broader reading of the human condition, it is in fact the latter which has been implicitly invoked throughout.

That Wordsworth's poem makes a powerful moral statement by invoking the paradox of "the weight of too much liberty" is obvious. As a parable pointing to all of life, however, it remains morally potent only by retaining in its application the specific context of its trope. Consider for example this misapplication which forgets that the notion of freedom is tied to *poesis:* The Gulag official welcomes his new arrival thus—"Here we shall generously relieve you of the burden you have been bearing for so long, the weight of too much toilsome freedom which has made so much trouble for you." Such a statement could be merely sarcastic—and thus stupidly cruel—or more deeply ironic in an Orwellian or Jesuitical mode, avowing its own apparent paradoxical quality with the saddened patience of a saintly inquisitor. (That liberty can sometimes seem a weight too heavy to want to bear is recognized in the Judaic law insisting on a harsh punishment for any slave who, preferring the security of dependence, refused manumission.) How can there be too much liberty? Is Wordsworth being as fatuous here as he would appear, in an ignorant reading, to be in the case of the weavers and spinners earlier?

The burden of liberty here is of course a different matter. It is the bewilderment of *apparent* freedom, not because there are too many options, but because there is no available principle of choice through which the freedom can be realized, and perhaps even no epistemological means for determining what an option is and what ones are where. Suppose that the Gulag official instead exclaims, "No, I have been base, base. I shall truly give you your freedom; tomorrow you will be flown to a point five hundred kilometerss from here and set down in a place where there are no roads to confine the unbridled spirit of your walking, no near landmarks to tyrannize over the quest of your gaze for vastness, but on the great, general, open rim of the horizon. The only epistemological restraints will be those imposed by your awareness of the sun and the other stars." Of course, the prisoner doesn't want *that* liberty; he or she would demand a crossroads with signposts and tourist guide and would want many choices to be ruled out by a desire to avoid danger or inconvenience or other unpleasantness. Frying pans and fires, rocks and hard places, devils and deep, blue seas are not what we feel we have bargained for in accepting the notion of choice (in fact, of course, we have bargained with nothing for nothing).

In art, freedom paradoxically manifests itself in the imagination's unbridled propensity to design new bridles for itself. Neither Pegasus nor the belated romantic Hippogryph which replaced him could have taken off without the bidding of the bit.

There is a freedom, then, which only certain restraints can yield up, as opposed to the excess of liberty which can in its zeal remove all restraints. Wordsworth's sonnet has worked through its tropes of itself as place and as instrument of work (in the sense, too, that a paradigm called "The Sonnet" is a wheel or loom for producing particular poems called sonnets), to return to a figure of place of another sort, a place of solace, of freedom from the *weight* of too much liberty. It is easy to make mistakes about this sort of freedom. Free verse, according to Robert Frost, is like playing tennis without a net, but that is true only of bad writing of any kind. Good free verse is like playing a new game, without a net but with an intricately mapped court, far more complex than that ruled by the lines of a tennis court, and a strict set of rules of another sort. (Or, in another correction of the analogy, it can use a tennis court and a net but involve hitting the ball both over and into the net, depending upon conditions provided by a complex set of rules.) Wittgenstein's related question "Can you play chess without the Queen?" is more to the point; the problems it calls to mind are like those of the Wordsworth sonnet's parable about art and life. Only by understanding "the weight of too much liberty" in its relation to the work of art (in both senses, *travail* and *oeuvre*) can it be understood other than trivially or crudely in its more general moral dimensions.

"The Sonnet," here a synecdoche for all short poems, is as much an element of nature (though Wordsworth would not have been able to say so explicitly) as the hills of the Furness-fells or the river Duddon. And the poem about what it is like to be solitary in its room is as far from being shoptalk of versifiers as "Resolution and Independence" is from being that of social workers. Its reading of its own paradigm as a romantic emblem is far from being narcissistic.

A scornful view of the sonnet evinced by Wallace Stevens's early Crispin condemns not its small compass but its old curriculum:

> Can fourteen laboring mules like this
> In spite of gorgeous leather, gurgling bells,
> Convey his being through the land? A more condign
> Contraption must appear . . .
>
> [Journal of Crispin]⁴

Wordsworth, however, does not argue for the fourteen-stringed instrumentality of the form. "Nuns fret not" considers the sonnet as a synchronic entity. In a later, more expository poem, Wordsworth looked back along its diachronic dimension to ask the sonnet form how it devolved upon him:

> Scorn not the sonnet; critic, you have frowned,
> Mindless of its just honours; with this key
> Shakespeare unlocked his heart; the melody
> Of this small lute gave ease to Petrarch's wound;
> A thousand times this pipe did Tasso sound;
> With it Camoëns soothed an exile's grief;
> The sonnet glittered a gay myrtle leaf
> Amid the cypress with which Dante crowned
> His visionary brow: a glow-worm lamp,
> It cheered mild Spenser, called from Faeryland
> To struggle through dark ways; and, when a damp
> Fell round the path of Milton, in his hand
> The thing became a trumpet; whence he blew
> Soul-animating strains—alas, too few!

Pragmatic schemata, like lists, catalogues, chronologies—usually ranked and ordered with respect to some taxonomic agenda—are expository devices. In poetry, they will be figurative, and a manifest principle of ordering may be overridden by a latent one, strangely inappropriate to the pattern of listing. Wordsworth's personal history of the Sonnet is additional idiosyncratic in that original artists always rewrite institutional literary or art history into a visionary poetic history of their own. Wordsworth starts with Shakespeare, whose sonnets were his only writing in purported *propria per-*

sona, his only poetry in which the word "I" is not framed in dialogue. (The modern view that the "I" of the *Sonnets* is a unique kind of fiction, more complex even than the sonneteer-muse pair of Petrarchan tradition, is not to the point here.) But the course of literary history is strangely mapped in the sequence of poets. Clio's arrangement would start with Dante, followed by Petrarch, Camoens, Tasso, Spenser, Shakespeare, and Milton. That Camoens is here, and not Ronsard, Du Bellay, Giovanni della Casa (for his influence on Milton's early sonnets, for example) or Sidney, is of no concern to the Muse of history. But that the chronology is so contorted by the zigzag line of Shakespeare–Petrarch–Tasso–Camoens–Dante–Spenser–Milton must mean that it is Calliope's list and that this is indeed poetic, or nonliteral, historiography. The sonnet's story is the evolution of its own prophetic role and power, and the telling of that story is aided by the unfolding of a series of tropes of instrumentality. The key to the heart in the chest, to the locked personal truth; the lute and pipe, both conventionally emblematic (lute as Renaissance equivalent of classical lyre and biblical harp, pipe for pastoral, which Wordsworth associates with Tasso's and Camoens' subepic modes). Myrtle and cypress are also commonplace tokens of *eros* and *thanatos,* respectively, as are the flickering, transitory, but in a minor way prophetic, glowworms. The trumpet is biblical, angelic, and, ultimately, final.

Instead of an octave-sestet division—here overridden by strong enjambment—there is a first group of four poets and a second of three: Dante, Spenser, Milton. It is not romance poets in the first group, English in the second, but rather a private sense of precursorship which would put Dante, Spenser, and Milton in that order, behind the *kind* of poem that the sonnet was for Wordsworth—the particular burden of the past with which the paradigm was freighted for him. The figuration in this poem is of the sonnet as a source of sound or light: the myrtle glittering in the dark crown the poet himself dons; the firefly lighting up a path through a poet's professional perdition. The ultimate postbiblical trumpet, more than merely the attribute of Fame—the "trumpet of a prophecy" as Shelley would call the instrument composed of himself and his west wind at the end of his ode made of terza rima sonnets—completes the sequence.

That Milton wrote "too few" of the sort of poem which Wordsworth would later want to write reminds us that there is another aspect of the brevity, the confinement, the flickering of the form. Wordsworth was himself wary of the sonnet's implicit transience. If sonnets are "transcripts of the private heart," as he wrote in another poem in the same year as "Scorn Not the Sonnet," a poem meant to be placed at the end of part 2 of his *Miscellaneous Sonnets* of 1827, they instill fears

> Breathed from eternity; for as a dart
> Cleaves the blank air, Life flies; now every day

Is but a glimmering spoke in the swift wheel
Of the revolving week . . .

—a terrifying revision of the productive spinning wheel.

With the key of "Scorn Not the Sonnet" Wordsworth could unlock only the doorway to the past: rhetorically, the poem is much more like dozens of position papers in sonnet scheme written during his later years than it is like "Nuns Fret Not." It is also a good bit closer to shoptalk, albeit readers' as well as writers'. Only in the mysterious groupings of the poem—of the poets and of the tropes of *son et lumière*—can the underlying metamorphic story be read. A key eventually becomes a trumpet, but without getting any larger, and such is the history of the sonnet, the instrument Wordsworth inherited and which is speaking for him now.

There is no question of freedom or constraint in this poem, and whatever chain or cord holds tradition together is more like a guy-rope, or the strand from the clew leading out of a labyrinth, than a rope to be bound in. And yet the figure of bondage looms nearby. I have observed elsewhere how Ben Jonson's metaphor of rhyme as handcuffs for syllables modulates, through later allusive revision of it by Milton, into fetters binding the poet to the practice or convention (and, later, in Blake's revision of Milton into personified Poetry when, in fetters, "fetters the human race").[5] Jonson's "A Fit of Rime Against Rime" has something of the panache of the escape artist's routine. But what Milton calls "the troublesome and modern bondage of Riming" has a subsequent history; Keats carries it one step further in the remarkable sonnet of 1819, where it is the language of English poetry itself (actually, the poem implies, "herself") which is shackled at the outset:

If by dull rhymes our English must be chained,
And, like Andromeda, the sonnet sweet
Fettered, in spite of painéd loveliness,
Let us find out, if we must be constrained,
Sandals more interwoven and complete
To fit the naked foot of poesy:
Let us inspect the lyre, and weigh the stress
Of every chord, and see what may be gained
By ear industrious, and attention meet;
Misers of sound and syllable, no less
Than Midas of his coinage, let us be
Jealous of dead leaves in the bay wreath crown;
So, if we may not let the Muse be free,
She will be bound with garlands of her own.

The bound female personages in this story are, successively, English; Andromeda; the Sonnet; Poesy; and the Muse. That English verse and sonnets in particular are bound up in rhyming—caught up in it—is as much a given as that Andromeda was chained to the rock and guarded by the here-unmentioned monster (himself, rock-to-be). Here again is the issue of sonnet vs. blank verse, and Keats, who had even more than Wordsworth been fussing about with rhyme schemes that would seem less schematic, comes up with an original way of loosening the links of rhyming's chains without actually breaking them or having them slip off. The story told by the first ten line endings is one of *chained/sweet/loveliness/constrained/complete/Poesy// stress/gained/meet/less.* The rhyming words here are separated by two or three lines with no other rhyming pairs intervening, so that the ringing of the terminal rhyming bell is muted, and the effect approaches that of blank verse. (Keats had indeed ventured a blank verse sonnet of the sort that Wordsworth fancied he heard in *Paradise Lost.*[6] But in it, three putative quatrains are marked out by lines of anaphora and full refrain—the poem is more chambered than by the brilliant rhymes of "If by Dull Rhymes.") The distant rhyme words themselves tell intercalated tales in the sonnet's unfolding story:

> *chained/constrained/*(then, four lines later, finally) *gained*
> *sweet/complete/*(then, four lines later) *meet* ("appropriate")
> *loveliness/*(then, four lines later) *stress/less*

—and the solitary *Poesy* is tenuously linked, across four interposed lines, with *be/free,* in the concluding quatrain's garland of *be/crown/free/own.* One way to put what the sonnet's fiction is about would be to call it the finding or unfolding of the quatrain, of that particular quatrain: *In truth, the bondage of our bodied minds / No bondage is.* This is manifestly part of the poem's "fit of sonnetteering against sonnets" aspect.

But the bound ladies in the poem call out for more attention, and we must inspect their chains more closely. The Sonnet is "sweet / Fettered . . ."—the "sweet" is adjectival, but it is also dangerously close, Miltonically close, to being itself adverbially chained to the following enjambed word, to meaning "sweet[ly] fettered." This is almost a subliminal effect, but its symmetry with the phrase "painéd loveliness" and its proleptic sense of the eventual sweetening of the instruments of present bondage are totally appropriate to the layers of nuance here.

The metamorphosis of the chains and fetters is the story told not only by this sonnet but, through synecdoche, by all sonnets, all fettered short poems, and, thereby, English poetry. (It might be called the topos of *vincula* becoming *catenae.*) Sonnet and Andromeda are alike in their fetters and perhaps in the etiology of their bondage as well: Cassiopeia's boasting of her own beauty caused bondage to be visited upon her daughter, and perhaps some primal Sonnet-Muse, some Beatrice-Laura-Stella-Dark Lady preened herself in sight of a vengeful Calliope. But the chains that fettered at the opening become complex thongs in the next trope. Perhaps the sandals occurred to Keats because of Perseus's winged ones, borrowed from

Hermes, which allowed him to kill the Gorgon Medusa and use her severed, petrifying head as an instrument for the liberation of Andromeda. Certainly the pattern in which terrors and constraints become instrumental in liberation has begun to evolve. The crossed thongs of sandals themselves modulate the notion of binding in such a way. And if rhyming, measured lines, with the weight of word stress falling—in English, unlike French, say—on the rhyming syllables, can be crossed upon each other and interwoven, the poetry can be said to be held, not in restraint, but together.

But gut and wire, thin and taut enough, are the stuff of instrumental string, restraining nothing more than unwanted frequencies of vibration of the air, and liberating song from the silences of the implicit. Tuning up involves tightening and listening carefully. Blake's Devil scorned the state of human affairs (death, the constraints of nature and limitation generally, the "year of dearth") which called on one to "bring out number, weight and measure," revising an older parable about prosody and moral control into one about consciousness itself. Keats's sonnet is sensible of how much the price of liberty is eternal vigilance, in art as well as in nations conceived in liberty. "Jealous," in the twelfth line, is used in the *OED* senses 5 and 6— "apprehensive, vigilant, mistrustful," and the whole line implies something of Keats's expressed desire to "load every rift with ore," to replace metrical and imaginative filler. The line itself exemplifies the process. Consider the peculiar, apparently redundant, "bay wreath crown": surely "laurel crown" would have served, iambically, designatively, and even alliteratively (with "leaves"). But the parallel grammatical and assonant weight of *dead leaves/bay wreath* was more to the point, the diphthong of "bay" awakening the vowel of "dead," as it were. Poetry must count, and prune, and lop and listen, and heed, and thereby control the limitations by the use of metamorphosed limitations themselves, so that the very word "bound" in the final line has lost its relation to chains and fetters. The fillet bound round the neoclassic hair binds in a connecting, supporting way, by unfelt constraint, rather like that of form, in certain Renaissance metaphysical stories, upon substance.[7]

Proust remarks on how the writer, "when in bringing together a quality common to two sensations . . . liberates their essence by reuniting them in a metaphor to protect them from the contingencies of time, and binds them with an indestructible chain of words."[8] Walt Whitman chants of spinning out lines of gossamer like a "noiseless, patient spider," to connect the spheres "till the bridge you need be formed, till the ductile anchor hold / Till the gossamer thread you fling catch somewhere, O my soul."[9] Catching a reader with a line (the pun on "line" being available and instrumental in English) is always a problematic matter, though. The "painéd loveliness" of the bound *poesis* is not wholly unconnected with the "poetic pains" of William Cowper's well-known lines in *The Task:*

> There is a pleasure in poetic pains
> Which only poets know. The shifts and turns,
> Th'expedients and inventions, multiform,
> To which the mind resorts, in chase of terms
> Though apt, yet coy, and difficult to win . . .   [2.285–89]

The *turns* in chase of the almost homonymic *terms* are the painstaking work of coping with the binding of scheme. Cowper is revising here Dryden's lines "There is a pleasure, sure, in being mad / That none but madmen know" (from *The Spanish Friar*), with both his own madness—and his poetry as a stay against it—in mind, and a sense of how maddening the dance of composition can be. (Hazlitt, interestingly enough, compounded out of the phrasing of both source and echo here, and from the trope of writing as painting further on in Cowper's passage, the opening of an essay: "There is a pleasure in painting which none but painters know," which he himself puts in inverted commas as if it were a quotation.)

The Muse, then, will in the end be bound—not, in Keats's last line, conventionally, expectedly, and rhymingly *crowned*—with complete, interwoven garlands of her own. And of her own making, I want to add, as well as of her own possession: the garlands are the evolved poems themselves, the interwoven terms twisted together by the turns of working art. Robert Frost's great sonnet "A Silken Tent" seems to gloss these complex figures of bondage with its simile of the woman caught in the moment of sensible freedom and the tent, both delicate in their strength, precariously maintained structures whose restraining ropes in fact support them. But the simile is itself even more tightly chained than usual: fourteen lines long, it is carried in one sonnet-long sentence, and the ending, like that of Keats's sonnet, brings back a delicate reminder of the sense of constraint in the network of ropes, of "constant silken ties of love and thought"

> And only by one's going slightly taut
> In the capriciousness of summer air
> Is of the slightest bondage made aware.[10]

Keats's sonnet and the "Nuns Fret Not" of Wordsworth are both monuments to "the figure," as Frost called it elsewhere, "a poem makes," discovering the consequences of—and for—work and love mandated by the parables of form that have moved far beyond the wit of palpable self-reference, the rueful puzzles of recursion. Yet one more sonnet continues the concerns of the three that we have been considering but starts bending its parable from the very outset. Dante Gabriel Rossetti's sonnet, written in 1880 and published as the introductory poem to his sequence *The House of Life* in the following year, commences with the narrowness of the schematic room but binds it immediately to the matter of occasion, a central question, we saw earlier, to both the history of the sonnet and for the concerns of Rossetti's premature modernism.

A sonnet is a moment's monument,—
  Memorial from the soul's eternity
  To one dead deathless hour. Look that it be,
Whether for lustral rite or dire portent,
Of its own arduous fulness reverent:
  Carve it in ivory or in ebony,
  As day or night may rule; and let time see
Its flowering crest impearled and orient.

A sonnet is a coin: its face reveals
  The soul,—its converse, to what power 'tis due:—
Whether for tribute to the august appeals
  Of life, or dower in love's high retinue,
It serve; or, 'mid the dark wharf's cavernous breath,
In Charon's palm it pay the toll to death.

"A moment's monument" is the monument *of* a moment, *to* a moment, and although the subsequent appositional gloss enforces the second of these readings, the first lingers on. The continued insistence of Renaissance sonneteering that "Not marble, nor the gilded monuments / Of princes shall outlive this powerful rhyme" (Shakespeare's formulation goes back through Spenser and Du Bellay to Horace's "Exegi monumentum aere perennius" [I have built a monument outlasting bronze])[11] is here acknowledged. The hour is both dead and deathless, like the frozen perpetual lovers and worshippers on Keats's urn; but Rossetti's revision of all these precursive figurations is remarkable in bringing back the trope of the material carving again, rather than asserting the greater durability of uncrumbling words. The occasion perpetuated in the sonnet, no matter what event in public history or private fable it constitute, is only made to outlast its moment by being married to the sonnet's own occasion, the absolutely unique, revolutionary event of the occasion of its being written, the occasion which Wallace Stevens called poems "the cry of." Sonnets, short poems in general, often avow a putative occasion and at the same time conceal one of their own: "Whether for lustral rite or dire portent," they remain "Of [their] own arduous fulness reverent." That "arduous" was "intricate" in an earlier printed version of this sonnet is significant, I think, for the very meaning of *arduous* here: the original phrase is a version of Keats's "interwoven" completeness, and the difficulty proclaimed in the revised text is that of working the intricacies. And it is these very difficult intricacies of its own, fetters and garlands both, with which the sonnet's own private occasion is marked. Rossetti himself, almost ten years earlier, had remarked in a letter that "I hardly ever produce a sonnet except on some basis of special momentary emotion," and certainly the excessively literal reader of sonnet sequences from Petrarch through Meredith would want to agree. The problem lies in what sort of emotion that might be—it is not merely that "ardent" could be substituted for "arduous," for example. Rossetti goes on, however, to observe,

> But I think there is another class admissible also, and that is the only other I practise; viz. the class depending on a line or two clearly given you, you know not whence, and calling up a sequence of ideas. This is also a just "raison d'être" for a sonnet; and such are all mine when they do not in some sense belong to the "occasional" class.[12]

It will be very difficult indeed for most literalists to understand that by "a line or two clearly given you" a poet could mean all sorts of schematic situations or problems which could be momentous as *données,* as momentous as turns and discoveries in an erotic romance. Varying the schematic structure of a sonnet is as crucial an occasion as a rebuked expression of desire in a love story the sonnets are alluding to, involving someone called "I," for example: Sir Philip Sidney's scholarly editors would, on the whole, not want to consider an encounter with a possible revision of a verse pattern in anything like the same light that a possible missed opportunity for erotic advance, or a moment of regret or self-rebuke, in the life of the literal poet would command. But in the sonnet world, the occasion of reworking a traditional conceit (for example, substituting Stella's eyes as source of truth for Laura's and thereby meaning English poetic authenticity, modeled on but freed from Continental tradition) is a crucial event. Likewise, a way of modulating the quatrain-and-couplet rhyme and syntactic structure by interlocking it with a binary octave-sestet one (some of Donne's *Holy Sonnets* do this very effectively) could dawn on the course of a sequence of poems like a new day of hope or a favorable glance from the Lady. And frequently, in the course of working through the scheme and working out the trope of a sequential poem, a deeper, more significant or powerfully generative occasion may be discovered. In one sense, it may matter little whether the intention preceded the representation or not. For example, in the crucial seventy-first sonnet of *Astrophel and Stella,* the concluding three lines present a remarkable instance of a conventional final couplet which is broken, syntactically, rhetorically, narratively, into two antithetical lines, the first of them forming an unrhyming "couplet" with the one which precedes it. I discuss this poem in the following chapter, but I only wish to suggest now that the "occasion" of breaking a couplet in that way, of breaking new structural ground, could as well have generated the "moment" in the fiction as it could have been discovered during the course of concluding the poem. Certainly, the "emotional" force unleashed by the rhetoric of the conclusion was created by the communing occasions of form and fable.

The sonnet, then, is the tomb of its occasion, its substance appropriate to the conditions of light or darkness which have ruled its moment. Its crest is not merely *flowered* (some carved garland at the top of a stele, for example), but, in the view of Time, to be eternally *flowering* and shining, which is to say that as an instrument of enduring it continually flowers in poetry, in the presentation of that which is to be apprehended interpretively. The gravestone is there, where someone is buried; the inscription identifies him or her and causes the traveler to halt for a moment, the busied passerby to remember death. The sonnet's crest, the poem's continuing shining evidences of artifice, will outbrave Time even more than will its material fabric and cause the reader to remember what remembrance must be.

In the sestet, the trope of a carved monument is revised and reduced in scale. The coin here is like one of Théophile Gautier's enamels and cameos, small works of the strong art of carving; "L'Art," which is his sonnet on the sonnet, as it were, engages some of the same figures of needed difficulty we have been considering:

Oui, l'oeuvre sort plus belle
D'une forme au travail
  Rebelle,
Verse, marbre, onyx, émail.

Point de contraintes fausses!
Mais que pour marcher droit
  Tu chausses,
Muse, un cothurne étroit.

Fi du rhythme commode,
Comme un soulier trop grand,
  Du mode
Qui tout pied quitte et prend!

[Yes, the work emerges more beautiful from a form
that resists working, verse, marble, onyx, enamel.
No fake restraints! but to go forward, Muse, don a narrow buskin.
Fie on the easy rhythm, like a shoe too large, of the
sort that every foot slips in and out of!]

But here the carving is a coin, both like Gautier's austere medal found by a laborer under the earth that reveals an emperor, and yet given more than memorial value by the authority of the figure under whose rule it was minted. Moreover, the matter of the coin having two sides is itself evocative of the octave-sestet division, as it descends through Milton and Wordsworth (despite his distrust of the binary form), as a scheme of propounding and revising, of qualifying a major statement with a shorter, subsequent one which nevertheless gets to have the last word.

It is in the sestet that the notion of the two sides of the sonnet as living in a heads-tails relation to each other is raised. But whichever face of the coin one considers at the moment, there is always a hidden agenda. There are Day sonnets and Night sonnets, but either can be the coin of any of three realms: one can pay taxes to what certain critics would today call "experience," or entry fees for a postulant in the triumph of love, or, inevitably, pay the final ferryman. The enabling Power is in each case the recipient of the coin's value; and while the payment a poem makes is one of signification, of an expenditure of "being about" something beyond its own arduous fullness, the matter of accounting here is sufficiently grim so as to make the final lines seem all the more inevitable. It also returns one to the apparent paradoxes of memorialization implied at the poem's opening. Monuments are more dead, as stone and worked language, than the living beings and feelings they memorialize; and yet when the latter are dead, the dead stone lives on. The competing powers here—the Soul, the triple rulers of Life, Love, and Death, the demands of its own being—are very like the competing grounds of interpretive stances. Each might claim, by its own peculiarly authentic method of accounting, to arrive at the bottom line. The soul is always there—every poem is "about" its author, always. But there is another side to the coin, and it will proclaim the poem to be "about" love or death or, indeed, anything else (Life's appeals are indeed august, imperial, wide-ranging). Yet Death has (and, in this instance, indeed *is*) the last word. One will never know what the poem's occasion is until that occasion is dead, and the poem has lived. And yet those medallions with two sides are *coins,* and something is being paid for something (nothing being got for nothing). Texts are handled and passed on by readers, who can use them as tokens or dwell on them as carved or stamped images. In any case, the coin is "merely" neither of these, and the older it is, the more value it has in both ways.

Like the other poems we have been considering, Rossetti's uses the occasion of writing a sonnet on The Sonnet for a deeper and broader purpose; sonnets are synecdoches of certain kinds of poetry in general, they are scenes of both repose and difficulty, they focus attention on the matter of labor and work, they yield discoveries, and so forth. A late, sad footnote to this sequence of texts is provided by a similar sonnet of Edwin Arlington Robinson, written in the 1890s and published in book form in *The Children of the Night* (1897). The poem seems all too painfully aware of its precursive tradition; in a poet like Robinson, for whom the history of great English poetry was a kind of heroic mythology of its own, this could be a crucial matter. Entitled simply "Sonnet," it starts out from the Keatsian notion of bondage, but in this case the bondage of the poet to the convention:

> The master and the slave go hand in hand,
> Though touch be lost. The poet is a slave,
> And there be kings do sorrowfully crave
> The joyance that a scullion may command.

> But, ah, the sonnet-slave must understand
> The mission of his bondage, or the grave
> May clasp his bones, or ever he shall save
> The perfect word that is the poet's wand.

The heavy archaisms ("there be kings"; "joyance"; "or ever" for "if ever," etc.), while much less stilted than those of Ezra Pound of a decade and more later, themselves manifest the touch of the grave. And with the turn away from the exploration of "the mission of his bondage" (and what, pray, is that? Tell us in the sestet), the trope of being out of touch with one's paradigmatic master, as well as out of touch with one's own work, becomes sadly literalized. It is all the more touching that the whole sestet, from the opening line, through the idiosyncratically contorted syntax and rhythm of the second one, to the inversion of the last clause, is almost pure Rossetti, whose sonnet on The Sonnet is the principal shape and echo haunting the workshop of this poem. For Robinson, The Sonnet is the scene of poetic failure, and the parataxis of octave and sestet and even of the trope of royalty (the *kings* of the octave and the *sad thrones* are connected only by hollow echo) somehow avows this. The hand of time on this poem is a deadening one: Stevens felt it in the lines about the laboring mules quoted earlier. The sonnet is a dead crown in a dead trope; the rhymes are decoration studded into the gold of Thought (no poet who writes in rhyme from Pope onward can believe *that!* this is the reductive view of literary journalism):

> The sonnet is a crown, whereof the rhymes
> Are for Thought's purest gold the jewel-stones;
> But shapes and echoes that are never done
> Will haunt the workshop, as regret sometimes
> Will bring with human yearning to sad thrones
> The crash of battles that are never won.

And yet it is in the Rossetti-haunted sestet that Robinson's sonnet reveals what power it has to engage the matter of working through bondage to something else. But his sonnet does not enact that work in the ways in which Wordsworth's and Keats's seem to, even though it sums the questions of "Scorn Not the Sonnet" with those of the schematic confrontations. The suppressed substance of "the mission of his bondage" may indeed be the sonnet-writing poet's diachronic struggles, his quest for originality. (The idea of bondage itself having a mission is very strange in any case, as compressed a figure as Hart Crane's bequeathed embassy in "At Melville's Tomb.")

And yet, sadly enough, the failure of this poem to be about more than poetic pains is interestingly involved with the one question that literalizing readings would misunderstand: this is *not* one of those self-regarding, recursive "exercises" in "poetic form," like "If by dull rhymes." Indeed, it cannot at first manifestly cope with the nature of the bondage, never revealing if the fetters are made of (1) not enough room to carry on in poetically, (2) repetitions enforced by the form and perhaps poisonous to the imagination, (3) the hard work of premature adjustment which seduces the spirit from its loftier flights, (4) etc. It is only in the sestet that the bondage is shown to be that of, and to, tradition. In its way, this is much more an American modernist poem than most American modernists would want to admit, saying more than it knows it is saying, rather as if it were the Browning monologue of an ambitious originator. Unlike Wordsworth's figures of space and instrumentality, Keats's evolving muse, making "bound" into "crowned," or Rossetti's transumption of the palpable monument into a trope of the living tomb of a once-living moment, Robinson's poem refuses to engage, save for the unacknowledged and perhaps unwitting matter of the Rossettian turn of the sestet, the formal, schematic questions. It flies too quickly up into abstraction, and as a consequence never escapes into the kind of potent moral generality that it clearly should like to.

But this reflects a more general question about poetry's allegorization of its sense of its own nature. Poetry presents to all implicit and explicit theorizing about it something very like the mind-body problem presented by human being. Different critical institutions have seized on one or another of a range of differentiations with regard to it: form/meaning; form/content; form/function; code/message. And whether form is body or mind depends upon the implicit metaphysical positions supporting the trope. In this and subsequent essays I shall revise the terms of such a distinction and invoke the ancient rhetoricians' differentiation of scheme, or pattern of surface representation, and trope, or shift of meaning. Poetry can contemplate itself as trope, as figuration, from atoms of local metaphor up through huge allegorical constructions or even as some allegorized process or force or impulse which builds atoms and allegories. Or it can, in the poems discussed here, confront itself in schematic terms. None of these sonnets on the sonnet engages the larger mythological questions posed by the origins of the form in the major mythopoetic sequences of Dante, Petrarch, Sidney, Du Bellay, Shakespeare, Tasso, etc. That is to say, that the myth of the sonneteer and the sonnet muse, the occasions for utterance and the array of available rhetorical stances provided by that story, the mode of self-analysis of both the "I" of the sequence and the poetic language that continually struggles with that "I" as to which of them has created, or empowered, the other (both of them deferring always to the Muse)—all of these problems which are so central to the origins of modern lyric, erotic or meditative, are available for consideration. It might be argued that their existence is implicitly conceded by Rossetti, and that his notion of a "moment" refers somehow to the moments—minutes, hours, days—of a sonnet sequence and to the individual sonnets of impassioned and self-aware experience in life remembered.

Perhaps a more interesting point could be made about the necessity for a self-descriptive sequence, rather than a particular sonnet purporting to contemplate sonnethood as a function of being-in-the-sequence. Christina Rossetti wrote a "Sonnet of Sonnets," a short sequence of fourteen poems, each one corresponding to a line of the paradigm. The whole of Dante Gabriel Rossetti's *The House of Life* is among other things a commentary on the history of sonnet sequences, particularly in regard to the outstanding problematic area of the relation of sonnet-occasions to autobiographical ones.

Most important of all, I should think, is Rossetti's precursor sequence, Meredith's *Modern Love* of 1862. Its revision of sonnet form (sixteen-line poems of four quatrains, 3 of *abba, cddc, effe,* and one of *ghgh*) into something "more" than the sonnet paradigm is a figure for something beyond, or transumptive of, the sonnet-sequence mythology (the weight of all this is carried by the "modern" of the title). Its strategy of anatomizing mid-Victorian adulterous passion and its modes of self-dramatizing self-deception for all involved is one with its deconstruction of the rhetoric of erotic poetry. Sometimes this association of life and text about life can be crudely ironic, as in the final line of the magnificent thirtieth poem of the sequence:

> What are we first? First, animals; and next
> Intelligences at a leap, on whom
> Pale lies the distant shadow of the tomb,
> And all that draweth on the tomb for text.
> Into which state comes Love, the crowning sun:
> Beneath whose light the shadow loses form.
> We are the lords of life, and life is warm.
> Intelligence and instinct now are one.
> But nature says: "My children most they seem
> When they least know me: therefore I decree
> That they shall suffer." Swift doth young Love flee,
> And we stand wakened, shivering from our dream.
> Then if we study Nature we are wise.
> Thus do the few who live but with the day:
> The scientific animals are they.—
> Lady, this is my sonnet to your eyes.

We are not only always in "the shadow of the tomb," but in the shade of our theology and science and poetry about death, and about that knowledge of death which distinguishes us from the animals. If the first half of the poem ends, with the seventh and eighth lines, on a note of one kind of irony (the "is" for the "it seems, in our deluded state, that . . ."), the final line of the poem, turning against a self-consumed tradition of love poetry, on the one hand, and against the very spirit of anatomy on the other, mutters in a different key altogether. Meredith apparently found it necessary to point up the relation between the life and the literature of eros in a prefatory sonnet, added to the reprint of *Modern Love* some thirty years after. In it he avows that the used-up tropes of the poetry of love are useless without metaleptic revision: "Now seems the language heard of Love as rain / To make a mire where fruitfulness was meant." But revision, as of the addition of two more lines as a figure for the addition of complex ironic perspective on the relation of life, novels, poetry, modernism, and tradition, can restore power to the original rebellious, antithetical, Satanic language:

> The golden harp gives out a jangled strain,
> Too like revolt from heaven's Omnipotent.
> But listen in the thought; so may there come
> Conception of a newly-added chord,
> Commanding space beyond where ear has home.
> In labour of the trouble at its fount,
> Leads Life to an intelligible Lord
> The rebel discords up the sacred mount.

The "labour" is that of birth, of human work after the fall into nature, and, at bottom, the labor of leading the rebel discords, the modern poems, back to the summit of significance again. The difficulty of the sonnet here is not the formal difficulty of commitment to a paradigm, of execution that must itself be design; rather it is the work of the redemptive and recreative imagination. Meredith is far closer here, as often, to Wallace Stevens than he is to Rossetti (it might be instructive to consider "Autumn Refrain" as the last of the sequence of texts we have been considering, a sort of blank-verse "Sonnet on the Sonnet on Nightingales"). And yet, for all the concern of Meredith's poem for the diachronic life of trope, for the revivification of poetry about love by means of the self-analytic turns of modernity, he cannot resist pointing out his own addition (like the mythical Terpander of Greek antiquity) of an additional string to the canonical lyre. If poetry, in an age of muddying language, can only be about love by talking about poetry about love, then this is also to be seen (reflected? embodied? a poet will always somehow feel that both are true) in the work of schematic revision. Meredith does not bother about rhyming here, or about readjusting the inner rooms of the sonnet pattern, as a figure for this general sort of work; his concern is rather a revision of the Wordsworthian one about space (in this case, demanding not so much *Lebensraum* as access to a world elsewhere, "beyond where ear has home").

One more point about the poetry of love might be made here. The revisionary task of modern poetic "aboutness," the need to designate forms and patterns and substances of life by allegorizing talks about forms and patterns and substances of poetic language, is probably a very ancient one. Sappho helps invent the grounds of erotic poetry by making the difficulty of talking about love a central part of the subject of the poetry and by revealing a desire for a language that would make present an absent object that is almost indistinguishable from the desire for the object itself. One Renaissance instance of a passage of poetry about love that is probably successful by means of its poetic self-reference has not heretofore been considered as such. Near the beginning of the sixth canto of book 3 of *The Faerie Queene* Spenser introduces a digressive account, adapted from a well-known idyll by the Hellenistic Moschus, of Venus's search for the lost Cupid. The digression is part of a most complex narrative strategy for leading the reader into the so-called core canto of the first of the books of his long poem which involves an anatomy of the erotic life, and in which sexuality is anything other than a set of pitfalls. This canto, the seventh, presents the generative mythological domain of the Gardens of Adonis, which is in itself a kind of energy source for much of the erotic mythopoeia in the rest of books 3 and 4 of the entire poem. It is also the place to which, in an aetiological fable about a pair of twins named Amoret and Belphoebe, Venus takes the former (as Diana will the latter) to be brought up in. In fact, the runaway Cupid will be found by Venus in the gardens when she arrives there with the infant Amoret. But it is the account of Venus's search which I wish to quote here:

> Him for to seeke, she left her heauenly hous,
>   The house of goodly formes and faire aspects,
>   Whence all the world deriues the glorious
>   Features of beauties, and all shapes select,
>   With which high God his workmanship hath deckt;
>   And searched euery way, through which his wings
>   Had borne him, or his tract she mote detect:
>   She promist kisses sweet, and sweeter things
> Vnto the man, that of him tydings to her brings.
>
> First she him sought in Court, where most he vsed
>   Whylome to haunt, but there she found him not;
>   But many there she found, which sore accused
>   His falsehood, and with foule infamous blot
>   His cruell deedes and wicked wyles did spot:
>   Ladies and Lords she euery where mote heare
>   Complayning, how with his empoysned shot
>   Their wofull hartes he wounded had whyleare,
> And so had left them languishing twixt hope and feare.
>
> She then the Citties sought from gate to gate,
>   And euery one did aske, did he him see;
>   And euery one her answerd, that too late
>   He had him seene, and felt the crueltie
>   Of his sharpe darts and whot artillerie;
>   And euery one threw forth reproches rife
>   Of his mischieuous deedes, and said, That hee

Was the disturber of all ciuill life.
The enimy of peace, and author of all strife.   [3.6.12–14]

The ad hoc, reflexive allegory here is about the source of authentic love
poetry. Just as Hobbes, in his "Answer to Davenant's Preface Before *Gon-
dibert*," had associated the "three regions of mankind, court, city and country" with the three "sorts of poesy," heroic, satiric, and pastoral, so Spenser
is elaborating just such a taxonomy of genre, with respect to the poetry of
love, in these stanzas. The true Cupid is not to be found in the world of
Court, and of the poetry of Court—Petrarchan forms, language, tropes and
rhetorical stances, expressive lyrics, and so forth, whose very clichés are
elaborated in the narrated complaints of the courtiers. Neither is Love to
be found in the characterizations of it, harsh and reductive and distrustful,
in satire, the realm of "Citties." And in the green cabinet of pastoral poetry,
she can well smile at the self-centered, erroneous accounts of the effects of
love by the "shepherd swaines" of pastoral conventions. He will, as it turns
out, be found only in a powerful, complex mythopoetic milieu (one like,
say, *The Faerie Queene* itself). This is to say that only intricate kinds of
allegory, capable of allegorizing prior modes of representation and even of
troping their own, can represent love. The other places, topoi, genres, conceptual worlds will either be misrepresenting him totally or else accurately
representing someone else, which is to say that you can't find Love in those
places. The recursive, or self-referential, undercurrent in these stanzas is
something like an encoded bit of grounding theory for the whole realm of
discourse that contains it. "The theory of poetry is the life of poetry," says
Stevens in his *Adagia,* to which he conjoins, "The theory of poetry is the
theory of life." Certainly this is the point in the matter of poets' allegorizing
their own technical problems, their kinds of work, their finding of freedom
in constraint.

In the case of the lines from Spenser, the poetry is "about" its original
genre, rather than its verse form. Moreover, it is "about" that in a secondary
way—that is, the ancient story is seamlessly worked into the narrative fabric
of Spenser's fiction, but its local allegory covers the whole realm of poesis
in which the text is conceived and at the same time points beyond the
allegorical moralization of place as genre to something larger. For to say
that a sort of literature, a way of talking, isn't about love, *really*, is not merely
to be indulging in literary warfare, but instead to be making a claim for
poetry itself as something different from mere literature. And beyond that,
it is to be saying something important about Love and Discourse generally.
In this case (as in the earlier instances of poems being about their own
formal structure in order to be about human work and freedom) we might
picture the interpretive recovery of the reference as a dual system, rather
like an hourglass or two congruent triangles joined at the apex. The fiction

reads down to being about the fiction itself, but then reads down further to an opening up of the representation. In her *Freud Journal*, Lou Andreas-Salomé remarks on how "psychoanalysis provides a plausible interpretation of those fairy tales in which something ugly or disgusting is transformed into something glorious (such as a frog into a prince): namely, that with the lifting of repression the sexual object is transformed by sexual love into something desired. Of course it is possible that here too sexuality has the role of symbol of symbols."[13] In other words, once we have read down to the sexual substrate, are we to stop reading? She goes on brilliantly and beautifully to suggest that in stories of this kind, sex can symbolize something else, and that here the parable may be one of an enchanted splendor in hiding in an outward appearance of banality and ugliness. The tenor of a metaphor may be itself the vehicle of another one; an allegorical level to which interpretation has carried one may itself be the surface of another fiction. This is certainly true, I think, in the case of true poetry "about" poetry. It is always propounding a wider parable out of its narrowed one and tells a story about itself in order to trope a much more general tale.

Given the history of the sonnet in modernity, it is not surprising to find the line from Wordsworth to (if I am right) Stevens coming to an end. Two notable examples of *Poems of Type A About Type A* are the sestinas on the sestina by Alan Ansen and Donald Hall; the first, of the tribe of "Scorn Not the Sonnet, Critic" not only recounting but formally enacting a history of generic and general literary decline, shrinks its line length in successive stanzas from seven stresses down to a final tornada consisting only of the end words, from an opening long line: "In the age of Arnaut when for God and man to be" down to the final, self-banishing "*Sestina order,* / Austere master, / Be Gone!!!" ("A Fit of Something Against Something").[14] The second, "Sestina," starts out with an echo of Ezra Pound on Browning, dutifully keeps to *ars poetica* in the first stanza, and then, at the point of the first repeated end word (in the seventh line), moves out into his general moral discourse about discourse, about conversation, itself seeming to discover later on that "The introvert sestina / May lose its voice by childishly supposing / It holds a hearer with self-conversation." But thus the first seven lines:

Hang it all, Ezra Pound, there is only the one sestina,
Or so I thought before, always supposing
The subject of them invariably themselves.
This is not true. Perhaps they are nearly a circle,
And they tell their motifs like a party conversation,
Formally repetitious, wilfully dull,

But who are we to call recurrence dull? . . .[15]

For modern poetry, the sestina and the villanelle were the two refrain-raddled forms, so beloved of later nineteenth-century versifying, which could be metaleptically and fruitfully readopted, and the sestina could be seen to be the ideal generic examplar of a scheme to be allegorized in the unfolding. But, like the sonnet on the sonnet, the sestina on the sestina is an extreme case of something yet more general in poetry.[16]

For true poems *represent* their literary genres in some of the same rich and problematic ways they represent actions, passions, perceived relationships and inferred ones, or any other aspects of nature. This is because, in the first place, genres, like the schemes by which they are defined, are themselves part of nature. (Forms like *sonnet* and *sestina:* their presence, their reasonably fuzzy boundaries, their changing surfaces are rather like those of *mountain* and *lake*.) In the second place, a mere examplar which we say "represents" a class by being a member of it usually does not represent the class in any other than the trivial way of instancing membership in it. A member is not necessarily even a synecdoche of a class (unless the class is itself a class of classes, for example, a set which is a proper subset). That is, if we say, "Let's select as a representative of humanity (*a*) someone selected at random; (*b*) an animal; (*c*) an image," only (*a*) will suffice. But if we ask for a representation, rather than "a representative," of humanity, then (*b*) or (*c*) will probably serve better than (*a*). And if we say that, in this case, (*a*) is also canonical, that "such a person authentically represents humanity *because* he/she was chosen randomly (rather than selecting the king or the prettiest baby)," that is already to make a critical statement about human-kindness itself.

In any event, we use "represents" in two ways: (1) as "exemplifies" (in which case, great works will be less exemplary of genre and schematic paradigm, often, than mere literature, and the world is made safe for formalism, perhaps), and (2) as "tropes." *Poetry tropes nature in part by troping literature,* just as, in a microlinguistic way, poetic language tropes ordinary language. Trope itself figures literalness, as fiction tropes truth. But this is not to say that the concept of figuration is that mysterious or frivolous. It is rather to say that *the mirror of art,* in a less-than-ordinary sense of that phrase, into which art gazes and contemplates itself, is always a focusing lens as well, transparent and refractive as well as reflective, shaped by the pressures of its own fiction, but to be used for reading through. To take the lens as a Narcissus-pool or, worse, as a mere jewel or bauble is not to be able to see poetry at all.[17]

Poetry's self-reflecting capacity can be localized in moments, as we have been seeing, that avow their own concerns. Or they can, as in the case of the lines from Spenser, carry the self-reference in an inner voice, so to speak, or as an accompanying gloss. Sometimes the self-reference can be carried in a moment of stylistic allusion. For example, Tennyson in "St. Simeon Stylites" has his monologuist declare that "Patient on this tall pillar I have

borne / Rain, wind, heat, hail, damp, and sleet, and snow." This establishes
complex overtones of the Hell in *Paradise Lost,* book 1, whose outer reaches,
when explored by the rebel angels, revealed "Rocks, caves, lakes, fens, bogs,
dens, and shades of death," in one of the most celebrated lines of monosyllables in the language (Tennyson even carefully revises the schematic force
of the internal *fens/dens* rhyme with his own *heat/sleet*). And yet, despite the
referential ironies, there is no self-reference, no adducing of the story of
how the poem got put together, and what that might mean.

But at another moment, Tennyson calls on Milton more subtly and more
powerfully even (because here, more generally, in a Virgil-Dante way), at
the end of "Tiresias." This is a passage which, as Christopher Ricks tells us,
Tennyson liked to quote as a "sample" of his blank verse.[18] When the un-
regainable heroic realm of the poem is being summoned up, Milton, as the
wielder of the stateliest English measure, is loudly invoked in lines that are
a near-pastiche of his enjambment style and syntax. One can hear Milton's
voice starting with the fifth line in the following passage (the preceding
ones being purely Tennysonian in cadence):

> and these eyes will find
> The men I knew, and watch the chariot whirl
> About the goal again, and hunters race
> The shadowy lion, and the warrior-kings,
> In height and prowess more than human, strive
> Again for glory, while the golden lyre
> Is ever sounding in heroic ears
> Heroic hymns, and every way the vales
> Wind, clouded with the grateful incense-fume
> Of those who mix all odour to the Gods
> On one far height in one far-shining fire.

It is in moving toward the matter of the poetry of the past, of *heroic hymns*
sounding in *heroic ears,* that the odors of Milton mix with Tennyson's own,
and that the blank verse starts telling the story of its own history. It is hard
to say whether or not some sense of the echoing in these lines was what
endeared them to their author. The distribution of assonance and alliteration in the final line of this passage, and of the poem, is all Tennyson's far-
shining fire, and the heroic hymning voice has been completely absorbed by
the later hymning ear.

When poetry dwells on its own formal schemes, then, it will be to read
them as emblems of representation in general. Representing is work, rather
than, in Hannah Arendt's terms, labor, and perhaps always a trope for all
productive human work. In human history, representations are themselves
part of nature; and as the world has become more cluttered with representations of a durable sort, the representation of those representations has
become part of the representation of nature itself. A rhyming scheme can

be no less personal and crucial a matter to a poet than a lover's token or a moment of revelation. Poetry can fetter randomness and bind possibility and link design to execution in chains of its own forging which, when worked through rather than slipped off, become garlands of its own achievement.

6 🙰

Necessary Hieroglyphs

There's nothing ornamental about the style of a real poet: everything is a necessary hieroglyph.

—A. W. Schlegel

The previous chapter considered some poems which addressed their own schematic arrangements—as if the canonical sonnet pattern provided a natural or material occasion, like a river or a ruin—and allegorized them in various ways. These sonnets were perhaps egregious instances of the extracting of primary matter from what poetry has always publicly proclaimed about itself as being contingent or secondary. "The greatest part of poets," said Sir Philip Sidney,

> have apparelled their poetical inventions in that numbrous kind of writing which is called verse—indeed but apparelled, verse being but an ornament and no cause to poetry, since there have been many most excellent poets that never versified, and now swarm many versifiers that need never answer to the name of poets.[1]

In Sidney's terms, sonnets on the sonnet, figurations of verse-schemes, would be like embodying clothing itself (not filling it with body). Francis Bacon distinguishes between poesy "in respect of words or matter," between fiction and scheme generally: "it is but a character of speech, for verse only is a certain kind of style and a certain form of elocution, and has nothing to do with the matter, for both true history may be written in verse and feigned history in prose."[2]

In every age, it is poets themselves who wish most to disentangle poetry from mere versifying and true poets from Chaucer's "drasty rhymers" or Wordsworth's "men ambitious of the fame of Poets." The highest poetry for Bacon is "parabolical"; for Shelley, its language is "vitally metaphorical," changing the world by interpreting it. To confuse rhyming with imitating (or, as we would want less confusingly to say today, representing) or making fictions is to be one of those "tuneful fools" (as Pope so tunefully—as will be noticed—called them) "who to church repair / Not for the doctrine, but the music there." It is mistaking the fashionings of scheme for the turnings of trope.

But perhaps I should turn at once to a formulation of this notion that has become central for modern American poetry. Emerson, attempting yet once more to distinguish between "men of poetical talents, or of industry and skill in meter" and "the true poet," remarks that his contemporaries are only "men of talents who sing, and not the children of music. The argument is secondary, the finish of the verses is primary." And he goes on in a famous passage from "The Poet" to explain,

> For it is not meters, but a meter-making argument, that makes a poem,—a thought so passionate and alive, that like the spirit of a plant or animal it has an architecture of its own, and adorns nature with a new thing. The thought and form are equal in the order of time, but in the order of genesis the thought is prior to the form. The poet has a new thought: he has a whole new experience to unfold; he will tell us how it was with him, and all men will be the richer in his fortune.[3]

By "argument" here Emerson of course means "matter," "subject"—what the poetry is all about—and not the structure of philosophical discourse. (For in a more limited sense of "argument," we might argue, as Wordsworth did, that the larger metrical patterns, the three-quatrains-and-couplet, of the Shakespearean, as opposed to the Italian, sonnet form were conducive to syllogistic argument, rather than to a unified flow of utterance. And see the previous essay.) And yet, as so often with Emerson, the word here partakes of a tincture of the other meaning of "argument," of a kind of disputation or mental fight. It is thus with a notion of fiction-as-contention that we may be dealing here.[4]

In any case, various sorts of formalist would want variously to argue that (*a*) there is nothing but a more generalized situation of "meter" to be discussed anyway; or (*b*) that meter is part of matter and the form of encipherment is indeed part of—not a sealed container for—the message; or (*c*) that all "matter" is a fictional notion ultimately designating nothing but moving within some meterlike matrix of relations. The extreme case of the first of these positions is that of the view of Jeremy Bentham that reduced the condition of being poetry to the textual condition of having, when inscribed, a ragged righthand margin. (It is by no means refreshing to discover that contemporary poetasters, scribblers, and their teachers seem to be unwitting Benthamites in this respect.) But it is not my intention to theorize about formalism here. Powerful criticism that is more than elementary parsing must avow that poems are by nature problematic in at least two ways: like persons, who may wryly but seriously be characterized as beings which will always present some kind of mind-body problem, poems are texts which present some kind of matter-meter problem. Poems also embody some kind of nexus of presence and memory that requires both synchronic and diachronic discussion, and to this degree, a poem is like a wave particle "of" light. I have elsewhere likened the relation between these two analytic dimensions to that between two sections of a tree trunk, taken at 90-degree angles to each other, save that neither the grain of the log nor the round array of growth rings would make any claims for authenticity over the other one. They would both be what they were, true pictures of what was there. It is tempting to try to think of the analyses of poetry's meter and matter cutting through a text, as it were, at similar right angles. But each of these notions, whether reinterpreted in more modern language as "form" and "content" or not, itself remains too complex and far too problematic for such a simple opposition. And yet these aspects of poetry present very traditional pictures of what is there.

In the following pages I shall explore further some of the consequences of Emerson's formulation of the "meter-making argument," both with a view to introducing a contrary notion which I believe holds true in certain significant situations and, more generally, to consider another distinction which may be far more useful in distinguishing poetry from mere writing in verse. If the claim for poetry's being the argument and not the meter means simply to hold that distinction to be central, there is nothing to be said against it. But the question of priority "in the order of genesis," as Emerson puts it, is another matter. In the case of mere versifying, a sonnet, for example, is a fourteen-line form, rhymed in one of a number of ways. A versifier can choose to write one and cast about for a subject, a matter, an argument, a substance to fill a sonnet-shaped-and-sized bottle with. Equally, he or she can start with a substance and, feeling in control of the processes of sonnet writing, can pour that prior stuff into the chosen container. The priority here is trivial, in any case. (Needless to say, I use *sonnet* to represent any recognizable formal structure, even if unrecognized as a conventional one by the very naive author.) But for a "true poet" of the sort invoked by Schlegel in the epigraph to this chapter the sonnet will become, as we have seen, a transcendental form—an institution, with a history, which must be imaginatively re-formed, an element of matter, not merely of meter. It is easy to see the poet's revisionary imagination at work in so exemplary a situation, for the sonnet is a form, a mode, an evolving line of genre, a continuing trope for a short poem generally. But there are more subtle and hidden places in which meter becomes not only practical but theoretical matter, and where the issue of the argument-making powers of meter, as it were, comes up in ways that are both elusive and profound.

Let me introduce this question by looking closely at one small element of an exemplary sonnet, the whole of which will have to be quoted. The climactic seventy-first sonnet of Sidney's *Astrophel and Stella* follows on an expression of erotic satisfaction, in the previous one (a poem which seems to have to defend itself against a charge of triviality in the absence of absence, in the presence of joy: "Sonnets be not bound prentise to annoy: / Trebles sing high, as well as bases deepe"). After this, Sonnet 71 gives strangely sudden praise to sublimation: Stella, so literally present (perhaps also in the embraced person of Sidney's beloved, but otherwise married, Penelope Rich) as to need no mention in the preceding poem, is now invoked as she has been earlier in the sequence. But where she had been a muse for English poetry, now she is the epitome of the Beauty in which Virtue is housed (rather than, say, the bog in which it gets entrapped):

Who will in fairest booke of Nature know,
  How Vertue may best lodg'd in beautie be,
  Let him but learne of *Love* to reade in thee,
Stella, those faire lines, which true goodnesse show.
There shall he find all vices' overthrow,
  Not by rude force, but sweetest soveraigntie
  Of reason, from whose light those night-birds flie;
That inward sunne in thine eyes shineth so.
  And not content to be Perfection's heire
Thy selfe, doest strive all minds that way to move,
Who marke in thee what is in thee most faire.
So while thy beautie drawes the heart to love,
  As fast thy Vertue bends that love to good:
  'But ah,' Desire still cries, 'give me some food.'[5]

Let us focus on the final couplet, in which a strange thing happens. Lines 12–13 seem to form a neat, concluding (though unrhyming) couplet of their own, summing up the platonizing strategy of the whole poem: "So while thy beautie drawes the heart to love, / As fast thy Vertue bends that love to good." The violent force of the interjection, in which Desire creeps in and blows down the whole now-complacent household with his unattenuated demand, manifests itself in an isolated sentence, breaking the normal mold of the couplet that contains and balances lines like the two preceding ones. I am not suggesting that Sidney set out to write a sonnet of the variant form *abba, abba, cdc[de], e,* say, and then asked himself, "What is the best story of interruption, given the general story of the sequence and sorts of local story generated in each of the sonnets, that can be told with this device?"—and then, presumably, "What interruption can best break apart a well-built and decorated chamber of self-consoling rationalization but Passion?" (Sidney's terms would have been *wit* and *will*.) It was too early in the history of English poetry for a metrical situation (here, a scheme of versification) to generate matter in quite this way. But certainly the whole question of breakage and abruptness is here, as regards both pattern and story. Certainly Desire, in a bout of successful stichomythia with the rest of the poem, has the disjunctive last word.[6]

Fractured couplets or quatrains, yielding dramatically disjunct terminal lines, have become conventional both in sonnets and in other modern lyric forms—Meredith's "Lady, this is my sonnet to your eyes" at the end of the thirtieth sonnet of *Modern Love,* mentioned in a previous discussion, for example; or Robert Frost's "And to do that to birds was why she came," pointed by the initial "And," which breaks a final couplet that commences with the poem's title line: "Never again would birds' song be the same." Frost varies the application of the scheme only slightly in the last line of his sonnet called "Design," where the penultimate question, "What but design of darkness to appall?" is—instead of being answered—abruptly qualified by "If design govern in a thing so small." James Wright's well-known sonnetlike poem with a deceptively long and literal title, "Lying in a Hammock at William Duffy's Farm in Pine Island, Minnesota," provides a further instance, wielding the scheme of abruptness and discontinuity with great skill. In a carefully modulated binary structure, with the second half enforcing a shift of both narrative and readerly attention from present to past and future, from fading sound to failing light, a penultimate pair of lines seems, like a couplet, to conclude the meditation appropriately, with a last personal report and an answering hieroglyph from nature. The final, short supererogation is devastating, yet schematically needed even as Sidney's last line was; it recapitulates the poem's opening scheme of an eleven-syllabled line followed by a six-syllabled one:

> I lean back, as the evening darkens and comes on.
> A chicken hawk floats over, looking for home.
> I have wasted my life.

It is as if the reader were being rebuked for thinking that such a serious meditation could end up in such an evasive, acquiescent, and even comfy mode of moralizing. Neither these nor the almost inevitable, long, concluding single line, a verse paragraph in itself, dropped below the rest of the text in the later poems of Robert Penn Warren are troped, as schemes, in the way Sidney's is. The dramaturgy of the separation—in Frost's case, there is a coy game being played with the last-line-as-footnote-which-is-really-the-heart-of-the-matter—is one thing, but fictions *about* the form are another. These are hieroglyphs necessary to the poem, but not to the poem's transcendental mode.

Yet there are many cases in which larger or smaller schemes do indeed become fictionalized. In Renaissance poetry, patterns of lines and stanzas and even cantos or books (as in the case of Spenser) are available for numerological exegesis and allegorizing. Dante's *terza rima* is itself moralized. On the other hand, a tiny bit of device can amplify its effects with such an accompanying fable about itself as device. Milton, as has frequently been noted, deploys a wide array of kinds of enjambment in *Paradise Lost*; but even in the most surprising and revealing of situations, he tends not to allegorize his scheme (which he calls "sense variously drawn out") itself. Yet look what happens at the end of Shelley's sonnet on England in 1819. The whole poem consists of a series of noun phrases, each a line or two in length, with the verb occurring only in the penultimate line:

> An old, mad, blind, despised and dying king,—
> . . . .
> Religion, Christless, Godless—a book sealed;
> A Senate—Time's worst Statue unrepealed,—
> Are graves . . .

But the remainder of that line, and the completed final couplet, enact an enjambment, pointed out by Stuart Curran,[7] of unusual force:

> Are graves, from which a glorious Phantom may
> Burst, to illumine our tempestuous day.

With the weight of the twelve lines of catalogued horrors all bearing down on the "are graves"—a figurative weight both syntactic and narrative—a strong pressure seems to be exerted on the "may / Burst." Thus the enjambment is not merely functional (that is, creating surprise—although not like many of Milton's, demanding a revision of meaning in the final words of the enjambed line). The surprise of the enjambment is troped here as the startling effects of an explosion on a hearer: the rest of the line, "to illumine our tempestuous day," will allow a realization that the explosion was the thunder of a cosmic storm of cyclic historical readjustment.

Even tiny schemes can partake of this: I discuss the momentary troping of a difference between direct and elliptical word order in a line of Milton's (below, pp. 189–91); throughout *Paradise Lost,* we are ever-conscious of how word order, placement and unfolding of clauses and qualifications are being used both to control our apprehension of truth and as emblems of the controlling process itself. Thus we tend to read a figure of *tmesis* (*adj¹-noun, and adj²,* instead of *adj¹, adj²-noun*), an ordinarily empty figure taken over from Italian verse, in two ways. Thus: "prefer / Before all Temples, th'upright heart and pure" (*PL* 1.18) can scan as (1) *pure* is predicate of the name *upright heart,* rather than sharing the predication with the other adjective, *upright,* and (2) with *pure* and *upright* conjoined as a pair of adjectives, the *purity* unfolds, in the reading, with a kind of heuristic force—it's as if one didn't get to learn of the purity until one had grasped, even worked through, the uprightness. The ordinary sequences *pure, upright* or *upright, pure heart* wouldn't have raised this question. This is even more complex in the phrase "human face divine" (*PL* 2.44), with its ellipsis of "and."

This kind of storytelling about formal pattern occurs very prominently even in instances where the scheme is not conventional, but ad hoc. Wallace Stevens frequently makes a figure of a fictive version of what a linguist would call ablaut, the internal vowel changes in, say, the sequence *ring, rang, rung*; he also does this with a sort of declensionlike series: "Pipperoo, pippera, pipperum, the rest is rot,"[8] which also makes "rot" follow "rest" as if an inevitable and declensional form of it. At a moment in "Le Monocle de Mon Oncle," however, in talking of love ("It comes, it blooms, it bears its fruit and dies") Stevens glosses not only his own parable, but the glossing of it as well: "This trivial trope reveals a way of truth." Here, not only the alliterating /tr/, but the very figure of alliteration, is characterized as essentially "trivial"; but the playing out of the linguistic sequence reveals a way in which /tr/ signals something else—truth (and not merely what is, as a logician might say, "trivially true"). The scheme, pointing to itself as trope as well as to the figure of the tree of love, takes a momentary walk along the way of a sequence of sound changes.

The use of a syntactic pattern in poetry can be very forceful and resonant without this self-troping, of course. Andrew Marvell's refrain in "The Mower's Song," "Juliana comes, and she / What I do to the grass, does to my thoughts and me," does indeed trope the strangely bracketed syntax of dependent clause interrupting the main one. The function of the pattern is to intensify the connection between Juliana's figurative, and the speaker's real, mowing. But the trope of the syntactic scheme is the physical movement of mowing itself, the reaching back in order to return forward. But an even more intense syntactic scheme, in "To His Coy Mistress," does not call attention to itself in the same manner:

> Thy beauty shall no more be found,
> Nor, in thy marble vault shall sound
> My echoing song . . .

In the marble vault, neither (*a*) will her beauty be found by any eye, nor (*b*) will his echoing song (including this poem) be heard. But here, it is as if the song were an echo to the sight: the architectonic centering of

> no beauty—marble vault—no song

is augmented by the undertone of *sound = test for depth* in the marble vault. But the deferred syntax of these lines does not make a figure of its own Latinate centering of the vault in spite of English word order.

This last pattern is rather close in some ways to the widely used and conventional figure of chiasmus, or crisscrossing of elements in a line or sentence. For our purposes here, it is a useful figure to consider.

As a scheme, chiasmus has no more meaning in itself than does any other surface pattern. *Chiasm* now refers to the inversion, in a line of verse, of the order of occurrence of any two elements just preceding, in some marked way; but until a particular moment of poetry has used it to help mean something in particular, the scheme remains figuratively silent. And yet, once we have heard the device tell a certain poetic story, that story comes to seem natural to it. Chiasm has come to be a scheme of schemes, a general paradigm of phonological, lexical, semantic, or even metalinguistic arrangement, usually represented as [*ab*:*ba*] (where *a* and *b* can be any small or large element). The patterned elements can be particular words, in which case the chiasm is total, for example, Brutus's "Remember March, the ides of March remember" (*Julius Caesar,* 4.3.18). Or it can manifest itself in a disruption of an expected syntactic parallelism, as in the example cited by Dwight L. Bolinger: "A superman in physique, but in intellect a fool,"[9] where the climactic force of the final word is gained at the expense of the inversion; the resulting ordering of [person quality:quality person] exemplifies the scheme.[10]

Early on in the history of rhetoric, the chiasmic figure called *antimetabole* is for Quintilian (9.3.85) evidenced by "non ut edam vivo, sed ut vivam edo," where the sense—"I don't live to eat but eat to live"—gives us the chiasmic ordering of the repeated words [live eat:eat live] with the necessary syntactic idiom *x* to [in order to] *y* is repeated without inversion. So in the Latin [*edam vivo:vivam edo*] is held together by the normal order of inflectional syllables -*am,* -*o,* -*am,* -*o.* A chiasmic pattern might be simply phonological: we could reorder the example "non vivo ut edam, sed ut vivam edo," giving us [*o am:am o*]. And indeed, the scheme has become generalized to cover almost any kinds of element, from prominent phonemes up through phrases, structures, and abstract entities like parts of speech. "In Xanadu did Kubla Khan" yields [*an u:u an*], or a scheme of rhyme. But aside from an incantatory tone, the lines signal not only that this is privileged speech, but that in the marked architectonics of the first line of the poem, its obvious phonological *structure,* there is a trope of the poet-Khan's kind of propounding of the pleasure-poem, of building by decreeing. That there is a phonological pattern at work in the narrative statement is obvious; less obvious, but poetically strong, is the way in which the presence of pattern itself is momentarily allegorized. But that the pattern is a chiasm, and what that might mean, is not part of the momentary schematic fiction in any way. The specifically chiasmatic character of the pattern is not interpreted.[11]

The language of Shakespeare's sonnets, riddling and riddled with ambiguous syntax that seems so often to be joking about certainty and doubt in both wit and will, puts its occasionally strict chiasmatic schemes to those more general purposes. In "Love's fire heats water, water cools not love"

(154) the repetition is almost totally strict, given the paraphrase of *heats* = *cools not*; and in "'Tis better to be vile than vile esteemed" (121), the inversion, as so often, admits of the possible adverbial reading of "vile." In the doubled chiasm of Sonnet 142's opening, "Love is my sin and thy dear virtue hate, / Hate of my sin grounded in sinful loving"—the [*love sin : virtue hate*] crosses [*feeling moral state : moral state feeling*], but is held together, at another level of abstraction, by an affective pattern of [+ − / + −]. The two lines taken together cross [*Love . . . hate : Hate . . . loving*] in an almost refrainlike return.

Chiasm is often used in wit to put down a previous speaker by imprisoning his or her last utterance in an unintended figurative cell. Moth, in *Love's Labors Lost* (1.2), responds to Armado's comment on his last joke ("Pretty apt") by troping one of its terms: "I pretty and my saying apt? or I apt, and my saying pretty?" where, again, the parallel syntax of *I . . . my saying / I . . . my saying* is superimposed on the chiasm. Marx, deriding the weakness of Proudhon's book entitled *The Philosophy of Poverty,* answers it with a work called *The Poverty of Philosophy.* Here, the inversion turns the formulation around as a Swiftian metamorphosis might turn something inside out. The momentary fiction is that the "philosophy" and "poverty" mean the same thing both times. Of course, they don't. In Roman Jakobson's perhaps echoic "Poetry of Grammar and Grammar of Poetry" there is only a faint troping of both terms, but the attack is implicitly against American structural linguistics and its distrust of diachrony and poetry.[12]

One of the most celebrated examples of the Shakespearean mode of the figure glanced at above, in which orderings of different categories of linguistic event are superimposed, occurs in the penultimate line of Pope's merciless account of the aged, sometime fashionable beauties at places like Bath:

See how the world its veterans rewards!
A Youth of Frolics, an Old Age of cards;
Fair to no purpose, artful to no end,
Young without Lovers, old without a Friend;
A Fop their Passion, but their Prize a Sot;
Alive, ridiculous, and dead, forgot. ["To a Lady," 243–48]

The succession of relentless syntactic parallels, all contrasting youth and age (the hovering sense of terminus in "end" is itself doubly artful), culminates in the *alive/dead* contrast of the final line. The penultimate one, however, imposes on the pattern a syntactic chiasm of [*object subject : subject object*] (the copula "was" being understood). Pope could well have written, "A Fop their Passion, but a Sot their Prize" (which still allows strong rhyming to arise). But here, the additional phonological pattern of assonance and alliteration [*monosyllabic /a/ initial /p/ : initial /p/ monosyllabic /a/*]—or, at another level, [*assonance alliteration : alliteration assonance*]—makes the pattern even more prominent. The penultimate line spits out its unrestrained venom before allowing the whole matter to sink—with a final hovering over the possibility that "dead" modifies "forgot" as well—into oblivion.

But the complex operations of chiasm need not be limited to such immediate ironic pointedness. The intensities of meaning that result from layers of simultaneous structure can work in other ways. In a line of Milton's discussed by Geoffrey Hartman in the past[13]—"Sonorous metal blowing martial sounds" (*PL* 1.150)—an ordinary parallel pattern of [adj + noun / adj + noun] is overlaid with a set of apparent morphemic identities in chiasm. [Son*orous* metal : *martial* sounds] gives a closer etymological likening of the outer pair than of the like-sounding inner one, and of these two words, the terminal -*al* syllable is a nominal stem ending in the first case and an adjectival suffix in the second one. But by whatever magical means, the action of the line manifests the implicit, initially designated qualities of the horns of Pandemonium in their realized sounds. Here the pattern again calls attention to itself in the course of its use. But except for the ultimate matter of *sound,* in both use and mention, turning the figure into an apparent phonological rather than inscriptional structure, the form of crossing or reversal is again unallegorized.

Similarly with a number of other elegant instances. Four well-known lines from Andrew Marvell's "To His Coy Mistress" deploy one chiasmic pattern as a musical echo to a preceding one, both to reaffirm its pattern and gloss its figuration. The lines are about how neither moral categories (like "honour"), motions of the will (like "lust"), nor, literally, sexual parts of bodies outlast death. They follow immediately upon the ones cited earlier, talking of what will happen in the grave:

> And your quaint honour turn to dust
> And into ashes all my lust.
> The grave's a fine and private place,
> But none I think do there embrace.

The punning "quaint" reifies the abstract "honour" into "parts of female honour (cunt)," as does the now-burnt-out lust as "cock," and the chiasm is manifestly one of [*living entity dead residue : dead residue living entity*]. But this is superimposed on another one:

honour   dust : ashes   lust

This groups the proverbial and biblical "dust and ashes" in the middle and suggests that the present "honour and lust" are an inevitably analogous pair, each term, as in the first instance, a paraphrase of the second. Even as the sexual difference of the two lovers has been polarized throughout the poem, it is undermined in the grave. The suggestion is thus that "honour" and "dust" are different synecdoches for something. (If that something is Life, then in fact they are, but at another level.) Moreover, the apparent crossing of [*abstract concrete : concrete abstract*] is superimposed on another one of [*live dead : dead live*], although the rhyme of "dust" and "lust" gives death something of the last word in any case. (This is aside from the greater concreteness, the substantiality, of the tropes of death.) It is only the punning reading, in which "honour" and "lust" are substantial flesh, which dissolves the apparent abstract/concrete chiasm. The subsequent couplet, with its own puns on "fine" ("attenuated," "narrow," and, of course, "terminal") and "private" (as in "private parts"), reinforces the complexities of the foregoing lines. This can be seen in its manifestly more innocently phonological and grammatical crossings of [/ey/ /ay/ : /ay/ /ey/] and [*noun adjective : adjective noun*] (although these are so grouped syntactically—noun [is] (adj + adj) noun—that the word order is sharply direct).

In the subtle and artful patterns of a little epigram on Hero and Leander by John Donne, an abstract chiasmatic scheme is buried beneath other more prominent patterns and yet does its own work of framing and intensifying. The dead lovers (one drowned in the literal crossing of the Hellespont) speak as a pair from beyond the grave:

Both robbed of air, we both lie in one ground
Both whom one fire had burnt, one water drowned.

The complexities of this start when the second line is added to the first, which is easily and conventionally arrayed. The two are both burnt only figuratively, by passion, and drown literally—Leander by accident, and Hero in grieving suicide. But the couplet is overloaded, in that even its fairly prominent pattern of the four elements is wittily interpreted, somewhat analogously to the association of the contrasts of abstract/concrete // alive/ dead in the lines from Marvell. Here, with the two lovers dead, only the two "hot" and impalpable elements, air and fire, are named literally, and thus seem more present. Earth and water are only implicit in the words "ground" and "drowned," which, respectively, designate what hides the unbreathing from the air and quenches the fires of passion along with the rest of life.

But what is not so apparent is the chiasmatic scheme that holds these parallels together, as if by a kind of cross-bracing. The words "both" and "one" are sad reminders of the condition of unity that the lovers had sought in life to attain, only to achieve it permanently in death. But these words also hold the conceited structure together by the way they are patterned. Their sequence of occurrence in the couplet is: *both both one / both one one*, or, abstractly, *aababb*, which is an interlocking scheme not actually chiastic.

But there is an implicit pattern of *meta-a* and *meta-b*, as it were, pointed up by the word order and by the arrangement of a more abstract pattern:

Both (airless) we're *both-in-one* (ground);
Both-in-one (fire) we're *one* (in being drowned).

By "meta-*one*" I mean the single predicate, either "both" or "one"; by "meta-*both*" I mean the doubled one "both–one". The chiasm above, then, is one of [*meta-one meta-both : meta-both meta-one*]. This cross-bracing is not apparent on the surface, but the fact that it mixes up the terms *both* and *one* and makes patterns of a higher (or at least, more abstract) concept of *both*-ness, is part of a commentary on the whole set of conventional erotic topoi being played with here, the figure of two-in-one, or the "Single nature's double name" of *The Phoenix and Turtle* of Shakespeare. But once again, no implicit parable about the scheme of chiasm itself emerges from this instance of it, save as a sort of emblem of mixture, of a connection deeper than would superficially appear. It is the ultimate dissolution—even of *both*-ness—in drowning which dominates the couplet, by its cadential role and by the sort of cold water it throws on all wit.

Many other instances could be adduced of occasional faint crossings, as well as prominent ones, with a range of functions. Barely discernible within its prominent parallelistic frame, for example, is the valedictory of Milton's Satan (*PL* 4.108): "So farewell Hope and with Hope farewell fear," where [*farewell hope : hope farewell*] recedes behind *farewell hope / farewell fear.* The interplay of English direct word order and Latinate lapidary word placement in the line is typical of *Paradise Lost* but is not allegorized here the way it is more generally in the rest of the poem. The function at this point is primarily to undercut Satan's rhetoric by having him inadvertently frame a repetitive and unfruitful utterance.[14]

More prominent, but more mild in its operation, would be a use of the scheme by Edwin Arlington Robinson in "The Sheaves": "a mighty meaning of a kind / That tells the more the more it is not told." Here the wit in the figuration of the second meaning of "the more" is almost minimal; and the conjoining of direct/inverted word orders, and the consequent active/passive verb confrontation (always an available mechanism of this scheme), are used but not made much of. This frequently happens when the scheme is used in prose. The early James Joyce is full of such patternings, but they are most often crossings of the sequence of pairs of adjectives, or of an adverb-adjective or adverb-gerundive pair, as from the lyrical coda to *The Dead*. Here one such scheme echoes and points up another, earlier occurrence of it. The snow ("general all over Ireland," in a phrase echoed from a casual use of it earlier in the story), was "falling softly upon the Bog of Allen and, farther westward, softly falling into the dark mutinous Shannon waves." It could be argued that there is an operative contrast here between the snow falling softly onto the soft land, but which—still soft in itself, and soft in its density, windlessness, and rate of descent—cannot fall softly onto, but merely fall into, the hardness of the wind-sharpened waves. Similarly, at the end of the paragraph, the protagonist Gabriel Conroy's "soul swooned slowly as he heard the snow falling faintly through the universe and faintly falling, like the descent of their last end, upon all the living and the dead."

Here the scheme occurs echoically, and there is even a reciprocal allusive phrase—"their last end"—also picked up from a remark dropped, at the party earlier in the story, in all unwitting innocence of its being echoed by a lyrical narrator and returned with refigured force. Here, too, the *faintness* of the falling, in what Gabriel Conroy figuratively "hears," is both an audition and a trope of the more literal and palpable *softness*. The faintness is that of metaphor itself, and it is appropriately applied to the way the snow falls, as it were, "through the universe." The final reversal—"faintly falling, like the descent of their last end"—lacks the pointedness of the contrast in the first pair and serves what it would be too easy to call a "musical" function, completing a pattern, acknowledging its presence, and closing out a larger, enveloping scheme: *falling [softly softly falling falling faintly faintly] falling*, a cadence of repetition and refrain.

In all of these instances, chiasmatic figures have been used to frame all sorts of tropes. The presence of the scheme itself has been variously prominent or receding, and its operation either engaged with or independent of other schemes. But I now want to turn to some uses of the figure which do more than call attention to themselves: they tell particular stories of what their pattern in itself means. That such stories are fictions goes without saying. But they are central fictions of poetry itself, akin to the emblematic readings of natural objects—that claiming of anything noticeable as a sort of hieroglyph, the constant work of interpreting anew every instance of even a conventional occasion—that are the imagination's noble work.

Here is what is perhaps a borderline instance of what I have been pointing to, a couplet of Pope's: "In Moderation placing all my Glory, / While Tories call me Whig, and Whigs a Tory."[15] Here, the parallel *plural-singular / plural-singular* cuts across the chiasm with satiric force: plurals are immoderate, the interrelation of schemes suggests, brandishing the singular forms of antithetical names. There is an implicit association here, perhaps aided by the force of the word "placing," of moderation and pattern-making, of putting words and extremes in their place: Alexander Pope the moderator is Alexander Pope the chiasmatician, who reveals how extreme positions engage in conflict only to their own confusion. Pope the wielder of schemes is no dialectician like Lenin or Blake—he is not turning the polar parties inside out to show how each contains the germ of the other. But he is making of *moderation* something more than a mere midpoint, something indeed more like the center of a whirligig. That the word "me" does not sit at the midpoint of the word order (matching the ":" of the scheme) is a function of the direct force of English declarative syntax; many instances of chiasm in the eighteenth century will generate interesting side effects framed by the word order. (Consider the example of chiasm from *Webster's New Collegiate Dictionary,* by Goldsmith: "To stop too fearful and too faint to go'—the sequence [*too fearful* + *too faint*] sets up a simultaneous cause-effect and spirit-body parallel as strong as the major crossing of *stop* [/f/—*hesitant*] : [/f/—*hesitant*] *go* itself.) But this direct word order also embraces the forceful "Tories call me Whig"—and whatever his protestations about being a moderate, Pope is indeed a Tory, and his virtue in being called out by his own party comes up front. In any event, Pope's couplet leaves us with a sense that the scheme is a tool of reason, of putting extreme positions in their proper schematic positions and places.

A number of examples from Spenser, however, will display an even more prominent range of allegories of the scheme. A borderline instance might be one from a lyric in Sidney's *The Countess of Pembroke's Arcadia* (3.37): "My heart was wounded with his wounded heart," says Colin, and here the reciprocity of feeling, the literal sympathy, is charged with something else. The mediating word "with" means at once "along with" (the matter of sympathy) and "by means of," which makes the other's injured heart a weapon to wound his own. Perhaps this momentarily depicts the mutual vulnerabilities of two dear friends, and its crossing the yoking of *philia.* But consider this line from Spenser: "He pip'd, I sung, and when he sung, I piped" / By chaunge of turnes, each making other mery" (Colin to the Shepherd of the Ocean, in *Colin Clout's Come Home Againe*). Here, the matter of "change" and "turns" cuts several ways, and the simultaneous schemes of *He-I* / *He-I* and [*piped sung : sung piped*] together embody a change of direct and crossed turns. Particularly since this is talking about their poetry, about the making and turning of verses here, the figure moves into the realm of trope. The fashioning becomes a turning—of the relation of nonrival poetries—itself.

It is because moments in *The Faerie Queene* so often discourse in barely concealed asides about themselves that the chiasms so often become tropes of poetry itself in its different aspects. The Latin etymon of *turning* in the word *verse* Spenser had played upon in his youth, in the "August" eclogue of *The Shepheardes Calender* ("How I admire each turning of thy verse," said in admiration of Colin's sestina). In a stanza from book 1 of *The Faerie Queene* describing Redcrosse's response to the arguments of the dreadful psychotherapist Despair advising suicide, the question of verse and poetry is again at issue and touches upon the chiasm in the final alexandrine:

> Well knowing true all, that he did reherse
> And to his fresh remembraunce did reverse

> The ugly view of his deformed crimes,
> That all his manly powres it did disperse
> As he were charmed with inchaunted rimes,
> That oftentimes he quakt, and fainted oftentimes.   [*FQ* 1.9.48]

It would be almost inevitable that we should come down to a literal reversal (of sequence, in the chiasm) at the end of the stanza. The reversing of "did reherse" in a similar phrase (*hearse* derives from an old word for a harrow; we are thus reminded that the coffin and the furrowed lines of verse do more than rhyme, although I don't think that Spenser knew the etymon necessarily) calls attention to rhymes, verses, charms, and their power generally. The last chiasm in which Redcrosse's reversed—and re-versed—reaction is framed makes a momentary picture of responses to verses as a sort of rhyming in reverse: *oftentimes* [*quaked*(/ey/) : [*fainted*(/ey/)] *oftentimes*. Guyon's responses are themselves a scheme. Without the framing of matter of verse and poetry and their rhetorical effects, this might be merely decorative; with it, the scheme is more than merely meaningful.

And so with the charm of the enchantress Acrasia, the Wicked Witch of Erotic Excess (in 2.1.55) as she invokes her victims in a spell: "Sad verse, give death to him that death does give, / And losse of love to her that loves to live." Her "sad verse" addresses, and arms, itself, providing an undercurrent of self-reference once more. Like other spells, it urges a latent magic into action, but here it immediately effects that magic in another way, by working on the names of the two victims, Mordant and Amavia, reinterpreting them into significances which are both necessary to the larger magic and, in addition, truths about the essences of the persons themselves. "Mordant," she reveals in these lines, means "death-giving" (*mort + dant*) and "Amavia" *amavi*, "I have loved." Yet up till now, their names seemed to mean "biting" (French *mordre*)—for the terrible pains this Knight has suffered— and "loves living," respectively. The paired chiasms concurrently constitute, empower, describe, and momentarily authenticate the appropriateness of the spell. The scheme of crossing becomes on this occasion a synecdoche for the language and potency of sympathetic magic, giving death only to the acutely nonimmune death-giver, etc. The spell, by awakening the true meanings of the victims' names, thereby increases their vulnerability.

Spenser's chiasmatic moments frequently draw upon a locally heightened consciousness of the artfulness of language, but the fables they come up with are by no means the same. One more example will suffice. In the Proem to book 5, the decay of the world through historical change is being lamented. A chain of chiasms depicts the loss of ancient virtues:

> For that which all men then did vertue call
> Is now cald vice; and that which vice is hight
> Is now hight virtue, and so us'd of all.

Right now is wrong, and wrong that was is right
As all things else in time are chaunged quight.   [5, Proem, 4.1–5]

Here the first two chiasms make a larger one as well:

VIRTUE *call : call* VICE :: VICE *hight : hight* VIRTUE

Lest we fall into the trap of thinking that these changes are merely those of
historical semantics, that only linguistic conventions have changed in time
(as, say, the words *meat* and *meal* have crisscrossed in their meanings of
"repast" and "substance thereof" since Spenser's day), the next crossing of
[*right wrong : wrong right*] uses the copula and plays no games with words
of naming. All the double senses of "right" and of phrases like "is right"
(+ "is 'right'") aside, we must notice the syntactic ambiguity of the final
line here—*all of the things that are "in" (or part of) time are all changed +
all things generally are changed "in time" (eventually + more magically "in
some crucible or region of time")*. It, too, points toward the story of the chiasm.
The crossings of terms are here seen as palimpsestic marks of decay (we
might think of them here as being like fossil matrices)—as if true, direct, *x
is non-y* predications stopped being possible after Astraea left the world at
the end of the Golden Age.

Milton can make his crossings seem like errors and puzzles, as when the
philosophers in Pandemonium

> reason'd high
> Of providence, foreknowledge, will and fate,
> Fixed fate, free will, foreknowledge absolute
> And found no end, in wandering mazes lost   [*PL* 2.553–56]

and the scheme momentarily feels like a maze itself. Satan plays with opposed terms like "evil" and "good" in structures that are frequently chiasmatic. But seldom do they reach the force of the narrator's invocation of
the "troubl'd thoughts"

> that stir
> The Hell within him for within him Hell
> He brings . . .   [*PL* 4.19–21]

The main scheme here is framed in a single line, a friezelike paratactic pattern with no verb. Two separate verbs are supplied in the adjacent enjambed
lines. This implies an additional surrounding scheme: [*verb hell-within-
him : within-him-hell verb*] and calls attention even more to the matter of
containment, the trope of internalization of place, which is the point here.[16]
Concentricity is the heart of the figure in this case, even as "the Cross"—
with perhaps an overtone of allusion to the name of the scheme itself—
becomes a momentary essence of it in the next example. Here the pattern

engages passive and emergently active verbal voice and literal and figurative
acts of "nailing":

> nail'd to the Cross
> By his own Nation, slain for bringing Life;
> But to the cross he nails thy enemies,
> The law that is against thee . . .   [PL 12.413–17]

In connection with the presence of the word "cross," two lovely lines of
Rossetti's from a sonnet on "An Early Annunciation" (a German painting)
gloss this last passage interestingly: "The loud flies cross each other in the
sun, / And the aisled pillars meet the poplar-aisle." Given the poem's ekphrastic program, the reading into the painting of the iconographic "cross
oneself" doubles the purely neutral, schematic patterning. The flies' symbolic gesture "cross each other" rubs off onto the purely formal reading of
the relationship of the two rows of verticals framed in the second chiasmatic
line.

Milton's Eve, in her narrative in the fourth book, falls into an important
chiasm as she describes her Narcissus-like encounter with her image in a
pool:

> As I bent down to look, just opposite
> A shape within the watery gleam appeared
> Bending to look on me . . .   [PL 4.460–62]

[*I bend-down-look : bend-down-look me*] is dispersed among three lines here,
rather than relentlessly arranged in one, and the nuance of ambiguity across
the enjambment (*appeared / Bending*—as if with a discovered sense of "appeared to bend or be bending") complicates it even further. But this may
be the locus classicus of the trope of *abba* as mirrored image. (One must
not be overliteral about this: any sequence of discernible marks, *ab*, on a
flat page will indeed read *ba* in a mirror placed perpendicular to the plane
of the page. Conjoining the sequence with its mirrored image will indeed
yield *ab:ba*. But it will only be the schema of abstract notation that will be
put in chiasmatic relation with its reflection.)

There is nevertheless something deeply compelling about this myth of
chiasm as mirror, particularly when whole words and phrases, rather than
sublexical elements, are being put into the pattern. The chiasmatic wisdom
of Keats's urn (the vexed textual question aside of whether the pot or the
poet comments on it by adding, "That is all / Ye know on earth . . . etc.")
is not mirrorlike and not really troped at all, although the "Beauty is Truth,
Truth Beauty" could be considered the near-palindromic result of an ekphrastic reading of an inscription—of rotating a vase first clockwise (*Beauty
. . . Truth*), then counterclockwise over the same area of surface (*Truth . . .
Beauty*).

But Robert Frost's remarkable revision of Milton's Eve and, through her, of Ovid's Narcissus in "Spring Pools" tells a canonically powerful story of chiasm as mirroring. "These pools that, though in forests, still reflect / The total sky almost without defect" are seen in the first stanza of the poem as mortal and transitory, "like the flowers beside them" soon to be absorbed by the forces of summer which darken the greenness of spring. But the relation of the mental and optical senses of "reflect," and the pool as a figure of consciousness, are put in place at the outset. The splendidly ambiguous syntax, aided by the enjambment, which yields (1) *reflect, almost perfectly, the total sky* or (2) *reflect the whole of the almost-perfect sky* suggests, in a Miltonic way, some natural sort of connection between object and representation—Eve said of what she saw behind the image in her pool that it "to me seem'd / Another sky." The pools also reflect the flowers beside them. In the second stanza, the chiasm of object and image is reinforced by all that has been said of light and darkness up to then. It is made more pointed, in its formal mode, by the intensely colloquial but slightly strange diction of "soon be gone . . . and yet not out . . . but up" and, even more markedly, of not "have it in them to," but a deferred version of that:

> The trees that have it in their pent-up buds
> To darken nature and be summer woods—
> Let them think twice before they use their powers
> To blot out and drink up and sweep away
> These flowery waters and these watery flowers
> From snow that melted only yesterday.

A question is raised by this penultimate line about whether the flowers are by now *in* or *on* the water (as with images colloquially "in" but actually "on" any mirror). But since the pools also reflect (intransitively) as human consciousnesses do, they thereby partake of what they reflect (transitively).[17] The figure is dual, for the "watery flowers" are both those on the rim of the pool ("watery" because they, too, are drunk up by summer) as well as, more prominently, their images in the water. We are never told what sort of flowers these are, but they seem to be narcissi, recalling their Ovidian avatar, who, Spenser memorably says,

> Was of himselfe the idle Paramoure:
> Both love and lover, without hope of joy,
> For which he faded to a watery flower.

(*FQ* 3.2.45)[18]

The chiasm embraces not only the flowers, the after-lives of the mistaken and betrayed reader of representation, but the poetry itself, which, by imagining Narcissus's condition, escapes his fate. For Thoreau in "Ponds" (from *Walden*) a lake is "earth's eye; looking into which the beholder measures the depths of his own nature"—as Narcissus sounded only its shallowness.

The mirror is human thinker, transient and mortal like that which he or she reflects and reflects upon. Frost's use of the figure here is canny and quizzical but nonetheless transcendental, full of what he himself called "the pleasure of ulteriority." It reminds us of so many other chiasmatic moments in English poetry. It itself reflects, in passing but thereby (for this is poetry and not philosophy) in ultimate purpose as well, on what Stevens called in "An Ordinary Evening in New Haven" (much more guardedly by its deployment of the line break), "The enigmatical / Beauty of each beautiful enigma." The enigmas of such figures are themselves flowers of our consciousness and part of nature itself. What poetry makes of them, as of whatever else it notices in and about its own language, is part of its very engagement with the world.[19]

7 &

Breaking into Song:
Some Notes on Refrain

Edgar Allan Poe, in "The Philosophy of Composition," told a fable of the genesis of "The Raven" which became symbolist, and eventually modernist, scripture. He speaks of having to start with what he calls a "point" (we would say a device or scheme or formal structure—but not a trope) of a purely musical sort, a timing device for a short (and thus, authentic) poem. Poe's "pivot upon which the whole structure might turn" proved to be a minimal refrain, a condensation of it, a synecdoche of a returning burden whose name, *refrain,* is etymologically *refractus,* broken back or rebroken: in short, a single word. We know how Poe—and with what mixed consequences in France—declared that the *o* and *r* of "Nevermore" (the most "sonorous" vowel and the most "producible" consonant) determined his choice of the word. This bit of visionary linguistics is phonetically nonsensical: the *o* and *r* he was characterizing are only those phonemes of the word *sonorous* itself. Moreover it represses a matter of allusive signification. Like the agent of a dream whose very sinews of meaning are woven on the warp of unacknowledgment, Poe's raven itself speaks deep and hidden truth. The author's account of the bird's utterance only stirs up the clouds. For Poe knew well that the squawk of the raven in the age of classical Rome's grandeur was rendered in Latin as "cras cras cras" (not "caw caw" as in English), and thus "tomorrow, tomorrow," thereby affirming the bird's true prophetic powers. Poe's raven knows, in the dreary light of what Harold Bloom would call romantic belatedness, that there is no poetic tomorrow ("a bird of ill-omen," Poe calls it), and so declares, albeit allusively. Perched on an emblem of wisdom washed out—not a beautiful, dark, haunted Pallas, but an anemic Athena—the poetic bird speaks of the limits of art for the man whose name is part "poe-t" only. It is the "lost Lenore" that is in the poem for alliteration and rhyme, not the word of the bird. "Nevermore" cancels and refigures "cras."

Poe went on to observe of his broken refrain that its "application"—as he called its syntactic, logical, and rhetorical role *in situ* of each strophe that it concluded—was to vary, even as the word itself remained unchanged. In practice, the whole refrain line varied, only the fragment "-more" remaining constant, the full clause ("Quoth the Raven, 'Nevermore'") occurring in only five out of eighteen instances. Poe's concern for his broken or refracted fragment as a device for breaking into an anxiety-ringed, hermeneutico-poetical circle of silence indicates a half-awareness that a formal element, or "point" previously used in song-texts, might itself be allegorized when employed in a true poem. In this case, the return of "Nevermore" denies the return of dead beauty to memory. In general, lyrics from the Renaissance on—poems whose relation to song-text is itself figurative—have tended more and more to trope the scheme of refrain, to propound a parable out of its structural role.

I am talking here of poetic, rather than merely schematic, refrain. This tradition starts perhaps with Theocritus, whose first idyll varies what Poe called the "application" of the repetend to signal phases of beginning, middle, and end of the whole poem itself. Thyrsis's song, it will be remembered, commences with (and I quote from Daryl Hine's splendid recent translation)[1]

> Start up the pastoral music, dear Muses, begin the performance
>
> [Archete boukolaikas Moisai philai, archet'aoidas]

which returns at intervals of from three to five lines, until it modulates, now avowing in the changed verb its own earlier form:

> Muses, continue the pastoral music, on with the performance
>
> [archete boukolaikas Moisai, palin archet'aoidas]

and, finally, to

> Muses, come finish the pastoral music, conclude the performance
>
> [lēgete boukolaikas Moisai, ite lēget'aoidas]

which reiterates and completes the self-referential effect.

Other early precursors of modern lyrical refrain are to be found in the "io Hymen Hymenaee" of Catullus's epithalamic poem (number 61) and in Virgil's eighth eclogue. There, following Theocritus, Damon's song is paced by an invocation to his pipe to start "incipe Maenalios mecum, mea tibia, versus") his lines of Maenalios and to finish them ("desine Maenalios, iam desine, tibia versus"); these are matched by the paired refrains of Alphesiboeus's song to Daphnis: "ducite ab urbe domum, mea carmina, ducite

Daphnum" (Bring Daphnis home from town, O my songs) and "parcite, ab urbe venit, iam parcite carmina, Daphnis" (Cease, Daphnis is coming from town, now cease, O my songs). But the earlier, Theocritus-like refrains of Damon are outdone by Virgil's own, purportedly less mediated imperatives. They are injunctions, not to the poetic skill of the pipe to start and end the songs, but for the power of the songs themselves to effect changes in the world. Alphesiboeus's song comes to an end because it has, indeed, brought Daphnis home.

But in both cases, the "iam" (now) is applied, like a brake, to the song's momentum. The imperative quality of these utterances in exercising control over the course of the song is characteristic of pastoral refrain. In the psalter, on the other hand, there is far less by way of refrain than one might expect. The famous "ki l'olam chasdo" (for his mercy endureth forever) recurs throughout Psalm 136 (and indeed, only four times in Psalm 118). Medieval refrains which are not specifically the burdens of carols are more rare. Most famous are the lovely, longing "l'alba, l'alba oc l'alba, tan tost ve" (the dawn, the dawn, yes the dawn comes too soon!) of the Provençal *alba,* or dawn-song, the recurring lines in Marcabru's famous *pastorela,* and the resolute "þæs ofereode, þisses swa mæg" (that passed away, so may this [and, finally, *these*]) of the Old English "Deor."[2] More frequently, the musical function of refrain will be effected by the repetitive structure of so much medieval lyric—ballades, virelays, rondeaux, whose melodic and strophic patterns will entail the repetition of lines or groups of lines. I have touched on some aspects of such forms in *The Figure of Echo*[3] and shall not expand on the matter here. But it might be observed that the French medieval lyric forms contribute to nineteenth-century English verse an interesting device that we see in the rondeau (but not in triolets, ballades, etc., where the refrain line remains independent and intact): the breaking off of part of an initial line and the reclaiming of the fragment as a refrain. Swinburne, who wrote a hundred examples of the variant of the form he called "roundels," examined the mode in a self-descriptive example entitled "The Roundel." It is worth quoting partly because of the consideration of the apprehended repetition in the last strophe (the evolving figure of the delicately wrought earring, parallel to Rossetti's sonnet-coin, will also be noted):

A roundel is wrought as a ring or a starbright sphere,
With craft of delight and with cunning of sound unsought,
That the heart of the hearer may smile if to pleasure his ear
     A roundel is wrought.

Its jewel of music is carven of all or of aught—
Love, laughter, or mourning—remembrance of rapture or fear—
That fancy may fashion to hang in the ear of thought.

As a bird's quick song runs round, and the hearts in us hear
Pause answer to pause, and again the same strain caught,
So moves the device whence, round as a pearl or tear,
      A roundel is wrought.

But modern lyrical refrain derives in good part from the medieval carol burden, whose reiterations have a literal quality: a leader-singer will sing the strophes, the choral dancers will each time respond with the frequently macaronic burden, which punctuates the periods of varying, and unfolding, monophonic material. Each occurrence of the danced-to burden increases its redundancy and tends to collapse it into a univocal sign: "That was all full of meaning; now meaning stops for a while and we all dance again." Poetic refrain, on the other hand, starts out by troping the literalness of the repetition, by raising a central parabolic question for all textual refrain: "Does repeating something at intervals make it more important, or less so?" Does statistical overdetermination—the criterion of redundancy-as-predictability—apply to such repetitions, or rather the interpreter's concept of overdetermination as implying an increased weight of meaning? It would appear that gradations of signification can appear, and operate, in any single case. We might suggest at first that the more complex the poem, the more it becomes necessary for it to confront the dialectic of these two emblematic readings of, say, the strophic *fa-la-la*. Feelings of "Oh, *that* again," "*We* know," etc. war with the incremental pain of each rapped knuckle; as we know, the ultimate story of modern, poetic refrain is, "What is it to mean *this* time around?" Wallace Stevens puts the deadening aspect of repetition in a concept not merely of scheme, but of metaphor deadened into convention or cliché:

The civil fiction, calico idea,
The Johnsonian composition, abstract man,
All are evasions like a repeated phrase
Which, by its repetition, comes to bear
A meaning without a meaning . . .[4]   ["A Duck for Dinner"]

The possibilities of renewal occur only as unsystematic returning fragments for Stevens, as will be seen shortly.

Refrain breaks into the unfolding or unrolling of any lyrical text. It partakes as well of that action of restraint invoked by our doublet word in English, *refrain* (Fr. *refréner*, for *se retenir*, literally, "to bridle oneself"). But the major tradition of poetic (some might say, "literary," some "self-conscious," some "writerly") refrain is rooted in a rhetorical self-consciousness. There is something allusive about all refrains, if only to their musical and conventionalized origins; and every attempt to make structures of permutation in what Poe called their application can only be a momentary confusion, a lie against repetition. We may perceive patterns of variation which are doomed from the outset to play themselves out, for example, Algernon Charles Swinburne's anaphoristic refrain pattern beginning with the scriptural "Watchman, what of the night?" and continuing through "Prophet, what of the night?," "Mourners, what of the night?," and on through the sequence "Dead men . . . ," "Statesman . . . ," "Warrior," "Master," "Exile," "Captives," "Christian," "High priest," "Princes," "Martyrs," "England," "France," "Italy," "Germany," "Europe," and, finally, "Liberty, what of the night?" ("A Watch in the Night" from *Songs before Sunrise*). Then there are those poems with paired refrains which depend upon a quasi-echoic rhyme; this is made a trope of decaying structure in Rossetti's "Troy Town" (of which I quote the first of fourteen stanzas):

> Heavenborn Helen, Sparta's queen,
>   *(O Troy Town!)*
> Had two breasts of heavenly sheen,
> The sun and moon of the heart's desire:
> All Love's lordship lay between.
>   *(O Troy's down,*
>   *Tall Troy's on fire!)*

The word "desire" terminates the fourth line throughout the poem, although as a half-suppressed subrefrain, unmarked by the formal position, the italicization, etc. of the other three lines. The effect is to have "desire" in the text lead to *"fire"* in the refrain; but aside from the growing significance of this in the narrative, the refrain's mode of application does not change.[5] It is the unvarying rhetoric of the Rossettian double-refrain (as in "Eden Bower," where it alternates in successive stanzas) which made it vulnerable to light-verse parody, as in Charles Stuart Calverley's "Ballad," the last stanza of which tweaks the nose of redundancy:

> The farmer's daughter hath soft brown hair
>   *(Butter and eggs and a pound of cheese)*
> And I met with a ballad, I can't say where,
>   Which wholly consisted of lines like these.

Aside from the matter of redundancy of application, there are questions of more specific allusiveness. Yeats, in many of his later lyrics, substitutes for the empty signaling of earlier poetical *fa-la-la*s, which signal only "refrain here, now," defiantly "unmusical" prosaic phrases ("Daybreak and a candle-end"). But allusive fragments can be turned into refrain in a similar way; this will sometimes constitute an initial interpretation of the nature of the fragment's canonical quality. Consider, for example, how Catullus's "nobis cum semel occidit brevis lux, / nox est perpetua una dormienda" (Ben Jonson gives it as "Suns that set may rise again; / But if once we lose this light, / 'Tis with us perpetual night") becomes for Thomas Campion a varying refrain in his far from mere translation, "My Sweetest Lesbia." It reinterprets the momentary memento mori that breaks into the argument for immediate bed:

> But soon as once is set our little light,
> Then must we sleep one ever-during night.

The second variation refigures the "night" as a moral and spiritual benightedness:

> But fools do live and waste their little light,
> And seek with pain their ever-during night.

The third and final stanza ends with a reliteralizing of the "night" and collapses eternity into mere hyperbole:

> And, Lesbia, close up thou my little light,
> And crown with love my ever-during night.

There are many questions about refrains in poetry which I shall not take up in these remarks but which should at least be considered briefly. One of these is a spectrum or scale of lexical or syntactic variation, or of rhythm of recurrence (at regular or irregular intervals), along which particular applications of refrains in poems might be arrayed. Another is a sort of referential scale, with one pole at what used to be called the "purely musical"—the *fa-la-la* mentioned earlier, a univocal sign of music returning to embrace narrative or analytic information in the strophes. The other pole of such a spectrum would be one of optimum density of reference, in which each return accrued new meaning, not merely because of its relation to the preceding strophe (their glossing of each other), but as a function of the history of its previous occurrences in the poem. Such a mapping would reveal an interesting relation to the rhetoricity of the lyric form as such—the refrains of what Yeats called "words for music perhaps" have, as historical revisions of the burdens of song-texts, a special structural, or quasi-musical, "perhaps"-ness of their own. But in all these taxonomies, historically belated or locally troped refrains would seem to have the property of remembering: their own previous occurrences in the poem, their distant ancestry in song and dance, and their more recent poetic parentage are recollected at each return.

There is a mode of easy irony which prevails in what look like antirefrains, whether partaking of particular parody (like Charles Stuart Calverley's quoted earlier) or more generally subversive of the form as such. A precursor of these is Don Quixote's triad of *coplas* in chapter 26 of book 1, each of which ends with two and a half lines of refrain, the first two rhyming with previous ones, the broken ultimate one egregiously unrhyming:

> aquí lloró don Quijote
> ausencias de Dulcinea
> del Toboso

The don's name rhymes throughout with grotesque, low-comic words like "pipote" (barrel). (You may remember that the hearers collapsed into laughter to think that if, when the don named Dulcinea he did not add "del Toboso," the stanza could not be understood—and such was the truth, as the don later admitted.) The effect here is to undermine the role of the applied rhyming return by attaching the broken parentheticl gloss, or even footnote: had "del Toboso" been made to rhyme each time with something like "hermoso," there would be no joke of this kind. But even this easy trick opens up some of the basic questions we have been considering—intrusions, extrusion, the repetend's manner of breaking and entering into an unfolding or development.

Sir Walter Scott's powerful verses from chapter 31 of *The Betrothed* are, despite their purported historical pastiche, biblical in cadence and antithetically proverbial in rhetoric. They get the strength of their refrain—unchanging in application throughout—from its allusive resonance, a direct undermining of the psalmist's great refrain (Psalm 136—but itself an echo of the opening verse, thrice quoted elswhere, of Psalm 106): *For his mercy endureth forever:*

> I ask'd of my harp, "Who hath injured thy chords?"
> And she replied, "The crooked finger, which I mocked in my tune."
> A blade of silver may be bended—a blade of steel abideth:
> Kindness fadeth away, but vengeance endureth.

The bardic stance here hides the antibiblical gesture, and the *fausse-naïve* repetition of the maxim serves in each instance to interpret the anecdote or poetic proverb preceding, giving it a strong, although reductive, reading:

> The sweet taste of mead passeth from the lips,
> But they are long corroded by the juice of wormwood;
> The lamb is brought to the shambles, but the wolf rangeth the
>   mountain;
> Kindness fadeth away, but vengeance endureth.

> I asked the red-hot iron, when it glimmer'd on the anvil,
> "Wherefore glowest thou longer than the firebrand?"
> "I was born in the dark mine, and the brand in the pleasant
>   greenwood."
> Kindness fadeth away, but vengeance endureth.

> I ask'd the green oak of the assembly wherefore its boughs were
>   dry and sear'd like the horns of the stag:
> And it show'd me that a small worm had gnaw'd its roots.
> The boy who remembered the scourge undid the wicket of the

castle at midnight.
Kindness fadeth away, but vengeance endureth.

Lightning destroyeth temples, though their spires pierce the clouds;
Storms destroy armadas, though their sails intercept the gale.
He that is in his glory falleth, and that by a contemptible enemy.
Kindness fadeth away, but vengeance endureth.

Refrains can, of course, be more directly allusive: the London cherry
vendor's street cry, "Cherry-ripe-ripe-ripe," works its way into the refrain
of Campion's "There is a Garden in Her Face": "Till 'cherry-ripe' themselves
do cry" (that is, the cherries of the lady's lips, in the poem's conceit); in
Campion's setting of the text for lute and voice, the street cry is reaffirmed
in full echo ("Cherry ripe, ripe, ripe" sung to the ascending minor third of
the actual sounds of the vendors).

Both lines of the two-line refrain of Thomas Nashe's well-known "Litany
in Time of Plague" are allusive: to the Office for the Dead and to the signs
put up on houses during the plague in the 1590s in London. They are
differently applied, however. The first inevitably completes a rhyming couplet and modulates its moral significance slightly at each occurrence. The
second stands unequivocally alone. Thus, in the first strophe:

Adieu, farewell earth's bliss,
This world uncertain is:
Fond are life's lustful joys,
Death proves them all but toys,
None from his darts can fly.
I am sick, I must die.
     Lord, have mercy on us!

Whereas in the third, the rhymed refrain is evoked by a more distant memento mori:

Beauty is but a flower
Which wrinkles will devour;
Brightness falls from the air,
Queens have died young and fair,
Dust hath closed Helen's eye.
I am sick, I must die.
     Lord, have mercy on us!

The changing modes of the application can be traced through the six stanzas. In another popular poem of the 1590s called "Tichborne's Elegy" a
continuing pattern of nearly oxymoronic paradoxes ("My feast of joy is but
a dish of pain," etc.) is broken three times by the refrain "And now I live,
and now my life is done" (the reputed author was awaiting execution in the
Tower). The refrain unfolds with increasing literalness.[6]

At this point I shall pass over the two great refrains of Spenser's, the varied, echoic burden of the poet's own wedding song, and the river refrain of the late, sad *Prothalamion;* there, the Thames is Time's running and Time's theme and Time's own poem, over which Spenser's song breaks for a little space, the major flood being repeatedly hushed by the refrain. But I shall discuss these in the following chapter.

Refrains, then, can time a poem, tolling its strophic hours in the tongue of bells that may be wholly foreign to the noises of the stanzas' daily life. And poetic refrains can enact tropes as well as schemes of time and memory. Our English words *memory, remembrance* contain the meanings of both *la mémoire* and *un souvenir* (that is, a phrase like "I have no memory of him" is ambiguous as to the nature of the verb's object). Thus we again observe that refrains are, and have, memories—of their prior strophes or stretches of text, of their own preoccurrences, and of their own genealogies in earlier texts as well.

The refrain lines of François Villon's ballades exhibit a range of syntactic and rhetorical modes of Poe's "application." But the whole of ballade structure seems almost to have been reinvented for, and by, the first of the ballades dispersed throughout *Le Testament* (it is also the foremost in the canon), the famous "Ballade des dames du temps jadis". I quote the first stanza:

> Dites moi où, n'en quel pays
> Est Flora la belle Romaine,
> Archipiades, ne Thaïs,
> Qui fut sa cousine germaine,
> Echo parlant quant bruit on maine
> Dessus rivière ou sus estan,
> Qui beauté eut trop plus qu'humaine.
> Mai où sont les neiges d'antan?

—for which I give Dante Gabriel Rossetti's splendid version:

> Tell me now in what hidden way is
>   Lady Flora, the lovely Roman?
> Where's Hipparchia, and where is Thaïs,
>   Neither of them the fairer woman?
>   Where is Echo, beheld of no man,
> Only heard on river and mere,—
>   She whose beauty was more than human? . . .
> But where are the snows of yester-year?

The pattern of ubi sunt catalogue proceeds forward in time from the dead ladies of antiquity toward Villon's own age, and the first refrain is introduced with the nymph Echo—"Echo parlant quant bruit on maine / Dessus rivière ou sus estan / Qui beauté eut trop plus qu'humaine"—who re-presents momentarily vanished voice (if we were to cry "jadis!" she would sigh "y" in return) and momentarily appears as a sort of muse of refrain herself.

Then come "les neiges d'antan," melting like Echo's body, in the post-Ovidian textual history, into mere voice, or even "melting" like sound into silent air. This is the bottom line, itself to be reechoed and remembered—even though in the poem-as-warhorse it is too easy to misremember the refrain as "*Et où* sont les neiges d'antan," an unstated but simple summary repetend, cancelled by Villon's with its qualifying "but." Villon's line calls wonderful attention to the way in which the refrain can incorporate the rhetorical features of a "that's that for the moment" with those of an "and then. . . ."[7]

The dialectic of memory and anticipation enacted by the scheme of poetic refrain can become prominent when the scheme has become most fully troped, or, to put it another way, when the formal occasion of redeploying the conventional lyric device, of making the words for music even more "perhaps," enters the allegory of the poem's own making. A magnificent example of this is the beautiful, problematic refrain of Trumbull Stickney's "Mnemosyne," a poem written fairly close to 1900 (I should guess) by a remarkable poet who died in 1904 at the age of thirty. The handful of powerful lyrics he left behind includes some sonnets which belatedly recapitulate an American romantic Hellenism—indeed, in a sonnet beginning with one of his favorite mise-en-scènes ("The melancholy year is dead with rain"), his own diction speaks of itself: "So in the last autumn of a day / Summer and summer's memory returns. / So in a mountain desolation burns / Some rich belated flower." His major summoning up of what he elsewhere calls "memory's autumnal paradise" is the poem originally called (on the manuscript) "Song," but then retitled:

It's autumn in the country I remember.

How warm a wind blew here about the ways!
And shadows on the hillside lay to slumber
During the long sun-sweetened summer-days.

It's cold abroad the country I remember.

The swallows veering skimmed the golden grain
At midday with a wing aslant and limber;
And yellow cattle browsed upon the plain.

It's empty down the country I remember.

I had a sister lovely in my sight:
Her hair was dark, her eyes were very sombre;
We sang together in the woods at night.

It's lonely in the country I remember.

The babble of our children fills my ears,
And on our hearth I stare the perished ember
To flames that show all starry thro' my tears.

It's dark about the country I remember.

> There are the mountains where I lived. The path
> Is slushed with cattle-tracks and fallen timber,
> The stumps are twisted by the tempests' wrath.
>
> But that I knew these places are my own,
> I'd ask how came such wretchedness to cumber
> The earth, and I to people it alone.
>
> It rains across the country I remember.

Structurally, the refrain here is complicated by the ambiguity of its role; starting out the poem, it seems more like a thematic, expository opening, immediately qualified (a) by the white space separating it from the tercet which it should else have joined to make a regular quatrain, and (b) by the implied opening-up of the syntax.[8] In the exposition of autumn as the condition of remembering summer, the full stop is almost put back two words, and "I remember" enjambed to the tercet.[9] With one's realization, at the first repetition, that a varying refrain has indeed been thereby instituted, comes the further problem of the Janus-like line in its very liminal placement. We have to ask whether the *rentrement* introduces or concludes, whether the line in its paradigmatic recurrence concludes its proceeding tercet or introduces its following one. The meticulously shaded echoic quality of the half-rhymes with the middle lines of the tercets, not to speak of the deep, inner resonance of the white space surrounding the refrain lines, underscores their liminal role. In their very placement, they control the mode of crossing from one chamber of remembrance, from one topos, to another. The white spaces are full of ellipsis: *But* (after the first tercet) "It's cold" or "*But now* it's empty" or "*Yet now* it's lonely." And yet the last two returns are not governed by those *and yets*—"*You see,* it's dark . . ." then leads to the vision of a ruined landscape in the next tercet, and the ellipsis of the refrain itself before the final one. The poem has a bipartite structure, controlled by the pattern of variation of the refrain line. Not only do we have the sequential narrative which leads us through the five successive predicates *autumn, cold, empty, lonely, dark.*[10] In addition, there is the mode of attributing the adjectives, which we come to hear as a superimposed sequence of varied predications: *it's . . . in, it's . . . abroad, it's . . . down. It's . . . in* returns to open the second sequence (followed by *it's dark about*), which concludes with the ellipsis of the last intermediate refrain and its displacement to the end of the poem, where it forms a kind of sonnet-sestet of the last two tercets, and moving beyond the predicatory sequences of both adjective and preposition in the previous ones. And so much is going on in those tercets: the introjection of the landscape cumbered by what has come to pass; the realization that "the ruin, or blank," as Emerson calls it, is in his own eye, which causes the speaker to reject the rhetorical posture of a Noah; and the rain of the *rentrement* which follows (I shall refrain from calling it, in the manner of my colleague Geoffrey Hartman, a ref-rain, despite its saturated allusiveness, of which more later), the rain which follows portends of no new deluge. (For the "wretchedness" came to "cumber" the earth in an array of that word's senses: *overwhelm, destroy, trouble, fill or block up, benumb with cold.*)

The second section of the poem is also distinguished by the only full rhyme in the sequence. The "lonely in . . . remember" and the "dark about . . . remember" lines embrace the remarkable trope of "staring the perished ember / To flames," which itself revivifies the latent allusion to Shakespeare's "glowing of such fire / That on the ashes of his youth doth lie," a precursor text of belated, autumnal, not-yet-totally posterotic meditation. The "ember" morpheme is elicited by punning analysis, from "remember." Emphasizing that analysis in the one perfect rhyme underscores an etymological trope of Mnemosyne's scene as one of flame reduced to its hotter spores, rather than one of re-collection or regathering. The poem organizes its own derivatively autumnal quality (the late September of Stickney's almost Parnassian romanticism) in specific relation to Shakespeare and Keats (its swallows as yet ungathered, but like swift Camillas that "skim" the plain); to its scene of present hearth and wasted outdoors; to its autumnal time-scale, in which recent summer seems so very bygone (one of the effects of the biblical diction evoking the "sister lovely in my sight");[11] and, of course, to its own schematic form of threshold refrain, of the chant of the word "remember" itself.

The interwoven narratives of tercet and repetend here are also effective in allegorizing the poem's structure. The movement from summer's remembered "here" to autumn's present "there"; the extended meditative and moralizing moment of the last two tercets and the way in which the interposition of the refrain between them would seem a transgression of some more than structural line; the final avowal of the mythological nature of "these places" (they are the speaker's "own," fully possessed, fully, in Wallace Stevens's sense, "abstract")—this movement is played out against the refrain sequence noted before, which could be said to name autumn and then unpack some of its store of predicates. *Autumn in . . . cold abroad . . . empty down . . .* (where the preposition is troped with such plangency), then the repeated preposition starting out the second part, in *lonely in . . . dark about* (with its echoes of "empty down"); then, the displacement, and, at the end (one wants to say, "in the end," for this is what it all *comes down to*). "It rains across the country I remember." The rain is out of sequence in that it is not one of the attributes of the scene, and the refrain is framing a very different kind of statement from the others. Whether projecting (again, echoically and thereby belatedly) an original introjection of Verlaine (as if to say: "Il pleut sur le pays / comme il pleut dans ma mémoire"); or momentarily realizing again the visionary geography of the now rainy country, Baudelaire's "pays pluvieux" (and, perhaps, "plus vieux" as well), the falling rain now plunging the whole poem in "l'eau verte du Lethé"; or indubitably evoking the refrain of rain raining every day in Feste's song in *Twelfth Night*—the final return is most complex. Apparently turning from emotional moralizing to the plenitude of plain statement, it cannot help but be overdetermined, both by virtue of and in demarcation of its terminal position. It is no longer liminal, save that on the other side of its threshold is the endless Lethean flood.

This remarkable poem by a rather young man fictionalizes his very youth as latecoming and therefore, figuratively, old enough to look—we cannot say, "back at" but rather "across"—such a long landscape. "Memory," said Swift, "is an old man's observation"; here, imagination is a young man's memory. And yet Walter Savage Landor's octogenarian observes, in a great poem called "Memory," that the names of his dearest surviving friends get lost to him. Specifically, they cumber like blocked river water the threshold between storage and retrieval: "To these, when I have written and besought / Remembrance of me, the word *Dear* along / Hangs on the upper verge, and waits in vain." And then Landor concludes: "A blessing wert thou, O oblivion, / If thy stream carried only weeds away / But vernal and autumnal flowers alike / It hurries down to wither on the strand." (If not, as for Spenser, "flowers = flow-ers, things that move in water," then at least the flow of what has been remembered into what is re-membered in the retrieval and articulation of it is seen as a flood that staves off the transverse flow of Lethe.) But for the young poet, there is no terror of a damming-up of the flow of eloquence. He is in sure control of the returning sequence of half-rhymes, and its own structural narrative (*slumber—limber—sombre—ember—timber—cumber:* framed by the *slumber* that comes to *cumber,* bracketed within that by the *limber* now felled to *timber,* mediated by the Janus faces of "remember").

Stickney's poem clearly allegorizes its scheme of refrain as a fable of memory, but less obviously it makes refrain a matter of autumn. Wallace Stevens's not-quite-blank-verse sonnet "Autumn Refrain" grapples directly with earlier voices (as if to say, "Where are the songs of autumn? Where are they?") and picks its way through sun and moon and evening and song and nightingale, hearing in these Miltonic and Keatsian tropes not available refrains, but burdens of the past. The poem itself employs only broken recurrences, true *refractions,* in its scattered repetitions of word and phrase.[12] The autumn in the poem is that of the poet's silent aftermath of eloquence, an autumn of stillness that is "all in the key of that desolate sound" that is the residuum of the voice of the fictions of the past. In a sense, Stevens's poem takes the trope of an autumn refrain and embodies it in an original scheme of belated structure—all the *tra-la-la*s, all the *forlorn*s, tolling like bells, lie about in bits of fractured echoic hearsay, in rumors of *rentrement*. In Stevens's sole poem of 1931, an aftermath of refrain makes for an extreme schematic pattern of a sort of through-composed stuttering, or of an un-gathering of the fragments which are collected into a full, line-terminal refrain in a passage from *Paradise Lost* (5.180–204).[13]

Stevens's general distrust of refrain manifests itself in a preference for anaphora over burden (as in "Sea-Surface Full of Clouds," where a repeated opening is the basis of variation, and a refrainlike reoccurrence of an ejaculation in French is never a repetition). Tennyson will allow a full, lyrical refrain to go on without any but the slightest accretion of meaning (as in "Mariana"). He can also cause a refrain to echo internally, as in the one from "Oenone"—"O mother Ida, many-fountained Ida, / O mother Ida hear me ere I die"—where the three syllables naming the mountain [*-er Ida*] are echoed in the nymph's last three words [*ere I die*]. Stevens will have none of such resonance, and even in the exuberant fresh air of a poem like "Fare-well to Florida," the opening phrase "Go on, high ship," repeated twice (*rondeau*-like, at the end of the second and third strophes), yields in prominence to a more self-conscious repetition: "The snake has left its skin upon the floor . . . . . the waves make a refrain / Of this: that the snake has shed its skin upon / The floor." The scheme of refrain is troped and retroped here, considered, allegorized, and finally—with a sense of the etymology of *refraction* noted above—broken in an enjambment. Stevens's true refrains are recurring fragments, like the "wide water" in "Sunday Morning," finally "inescapable."

But I should like to move back in time, to a poem with another kind of refrain structure, and another way in which autumn, memory, and schematic return enter into figurations of each other. Composed sometime between 1913 and 1917 (almost midway between Stickney's and Stevens's poems), Thomas Hardy's "During Wind and Rain" presents a typically problematic Hardyian formal face: as always, we want to ask, with a kind of modernist (but perhaps callow) earnestness, how he ever allowed himself to get trapped in his singsong stanzas' awkward rooms. Frequently some marvellous lyric or short-story-in-verse of Hardy's will seem to have been composed by letting an opening take up a self-generated formal space, and then passively accepting the strophic fiat for the successive stanzas. But many do not, and the scheme of this poem, its pattern of minor and major variation, and its remarkable metarefrain in the ultimate line of each stanza, mark out the places of remembering and the moments of judgment of what has been summoned up in a way totally different from Stickney's.

> They sing their dearest songs—
> He, she, all of them—yea,
> Treble and tenor and bass,
>   And one to play;
> With the candles mooning each face. . . .

Ah, no; the years O!
How the sick leaves reel down in throngs!

They clear the creeping moss—
Elders and juniors—aye,
Making the pathways neat
   And the garden gay;
And they build a shady seat. . . .
   Ah, no; the years, the years;
See, the white storm-birds wing across!

They are blithely breakfasting all—
Men and maidens—yea,
Under the summer tree,
   With a glimpse of the bay,
While pet fowl come to the knee. . . .
   Ah, no; the years O!
And the rotten rose is ript from the wall.

They change to a high new house,
He, she, all of them—aye,
Clocks and carpets and chairs
   On the lawn all day,
And brightest things that are theirs. . . .
   Ah, no; the years, the years;
Down their carved names the rain-drop ploughs.

The four strophes of the poem frame four vignettes of an elliptical family
novel, presented in strains interrupted by minimal, fragmentary refrains—
"yea" and "aye" of ironic assent in alternating strophes, "Ah, no; the years
O!" alternating with "Ah, no; the years, the years," and the repetition of
"He, she, all of them" in the last stanza bringing full rondure, albeit with
the "aye" now replacing the initial "yea." The refrains seem to be uttered
by almost antithetical voices, the second one recoiling with ironic dismay,
even disgust, from the initial affirmations and particularly, in the even-numbered stanzas, from the punning reading of "aye" as "ever" (rather than
"ay," perhaps from the "I" of voice-vote: "Ever, eh?—Ah, no; the years, the
years"). And then the problematic closures, the terminal lines which, for
each stanza, are summary, interpretive, offered by the second voice as if in
evidence, or as cause, of its distaste. These four lines are like one-line poems
in their own right. The novelistic vignettes—two indoors, two outdoors;
the first, which might be a cheerful winter evening, the other three, of spring
and summer—move chronologically toward greater wealth, the proliferation
of generation, the sense of in-dwelling rather than merely inhabiting. The
first refrain is merely schematic, merely an exercise of the rhetoric of verse
rather than prose; the second refrain, as syntactic herald of the terminal
line, is the voice of the poet reminding the novelist that he has suppressed

exactly what his characters have. Seasonal cycle may unroll in strophes, as the providential cycle of the months unfolds its pageant of the working year in *Les Très riches heures du duc de Berry,* but such cycles are often rooted in spring or summer without knowing or avowing it. The chronicler in this poem purports to believe in the beneficence of cycle, of seasonal pattern, of unrolling, of (and here Hardy shudders) *developing* time. The poet reminds him, in the terminal lines, that it is always autumn and that, indeed, chronicle of the foregoing sort is always being recounted as a defense against the autumnal sense of the entropy of consequence. The poet of the terminal lines reads the genre-scenes in the brightly painted stanzas and groans as he sees that each is an unwitting memento mori.

The first of these repudiating monostichs is emblematically autumnal and at the same time merciless in its figure—via Shelley's "Ode to the West Wind"—of sick leaves ("Yellow, and black, and pale, and hectic red") in throngs ("pestilence-stricken multitudes") as dying generations. The terminal line sings for Hardy's poet the Shelleyan refrain. Formally considered, these terminals rhyme only with the stanzaic openings, six lines back. The effect is to render them almost blank, but then, on reconsideration, to link them in a violent antithetical couplet with those openings ("They are blithely breakfasting all": "And the rotten rose is ript from the wall"). Rhetorically, each subsequent emblem of autumn and decay underlines its own mode of pseudo-refrain in that the expected return is, in each case, an autumnal emblem as the accountant's bottom line of a cheerful and hopeful scene, of *luxe* and *calme* (*volupté* not sorting well with the others in England, even in dream). And the bottom line of the emblem-sequence is the most self-aware, rhetorically: culminating the sequence of powerful verbs—*reel, wing, is ript*—comes the terrible *ploughs* of the terminating trope of rain. The rain which conventionally weeps over tombstones here plows down the already furrowed, text-blossoming stone, apparently to trace names out with a commemorative finger, but actually with the effect of eventually effacing them altogether. Here again, as in Stickney's poem, the falling rain sings the final refrain and claims the role of autumn's ultimate emblem.

This resonant raining engulfs a welter of allusive streams. The wind and rain of the title are those of the poem's formal paradigmatic precursor, Feste's final song in *Twelfth Night.* There, the paired alternating refrains, "With hey, ho, the wind and the rain" and "For the rain it raineth every day," enact the figure of refrain as marking a redemptive cycle and a reclamation of the generality of rain from autumnal and wintry claims to it. Feste's vignettes of the phases of life are framed by his music of figurative rainfall. For Hardy, the usurpation by autumn of all scenes of remembrance has long been irreversible. In addition, the short refrains of "During Wind and Rain" echo those of a slightly earlier poem, "The Change," which similarly looks back grimly at moments of innocent pleasure and calm ("And who was the mocker, and who the mocked when two felt all was well?") and similarly employs narrative material from the life of Hardy's first wife, Emma Gifford (a scene of candlelit singing, in this case, of duets with her sister). The sequence of refrains both modifies and alternates: "Who shall read the years O!"; "Who shall spell the years, the years!"; "Who shall unroll the years O" "Who shall bare the years, the years!"; "Who shall lift the years O!"; finally coming down to "Who shall unseal the years, the years!"—and thus framing the whole lyric in the textual tropes of reading and unsealing. Hardy echoed this refrain and its very mode of alternation ("the years, O" and "the years, the years") in the later poem, but he assigned it to the lyrical ironist of his final lines rather than to his putative chronicler of the vignettes. The terminal, image-bearing lines of each stanza are, as has been observed, quasi-refrains in that they time, pace, and return to their mode of moral-izing-by-riddling, as it were (rather than moralizingly interpreting the tropes they adduce). Their return is like a bell at the end of a line of manual typewriting, rather than Feste's wind and rain refrain, which tolls like a church bell in certain fictions of simple, organic village life finding a prov-idential comfort in reminders of transcience.

A glance at Hardy's revisions of his original text of the poem, by the way, shows how he came to realize the different schemes of the refrain sequence. Originally, the odd- and even-numbered stanzas were identical in their re-petends—"aye" was "yea" throughout, as was "the years O." (These revi-sions may have accompanied, or followed by some time, those of "The Change," which likewise introduced the alternation of the two half-lines.) But more significant, the rhythm of the terminal lines can be seen to have emerged from an earlier, more regular conception, notwithstanding the changes in diction. The terminal lines originally read, "How the sickened leaves dropped down in throngs!"; "See the webbed white storm-birds wing across"; "And the wind-whipt creeper lets go the wall"; and, at first, "On their chiselled names the lichen grows" (in manuscript), then, "Down their chiselled names the rain-drop ploughs." The acephalic pentameters yield to tetrameters with a starting dactyl or anapest, which catches up the bits of triple movement throughout the poem and allows the monostich of the terminal lines to return an echo of these mingled with the sobs, in all but the third one, of spondee.

Hardy's and Stickney's unrolling patterns of refrain in their respective autumnal songs are ultimately descendants of Poe's in that his "Nevermore" was avowing the *poetic* impossibility of merely formal—others might have said, merely "musical"—refrain. Nevermore can refrain be merely *tra-la-la,* stand for "now everybody sings," trope the turning of a page to a new chapter, allow the singer to rest. Poe claimed falsely that his refrain was a true *fa-la,* a true bit of verbal music, but his schematic arguments for its varying "application," the ways in which "Nevermore" continues to answer every question the speaker puts (and thereby reveals the rhetorical nature of each question), merely go back to the echo-device which descends from Ovid through the Renaissance. For Poe, refrain is the trope of reiteration of reiteration, of how "jadis!" is the only musical cry. For Stickney and Hardy, it is a much more complex matter. Memory, time, autumn, penulti- mateness, all enter into the structure of their fables of refrain. And the ultimate point is that for poetry, rather than mere verse, to employ a refrain, it must thereby, therein, therewith propound its own parable of the device itself, its etiology, or its effect, or its emblematic reading. In a sense, a new meaning of the concept of refrain must arise, along with a new mode of application.

8 ᥩ

Spenser's Undersong

Avenne poi che, passando per un cammino, lungo il quale correva un rio molto chiaro d'onde, giunse a ma tanta volonta di dire, che cominciai a pensare il modo ch'io tenessi.

[It then befell that passing by a way along which there coursed a river of most clear waters, so great a desire to speak possessed me that I began to ponder on the style I should use.]

Dante, *La Vita Nuova*, 19.

The undersong in question is the refrain of *Prothalamion,* that magnificent spousal verse that Spenser wrote on the occasion of the announced marriage of the two daughters of the earl of Somerset in the fall of 1596. It is a poem that descants upon itself obliquely, but with a sad power that not even Spenser's earlier *Epithalamion,* sung by the bridegroom and addressing itself as a text and as a trope for a masque or pageant, at the very end, could summon up. *Prothalamion* sings, you will remember, of these incipient paired marriages in an account of a walk along a river—*the* river—and an encounter first with nymphs gathering flowers on the bank as if for their own wedding day, then with a pair of swans swimming along the river, and a continued procession of swans, nymphs, and narrator along the river to Essex House, where the two bridegrooms receive their two "faire Brides," the two allegorical "faire birdes" having shed their figuration by metathesis of the letters *r* and *i* (of such words as "river" and "rival"). But the poem broods throughout over the poet's own "sullein care" and "freindlesse case" and "long fruitlesse stay / In princes court."

The poem's celebrated refrain is called an "undersong" at only one point. One of the nymphs sings what is in fact a monostrophic epithalamion embedded in the larger poem, occupying the sixth of its ten strophes (of eighteen lines each, a number Alastair Fowler has associated with Gemini,

the twins of the swan and Leda, and hence with the geminations and dou-
blings throughout the poem). The daughter of the flood—one of the group
whom the poet, in the second strophe, encounters as they gather flowers,
all looking themselves bridelike—sings this:

> Ye gentle Birdes, the worlds faire ornament,
> And heavens glorie, whom this hapie hower
> Doth leade unto your lovers blisfull bower,
> Joy may you have and gentle hearts content
> Of your loves couplement:
> And let fair *Venus,* that is Queene of love,
> With her heart-quelling Sonne upon you smile,
> Whose smile they say, hath vertue to remove
> All Loves dislike, and friendships faultie guile
> For ever to assoile.
> Let endlesse Peace your steadfast hearts accord,
> And blessed Plentie wait upon your bord,
> And let your bed with pleasures chast abound,
> That fruitfull issue may to you afford,
> Which may your foes confound,
> And make your joyes redound,
> Upon your Brydale day, which is not long:
>   Sweete *Themmes,* run softlie, till I end my Song.   [91–108]

Five previous occurrences of the great refrain have already made it resonant: the "not long" of the bridal day has been both "not far off, not long
in coming," and "not long, certainly not as long as the long midsummer
day of my own marriage poem." And the possessive pronoun of "my song"
has been, until the nymph in either fictional innocence or a sort of neoclassical allusiveness made it her own, purely Spenser's, in as *propria persona*
as he gets. But then, starting the next strophe, the poet calls attention to
the refrain. The other nymphs take it up chorally and reinterpret the coming
bridal day as their own. The river bank affirms and authenticates the word-
ing. And the whole account resounds with consciousness of the degree to
which the refrain itself is an unwitting echo, both for the nymph and to the
degree that every refrain per se echoes its first occurrence.[1] This is how he
does so:

> [Sweete *Themmes,* run softlie, till I end my Song.]
> So ended she; and all the rest around
> To her redoubled that her undersong,
> Which said, their brydale daye should not be long.
> And gentle Eccho from the neighbour ground,
> Their accents did resound.   [109–13]

—And then, speaking of the pair of swans he has encountered, the Somerset
sisters both literally and figuratively "bred of Somers heat"—

> So forth these joyous Birdes did passe along,
> Adowne the Lee, that to them murmured low,
> As he would speake, but that he lackt a tong
> Yet did by signes his glad affection show,
> Making his streame run slow.   [114–18]

The "Lee" down which the swans are swimming—and they are designated as doing so at their first appearance in the opening lines of the third strophe—is remarkably problematic throughout the poem; current scholarship is in debate about whether it means a leeward shore, the lea or meadow through which the river runs and in which the nymphs are first encountered gathering flowers, or, as here, the river Lee itself, which runs into the Thames at Greenwich. As Angus Fletcher has pointed out, the complicated geography of the poem's itinerary implies that the Spenser who walked forth to ease his pain "along the shoare of silver streaming Themmes" would be walking upstream in the course of the ode, starting from Greenwich, following the procession of attendant swans who have joined the first two after they have somehow turned into the course of the Thames.[2] Upstream, past the Temple, whose towers once housed the chivalric Templars and now remain emblems of how "they decay'd through pride," as well as houses "Where now the studious lawyers have their bowers." Upstream past these to Leicester House, built by Spenser's patron ("Where oft I gayned giftes and goodly grace / Of that great lord which therein wont to dwell, / Whose want too weel now feeles my freendles case" [138–40]), now belonging to the earl of Essex, the victor of the Battle of Cadiz, the Devereux whose name puns on "endless happinesse," but who, and whose head, would fall two years after he had had to pay for Spenser's funeral. Upstream with time, encountering on the banks the souvenirs of decayed hopes, expectations, tropes (Artegall replaced by the tribe of Coke and Bacon!). Upstream, and yet, the Thames being a tidal estuary, with the tide (which in Middle English means "time" and "season" as well), which forms its own countercurrent.[3]

Consciousness of the current, the flow of the river, keeps breaking through the account of the poetic walk to the intermittent refrain. In considering it, one wants to listen for a moment to the earlier refrain of *Epithalamion*, the great "song made in lieu of many ornaments" for his own wedding, the transcendental epithalamium that he figuratively sang as poet-bridegroom and into which he imported a mythological pageant. In place of the conventional "io Hymen Hymenaee" of Catullus's epithalamium, we hear the characteristic Spenserian alexandrine of closure, always rhyming with the word "sing" in the penultimate short line of the long, complex stanzas: "So I unto myself alone shall sing / The woods shall to me answer and their echo ring" (17–18). This refrain refigures an echo of affirmation (which comes from Theocritus and Virgil—not an Ovidian, mocking echo) in several ways. First, it adds an answer to the echo (rather than going, say, "The woods shall to me answer, by their echoing"). Second, it schematically embodies echoing (1) in the way in which the rhyme-word "sing" is answered by "ring," and (2) in the bipartite, reciprocal patterning of clauses across the caesura as a figure of echo itself.

In addition, there is a faint bit of lingering grammatical ambiguity: "ring" is transitive ("echo" being the object) and also intransitive, with "echo" the subject, and a more prominent ellipsis of the auxiliary "shall" but with direct word order. In its hovering between "woods" and "echo" as the source of the ringing, the syntax moves into one of those momentary tropes of a scheme considered earlier in this book. The oscillation between object and subject, and between direct and inverse word order, becomes a momentary story of voice and transformed echoing answer.

But the echo-refrain of this earlier poem, despite its role in the marking of the hours of the day, and (as A. K. Hieatt showed some time ago) specifically those of daylight on the midsummer occasion of the wedding, is largely unconcerned with time outside the poem (save for the last line of the poem, about being "for short Time an endlesse moniment," the one terminal beyond refrain).[4] The mellower, yet more anxious concerns of the *Prothalamion* undersong, however, point to its own demarcation of period. The whole sui generis song of the therapeutic walk upstream is a forerunner of romantic crisis lyrics: I can think of no earlier nor more momentous source of the notion that a poet might take a walk "to ease my payne" (and surely not in the *Natureingang* of medieval German lyrics, which is another matter entirely). The timing effect of the later undersong is deeper and more figurative. It is as if the cheerful numerology in the hermetic subplot of *Epithalamion* were being remembered in a late sadness, and being caused to yield up the suppressed consequences of what Harold Bloom called, à la Nietzsche, "lying against time." The earlier refrain's introductory verb, "sing," rhymes chorically with everything; but "undersong," or any kind of song, rhymes with "belong," "long," "wrong," and—strangely—"strong," and yet we never find a "strong"-ly rhymed "undersong" in Spenser or any later writer using the word.

The earlier refrain is, as was observed, an alexandrine; the song by the Thames exhibits a recurrent pentameter, although T. S. Eliot, ironically quoting the refrain in "The Fire Sermon" part of *The Waste Land*, reechoes it in an oddly poignant, interpretively augmented alexandrine: "Sweet Thames run softly, for I speak not loud nor long"—as if this were the way it should have gone all the time. "Sweete Themmes runne softly, till I end my song"—surely one of the sets of resonances struck by the line in subsequent poetry comes from the overtone "sweet theme," which later on in the seventeenth century, Sir John Denham, with neoclassical tact, would merely predicate ("O could I flow like thee! and make thy stream / My great

example, as it is my theme") and safely rhyme with the name of a synecdoche, rather than more powerfully and Spenserianly punning on the name
of the river itself. But Donald Cheney, a modern scholar with a fine Spenserian ear, hears "Sweet Time" lurking in the epithet. We might remember
here the brooding ambiguity of "not long in coming/not long in duration,"
noted earlier, of the refrain's first half-line.

But the Thames, unlike the woods, does not echo the poet's song. Moreover, the refrain is of the sort whose grammar is an imperative operating in
ways previously discussed. This mode, it will be recalled, is exemplified by
pastoral refrains in Theocritus and Virgil, and by Catullus's Parcae, as they
sing their chant, "perfidiae quod post nulla arguet aetas" (which no tract
of time shall belie) for the wedding of Peleus and Thetis. That refrain,
"currite ducentes subtegmina, currite, fusi" (run, drawing the thread out,
spindles, run) is an undersong that urges the completion of the song itself.
The fatal spindles have replaced the Muses of pastoral as the empowering
deity to be invoked, and the yarn they spin, the story they tell, is not only
the stuff of fable, but, we must always remember, the stuff of life itself. In
Spenser, the Thames is commanded, not to generate the song, not manifestly
to aid its production, nor even, in direct opposition to that, to desist while
the poet sings. Rather, it is asked to lower its voice, in order to provide
what we should today call an accompaniment to the voice of the singer,
whether in the frame song or the inset epithalamium sung by the nymph.
Such a modern notion of accompaniment—the piano part of "Wohin?" with
its brook noises, in Schubert's setting of *Die schöne Müllerin,* as it were—
was not a musical actuality in Spenser's day, although a notion of compan-
ionship is represented everywhere in *The Faerie Queene.* In this case, we are
not told what the Thames might have been implying in the sounds of its
motion. But mythologically, it surely derives (in all senses) from the common source of all poetic rivers, whether Petrarch's Rhône, Milton's revised
Alpheus in *Lycidas,* or all of the rivers discussed so eloquently by David
Quint.[5]

The very metaphor of a flowing river continues to flow through post-
Renaissance English poetry. A river can be time itself or eloquence itself.
For Francis Bacon "the truth is that time seemeth to be in the nature of a
river or stream, which carrieth down to us that which is light and blown
up, and sinketh and drowneth that which is weighty and solid."[6] But Milton's conceit moralizes differently: "Truth is compared in scripture to a
streaming fountain [Ps. 85: 11]; if her waters flow not in a perpetual pro-
gression, they sicken into a pool of conformity and tradition."[7] The voices
of preromantic rivers, on the other hand, tend to recall and speak to dormant
memory. Thus Macpherson's Ossian (1760): "I hear the river below murmuring hoarsely over the stones. What doest thou, O river to me? Thou
bringest back the memory of the past."[8] For Tennyson, rivers frequently

provide instrumental accompaniment, as if taking back from Schubert the piano's figurations: "'Tirra-lirra', by the river / Sang Sir Lancelot" from "The Lady of Shalott" combines an echo of Autolycus's quotation of an erotic refrain ("The lark that tirra-lirra chants") with an almost Spenserian ambiguity of word order (that is, is "by the river" part of the song or not?). Or Tennyson again, "O that 'twere possible," from *Maud:*

> She is singing in the meadow
> And the rivulet at her feet
> Ripples on in light and shadow
> To the ballad that she sings[9]

But even here, with Tennyson's characteristic doubling of visual and auditory images, there is an overtone of convention, if not of history, in the river's movement.

The undersong also affirms, then, the Thames as the flow of English poetic eloquence, the Thames with whose marriage to the Medway Spenser had concerned himself probably from 1580 on. Drawing not only on the ancient trope of flowing water for discourse (as opposed to standing pond and reflective pool, with their silent surfaces and depths, for thought), the Thames here replaces earlier poetic rivers, even those that had been intimately associated with the scene of writing for him (the "*Mulla* mine, whose waves I whilome taught to weepe").[10] But it also replaces in a different way the central poetic river of Greek mythology, by repeated allusion: first by likening the whiteness of the swans to that of the snow on Mount Pindus in Thessaly whence it springs, then to Peneus itself, flowing through the plain of Tempe (in connection with the nymphs gathering flowers), the river of the father of the nymph Daphne, and hence father as well of all the poetic consequences of Apollo's loss. (Petrarch had also invoked Peneus in just such a context. In *Canzoniere* 23 he juxtaposes the white feathers of Cygnus—associated in Ovid with the Po—with Peneus and the Rhône, as Spenser does with the Thames.)

But if these poetic rivers are tributary in a figurative sense, the literal influx of the river Lee, "The wanton Lee, that oft doth loose his way" (*FQ* 4.11.29), is also significant. Regardless of the primary meaning of the phrases "downe along the Lee" (and perhaps there is an overlay of the down of swans here?) and "adowne the lee," the minor river flows into the poem from one of its precursor texts. *A Tale of Two Swans* by William Vallans, published in 1590, overflows with awareness of its own precurrent text in Spenser's unpublished *Epithalamium Thamesis,* the work he contemplated writing in quantitative meters in 1580. Vallans's blank-verse itinerary of the course of the river Lee from its sources until it runs into (and in his Spenserian fable, marries) the Thames starts with an etiological myth of the swans in England: Venus, seeing the beauty of the river "and the meades thereof / Fit for to breed her birdes of greatest prise" (15–16), sends Mercury to get two cygnets of the best from "Cayster, silver streame," a Boeotian river that associates twice with crowds of singing swans. There is indeed a "commodious vicus of recirculation" in Vallans's stream feeding on and later back into Spenser's,[11] as there is indeed a rearrival, in *Prothalamion,* of the figurative flow of life, when the whole procession comes to what the poet calls "mery London, my most kyndly nurse, / That gave to me this lifes first native sourse" (127–28). The river, then, like the flow of poetic life, gliding by its rival banks that are set with emblems first of poetry and love and beauty, then of the objects of "expectation vayne / Of idle hopes" (7–8) must inevitably sing out for a while under each strophe, invoked in, and seeming to become, its undersong.

But here I should like to dwell on the word itself. *Undersong* is one of those Spenserian coinages that, reechoed and redoubled by subsequent poets from Drayton and Browne through Wordsworth, Coleridge, Keats, and Emerson, emerges from a private life in the poetic ear into the more general air.[12] As its first occurrence in English, it means nothing but "refrain," a refrain specifically linked to the tradition of pastoral refrain stemming from Theocritus and Virgil. In the "August" eclogue of *The Shepheardes Calender,* a "delectable controversie"—as Spenser refers to the subgenre of amoebaean or alternating song—takes place between Perigot and Willye. The two shepherds compete, as you will remember, in a singing contest for a prize to be awarded by a cowherd, Cuddie, and at the completion of their bout, Cuddie himself sings a sestina, "a dolefull verse / Of Rosalend (who knows not Rosalend?)" (140–41) composed by Colin Clout, or Spenser himself. What is unusual about their contest is that they do not, unlike their classical precursors, compete in kind (as in Virgil's seventh and eighth eclogues, where quatrains, or whole songs, alternate—in this latter case, each song has its own refrain). Instead, Perigot sings the first and third lines of a balladlike song, and Willye sings a refrainlike second and fourth, always starting up with an unvarying "hey ho" and always picking up a phrase or notion from Perigot's first line and playing with it. Here, for example, are a few exchanges from the beginning of their joint effort:

> *Perigot.* It fell upon a holly eve,
> *Willye.*   hey ho hollidaye,
> *Per.* When holly fathers wont to shrieve:
> *Wil.*   now gynneth this roundelay.
> *Per.* Sitting upon a hill so hye
> *Wil.*   hey ho the high hyll,
> *Per.* The while my flocke did feede thereby,
> *Wil.*   the while the shepheard selfe did spill:
> *Per.* I saw the bouncing Bellibone,
> *Wil.*   hey ho Bonibell,

Per.	Tripping over the dale alone,
Wil.	she can trippe it very well:
Per.	Well decked in a frocke of gray,
Wil.	hey ho gray is greete,
Per.	And in a Kirtle of greene saye,
Wil.	the greene is for maydens meete:

["August," 53–68]

The competition here is between the powers of the primary and the antithetical, the phraser and the echoing, mocking paraphraser;[13] in the improvisatory tradition of jazz, it is like what is called a "cutting session" between two soloists. Moreover, Willye's opening pair of lines invoke the clocking, pacing function of the classical pastoral refrain, the signaling effected by modulating the refrains not from positive to negative, as in *Epithalamion,* but by Theocritus's refrain in his first idyll, which, as we saw in chapter 7, changes from "Start up the pastoral music, Muses" to "Continue the pastoral music" to "Finish up the pastoral music" during the course of the idyll. The measuring quality of this sort of refrain, particularly when the recurring line is an imperative sentence allegorically addressed to the poem being uttered itself, is most important, and I shall return to it later on. At this point, I shall observe only that in the radically experimental revisionary uses of schemes and subgenres that mark *The Shepheardes Calender,* the contention of verses and refrains, while seemingly an elegantly technical matter merely, is instead a very deep one, a testing out of a dialectic of paradigms of the sort that will, in *The Faerie Queene,* involve vast patterns, patrons, presences, and forms. And it is here to be observed that Colin, and thus Spenser himself, outdoes this "delectable controversie" with an examplar—and a unique variation on the canonical form, at that—of that most intricately arrayed set of one-word refrains, the sestina. In a sense, he resolves the dialectic at a level higher than that of mere contention, first splitting the prize between the two contestants and then incorporating refrain and main text in a form whose every new line is in fact a refrain.

It is in bestowing his split award that Cuddie remarks, "Little lacketh Perigot of the best, / And Willye is not greatly overgone, / So weren his undersongs well addrest" (126–28). The word is remarkable here, as elsewhere, because of its paired meanings. (Spenser has no other word for *refrain* throughout his works: the very word *refrain* is used in our modern verbal sense of "desist" or more literally "rein in" [from *refréner*] throughout Spenser, and the word *burden* only to mean "lead" [as derived from OE byrthen and ultimately from the same root as the verb one bears it with].) E. K. in his gloss remarks that "Willy answereth every under verse," in the sense that, in writing, a line that follows another comes under it; but Willye's continuing stream of refrain is also like a sort of drone, not a returning *ostinato,* but a continuous sound of the kind invoked by the other etymology of the other meaning of *burden* (from *bourdon,* "drone pipe"). The two senses are clearly different, in that one must wander away from something in order to return to it: the river I walk beside, perhaps singing as I go, can provide a drone, or *bourdon,* but only the fountains placed at measured intervals along the paved walk I take can assent to my sung blues with refrains of their own. But Willy's undersongs have been both refrainlike and dronelike, and the resonance of the word, the interrelations of its meanings, and the reinterpretations of those in later poems all help us to hear some of the remarkable resonances of the undersong of *Prothalamion.* Intermittence can be a trope of bouts of strife, but it can also become the alternations of task, of assistance in work and in love. So, at any rate, does it become in a very different version of pastoral alternation in *Colin Clout's Come Home Again,* for example. Colin's chiasmic formulation (mentioned in chapter 6) represents his relation to the Shepherd of the Ocean (and, therewith, Spenser's relation to Raleigh): "He pip'd, I sung, and when he sung, I pip'd, / By chaunge of turnes, each making other mery" (76–77). The piping here becomes the returning, purely melodic, less densely textual utterance; but it is also something else, an accompaniment, our word for which is not used in a musical sense before the middle of the eighteenth century. (Some of the consequences of this for Spenser will reemerge a bit later on, when we must glance at the possible parsing of the phrase "tune his pipe unto the water's fall.") In *Colin Clout's Come Home Again,* Colin describes a poem by that same mariner shepherd, a "lamentable lay . . . Of Cynthia, the Ladie of the Sea," and observes that

> And ever and anon, with singults rife
> He cryed out to make his undersong:
> Ah my loves queene, and goddesse of my life
> Who shall my pittie, when thou doest me wrong?   [168–71]

Here the primary sense is "refrain"; and yet there is a tinge of that figurative sense that "the burden of his song" began to take on in the seventeenth century, that rhetorical sense of a continuous point, apparently being returned to but, for the listener, continually droning on, beneath the surface of apparent argument and exemplification. This reductive sense of a burden is implicitly directed against eloquence itself, implying that it always has holes through which a continuous drone breaks out in what appears to be a mere recurring refrain. It is this reductive relation between the senses of drone and fragmentary recurrence that has always been most common.

Spenser's most significant invocation of refrain as an "undersong" is in the very refrain that so designates itself. The complaint of Alcyon, the allusively Chaucerian man in black, for the dead Daphne in Spenser's 1591 *Daphnaïda* is composed of seven sections of seven stanzas of seven lines;

each section ends with a stanza that concludes with the refrain, as in the case of the first of these:

> She fell away in her first ages spring,
> Whil'st yet her leafe was greene, and fresh her rinde,
> And whilst her braunch faire blossoms foorth did bring,
> She fell away against all course of kindes:
> For age to dye is right, but youth is wrong;
> She fel away like fruit blowne downe with winde:
> Weepe Shephearde weepe to make my undersong.

[11.239–45]

This beautiful and highly architectonic stanza shifts the position of one line in the traditional rhyme-royal to produce a pair of terza rima tercets with a concluding extra line (as in the last seven lines of the *Paradiso*). In this instance, the refrain line, "Weepe Shephearde weepe to make my undersong," seems at first to refer to the anaphora of "she fell away." It is only as the dirge unfolds that it is seen to be self-invocatory; rhyming in alternate sections with "wrong" and "long" and once with the verb "prolong," its last occurrence is in the modulated form familiar to readers of Virgil's eighth eclogue: "Cease Shepheard cease and end thy undersong." The "Shepheard" in question has been the pastoral narrator whose account of meeting Alcyon frames the elegy; the shift from "my undersong" to "thy undersong," at the end, avows that the audient attendant accompanist—who in Spenser's modernist modulation of Theocritus takes the place of the pastoral Muses themselves—implicitly reclaims the responsive refrain when the song itself is done.

Moreover, the undersong is "made" of weeping, that is, of Colin Clout's "singults," or sobs, and the flow of tears. Together they make up the essential Spenserian occasion of eloquence, music "tuned to" the sound of water. Colin's "laye" in the "April" eclogue was so composed, we are told: he "tunèd it unto the waters fall," in a phrase so resonant that every Spenserian for the next seventy years or so would work it into a poem of his, sometimes more than once, the phrase having become a covert Spenserian trademark even as the alexandrine would always be. (That the first occurrence of the phrase in Spenser is to be found in his earliest known writing, the verse translations for the *Theatre for Worldlings* of 1569, is remarkable; that it emerges in the first alexandrine in all of Spenser's poetry, itself occurring as an apparent *lapsus metricae* among nothing but pentameters, is spooky, as is detailed below, pp. 173–76.)

That the undersong of *Daphnaïda* should be literally a refrain and figuratively both the command to the poem itself to get itself written, which all imperative refrains seem to be enacting, and the association of intermittent sobs with the continuous drone of falling or flowing water is, I think, important. The word used here seems to be a confluence of some of the streams of meaning that have come up: accompaniment, but then again, drone. In addition, the *under* part of the word suggests that, at bottom, the sound of moving water is the ground—musically as a bass, epistemologically primary, mythologically as an *Urgeräusch* or primal sound of poetic discourse. (I find it interesting and puzzling that the scheme of *epizeuxis*—for example, Tennyson's "the woods decay, the woods decay and fall"—a repetition rather like that of refrain, Puttenham calls "the underlay or cuckoo-spell.") A sound going on *underneath* discourse implies a lower polyphonic part, at a metaphorically "lower" pitch, and placed spatially below others in staff notation, and/or one that is "lower" in volume and goes on at a lower level, as it were, of audibility. The introduction of the technical acoustical term *overtone* by Helmholtz in the nineteenth century led soon to figurative uses of both that word and an analogous *undertone* (but Keats in *Lamia* 2.291: "'Fool!' said the sophist, in an under-tone / Gruff with contempt," where it means simply "sotto voce"). *Undertone* begins to take on implications of implication itself, of a latent meaning or purpose or intent flowing along "below" (in an incipient layering of structures of consciousness) the manifest, and it reflects an earlier Renaissance sense of the most important matters being necessarily half-hidden. That excellent Spenserian James Russell Lowell (a better poet, perhaps, when he discoursed on allegory in prose than ever in verse) spoke of great poetic allegory as "not embodying metaphysical abstractions, but giving us ideal abstracted from life itself, suggesting an under-meaning everywhere, forcing it upon us nowhere" (this rare word is also used by Ruskin, in *Sesame and Lilies* 2, par. 93). Even the common use of *undercurrent* in an extended sense to invoke a layer of significance is pointedly post-Spenserian, I think (an early *OED* citation is from Coleridge, *Biographia Literaria:* "Our genuine admiration of a great poet is a continuous undercurrent of feeling" [1.1.23]).

Other post-Spenserian undersongs resonate with some of these implications. Although some poets merely dutifully employ the word in a pastoral context, alluding to Willye's refrain in "August" (thus Drayton, Eclogue 9 G.3b: "When now at last . . . Was pointed who the roundelaye should sing / And who againe the undersong should beare"; or Dryden, translating Virgil's third eclogue's "incipe Damoeta; tu deinde sequere Menalca," "The challenge to Damoetas shall belong: / Menalcas shall sustain the undersong"; or, following directly in this line, Ambrose Phillips: "As eldest, Hobbinol, begin: / And Lanquet's Under-Song by Turns come in" [Pastoral 6.7–8]), others trope Spenser's later implicit senses of the word in *Daphnaïda* and *Prothalamion*. Wordsworth, at the end of the first sonnet of "Personal Talk," turns off the switch, as it were, of social noise to provide a scene of meditation:

Better than such discourse doth silence long,
Long, barren silence, square with my desire;
To sit without emotion, hope, or aim,
In the loved presence of my cottage-fire,
And listen to the flapping of the flame,
Or kettle whispering its faint under-song.   [9–14]

On the other hand, it is just the sound of conversation forsaken by Wordsworth that Keats incorporates into the concerted music at the banquet in
Lamia:

Soft went the music the soft air along
While fluent Greek a vowelled undersong
Kept up among the guests, discoursing low
At first, for scarcely was the wine at flow.   [2.199–202]

In "Isabella," Lorenzo's ghost appears speaking with a strange voice, "And
Isabella on its music hung":

Languor there was in it, and tremulous shake,
  As in a palsied Druid's harp unstrung,
And through it moaned a ghostly under-song,
Like hoarse night-gusts sepulchral briars among.   [st. 36]

(And here the untuned, abandoned instrument in the Gothicized version
of the harp of Psalm 137 in the process of becoming Aeolian, produces not
intrumental or vocal music, but poetic "under-song.")

Nevertheless, the most significant extended uses of the word seem always
to occur in the presence of moving water. William Browne's river in *Britan-
nia's Pastorals* praises his love, "his hasty waves among / The frothied rocks,
bearing his undersong" points specifically to the literal "refrain" with its
verb "bearing" (2.3.1028). The water-as-swain is really less Spenserian than
the swain undersung by water. Coleridge's Spenserian stanzas to Joseph
Cottle map out a poetic landscape, with a Parnassian-Heliconian-Acidalian
hill, a poisonous Lethean stream, and, above that but still on the lower
slopes, a meadow with another sort of brook:

Nor there the Pine-grove to the midnight blast
Makes solemn music! But th'unceasing rill
To the soft Wren or Lark's descending trill
Murmurs sweet undersong mid jasmine bowers.[14]

But most significantly for this discussion, Coleridge blends the voice of
the river Greta, in the later "Recollections of Love," with that of a putative
beloved and of personified Love itself. Hearing, after an absence of eight
years, "quiet sounds from hidden rills / Float here and there, like things

astray," he half-remembers a presence; and in lines that themselves, with their striking anacoluthon, replace a person with a river, calls that very memory into deep question.

> You stood before me like a thought,
>   A dream remembered in a dream,
>   But when those meek eyes first did seem
> To tell me, Love within you wrought—
>   O Greta, dear domestic stream![15]

It is the sound of that "dear domestic stream," a voice quite other than that of the Spenserian lyric water muse, or even that of the Thames of poetic tradition, that is addressed in the final stanza.

> Has not, since then, Love's prompture deep,
>   Has not Love's whisper evermore
>   Been ceaseless, as thy gentle roar?
> Sole voice, when other voices sleep,
>   Dear under-song in clamor's hour.

The "ceaseless" essence of the undersong here is no longer a matter of a droning bourdon; for only the desire for death would hear the hum of life, or sounds of its tributary streams of love and memory, as oppressive drone, and one of the secondary undersongs of the Thames in *Prothalamion* has occasioned a new and revised audition.

Emerson carries the romantic revision of the Spenserian undersong one stage further; in "Woodnotes II," the pine tree, singing the song of "the genesis of things," of how

> The rushing metamorphosis
> Dissolving all that fixture is
> Melts things that be to things that seem,
> And solid nature to a dream.
> O, listen to the undersong,
> The ever old, the ever young;
> And, far within those cadent pauses,
> The chorus of the ancient Causes!   [112–19]

If Coleridge's Greta sang her undersong to the listening of loss, Emerson's undersong is that of no particular river, no local or national voice, but that of flux itself. It does reecho the "sweet Time" that Cheney hears in Spenser ("The ever old, the ever young"), and it seems remarkably attentive to the notion of continuous drone intermittently making itself heard as periodic refrain: "And, far within those cadent pauses, / The chorus. . . ." The "cadent pauses," each rumoring, but only falsely, of final, cadent closure, each marking pace and time, each falling into place with the water's fall, allow the united choral voices of the conditions of Creation to arise as repeated chorus after the unrolling of each successive epochal strophe. (Emerson uses "undersong" once again, more trivially, in the Concord "Ode" of 1857: "'United States!' the ages plead,— / Present and Past in undersong" [17–18]. But even here, the stream of time is clearly the source of the Spenserian undersinging.)

A final transumptive elicitation of one of the undersongs of sense in Spenser's word appears in Robert Frost's etiological fable—post-Ovidian, post-Spenserian, post-Miltonic all in different ways—of the institution of meaning in natural noise. "Never Again Would Birds' Song Be the Same" does an end run around Virgil's Tityrus teaching the woods to echo the name of Amaryllis, but like all such preposterous etiologies, it resounds with the Spenser who has come between: Frost's sonnet tells of how Adam

> Would declare and could himself believe
> That the birds there in all the garden round
> From having heard the daylong voice of Eve
> Had added to their own an oversound,
> Her tone of meaning but without the words.   [1–5]

Here, I cannot help but feel, the "oversound," playing against the modern figurative sense of "overtone," is returning "undersong" in a strangely inverted way.[16]

The song of the river—the sound of water generally—outlasts all others and, in narrative and descriptive accounts, frequently concludes catalogues of harmonizing natural noises by being placed below them. So with the sounds at the beginning of Wordsworth's "Resolution and Independence":

> The birds are singing in the distant woods;
> Over his own sweet voice the stock-dove broods;
> The Jay makes answer as the Magpie chatters;
> And all the air is filled with pleasant noise of waters.   [4–7]

—where the water sound underlies and underscores the others in a Spenserian alexandrine. No more than a month or so later, Wordsworth recalled the stock-dove's consciousness of its "own sweet voice" (perhaps *its* undersong was some dove-talk version of "So I unto myself alone shall sing") and finally brought it down into the bottom line, in the Westminster Bridge sonnet's "The river murmurs at its own sweet will," Spenser's prothalamic Thames, taking its own sweet time. To varying extents, all of Wordsworth's discursive rivers partake of Spenser's Thames. From the Derwent in book 1 of *The Prelude,* the voice that flowed along his dreams, that made

> ceaseless music through the night and day
> Which with its steady cadence, tempering
> Our human waywardness, composed my thoughts
> To more than infant softness, giving me

Among the fretful dwellings of mankind
A knowledge, a dim earnest of the calm
That nature breathes among the hills and groves.・   [1805, 1.279–85]

—to the Duddon, which Wordsworth twenty-five years or so later diverts into being a master trope for a series of sonnets variously composed, the Thames's undersong is never far away. The "After-Thought" sonnet to the river Duddon sequence refigures the river not as Heraclitean time, but as the history of consciousness:

For backward Duddon! as I cast my eyes,
I see what was, and is, and will abide;
Still glides the stream, and shall for ever glide;
The Form remains, the Function never dies.   [3–6]

And here the silence of the water ("Still glides the stream") cannot help but entail, through an inevitable and unwitty pun, the ceaselessness of its current, the eternity of the form and function, as contrasted with the feeble mortality of the mere substance, of discourse.[17]

I mentioned earlier both the Spenserian signature trope of "tuning" a poetic voice or instrument "to the water's fall" and Vallans's *Tale of Two Swans*. They converge here most significantly. Vallans's poem sought to make restitution for a missing Spenserian river poem (even as it was itself followed by a very great one), and at the crucial moment toward its beginning, when Venus receives the pair of swans, she

like the Goddesse of great Love,
Sate lovely by the running river side,
Tuning her lute unto the waters fall.

The trope of singing to the water, attuning or according with it, also involves addressing it. The figure constitutes a hidden undersong for Spenser's actual and remembered oeuvre. It is exemplified most audibly in *Prothalamion*, a poem that tunes its own utterance to the water's fall, although always in full cognizance of the greater power of the river: its audible volume, physical force, and long, long duration, both backward, preexisting Spenser's poem as an almost natural trope of poetic discourse (the books in the running brooks are the oldest ones) and forward, outlasting any human voice that, like Spenser's, could speak to, or of, or for it.

Moving water is in the Spenserian undersong, at least as the deep, private scholarship of poets seems to have perceived it. And so is poetic self-reference. Hart Crane's reposing river, now turned into a meditative pool by having run into the sea, remembers not its own voice but the "slow sound" carried by the willows on its banks, "A sarabande the wind mowed on the mead." But had the poet not become the river, in order, so late in the poetic day, to join it rather than to succumb to it, it should itself have spoken. Like the raving of Shelley's Arve in its "dizzy ravine"; like the river Duddon, playing in Wordsworth's sonnet the role of the wide water of *Il Penseroso* for the poet for whom "the summits hoar / Of distant moon-lit mountains faintly shine, / soothed by the unseen River's gentle roar." Or the sound of water with which, when conjoined with the sound of the wind in the pines, all pastoral is initiated (in Theocritus I); the plaintive mythological streams of Spenser's early pastoral, whose "song" rhymes with lamented "wrong"; his local Irish river, which he loved both in actuality and in trope ("Mulla whom I whilome taught to weepe"); the everlasting universe of things running through the mind, the trope of that flow in the actual river that runs on "with a sound but half its own"; the schoolbook lesson of Spenser-for-the-young in the undersong of Tennyson's brook ("O men may come and men may go / But I go on forever"); the underground sacred Alphs that break out from time to time for all of us, an accompaniment breaking out into refrain between strophes, a refrain becoming the argument it was measuring out, an ancillary sound that recurrently rises into mastery, as it does for Mrs. Ramsay in *To the Lighthouse,* reading the story to James, "reading and thinking, quite easily, both at the same time; for the story of the Fisherman and his wife was like the bass gently accompanying a tune, which now and then ran up unexpectedly into the melody."[18] Only Stevens's river of rivers "that flows nowhere, like a sea" can be so silent, refusing to follow the course of the old trope, but the sound of the flowing rises again into refrain, one of the only natural refrains, even after the song of its unsinging has been ended.

9 🐚

The Footing of His Feet:
A Long Line Leads
to Another

Generic forms, like sonnets or odes, general rhetorical categories, like questions and answers, implicitly complex lyrical devices, like refrains, momentary phonological and syntactic structures, like chiasms or tmesis, are all
modules of poetic structure of various size and complexity. As has been
shown, they not only provide the special linguistic framework for poetry's
fictional guiles, but are themselves momentarily made fictional, or allegorized. One of the differences between a mere formal or rhetorical convention
or topos and a comparable device in the work of two or more poets of
originality lies in the fact that in the latter case, a poet will recognize a
moment of extraordinary figuration in the work of another one. A special
chord will be struck, and a response given; but neither of the two poets'
contemporaries may hear what has been heard and take it up. Poetically
accepted, we might say, the device never becomes conventionally received.
This kind of response I have written about elsewhere, in *The Figure of Echo,*
as a trope of pointed allusive resonance (as opposed to the use of echo in
ironic scheme). In the following pages I should like to trace, through a
problematically egregious line—a kind of blunder—by one poet, an allusive
relation to an earlier poet's metrical device that afterward became a conventional one. And yet looking back from a single line of Milton's to a post-
Spenserian convention—and further back still to a moment of Spenser's own
origination—will reveal an uncanny relation between an atom of scheme
and a tissue of trope as well as between two great poets' fascinatingly overdetermined mistakes, or slips, that in a more general and mysterious way

seem to stand as voice and echo. But first a bit more on intertextual echo itself.

By poetic allusion I mean not so much to indicate allusions, quotations, and so forth *in* poems, but rather the poetic or figurative operations of certain unavowed, or barely acknowledged, fragments of earlier poetry which are worked into a later text. (In the taxonomy of *imitatio* in Thomas M. Greene's *The Light in Troy,* this should constitute that Renaissance type which he calls "dialectical.") We commonly use the acoustical term *echo* metaphorically to invoke such sorts of allusion, and it may be observed that Renaissance poetic practice is full of moments at which literal or mythological invocations of echo or the use of echo schemes of formal or informal kinds will be accompanied by such allusions and will frequently produce them in later texts. To adduce one example not previously discussed: Ben Jonson, in the fourth poem of his extravagant *Eupheme* (a cycle in praise of Lady Venetia Digby), addresses his mythologized heroine as follows:

> The voice so sweet, the words so fair,
> As some soft chime had stroked the air;
> And though the sound were parted thence,
> Still left an echo in the sense.   [ll. 37–40]

This is not the nymph Echo of post-Ovidian mythography, but neither is it the literal acoustical phenomenon. We may admire the delicate syntactic ambiguity of "Still left an echo *in the sense*"—in the hearer's own sense of hearing (in sensation, *im Gefühl*) and in the sense, the meaning (*Sinn, signification*) of the text. Alexander Pope had certainly "heard" these echoes of this echoing. In his famous formula (in *An Essay on Criticism,* 364–65) directed against the cultivation by "tuneful fools" of what he treats as poetic musicality in spite of meaning, he himself echoes Jonson's line:

> 'Tis not enough no harshness gives offense,
> The sound must seem an echo to the sense.

This is a sharp, expositorily tactful (note the "must seem") but reductive revision of Jonson's far more resonant trope of memory, or abstraction, even to troping itself. Where Jonson is plangent, Pope is merely striking. It is one of many instances in which poetry *about* echo elicits intertextual echoes later on.

Yet we cannot help but observe that a relatively minute particular of poetic language—the sequence "sound"–"echo"–"sense"—engages the poetic attention of a later writer, and that such minutiae are easy for the reader to overlook. The philological scholar, in the earlier history of the academic study of literature, would frequently note echoic phrases or uses as linguistic evidence of, or exceptions to, some convention he was trying to identify.

Intrinsic theories of reading, including extreme "new-critical" responses to a text, would, perhaps even unwittingly, tend to write as if in each poem, language were born anew, ex nihilo (even though the trope of birth out of nothing seems sterile in its self-contradiction). The philological scholar wields his *confer* footnote in such a way as to make the poet ask, "So what?" The new critic abandons the device as an instrument of inauthenticity. But the poetic reader—a strange blend of Lessing's critic, philosopher, and (in the oldest sense of the word) *Liebhaber*—will always be hearing bells that sing out, "compare, compare," sometimes at the tiniest but often peculiarly sharp points of language. I believe that the poetic process is deeply associated with awareness of this kind, whether actively displaying the interconnections of allusive use or interestingly and significantly suppressed.

But I shall proceed at once to a minutely particular instance, a line from Milton's *Il Penseroso,* from the passage celebrating the Imagination's nighttime at the heart of the poem. This section, running roughly from lines 75 through 122, has obsessed English and American poetry from Collins to Yeats and Stevens; from

> I hear the far off *Curfew* sound
> Over some wide-water'd shore,
> Swinging low with sullen roar

—whose echoes are heard in the "sullen horn" of the may-fly in Collins's "Ode to Evening" and in the repeated "wide water, without sound" of Stevens's "Sunday Morning"—through the place

> Where glowing Embers through the room
> Teach light to counterfeit a gloom

and to generate the interior illumination of the figurative, the passage then continues into the realms of tragedy and romance.

But at this point, the power of Melancholy is invoked as being unable to call up the power and the persons of poets in the way in which the figure of "Gorgeous Tragedy" had been able to represent tragic poets by presenting their plays:

> But, O sad Virgin, that thy power
> Might raise *Musaeus* from his bower,
> Or bid the soul of *Orpheus* sing
> Such notes as, warbled to the string,
> Drew Iron tears down *Pluto's* cheek,
> And made Hell grant what Love did seek.

It is interesting to observe that the parallel evocation of Orpheus in the closing lines of *L'Allegro* calls up music and lyric poetry to make one

> hear
> Such strains as would have won the ear

Of *Pluto,* to have quite set free
His half-regained *Eurydice.*

We are reminded that the formulation in *Il Penseroso* suppresses the fact that
Hell granted to poetic power only half of what Love did seek, and it is all
the more touching that, as Milton's meditative consciousness moves on, the
matter of suppression, of telling half a tale—or perhaps half a truth—of
poetic incompleteness, in short, emerges as a central question. The lines
continue:

[And made Hell grant what Love did seek.]
Or call up him who left half told
The story of *Cambuscan* bold,
Of *Camball,* and of *Algarsife,*
And who had *Canace* to wife,
That own'd the virtuous Ring and Glass,
And of the wondrous Horse of Brass,
On which the *Tartar* King did ride . . .

The poet invoked here is of course Chaucer, but as author of the half-told
Squire's Tale—a very strange choice indeed to juxtapose with the exemplary
works of the tragic dramatists, those central matters of Thebes (for Soph-
ocles), the line of Pelops (for Aeschylus) and of Troy (for Euripides). We
may well ask why this is so, and a glance at the following lines will lead to
an answer as well as to the crucial and problematic line:

And if aught else great Bards beside
In sage and solemn tunes have sung,
Of Tourneys and of Trophies hung,
Of Forests, and enchantments drear,
Where more is meant than meets the ear.
Thus night oft see me in thy pale career . . .

The "great Bards" are only one, Spenser, the suppression of whose name is
a very different matter from reducing Chaucer's to "him that left half
told. . . ." It has been frequently remarked that the epithet "sage and solemn"
was one which Milton himself recalled, probably a decade or more later, in
a passage in *Areopagitica* to which we must return, when he invoked "our
sage and serious poet Spenser." Indeed, possible allusions to Ariosto and
Tasso fade before the strength of Spenser's presence here. "And who had
Canace to wife" is itself answered by the text it echoes, from book 4, canto 3
of *The Faerie Queene:* "For Triamond had Canacee to wife" (st. 52), and the
importance of the allusion to the *Squire's Tale* is now apparent. It is that
half-told story which Spenser completes in book 4 of *The Faerie Queene* and
which he uses as an occasion for acknowledgment of his major precursor,
Chaucer, "Well of English vndefyled." Milton chooses the half-told tale of

Chaucer because of its influential power on Spenser as well as for its incompleteness; at the same time, Spenser is himself unnamed and undesignated here. Given that, as Dryden observed in a famous moment in the preface to the *Fables,* Chaucer's relation to Spenser was that of Spenser to Milton (his "original"), it would seem that this whole passage would constitute an important constellation of acknowledgments.[1]

That Spenser goes unacknowledged, then, save perhaps through the screen of Chaucer's presence, is strange. Spenser confessed that he could not dare to strive for poetic eminence "but through infusion sweete / Of thine owne spirit, which doth in me surviue," as he says to Chaucer, adding that

> I follow here the footing of thy feete,
> That with thy meaning so I may the rather meete.   [4.3.34]

But at the analogous point of acknowledgment, Milton loses his own footing, in all the senses of the word which Spenser had employed.[2] When he moves away from the half-avowed Spenserian scene "Where more is meant than meets the ear," he does so with a curious metrical limp, a lapse of an almost unique sort in all of Milton's verse. The hypermetrical line "Thus night oft see me in thy pale career" is egregious not only for its extra syllables—it is a strict iambic pentameter thrusting out from the well-trained herd of octosyllabics in both *L'Allegro* and *Il Penseroso*—but also because it continues on with the rhymes of the previous couplet, an infelicity elsewhere scrupulously avoided. I find it interesting that no editor since the eighteenth century has remarked on the line, and then only to observe that its role was to introduce a new section. But no new section in either of the companion poems is introduced in this fashion, and we are clearly dealing with a matter of meeting meaning in a deeper way.

For Milton's is no ordinary error, no mere lapse in prosodic control nor violation of his own carefully drawn ground rules. Rather it is itself an interpretive reminiscence of Spenser, and a strong defense against the very defensive suppression of acknowledgment which has just occurred. Like the one other, far better known slip of Milton's, which also occurs with respect to Spenser, some slight souring of the "infusion sweete" is going on, though ultimately with an even more quickening effect. In the most famous passage, perhaps, in *Areopagitica,* which I mentioned earlier, Milton's celebrated lapse of memory causes him to include Guyon's palmer on the excursion into the Cave of Mammon (as Spenser does not) as well as into the Bower of Bliss. The whole passage, which starts out with celebrated dispraise of the "fugitive and cloistered virtue, unexercis'd and unbreath'd," deals with necessities of moral and spiritual risk, of imaginative enterprise; "that which purifies us is triall, and triall is by what is contrary." I continue with the famous sentences:

> That virtue therefore which is but a youngling in the contemplation of evil,

and knows not the utmost that vice promises to her followers, and rejects it, is but a blank virtue, not a pure; her whiteness is but an excremental whiteness; which was the reason why our sage and serious Poet Spenser, whom I dare to be known to think a better teacher than Scotus or Aquinas, describing true temperance under the person of Guyon, brings him in with his palmer through the cave of Mammon, and the bower of earthly bliss, that he might see and know, and yet abstain.

It is not surprising that, at such a crucial imaginative moment, Milton, whose earthly father was a musician and a money-lender and whose spiritual or political father was Spenser,[3] might reach out for a succedaneum and prop by remembering one—the assistance of the reasonable palmer—that had not been there. The cave of Mammon, in particular, is charged for Milton with implicit significance: it probably plays a greater formative role in the generation of the Hell of *Paradise Lost* than has been acknowledged and is in any case a highly charged topos for an ambitious poet.

The significance of Milton's mistake has been variously discussed by historical scholars like Ernest Sirluck and poetic interpreters—Harold Bloom and, more recently, John Guillory.[4] I shall not dwell on it any further but return to the long line in *Il Penseroso*. In its Spenserian environment, it presents as many features of a fiction as of an error (like the cave of Mammon slip and, indeed, like any dream). Looked at more closely, it can be seen to seal a kind of closure as much as to commence what Warton in the eighteenth century called the "second part or division of the poem . . . ushered in with a long verse."

> Of Forests, and enchantments drear,
> Where more is meant than meets the ear.
> Thus night oft see me in thy pale career . . .

The "thus" can look backward, syntactically, as well as forward, and the repeated rhyme of the previous couplet, carried through in the following long line, suggests a compelling and familiar way of closing down a stanza. Suppose that we pad out the lines as follows:

> Of forests and of dire enchantments drear,
> Where more is meant than merely meets the ear—
> Thus night thou oft dost see me in thy pale career.

The Spenserian closure, which had operated so strongly on Milton in "On the Morning of Christ's Nativity," as Kenneth Gross has so admirably shown,[5] returns here in synecdoche: a triad of lines of 8, 8, and 10 syllables, linked in rhyme to what proceeds, is here made to represent what had been 10, 10, and 12. The line in which the speaker rejoins the text of *Il Penseroso* after leaving it at night in his high, lonely tower "Where I may oft outwatch the *Bear*" (line 87) is not merely hypermetrical, but Spenserianly so. Stylistically speaking, the absence of Spenser's name even in pronominal allusion (as with Chaucer's) is a question of suppression; poetically it is another matter, and the Spenserian close enters the poem in a return of the *repressed*.

Milton's line, then, is in itself a metaphoric version of Spenser's alexandrine, and is, in its role in *Il Penseroso*, playing an important part in the drama of authorial priority in that poem, and in Milton's early career generally. Humphrey Moseley, the publisher of Milton's 1645 *Poems* in which it appears, boasts of having been able to bring "into the Light as true a Birth, as the Muses have brought forth since our famous Spencer wrote; whose poems in these English ones are as rarely imitated, as sweetly excell'd." And while neither of these is strictly or significantly true, it is clearly the Spenserian presence which shadows so much of the light of these poems. It may seem strange to suggest that Spenser—or his returning shade—can enter them by the waving of so slender a wand as a single alexandrine. For a historian of form, identifying Spenser with the English hexameter line might seem irresponsible or capricious. Yet for English poetry from the mid-1580s on, this identification was clearly at work: poets grasped and wielded the minutiae which later learning might overlook.

In early Tudor poetry, the hexameter line introduced the rhyming couplet form called by George Gascoigne the "poulter's measure," the twelve-syllable six-stressed line rhyming with the following fourteener. (We may remind ourselves of the rhythmic effect of this by distinguishing between the full couplet of fourteen-syllable lines: "Fourteeners, cut from ballad stanzas, don't seem right for song: / Their measure rumbles on like this for just a bit too long" and "A poulter's measure (like a "baker's dozen") cut / One foot off a fourteener couplet, ended in a rut.")[6] But the independence of the six-foot line would not emerge until well after the earl of Surrey had given the English pentameter a canonical form. The first English poem in alexandrines I know of is Surrey's translation of Psalm 55; the first original one is George Turberville's "Of Ladie Venus" (a version, perhaps via Poliziano, of Moschus's "Idyllion of wandring Love"—as E. K. calls it in a note on the "March" eclogue of *The Shepheardes Calender*), published in 1567.[7] Ten years after that, we find Sidney and Spenser first employing the line at about the same time: Sidney in several places in the original *Arcadia* and Spenser, for the first avowed time, as the closing line of the opening "January" eclogue of *SC*.[8] This last instance is most significant: Spenser associates the alexandrine with closure of a pentameter rhymed stanza, albeit only once, at the very end of the whole poem, which is itself by way of being the entire *Shepheardes Calender* in prefatory microcosm. The anticipation of the ultimate shaping of the alexandrine and its role in the stanza form of *The Faerie Queene* is clear.

Sidney used alexandrines not infrequently in the sonnets of *Astrophel and Stella* (sonnets 1, 6, 8, 76, 77, 102, as well as the first and third songs), but more and more, particularly after the publication of *The Faerie Queene* and of *Epithalamion,* the English alexandrine seems to ring with Spenser's name. The intricately rhymed alexandrines of the lament for Sir Philip Sidney, *The Mourning Muse of Thestylis,* by Spenser's friend Lodowick Bryskett (written in 1587 or after); the choice by the devotedly Spenserian poet Michael Drayton of alexandrines for his devotedly Spenserian topographico-mythographic *Poly-Olbion;* the use by even so anti-Spenserian poets as Donne and Jonson of alexandrines to terminate strophes of epithalamia and odes—in all of these instances there is some echo, however muffled or suppressed, of the older poet.[9] Milton's self-consciously Spenserian alexandrines have recently been discussed in detail. Abraham Cowley used the alexandrine frequently among the heroic couplets of his youthful *Davideis,* not with an eye to their power of closure, but, interestingly enough, to trope augmentation. In a note to one of these lines in book 1, Cowley apologizes for the intrusion of the long line, protesting that "it is not by negligence that this verse is so loose, long, and as it were, vast; it is to paint in the number the nature of the thing which it describes." Cowley cites at this point a number of such lines, including one from the fourth book, "Like some fair pine o'erlooking all th'ignobler wood," which caused Dr. Johnson, in his "Life of Cowley," to observe that he could not discover "why the *pine* is *taller* in an Alexandrine than in ten syllables." But Johnson went on to praise, as an example of "representative versification," the conclusion of these couplets:

> He who defers this work from day to day,
> Does on a river's bank expecting stay
> Till the whole stream which stopp'd him should be gone
> Which runs, and, as it runs, for ever will run on.

Here, the last line so clearly applies to itself, to verse in general, and to running water as an ancient figure of eloquence, that Johnson's conviction that verse "can imitate only sound and motion" gives way. Cowley used the alexandrine, later on, conspicuously to terminate strophes of his "Pindarick" odes, and from a remark by the poetaster Dogrel in his play *The Guardian* (1650), in re one of his own lines of verse ("The last is a little too long: but I imitate *Spenser*"), the association remains strong for him.

When John Dryden comes to discuss the alexandrine's use as the third line of the occasional, pace-modulating triplet in Augustan verse, he makes clear this same association: "Spenser has also given me boldness to make use sometimes of his *Alexandrin* line, which we call, tho' improperly, the Pindaric, because Mr. Cowley has often employ'd it in his *Odes,*" he observes in his dedicatory essay prefixed to his translation of the *Aeneid.* He goes on to add that it gives "a certain majesty to the verse, when 't is us'd with judgment, and stops the sense from overflowing into another line." Dryden's triplets that conclude with hexameters, then, are like the closes of Spenserian stanzas: the effect of an alexandrine for him is clearly cadential. It is perhaps more than merely amusing to note what may be the earliest instance of an alexandrine at the end of one of Dryden's triplets; in 1670, in the fourth act of his heroic drama *The Conquest of Granada,* his hero Almanzor counsels the queen of Granada not to look before she leaps:

> True, 'tis a narrow path that leads to bliss,
> But right before there is no precipice:
> Fear makes men look aside, and then their footing miss.[10]

Dryden knew well the passage in *The Faerie Queene,* book 4 cited earlier and seems here to be following the "footing" of Spenser's "feete" in a way that strangely surfaces, some twenty-seven years before he wrote the introduction to his translation of Virgil. In his nondramatic verse, Dryden did not use the longer line to complete a triplet much before 1682 (lines 90 and 166 of "The Medal"). In the following year, he concludes the final couplet of the great elegy on John Oldham that begins "Farewell, too little, and too lately known" with a line imitated from Virgil (having used one for a triplet earlier in the poem): "Thy brows with ivy, and with laurels bound, / But fate and gloomy night encompass thee around." Here, the echo of Virgil's specific account of the shade of Marcellus in book 6 of the *Aeneid* ("sed nox atra caput tristi circumvolat umbra")[11] points back to the mention of Marcellus by Dryden earlier, and itself *circumvolat,* wraps up, the whole poem in the Spenserian closure.

During the next twenty-five years, the cadential power of the alexandrine at the end of the occasional triplet in Augustan heroic couplets had become weakened by convention. Pope, in the famous passage from *An Essay on Criticism* quoted earlier, heaps his scorn on such concluding devices: "A needless Alexandrine ends the Song, / That like a wounded Snake, drags its slow length along," brilliantly slowing up his own line with the "slow length." It is interesting to observe that, less than twenty lines later (370–73), when Pope is using the same sorts of self-descriptive lines to represent beneficial, rather than harmful phonetic devices, he introduces a "quick" rather than a "slow" alexandrine. Like all the lines in this passage, it directs its energies toward a particular bit of narrative:

> When Ajax strives, some Rock's vast weight to throw,
> The Line too labours, and the Words move slow;
> Not so, when swift Camilla scours the Plain,
> Flies oe'r th'unbending Corn, and skims along the Main.

Swift Camilla's fast six feet are uncontaminated by any belatedly Spenserian closure here, and one can't help wondering whether the serpentine presence in the bad, slow "closing" alexandrine has not wandered into the example from Spenser. A serpentine line of gold thread in one of the erotic tapestries in Busirane's house in *FQ* 3.11.28 is described as making its way among the threads of other hue "Like a discoloured Snake, whose hidden snares / *Through the greene gras his long bright burnisht backe declares*" (my italics). Perhaps questions of discoloration and long bright backs might have resonated for Pope against overtones of woundedness and crippled incapacity. Or perhaps the wounded snake comes from Spenser via Milton: the stanza in *FQ* 1.7.31, describing Arthur's helmet, ends with the dragon on it, "And scaly tayle was stretcht adowne his backe full low." The "old Dragon under ground," in stanza 18 of Milton's Nativity Hymn, at stanza's end "Swinges the scaly Horror of his folded tail" in echo of Spenser. Pope's needless alexandrine is related to these lines; his effectively swift one has been purified by Virgil and by Dryden.[12]

In any event, the alexandrine continued to resonate, however faintly, with Spenserian allusiveness throughout the seventeenth century. We may well want to ask if Spenser himself even gives evidence of being aware of his own possession, as it were, and, if so, where and when. Without knowing anything of the formal structure of Spenser's "lost works" like the *Dying Pellicano* or the *Dreames,* we may turn to the verse epilogue to *The Shepheardes Calender,* in six alexandrine couplets, beginning, "Loe! I have made a Calender for every yeare, / That steele in strength, and time in durance, shall outweare." (The poem is divided in two by the opening of the fourth couplet, "Goe, lytle Calender! thou hast a free passeporte," which echoes the already formulaic "Goe, little booke: thy self present . . ." of the opening invocation "To His Booke."[13] The six tetrameter triplets of the opening invocation contain the same number of syllables as the six hexameter couplets of the closing one.) The form to which that epilogue is attuned is by no means a trivial matter; but in any case, I should like to consider one unique earlier instance of an alexandrine line in Spenser's earliest published writing. Both for the remarkable question of the occasion of its occurrence and for the uncanny relation it bears to the egregious pentameter line of Milton's, it deserves the attention it never seems to have received.

In 1569, Spenser at the age of seventeen had graduated from school and was on his way to university, and it is at this early moment in his far from pale career that he translated some poems of Marot and Du Bellay for an English edition of Jan van der Noot's *Theatre for Voluptuous Worldlings*—a kind of emblem book with woodcuts accompanying the poems and an extended, polemically protestant commentary. Spenser's version of the Marot lines (themselves a translation of Petrarch's "Standomi un giorno solo a la finestra") is in rhymed iambic pentameter. But in the fourth of the so-called epigrams into which it is divided, a "spring of water" is described,

Whereto approched not in any wise
The homely shepherde, nor the ruder clowne,

But many Muses, and the Nymphes withall,
That sweetely in accorde did tune their voice
Unto the gentle sounding of the waters fall.

Here once more (for us), but first (for Spenser) is an egregious alexandrine,
the only one in all of the 294 lines which Spenser contributed to the *Theatre*.
It represents a strange sort of mistake, for the French is decasyllabic:

N'osoient pasteurs ne bouviers approcher,
Mais mainte Muse et Nymphe seulement,
Qui de leurs voix accordoient doulcement
Au son de l'eau . . .

Spenser radically expands Marot's half-line in what is his first, apparently
unwitting alexandrine. This would be of little interest were it not for its
origination, for the rest of the poet's oeuvre, of a thematic topos as well as
a formal one. A singer "tuning" his or her voice to the fall of water—where
tune means both "to sing" or "sound" (*OED* sense 3) as well as "to attune"
or "adapt to" (*OED* 1a or b, *accorder*) and *fall* has an additional musical
sense of "cadence"—is a recurring presence. Ten years later, in the "Aprill"
eclogue of *The Shepheardes Calender*, the shepherd called Hobbinol says of
his friend Colin Clout,

then will I sing his laye
Of fayre Eliza, queene of shepherdes all,
Which once he made, as by a spring he laye,
And tuned it unto the waters fall.

This was an important trope for the young poet.[14] In an ambitious and
radically experimental book, Colin, the figure "under whose person the
Author selfe is shadowed," both intones his song to the moving water and
accords his singing with it. Tityrus, in Virgil's first eclogue, "at ease in the
shade teaches [with his piping and singing] the Woods to reecho the name
of lovely Amaryllis" (lentus in umbra / formosam resonare doces Amaryllida
silvas). In the *Calender*, "Tityrus" stands for Virgil, and the Virgilian trope
of imprinting human significance on the mute nature of the pastoral world—
the institution of the pathetic fallacy, as it were—is powerfully revised in
Spenser's transumption of it. Colin addresses—and thereby extends authorial power over—the moving water of poetic tradition, even as he ac-
commodates to it. (One of these senses of *tune* makes this an emblem of
Eliot's "Tradition and the Individual Talent," the other, of Bloom's *The
Anxiety of Influence*: Spenser's figure subsumes the dialectic between these
views.) Hobbinol tells us that the "laye" so attuned was not about Colin's
love Rosalind, but of "fayre Eliza" herself, which suggests a major conse-
cration to a Muse outside the "greene cabinet" of the *Calender*. In addition,
the quatrain's *rime riche*, unusual in that book, of "laye" (poem) and "laye"

(reclined) underscores the trope of according and the association of pastoral *otium* and pastoral poetry.

The figure returns in the "June" eclogue of *SC* (ll. 7–8): "The bramble bush where byrdes of every kynde / To the water fall their tunes attemper right." It reappears in *Virgils Gnat* (Spenser's translation of the pseudo-Virgilian *Culex*) where, at the opening, the falling water is clearly revealed as poetic tradition: "We now have playde [Augustus] wantonly, / Tuning our song unto a tender Muse." And at a high and important moment in book 6 of *The Faerie Queene,* Sir Calidore encounters a stream at the foot of Mt. Acidale, where he is about to be vouchsafed one of the poem's major and central visions:

Ne mote wylde beastes, ne mote the ruder clowne
Thereto approach, ne filth mote therein drowne:
But nymphes and faeries by the bancks did sit,
In the woods shade, which did the waters crowne,
Keeping all noysome things away from it,
And to the waters fall tuning their accents fit.   [6.10.7]

Here there is a direct reminiscence of the Marot translation, of the privileged scene of a vision of eloquence not to be transgressed upon by "the ruder clowne," the bad poets. Spenser had, probably in the early 1580s, reworked his contributions to the *Theatre* volume, and these revised poems were published much later in his volume entitled *Complaints*. In this later version, the lines about the nymphs read, "That sweetly in accord did tune their voyce / To the soft sounding of the waters fall," the alexandrine being corrected. In addition, his later *Visions of Bellay* recast into sonnet form the blank verse he had originally used for them in the van der Noot book.[15] In the early, unrhymed Englishing of one of the *Songe* sonnets, the same figure turns up:

Hard by a rivers side, a waling nymphe
Folding her armes with thousand sighs to heaven
Did tune her plaint to falling rivers sound.   .

In the later text, this becomes

Hard by a rivers side a virgin faire
Folding her armes to heaven with thousand throbs
And outraging her cheekes and golden haire
To falling rivers sound thus tun'd her sobs.

Du Bellay's French seems to provide a possible paradigm for the alexandrine expansion of the Marot tuning-to-the-water line: his "Nymphe esploree . . . / Accordeit ceste plainte au murmure des flotz," and Spenser may have had the cadence of the French *alexandrin* in his ear as he worked with the uncannily similar text from Petrarch via Marot, where one "waling nymphe" gave way to many.

Be that as may be, their song was in his line; and just as the terminal alexandrine would always seem a Spenserian echo, the trope of tuning poetry to the flow of poetic waters became, for many of Spenser's followers, a kind of colophon or signature to be acknowledged. Thus, three years after the publication of the first edition of *The Shepheardes Calender,* Thomas Blener-hasset (in *A Revelation of the True Minerva,* 1582): "Take lute in hand, tune to the waters fall." Lodowick Bryskett's elegy for Sir Philip Sidney in alex-andrines, mentioned earlier, makes the water that of his local, Irish poetic river; the nymphs he invokes at his poem's opening seem figures for the poetic of his friend Spenser: "Help me to tune my dolefull notes to gurgling sound / Of *Liffies* tumbling streams. . . ." George Peele's *A Farewell* (1589): "So couth he sing his layes among them all / And tune his pype unto the waters fall." William Vallans (*A Tale of Two Swans,* 1590): "Where Venus . . . / Sate lovely by the running river side, / Tuning her Lute unto the waters fall." *The Returne from Parnassus* (part 2, 1606) invokes Spenser directly: "While to the waters fall he tun'd her fame" (act 1.2), and, later on (act 4.4): "Weele tune our sorrows to the waters fall." Spenserians like Drayton, William Browne, and George Wither repeat the figure several times.[16]

What we have seen in the resonance of Spenser's early, mistakenly long alexandrine exhibits a somewhat ghostly quality: the anticipation, at an early point in an artist's work, of what might come to seem synecdochic of it by others. There are other such instances of overprivileged—and perhaps ov-erdetermined—minutiae in Spenser which, by self-echoing, he seemed to avow. One of these is the rhetorical formula, used in a quasi-mythographic context, "Who knows not X?" Spenser uses it to institute a central fiction—to introduce it and to make an ironically guarded claim for its prior estab-lishment by the two-edged means of a rhetorical question. Its first use in the "August" eclogue of *The Shepheardes Calender* involves "a doeleful verse / Of Rosalend (who knowes not Rosalend?) / That Colin made." (Colin-Spen-ser has a "love and mistresse" with the "feigned name" of Rosalind.) This initial instance of the little scheme is protected by the fictional extension of the question "Who knows not?" That question is uttered by Cuddie, one of the shepherds in the eclogue, about another, Colin, and his mistress: in Cuddie's world, her name is echoed by every stream. When Spenser comes later on to echo his own formula, the two other occasions, while evoking versions of a Colin-Rosalind situation, are nonetheless far more audacious.

In the first of the *Cantos of Mutabilitie* (7.6.36), Spenser as narrator first names the sacred spot, the hilltop whereon a legal proceeding with cosmic consequences is to take place. The hilltop "shadowed," as Spenser would have said, by the hill in the poem was a place near and dear to him—

Gullymore, near his own home at Kilcolman—but renamed in the poem from the valley beneath it, and thereby refigured. The spot "That was, to weet, upon the highest hights / Of Arlo-hill (who knows not Arlo-hill?)" stands to the poet as Rosalind to his own persona, Colin; it bears a feigned name which also, "being wel ordered, will bewray the very name" of a personal place. The rhetoric of questioning here is much more complex than in the first instance. First, the height has been renamed from a stream of water at its base: readers could be said to know and not know it at once, depending upon whether what Spenser elsewhere calls the "feigned colours" or the "true case" is meant. Second, the narrator here, unlike the naïf Cuddie in the *Calender,* knows well that the scoffing answer ("Nobody") and the plain answer ("I don't") are both subsumed by the wise answer ("We all do, now that you mention it").

The second reechoing of the formula occurs in book 6 of *The Faerie Queene,* a few stanzas after the reoccurrence of the tuning-song-to-the-waters'-fall figure we just considered. The scene is the top of Mt. Acidale itself, where Sir Calidore has come upon his fragile vision of the hundred naked girls dancing in a ring around the Graces, who concentrically surround an unnamed lady in the process of being "advaunst to be another Grace":

> She was, to weete, that jolly shepheards lasse,
> Which piped there unto the merry rout;
> That jolly shepheard which there piped was
> Poore Colin Clout (who knows not Colin Clout?) [6.10.16]

And who remembers not Rosalind, who need not be named? At this astonishing moment of encounter between a pure fiction (Sir Calidore) and his own persona, the narrator names that persona by means of the formula applied to his "love and mistress" by a surrogate shepherd-poet earlier in Spenser's career.

It is no wonder, then, that this poignantly returning figure should have been picked up—as the tuning-to-the-water had not been—by Milton, at a moment of flagrantly Spenserian mythopoeia. In discoursing of the genealogy of his version of Comus in *A Masque Presented at Ludlow Castle,* the Attendant Spirit tells of how Bacchus

> On *Circe's* island fell: (Who knows not *Circe,*
> The daughter of the Sun? Whose charmed Cup
> Whoever tasted, lost his upright shape
> And downward fell into a groveling Swine.)

The long parenthesis, incorporating the mythographic footnote into the text itself, anticipates what would be a major strategy in *Paradise Lost.* The allusive use of the Spenserian device is rhetorically complex as well: by interpretively echoing Spenser's rhetorical question, Milton can displace his own mythographic uneasiness. Instead of asking, "Who knows not Comus?" about his masque's character (the one he had so radically transformed from the belly-god of Ben Jonson and the delicate youth of Philostratus), he can redirect the question to one about Circe. He is thus able to ask it with the singular candor of Spenser's Cuddie.[17]

The Spenserian topos of tuning-to-the water is, like the "who knows not?" scheme, more than merely one of what Thomas Warton called "Spenser's imitations of himself": it was recognized as such, as we have seen, by subsequent poets of the kind whose ear is tuned to the frequency at which poetic echo is transmitted. What seems so strange about the original alexandrine in the *Theatre* of 1596 is that the young poet's schoolboy pentameters should stumble over just that place. When Colin Clout, ten years later in the *Calender*, can tune in on his central precursors through the tutelage of a "Tityrus" who is both Virgil and Chaucer, Spenser is troping the pastoral convention of the accord between natural voice and shepherd's piping. The "water's fall" had not yet become the major stream of full, assured poetic eloquence, the Thames, which would provide for the poet at the end of his life so resonant an undersong. But this poignant moment of being metrically out of tune would in fact generate just such a figuration of poetic accord. Both the long line and the trope of tuning poetry to moving water would always stay with him.

Even if the alexandrine seems to remain Spenser's property in subsequent verse, I do not mean to suggest that all egregious long lines, or versions of them like the one of Milton's that has led us to this pass, are willful and manifest Spenserian allusions. But for a certain kind of English poetic ear, the very line is like a spell. Even after the flood of eighteenth-century Spenserian verse had turned the stanza form into a trivial container, Wordsworth, Blake, Byron, Shelley, and Keats could reanimate it in powerfully different ways. Keats, in particular, returned to the Augustan practice of pacing heroic couplets with the occasional alexandrine (in *Lamia,* part 2). But one particular instance of an egregious alexandrine is, in light of the previous discussion, a most touching one.

Keats's line—or rather lines, for it is a pair of them, a Drayton-like *Poly-Olbion* alexandrine couplet, in fact—reaches out from the meter of his verse letter of 1816 to Charles Cowden Clarke, who, Keats says,

> first taught me all the sweets of song.
> The grand, the sweet, the terse, the free, the fine;
> What swelled with pathos, and what right divine;
> Spenserian vowels that elope with ease,
> And float along like birds o'er summer seas;
> *Miltonian storms, and more, Miltonian tenderness;*
> *Michael in arms, and more, meek Eve's fair slenderness.*   [11.53–59]

The alexandrine couplet is interestingly displaced here from the lines which invoke, with a sort of Popean "representative versification," Spenserian vocalic prominence, onto those lines characterizing Milton's style. Second, they are far from Miltonic in themselves: the architectonic quality of the couplet resounds with Sidney and Spenser. The pattern in which the stylistic modes (concrete "storms," abstract "tenderness") are exemplified in the following line by the near-rhyming instances (concrete "arms," slightly more general "slenderness") can be rendered thus:

| Miltonian storms | (and more) | Miltonian tenderness |
| Michael in arms | (and more) | meek Eve's fair slenderness |

The more precise (masculine?) rhythmic echo of the first four syllables of line two is modulated by the slower, rhythmically more ambiguous (feminine?) half-line about Eve. And yet they are both aspects of the Miltonic voice, even as they are revealed in a Spenserian schematic pattern, arrayed in the alexandrine line that for poets would always be Spenser's own. As we have seen, Milton himself, at a moment of authorial anxiety, of suppression of the proper acknowledgment of his poetic father, himself falls into the "footing" of his precursor's "feete" and causes his verse to cast a shortened but unmistakable shadow of the Spenserian line. The line from *Il Penseroso* is a momentary revisionary version—I should call it a metalepsis—of a line of Spenser's whose own origination lies in a mysterious moment of overdetermined error.

In following the thread of Milton's line, we may seem to have wandered into, rather than out of, a labyrinth; I hope it has not been too confusing to discover that one was holding on to a line of Spenser's for most of the journey. One of the dangers has been the risk of concern with the sort of historical detail that caricatures philological research—the risk of becoming what Pope called one "who reads not, but who scans and spells," a "word-catcher that lives on syllables."[18] Formal matters of prosody and versification concern verse, not poetry, which is to say that poetics is involved with trope, rather than with theme or scheme. But the mysterious way in which poetry animates the otherwise lifeless image of verse form has always been something that poets have perceived in each other's work and have been reticent about addressing openly. Occasionally, as at moments of metrical pathology like the two we have pursued so relentlessly, these perceptions may surface, and we may conclude that the loss of footing has been a slip not of ordinary nor of unusual skill or craft, but a stumbling over a block set up by the Imagination itself.

10 ❧

Dallying Nicely with Words:
Poetic Linguistics

The figurative role of scheme—no less than that of theme (or genre or mode or occasion)—is, as I have been suggesting, ubiquitous, like the troping of informal or ad hoc patterns of written language in verse. One is tempted to say that poetic language represents itself as being in part or whole something other than what the metalanguages of linguistic analysis would hold it to be. In this chapter, I should like to consider some aspects of figurative, or poetic, linguistics.

By that I do not mean to expand on either half of Roman Jakobson's chiastic title "Poetry of Grammar and Grammar of Poetry" so much as to suggest that particular bodies of poetic text seem implicitly to theorize about language, recasting categories of *langue, parole,* and, certainly, *écriture* in terms of each other and inventing fictional new ones. A poet's relation to his or her language is certainly not like that of a linguist, and, as we shall see in a later chapter, a philosopher, or indeed even a humbler expositor. "Good prose is like a window pane," said George Orwell, and we might add that only when it breaks are there concomitant refractions and opacities. But poetic language is as much mirror as window, and for poets, words are often like some agents in a larger fiction, not so much an epic or drama, but more a complex romance, of language. It has been pointed out over the last twenty-five years that the ways in which poetry revises other forms of discourse include troping them, and that this may involve figuration of structures and processes that linguistic study has classified and analyzed. Donald Davie in *Articulate Energy* and Christine Brooke-Rose in *A Grammar of Metaphor* stopped short of characterizing poetic language as deploying fictional or notional syntax and accidence, yet such scholars as Marie Borroff have gone further in suggesting that in both diction and the formation of fictional names and epithets an analogue of folk etymology can be at work.[1] But let me turn to an observation, at once poetical and theoretical, about the behavior of poetic words.

At the opening of act 3 of *Twelfth Night*, the two poetical characters, Viola and Feste the clown, neither of whom speaks *in propria persona* for most of the play, exchange words and coins for the first time. After an introductory bout of wordplay turning on innocent locative and problematic instrumental uses of the preposition *by*, the Clown observes, with regard to the very rhetoric of their punning, "A sentence is but a chev'ril glove to a good wit. How quickly the wrong side may be turned outward!" To this Viola replies, "Nay, that's certain. They that dally nicely with words may quickly make them wanton." This is a kind of metawit, and poetically intense, at that. Both *dally* and *wanton*, like the word *sport*, have, in the late sixteenth century, erotic insides. Feste is coy in calling such an inside "the wrong side," treating with kid gloves what should—had the technology been available—have been more properly figured as a reversible coat. *Wanton*'s oldest general sense (wan + towen [= "discipline" or "train"]) is of unruliness, although the *OED* distinguishes among a number of states of negatively valorized activity: unruly, frolicsome, capricious, self-indulgent, insolent, arbitrary, gratuitous, changeable, and, of course, erotically unsubdued (*OED* sense 7, "luxuriant," seems to double in sense with "erotic," at least in the examples cited). Viola asserts that playing with words (as opposed, perhaps, merely to using them) will cause them to lose control of themselves and thereby perhaps our control over them. But *dally*, primarily applied to discourse, has erotic overtones as well, and Viola's very words themselves imply that "nice," precise, delicate wordplay will cause language to heat up erotically, if not (anachronistically) with the return of the repressed, then at least, figuratively, with an analogously turning of insides-out.

Feste picks this up immediately in his return, and the remainder of the exchange is instructive:

Viola. Nay, that's certain. They that dally nicely with words may quickly make them wanton.
Clown. I would therefore my sister had no name, sir.
Viola. Why, man?
Clown. Why, sir, her name's a word, and to dally with that word might make my sister wanton. [+ *want one?*] But indeed, words are very rascals since bonds disgraced them.
Viola. Thy reason, man?
Clown. Troth, sir, I can yield you none without words, and words are grown so false I am loath to prove reason with them.

Words not only get out of hand, but their unruly activity eroticizes what they signify. The bonds—sworn legal instruments, instead of one's word plainly and honorably given—put words into bondage. Such fetters improve neither the behavior of language nor, certainly, its reputation. There is a final oblique reflection on words at the end of the scene. Viola gives Feste a coin, and he asks, "Would not a pair of these have bred?" to which Viola replies, "Yes, being kept together and put to use." *Use* is itself used commonly in an erotic sense by Shakespeare (*OED* sense 3b), and two coins rubbing up against each other will breed, implies the clown, even as the sum of their two values will breed usuriously. And so with wanton words, at least in the fictional linguistics that momentarily surfaces in the two word-mongers' exchange of serious wit.

Another, very different poet, Friedrich Schlegel, wrote in his essay on incomprehensibility (*"Über die Unverständlichkeit"*) that "words often understand themselves better than those who use them," and this personification by poetic thought of the elements of language typifies a kind of romance in which signifiers become agents, or even scenes.

I am not considering at the moment such issues as those of private or fictional dialects in which poets from Theocritus through Burns and Chatterton to Hugh Macdiarmuid have written, nor, in the case of Spenser (whom Ben Jonson accused of having "writ no language") the distribution of archaisms, coinages, and unstable spellings in the interests of multiple readings that make it impractical to modernize the text of *The Faerie Queene*. Nor, indeed, shall I discuss here the metaphoric use of linguistic terminology in Hart Crane's poetry, for example. Rather, I want to consider some phenomena resulting from what I. A. Richards in *The Philosophy of Rhetoric* called "the interinanimation of words,"[2] one specifically erotic aspect of which Viola invoked. Released wantonness can be libertine in another way, and here again I quote Schlegel (*Critical Fragments*, no. 65): "Poetry is republican speech: a speech which is its own law and an end unto itself, and in which all the parts [*Redeteile*] are free citizens and have the right to vote."[3] The fictional morphology of Spenser's naming of persons and places is more to this point. It is not just the pre-Carrollian portmanteu words that I am thinking of, nor the Joycean play across languages, whereby, for instance, the Lady in book 5 of *The Faerie Queene* in thrall to the tyrant Grantorto is called Eirena, her name bringing together with ringing English irony the Celtic name of Ireland, or Erin, and the Greek *eirene,* or "peace." But the knight who is her champion is named Artegall, because of an Artagallo who in Geoffrey of Monmouth's chronicle was a half-brother of King Arthur, and his name gets implicitly etymologized as *Art + egal* or "equal to Arthur," and as something like *l'art d'egalité,* or judgment of equity. Yet Artegall's name reacts erotically with that of his own lover, Britomart, a name from Virgil originally, but understood as a Martial Britoness (she fights battles disguised in armor as a knight). The first morpheme of "Artegall" arouses the last three phonemes of "Britomart"'s final syllable, and they declare independence, in Schlegel's way, from the [*mart*] morpheme, so that, as James Nohrnberg has observed, the eventual married condition of the bearers of the two names would produce a *Britomartegall* (even as another pair of lovers, in the same mythological region of the poem—Scudamor and Amoret—form a hypogrammatic *Scudamoret* at one point).[4]

Spenser's visionary linguistics alone would be an instructive matter: typically, we would find it to be totally synchronic. But I should like to discuss some other kinds of fabulous grammars evoked at moments by poets' language. I shall skirt for the present the whole area of tone in poetry, whether in pursuit of what Robert Frost called "the sentence sound," or, with Dwight Bolinger's *Intonation and Its Parts* in one hand and a number of samples of fine accentual-syllabic verse in the other, in a consideration of how the relations between voice and verse generate competingly powerful but virtual intonation patterns of their own at a new level, while still sharing the stage with the literally phonological ones. There might be a certain timeliness in this: at least in the United States, a whole new set of intonational phenomena seem to be arising, not in speech, but in the public performance of even minimal prose texts. Primarily in television newsbroadcasting, language has been overwhelmed by grimacing visage even as truth has by packaging. As a result of this, the ability to read aloud for sense—providing the discursive and prosaic basis of Frost's "sentence sound"—seems almost to have become a disabling skill among younger persons employed to read aloud from the admittedly minimal syntax of the teleprompter. Idiolectal and random junctures, for example, occasioned by the inability to anticipate a line break in the copy (something all radio people were trained to do) sound rather like illiterate attempts to read across enjambments, and every day one hears new entities being brought into being by inept performance. Thus, even on radio now, you get an announcement of a dance at "the Martin Luther King # Junior High School," displacing the "Jr." from its role in the dedicatee's name and changing the nature of the school. One might say that this was an exercise of poetic *techné* analogous to the deft articulation of enjambments by Milton, for example. But as Quintilian reminds us, every inadvertent trope is a solecism;[5] but in the realm of poetry rather than of rhetoric, Freud's view that solecisms are inadvertent tropes seems more to the point. It might be only with respect to schemes that the other formulation remains true of poetry. In such a world of public language, one almost despairs of addressing even the old modernist criterion of the sound of speech as poetry's antidote to the old poetical diction (an inadvertently warmed-over serving of a Wordsworthian "language of men"), let alone the subtler matter of "sentence-sound." A line of Frost's from "The Code," in which intonation pattern is crucial to both metrical and semantic construing, would simply get lost in the world of contemporary oral performance: "But I know you don't understand our ways." Without a sense of the contrastive emphases, the line would fall out of pentameter status into a [˘ ˘ ´ ´ ´ ´ ˘ ˘ ˘ ´]; in fact, it needs [ˈ ' ' ' ' ' ' ˈ ' '] ("But *I* know *you* don't understand *our ways*") both to scan as pentameter and to come into rhetorical focus. But these were some of the interests of structural linguistics, with its synchronic biases and its concern for spoken language, as applied to poetry thirty-odd years ago. Instead, I want to take a different sort of look at the implicit linguistics of various schematic situations in poetry.

In these pages I have been considering the ad hoc troping of schemes in poetry: how, for example, the ways in which such observations as those of the late W. K. Wimsatt about rhyme—and those in a fine essay by William Harmon—were indeed instances of something more general.[6] Rhymes, by exploiting linkages between words, propound fictional ones between their referents—as in Latin verse, patterned juxtaposition of nouns and adjectives, irrelevant to syntax, plays a pseudoattributive role. (These linkages, of course, may be antithetical as well as associative.) But in certain situations, the instrument of rhyming, and the sort of linkage it enforces, becomes allegorized as bondage—by Ben Jonson, for example, as fetters between words, and thereby, between lines, or by Milton, as fetters binding the poet to a Jonsonian neoclassicism (although Milton cleverly screens this by associating rhyme as an institution with medieval barbarism).

Emerson, in a remarkable journal entry for June 27, 1839, makes rhyme a trope not only of poetic form generally—as Keats does in his sonnet on the sonnet—but, indeed, of mythmaking—a particular scheme troped not to mean even all schemes, but trope itself.

> Rhyme.—Rhyme; not tinkling rhyme, but grand Pindaric strokes, as firm as the tread of a horse. Rhyme that vindicates itself as an art, the stroke of the bell of the cathedral. Rhyme which knocks at prose and dullness with the stroke of a cannon-call. Rhyme which builds out into Chaos and old night a splendid architecture to bridge the impassable, and call aloud on all the children of morning that the Creation is recommencing. I wish to write such rhymes as shall not suggest a restraint but contrariwise the greatest freedom.

Rhyme, he says, must be not conventional (the "tinkling of piano strings" part 1 of his later poem, "Merlin"), but original (as elaborated in part 2)—not half-heard, but *striking,* in various senses of the word which he then proceeds to draw out. Then the linkage of rhyme becomes newly allegorized as a bridge (Hart Crane's myth seems to grow in part from such a notion), and specifically as a piece of satanic architecture (the words "Chaos and old Night" are from *Paradise Lost,* 1.543).

But there are countless other tropes, less grand and spectacular, for rhyming that crafty verse enables, and good poetry requires, the imagination to fashion. Two rhyming words (or phrases or lines or even larger syntactic units the words terminate and are synecdochic of), say a_1 and a_2, may be so deployed in a poem that they imply any one of a number of nonce theories of the effects of rhyme: for example, a_2 is the echo of a_1; or a_1 and a_2 are in some kind of cause and effect relation, whether empirical or scholastic (that is, a_2 is made up of a_1 or a_1 invented or formed a_2 or whatever); or a_1 is the soul, or the body, of a_2; or a_1 is a text and a_2 a commentary on it, or indeed, in a bitestamentary relation, the fulfillment of it; or a_2 is a hidden or un-acknowledged part of a_1 (or vice versa), and the rhyming occasion is a moment of analysis or revelation. So that rhyming enacts some local verbal magic *with* the words in question, but, beyond that, implies some general principle, some theory of rhyming. This can be as powerfully figurative as the local trope whose epistemological grounding the theory would purport to explain.

Sometimes another scheme, itself tropically neutral until actually employed in poetry, will catalytically enable such an extension to occur. In George Herbert's "Deniall," for example, each tightly rhymed stanza ends in a four-syllabled, unrhymed, noniambic line: "And disorder" // "Of alar[u]ms" // "But no hearing" // "Discontented," each touching on a question of the failure of language (in this case, in prayer). When, in the final stanza, a metaprayer for the efficacy of the prayer envisions a fortunate conclusion, rhyme, meter, broken scheme, and broken hopes are repaired:

> O cheer and tune my heartless breast,
>> Defer no time;
> That so thy favours granting my request,
>> They and my mind may chime,
>> And mend my rhyme.

Even the muted chiming of the two whole phrases "mind may chime / mend my rhyme" is operative here, aside from how self-referential the *chime/rhyme* pair is. It helps establish the fiction that rhyming is, far from being bondage, a kind of elemental discursive force, holding together the surface structures of utterance, their relations to the deep structures, and the whole rhetorical matrix within which utterance is framed. Interestingly enough, this fable of rhyming is established by the marked form of its abruptly revealed absence. But ultimately, the final line turns on three senses of the word *rhyme*, (*a*) the instance of rhyming two line termini, (*b*) rhym*ing*, or the process itself, and (*c*) the entire poem; it is through this last that the figuration of authenticity of discourse is finally accomplished.[7]

A more egregious and original scheme, in Herbert's "Paradise," again sees rhyme as elemental, but specifically functional. In this poem which meditates on what protective enclosure is, the rhymed triplets successively pare down the monosyllabic terminal word of the first line by a letter each time.[8] (The scheme is one of aphaeresis or *ablatio,* save that a phoneme, rather than a syllable, is removed.) Thus:

> I bless thee, Lord, because I GROW
> Among thy trees, which in a ROW
> To these both fruit and order OW.

It is as if each rhyming move revealed something crucial and implicit in the previous word. The fruit of this process is order itself—"ROW" plucked from "GROW," for instance, or, in the second tercet,

> What open force, or hidden CHARM
> Can blast my fruit, or bring me HARM
> While the inclosure is thine ARM?

There seems to be harm and danger hidden in the spell of charm, but hope lies in a refiguration of enclosure, not of words within words or effects implicit in causes, but a figuration of a transcendent sort which wraps the word contained around the container (God's ARM, not a mere human limb whose power to enclose and thereby protect someone else is contingent upon its signifier's being itself "inclosed" within HARM and, ultimately, CHARM).

It is only in the last two tercets that the very process is finally and canonically troped. In the penultimate one, the prelapsarian work of gardening even in Paradise is invoked, the basic task being pruning of trees:

> When thou dost greater judgments SPARE,
> And with thy knife but prune and PARE,
> Ev'n fruitful trees more fruitful ARE.

The analytic story tells us that in order to spare the coming fruit, one must pare down the present branches, that PARE is at the heart of the matter of SPARE, and that, ultimately, the ARE of "fruitful are" will emerge. But the poem, and the allegorization of the scheme, cannot end here, if only because the specific mode of reduction, of word-pruning, has not been addressed. Inevitably, then,

> Such sharpness shows the sweetest FREND:
> Such cuttings rather heal than REND:
> And such beginnings touch their END.

In the revealed teleology, finally, the end of this kind of friendship, protection, enclosure—as well as the end of what could falsely be construed as rending, rather than closing up—is the end of ends itself. Cutting back the extraneous front matter to disclose the final truth in the penultimate line leads to the final trope of regained paradise in—for Herbert's Christian vision—eternity as well as in a termination of the poem: at once *le fin* and *le but,* termination and half-hidden objective.

Herbert is an exemplary allegorist of scheme and pattern, and one could go through *The Temple* and show a multitude of instances of this. (For example, the figuration of the scheme of anadiplosis, which Puttenham calls the "redouble," in the poem titled "The Wreath," where it partakes of a dialectic of crooked-and-straight because of the governing emblem of weaving an utterance of praise, and reinforced by a strange chiasmatic scheme of repetition of rhyming words.)

Not only other schemes, but whole orders of scheme, are susceptible, like rhyme, to reflexive troping and, even more, to the generation of ad hoc theorizing about the scheme. And, as has been suggested, that very fragment of rhetorical theory may itself point back to some central figure of an entire poem. The orders of scheme I have examined could range from whole verse forms (considered synchronically, of course, and without regard to their inevitable allusive dimension), anaphora, refrain, rhetorical question, stanzaic closure, to patterns like chiasm. It will be remembered that none of these is naturally (by which I mean canonically) figurative. They all—again, like rhyming—enable troping to occur but do not necessitate it. Neither are schemes naturally self-referential or reflexive: it is only the tropes of poets which make them so, and to which they return figuration.

As with the paranormal sequences of schemes, so, as we have seen, with words and sublexical elements. Assonance and alliteration are most obviously like rhyme—and may, indeed, be variously figured as subcomponents of it—in this respect. As in the case of Wallace Stevens mentioned earlier, consider how an inferential pattern of linguistic analysis can serve as a scheme in a similar way, as in this beautiful stanza of Geoffrey Hill's (from *The Mystery of the Charity of Charles Péguy*):

> Patience hardens to a pittance, courage
> unflinchingly declines into sour rage,
> the cobweb-banners, the shrill bugle-bands
> and the bronze warriors resting on their wounds.

"Patience" hardening to "a pittance" entails a parable about sound-change. In the fabulous linguistics of the quatrain in question, ablaut is not morphological but moral, the soft fruit of forbearance shriveling into its own pit. In the second, appositive figure, "courage / unflinchingly declines into sour rage," the implication is diachronic, as if "sour rage" were a suffixed, /au/-grade form, as it were, reflected in some latter-day satem language. But just as both instances denote a degenerative change occurring over time, the second has an overtone of the synchronic analysis of the "patience"/"pittance" ablaut, for the process exemplified is both declension and declination. (There are other residues of the decay of courage into inane expressions of what is no longer there to express—"the cobweb-banners, the shrill bugle-bands / and the bronze warriors resting on their wounds." The great effectiveness of this last line depends upon the surprising substitution for the expected word ["spears"? "shields"? "laurels"?] the unpleasantly softening "wounds.")

One of Wallace Stevens's many ablautlike schemes ("Pipperoo, pippera, pipperum") was mentioned in chapter 6. In H. D's "The Flowering of the Rod," a spell of sympathetic, prophetic magic is woven in Kaspar's lines "through my will and power / Mary shall be myrrh"—it is as if "myrrh," in the catalytic presence of a word sounding like "power," were revealed as a declensional form of "Mary." Yet such devices are not limited to modernist verse. Christina Rossetti's opening line of the tenth sonnet in "Monna Innominata"—"Time flies, hope flags, life plies a weary wing"—is more than merely a Tennysonian sort of "representative versification." The *flies/flags* is declensional in tone; but the "life plies" gathers up the /ay/ + /ay/ vowels of the first spondee and permutes the junctural consonants /p/ + /fl/ of the second, even as, conceptually, *life* contains the perception of both *time* and *hope*. Bearing the weight of that containment is heavy, tiring work, though, and the word "weary" resonates, in an almost Popean way, with a final sense of tired phonological articulation as well.

There is a blending of the morphological and the historical in the fictions about sound-change here. Certain poets' mythological grammars do indeed incline either toward the synchronic or the diachronic in their fables about interinanimated words. I have discussed elsewhere how, in A. E. Housman's clause "The chestnut casts its flambeaux," the Latin etymon of "chestnut" (*castanea*) is redoubled in the presence of the delicate, unasserted pun on the verb "casts" (purely Germanic in origin), so that a hypogram, a notional *castanea casta* (the Latin *casta* = "chaste" being likewise unrelated to *castanea*), is conjured up and momentarily flowers in a sort of "chaste-nut."[9] This is a recognizably Miltonic kind of move, playing on English word and Latin etymon, flower and root, what meaning was then and is now, although there is no allegorizing of the etymological process, as there is in *Paradise Lost,* no valorization of the relation between past and present usage. It is as if Latin and English coexisted synchronously (as they did, for Housman, in his writing in prose). But I want here to continue with the matter of the latinate syntax which is so beautifully and tactfully engaged by the remainder of the sentence:

> The chestnut casts its flambeaux, and the flowers
> Stream from the hawthorn on the wind away.

Even before the hyperbaton of the second line is revealed, the "flowers" seem momentarily to be the chestnut blossoms, now no longer torchlike, on the ground. But after the enjambment, the flowers that should in normal syntax stream either away from the hawthorn on the wind, or else on the wind away from the hawthorn, now, more generally, stream away (a nonce verb modeled on the intransitive form of "blow away"). Also, we encounter the subphrase "the hawthorn on the wind," which is part of the picture. (An effect like this, with syntax like this, e. e. cummings would have had to underscore with violent bracketings of format.) This sort of thing happens in Latin poetry as normally as rhyming in later vernaculars. But Housman just makes it happen, without any built-in reflexive, interpretive glossing. Two kinds of syntax are contrasted here. First is the direct svo of the chest-nut's actively casting its flambeaux, marked by the fictional etymon seeming to connect subject and verb and by the assonance of verb and object. Op-posed to it is the hyperbatic, ambiguous rearrangement of the intransitive streaming away of the flowers. But Housman never actually does what Mil-ton so often contrives in his local tropes on syntactic patterns, where there is always some larger moralization being pointed at.

Take, for example, a line from the middle of a passage in *Paradise Lost,* book 2 describing the activities of the fallen angels in their newly organized, proleptically neoclassical civilization which might be called the culture of Pandemonium.

> Others more mild,
> Retreated in a silent valley, sing
> With notes angelical to many a harp
> Their own heroic deeds and hapless fall
> By doom of battle; and complain that fate
> Free virtue should enthral to force or chance.
> Their song was partial, but the harmony
> (What could it less when spirits immortal sing?)
> Suspended hell, and took with ravishment
> The thronging audience. In discourse more sweet
> (For eloquence the soul, song charms the sense,)
> Others apart sat on a hill retired,
> In thoughts more elevate, and reasoned high
> Of providence, foreknowledge, will and fate,
> Fixed fate, free will, foreknowledge absolute,
> And found no end, in wandering mazes lost.   [546–61]

I pass over the typical effect of the inversion discovered at the enjambment of "that fate / Free virtue should enthral to force or chance," a typically neo-Virgilian device, to consider the pivotal line about the relation of philos-ophy and poetry: "For eloquence the soul, song charms the sense." Richard Bentley, the eighteenth-century classical scholar who edited Milton and emended everything of poetic interest that he could find, rewrote the line as "Song charmes the Sense, but Eloquence the Soul" (objecting that "the Verb ought of right to be in the first *Colon* of the Sentence").

For Bentley, the representation of the proposition in Milton's verse is nastily opaque, and for Bentley there is no problem in the platonizing ele-vation of prose eloquence, or philosophy, more sweet (in the Renaissance musical sense of being well tuned) than the music of poetry. But Milton knows that there *are* problems here: abstract and concrete, mediated and direct, absence and presence, all enter into the dialectic, and the syntax of the line becomes both instrumental and figurative in its behalf. If this were only a matter of style (as, less for Bentley than for the uncomprehending Ezra Pound), the high mode might have asserted itself in a more usual inversion: "For eloquence the soul charms, song, the sense" would be perhaps a bit Popean in its rhythm and its evenhanded balance.

It is amusing to note, incidentally, Pope's taming of Milton's device in an analogous conceptual situation: "Survey the WHOLE, or seek slight fault to find / Where Nature moves, and Rapture warms the mind." The strength of this depends upon the simultaneous transitive and intransitive uses of "moves," so that Rapture moving the mind could be one consequence of Nature's motion (intransitive "moves"), or part of a joint operation on it, or both. That "Na*ture*" and "Rap*ture*," not usually associated because of their deep categorical estrangement, are here related (mother and daughter?) by their suffixes' becoming a sort of surname, is a Spenserian device.

But for Milton, first things come first, and for him, syntactic order, as Donald Davie and Stanley Fish and others have demonstrated,[10] is always to be read for its parabolic narrative, epistemological, historical, and teleological.

What is the story of this line, then? The ellipsis of the verb "charms" from the first clause is filled by the extension of its most direct normative position in the second one. But that position, immediately following its subject, "song," awakens the Latin etymon lurking in "charms" (<*carmen,* "song") and patent still in the modern senses of "incantation" and "spell." Poetry, song, sings directly to sense, whereas eloquence, philosophy, charms the soul in another, higher way, in which the music of poetry is not literally there, just as the verb "charms"—even in its extended senses of delighting, alluring, bewitching—is not literally "there" in the clause describing the action of philosophizing on the soul, and, finally, as soul is less literally present than sense. The charm of philosophy is less literally "charm" in the prior sense of "song," then, and the usual parable of linguistic diachrony in *Paradise Lost* is at work here as well. The primary sense of things is present (in both meanings of the adjective); the prior sense is absent, and must be secondarily derived. But presence somehow gets it all wrong, and it is this dialectic that the fictional linguistics of the poem is always assisting the rest of its system of figuration to undo. Ultimately, the fallen angels in book 2, whether composing epics or debating on their fiendish Areopagus, are getting it all wrong, in any case, and the issues of Fate and Freedom perplex them both. But in the course of dealing with the rhetorical activities of what are, after all, two different kinds of writing, Milton applies an ad hoc theory of syntax, based on a troping of SVO as an emblem of literalness, as opposed to the figurativeness of displacement.

The contention between current and obsolete, original lexical use that Milton is constantly staging is a reflection of Satan's dubious battle with God over the nature of authority. We might say, given the consequences of romantic theories of originality as self-origination (a domestication of Satan's view, in any case), that this is a dialectical struggle between two antithetical concepts of originality—that of prior, but absent source, and primary, present given. It is not that Milton always allegorizes semantic change as a figure of the Fall itself (in the case of "charms" there is no such mapping). But such an interpretation is paradigmatic for other figurations.

Andrew Marvell, in his prefatory poem to *Paradise Lost,* shows himself to be aware of how Milton momentarily allegorizes not only schemes like chiasm (so, as we have seen, does Marvell himself), but other grammatical situations. In this case, the issue is not etymology, but word order within the line. At the beginning of his poem, Marvell expresses his original doubts, before reading Milton, about the success of so ambitious and problematic a task, doubts how "In that wide Field how he his way should find / Through which lame Faith leads Understanding blind." The chiasm, of course, is effective in ways previously noted, partially because the "blind" might modify—adjectivally and adverbially—either "Faith" or "leads" or both, thus providing an effective countercurrent to the old figure of the paired incapacities. But the preceding line, all monosyllables, involves Marvell's acknowledgment of Milton's trope of a scheme of monosyllabism. The survey of Hell in the second book of *Paradise Lost* yields a famous prospect in a celebrated line: "Rocks, caves, lakes, fens, bogs, dens and shades of death." The reader's progress through the metrical construction of the syntax of listing, even though aided by the final phrase-stress and the internal rhymes and assonance, is itself a figure for contemplating this "universe of death." Pope thought of the syllabic paradigm of this line in his self-descriptive "And ten low words oft creep in one dull line," and John Dyer, in *The Fleece* (1757), simply alludes to it: "Woods, tow'rs, vales, caves, dells, cliffs, and torrent floods," borrowing, at most, a tincture of sublimity at the end. But Marvell's "In that wide Field how he his way should find" is immediately applicable to the question of a reader's finding his way through Milton's syntax, blank-verse paragraphs, and complex similes. And it is beautifully handled in closing the rhymed couplet that *Paradise Lost* itself disdained to use. Marvell's glossing of Milton's style is more than an allusive echo, but rather an instructive following by an expositor of the footing of a poet's feet—perhaps even in so crude a way as placing one's own feet in some hardened figurative footsteps in order to demonstrate what it looked and felt like to walk in such a way as to produce them.

The peculiar effect by which English "song" summons up the *carmen* in "charms" is expanded in a fourfold way by G. M. Hopkins, whose morphophonemic fictions are far more complex than the rhythmic packing which frames them. At the opening of a poem called "Binsey Poplars," Hopkins addresses the dear trees, which

Quelled or quenched in leaves the leaping sun,
All felled, felled, are all felled,
　　Of a fresh and following folded rank
　　　　Not spared, not one . . .

The word "folded" follows the word "following" and, ultimately, the reiterated "felled" with most remarkable consequences. In the first place, it is as if there were some typical Germanic strong-verb ablaut at work here, yielding (once, or formerly) "folded" as a strange historical participle of "felled." Then there is the matter of "folded" itself, lexically speaking: the rank is folded over in the sense that it is staggered, or wrapped onto itself [fold¹ < OE *faldan*]. But the trees are also folded not in another sense of the same word, but homonymically, like sheep [fold² < OE fald] following each other in a linear flocking. The "leaves" in the first of the quoted lines exerts some other pressure on "folded," causing it momentarily to resonate with an echo of *folium* (even as there is a trace of another Latin false—but figuratively relevant—etymon, *fello* in "felled": the chopping-down of the trees having been accomplished by fell, as well as felling, blows. All the other etyma here are Germanic, and the Latin false-roots only provide evocative shadowing. (Nevertheless, as the poem progresses, puns on a Latin etymon—as in an insistence on the *specere* of "seeing" in the repeated word "especial" and, particularly, in the identification "self" and *sylva* in the insistence on how the "strokes of havoc únselve / The sweet especial scene"— become central.)

Etymology—not, as Curtius discussed it, as "a mode of thought,"[11] but more specifically as a frame for trope—is foregrounded here, and the sequence "felled/felled/felled/following/folded" engages both diachronic and synchronic fables of sound-shift. But Hopkins is perfectly capable of leaving words almost totally at linguistically referential ease: notice that "rank," which is only faintly agitated by being rhymed later on with "sank" and "bank," is never called on to breed a punning overtone on its adjectival homonym, "rank" = profuse, excessive, offensive (< OE *ranc*). And observe that the wonderful patterning of the first line engages no historical linguistics whatsoever; its visionary morphology is all synchronic, and the momentary narratology of the alliterating /l/ and where it goes, and the assonant pairs of /e/ and /iy/ and finally, the /n/ that underscores the appropriateness of "quenched" for the "sun" assumes that no word ever meant anything else nor had any other form.[12]

It is this sort of purely synchronic attention to words that characterizes so much of what, following Dr. Johnson, we have called "representative versification," the purely associative analysis which legislates morphophonemes and symbolic values for them in the idiolect of a particular poem, and, often, of a single line.

Hopkins's interinanimated words are like Milton's in that they all have personal histories and in that, as with modern psychologies, authentic inner states and essences are referred to stages in past lives. Poets like Spenser and Wallace Stevens tend to have more purely synchronic poetic grammars. Minor verse will seldom exhibit much of this fictive linguistic thought, seeking to attain a style without raising any disturbing questions about it. Words that work and play and breed and brood together will naturally take their phonological bodies very seriously indeed, even as their poets who dally nicely with them always do. The Duchess's advice to Alice, "Take care of the sense and the sounds will take care of themselves," is as compromised by economic actuality as its prototype about pence and pounds got to be by the nineteenth century (it was coined, I believe, by William Lowndes around 1700). Taking care of the pence will keep your mind off the pounds you'll never have, and, for bad poetry, the situation is indeed analogous. Only the rich can offer such advice, and only someone whose word-hoard is sufficiently rich can afford to take what the Duchess has to say without danger.

11 ❧

The Poetics of Character

The guiles of poetry extend from fictions about language—about elements and uses and patterns—to the larger matter of feigning person, place, thing and the compounding of these three in narrative. Ultimately, they reach the largest notion of poetic "argument," or ultimate mythmaking, itself. Of these greater linguistic constructions two things might be observed: that they are designated by the more usual use of the term *fiction* to mean prose narrative, and that their linguistic nature is normally suppressed in the apprehension of them. Fictional character, for example, feels less like a matter of written language than even a chronicle does. Modernist and later literary theory, unhappy with romantic acceptance of fictions of person (Shakespeare being perhaps the focal point here), have for decades been decomposing characters into complex polymers of discourse, as it were. But more recently, imaginative criticism has had some fascinating things to say about the phenomenology of persons in books, as well as claiming that the phenomenology was important per se. Martin Price's elegant and powerful *Forms of Life* recently rescued a good part of the notion of fictional character from zealous deconstruction. John Burt, in two excellent essays, has also begun to reconstruct appropriate ways of dealing with fictional persons in regard to the power of their own discourse—as well as their authors'—to feign personal presence.[1]

The following observations on the poetics of character will stipulate simply that characters—rather than spirits, Muses, Dantean shades, and the personages of romance—are elements of stories first invented for modernity by Chaucer, then lost and reinvented even more grandly by Shakespeare. Literary characters seem to invent, and consequently control and even transform, themselves by what they say and by their apparent knowledge of what they have said. The old-fashioned dissolution of character by, say, L. C.

Knights in a celebrated essay of an earlier era called "How Many Children Had Lady Macbeth?" was no more effective than the newfangled ones have been; the notional "children" of literary characters are frequently born in subsequent books by subsequent authors, their determining substance being not DNA but convention. Just so do their lost childhoods appear in prior figurations: Falstaff's determining childhood lies not in something gleaned from after-the-fact psychoanalysis, but in the more primitive *miles gloriosus,* the swaggering bully of earlier drama.

In any event, the census of Lady Macbeth's get, on both sides of the blanket, is an ongoing, open-ended task of literary criticism. But I am not concerned with that arena of literary theory in the banlieux of good sense where nothing refers to anything, and where the pious still abstain from utterance of the forbidden tetragrammaton *word,* substituting the euphemistic *sign* instead. It shall thus be assumed that the question of whether literary characters are more characteristic of the books they inhabit or of elements in the lives of their authors and readers is an important and open one.

Contemporary critical fashion among younger academics often tends to read these literary tropes we delight to continue to call characters as signs, but of other sorts. Talking of, for example, Panurge or Pangloss, Moll Flanders or Molly Bloom, Dorothea Brooke or Little Dorrit, Ivan Karamazov or Miss Lonelyhearts as semaphors whose signs are only proclamations of their own inability to designate anything interesting is going out of fashion now, despite the continuing barking of antiintellectual watchdogs. Instead, the pressures of critical fashion are now of another sort, and we now see reduction of fictional persons to emblems of class or sexual difference—two different kinds of interpretive bottom line. It is almost as if two crudely reductive versions of something like reality were exacting a heroic revenge for having been banished from another reductive referential agenda.

On the other hand, some critics would link the notion of character with history.[2] This could lead to a fascinating consideration of historiography with regard not so much to its narrative figurations, but to its conception of person or agent. Or it might suggest, at least as a preliminary, a study of the history of the idea of fictional *character* in the abstract: Aristotle's term *ēthos,* which is usually translated as "character," seems to come about from a notion of habitual manner or disposition—an as it were characteristic something about someone which is his or her manner. In the *Poetics* (6.24), he is concerned to distinguish between character and fictional characters— *ēthe* are not *prattontai,* or agents, and agency itself is not "character," because it does not necessarily embody choice. But when we think of fictional persons, the fate of our language leads us to use, not a word derived from *prattonta,* but instead one derived from the other Greek word that for us

covers just those two concepts which Aristotle wished in the *Poetics* to separate. It is through our modern word *character* that I should like to consider
something of the poetics of person.

For poetry, words—like the complex structures of words called books—
are as much like people as like things, and the very word *character* has a tale
to tell of itself—indeed, as much of a tale as any Shakespearean character
might. The Greek word *charactēros* means a sharp stylus and, by extension,
the incised mark it makes. (Hence our term "written characters".) Even in
Greek the sense got extended to include a significant attribute that figuratively "marks," distinguishes, or even (to use another word whose modern
general sense seems to derive from that of an impressed or cut image) *typifies*
a person or thing. One could easily mistake this as the direct source of all
our modern uses of the word, including: "characteristic," the peculiar character of a person, an extension of that to mean something like "character-
isticness" as well as our sense of "fictional person." (Of a final sense of
someone's having "character" by way of bearing "characteristic moral
strength of some sort, moral weight," I shall speak a bit at the end.) And
yet character *types,* moral semaphores who bear only their distinguishing
marks (whether of Jonsonian humors comedy, the commedia dell'arte, the
opera, etc.), seem just not what we mean by literary characters, by persons
made of an author's and their own words, but who seem to stand midway
between being mere words and actual people.

A type is more of a corpse of a character than a living being. Yet it is by
another historical route than that which extends directly from the sense of
"mark" or "inscribed sign" that our word for the nature of particular personhood reaches us. The so-called Theophrastan character—the "sketch,"
or quick, summary, and exemplary description of a personal or social type—
originates with the eponymous third- to fourth-century Athenian writer and
his descriptions of human vices. The form flourishes in England in the early
seventeenth century, coincidentally with the drama; the word itself comes
to mean, first, the piece of writing, then, its topic. John Earle's *Microcos-
mography* (1633) contains a Character of a Child which begins

> Is a man in small letter, yet the best copy of Adam before he tasted of Eve or
> the apple; and he is happy whose small practice is the world can only write
> his character. He is nature's fresh picture newly drawn in oil, which time, and
> much handling, dims and defaces. His soul is yet a white paper unscribbled
> with observations of the world, wherewith, at length, it becomes a blurred
> notebook.

The obsession of this passage with writing, its tropes of the written character of characteristics, and, most particularly, the apparent prefiguration of
Locke's epistemological *tabula rasa* in an ad hoc conceit cannot help but

catch the contemporary eye, with its sensitivity to questions of representation. Indeed, the sketch continues in a prophetic way:

> Nature and his parents alike dandle him, and tice him on with a bait of sugar to a draught of wormwood. He plays yet, like a young 'prentice the first day, and is not come to his task of melancholy. All the language he speaks yet is tears, and they serve him well enough to express his necessity. His hardest labour is his tongue, as if he were loth to use so deceitful an organ; and he is best company with it when he can but yet prattle. We laugh at his foolish sports, but his game is our earnest; and his drums, rattles, and hobby-horses, but the emblems and mocking of man's business. His father hath writ him as his own little story, wherein he reads those days of his life that he cannot remember, and sighs to see what innocence he has out-lived.

But let us notice the way in which the meaning of the word *character* shifts. It comes to mean not merely, as here, the genre of the descriptive prose sketch, nor even the outward marks of the person the sketch delineates, but rather some kind of essential nature—of, indeed, a *type* of person, whether defined by biology or by culture, by age, sex, physical condition, caste, role, métier—propounded in, and by, the piece of writing. An internalizing of the meaning of *character*—a move from a perceptible mark to a definitive inner state far more subtle than a physiological recipe of humors— soon follows. But it is not until the mid-eighteenth century that we find *character* designating a well-known or fictional personage: the *OED* lists Henry Fielding, in 1749, as a source of the first attestation, and perhaps appropriately so.

Our notion of character, in short, involves precisely what cannot be pinned down by a Theophrastan sketch, whether Samuel Butler's hilarious and almost endless *Character of a Hermetic Philosopher* or Wordsworth's "The Character of the Happy Warrior." Here is a modern novelist on this question:

> Begin with an individual, and before you know it you find that you have created a type; begin with a type, and you find that you have created—nothing. That is because we are all queer fish, queerer behind our faces and voices than we want anyone to know or than we can know ourselves. When I hear a man proclaiming himself an "average, honest, open fellow," I feel pretty sure that he has some definite and perhaps terrible abnormality which he has agreed to conceal—and his protestation of being average and honest and open is his way of reminding himself of his misprision.

In these opening lines of Scott Fitzgerald's fine story "The Rich Boy" the last sentence treats an aspect of self as if it were a text, the purer dialectic of Freud's Reaction-formation is interestingly revised, and the implications of the phrase "abnormality which he has agreed to conceal" ("agreed"? and with whom?) slip casually but resonantly by. For a rhetorician, this is all a simple matter. For a novelist, someone committed to a tale whose agents are characters rather than tropes, the ways in which persons make representations of—and to—themselves is crucial.

The character of our idea of character itself is indeed elusive. The written characters in which spoken language (and not only that) is encoded, and the human characters who live by—or at least in among—codes of another sort, both partake of having been written. And while I share John Bayley's distaste of the critical stance which would add that there was nothing more to say, I nevertheless want to continue to brood over what the fictiveness of characterizing essences, and of persons embodying them, and of persons transcending them, might all mean. Alasdair MacIntyre's interesting stipulative redefinition of *character* (in *After Virtue*) involves an association of role and code: for him characters constitute "a very special type of social role which places a certain kind of moral restraint on the personality of those who inhabit them."[3] Then consider the ever-varying pas-de-deux of role and personality played out in novelistic and dramatic characters, and the strange notion of personality exhibited by film-star acting, in which the character of the player speaks through the ad hoc mask of a particular movie's role, in another sense of the word. (This last also reminds one that the etymology of *persona,* the actor's mask, from *per* + *sona,* or voice sounding through, is a poetical fancy—we are assured today that it was an Etruscan word and hence etymologically ineffable.)[4]

And this leads to what I suppose must inevitably have been my own poetic concerns in this matter. I do not of course invoke what William Collins called "the poetical character" in his famous ode thereon, where the sense of the word hovers mysteriously between a half-allegorized, post-Theophrastan essence and the personified romantic Apollo of the "rich-haired youth of morn" in the poem. I allude rather to that fascinating array of literary characters—*carminis personae* perhaps we might call them—all referred to as "I" in lyric poetry. We might put it another way by observing that a character-type, or paradigmatic figure, is invented for subsequent poetry by the Greek lyrists (Sappho, Archilochus, Alcaeus, and their followers) and in the Psalms. All the great "I"'s in the history of our poetry—those of Horace, Catullus, the Roman elegists, medieval love poetry, Dante, Petrarch, Sidney, Shakespeare, and practically everyone thereafter—are in some way revisions of those Greek and Hebrew prototypes. They are, moreover, as self-conscious, as aware of their own revisionary status, as any great dramatic character is. The "I" of Shakespeare's *Sonnets* represents as complex a transumption of Du Bellay, Sidney, and Spenser, as, say, Hamlet does of Kyd's Hieronymo or Falstaff of a stock *miles gloriosus.*

On the other hand, dramatic lyrics per se—not songs from plays, but lyric poems independent of any dramatic text—are like dramatic monologues in that situations, and indeed characters as well, lie latent in their utterances. The act of reading entails the interpretive "reconstruction" of something—

a play, a novel—which was never in fact ruined. But whereas in dramatic monologue, the implicit material can be narrative and/or epistemologically meditative, in dramatic lyric the external situation is largely trivial. It is instead an internal state, a condition of a certain kind of consciousness, which is to be inferred from an expression of it. (In this, lyric poetry is indeed lifelike: how else, outside of literature, do we have access to other minds? Yet in our inability to ask questions of, and get answers from it, lyric poetry is not at all lifelike, but picturelike: once having sung, it is mute.)

But it is now generally, and reasonably, agreed that all lyric personae, no matter how *propriae,* are essentially dramatic ones. (The lyric "I" was being deconstructed by modernist criticism before those who coined the term could read.) The "dramatic" context of the lyric ego can be minimal—some kind of *Ich-Du* relation—or quite complex, with many other ghosts of characters, summoned up by various incantations of allusion, haunting the stanzaic room. These may be momentarily present as personages, like those of romance, rather than novel or drama: Fräulein von Kulp, in Eliot's "Gerontion," a creature of one glimpse, or the Canon Aspirin of Wallace Stevens. But long lyrical cycles (*La Vita Nuova,* Petrarch's *Rime, Astrophel and Stella, The Temple, Song of Myself,* Emily Dickinson's *MSS*) are, whether precursors or inheritors of major long poems, romances in themselves. Perhaps the most minimal situation in which the lyrical ego is generated occurs in rhetorical address, the mode of prosopopeia engaged by putting any noun into a vocative (in English, "O [Noun]!"). The persona of the speaker is a kind of shadow cast by the prosopopeia, outlining the stance taken toward it by the utterer of the "O—!"

The relations of the dramatic to the literal propria persona it usually purports to be are very complex. They lead to that peculiar dialectic of "biography" in powerful readings of poetic texts: the personal "truth" of the poem must, at a first stage of reading, be held in abeyance, and the "I" treated as a fiction. (This is perhaps to say that the hermeneutic principles of Brooks and Warren's *Understanding Poetry* must remain a necessary primer.) Only the bottom rungs of the ladder, at which all I's—whether designating Yeats as "sixty-year-old, smiling public man" or Crazy Jane— are fictional characters, will give access to the higher ones, from which we indeed can recover the Browning in his Andrea del Sarto, the Frost in his own "I." And indeed, our process of interpretive recovery is probably identical in the two situations, although partaking more of "analysis interminable," as Freud put it, in the second one. It might be added that contemporary literary verse of that literal-minded, "confessional" sort presents none of these interpretive problems, probably because it is not true poetry.

This general matter of the relations between the "characters" of lyric and meditative poetry, on the one hand, and fiction and drama on the other may be considered in the light of another relation, that of personification to characterization. Personification is the trope of *prosopopeia:* George Puttenham, the sixteenth-century rhetorician, called it the "counterfeit in personation" (as opposed to "the counterfeit countenance," or *prosopographia,* by which he meant fictional character). Personification can be considered a central figure of that expanded mode of lyric which is the poetry of our modernity. This is all the more true if what we might call the figures of location and reification—of loosely and analogously allegorizing places and objects—are considered as being ancillary modes of it. What is most poetic about *personifying* is the way in which it avoids or transcends or tropes what in a more abstract sense of our word we call *characterizing.* Giving to a mode of feeling or believing, or a shade of consciousness, a counterfeit countenance is actually to refuse it a reductively abstract sort of essence. The "figure of capable imagination" who rushes down the hill of vision, past the nay-saying Mrs. Alfred Uruguay making her velveted, asinine way up the Montevideo of the real (in Wallace Stevens's wildly funny poem) is a poetical person with more at stake in him, and on his riding, than his youth, his phosphorescent hair, his poor dress, and his verbal silence might suggest. He may typify the poetical character in rushing downhill from certain kinds of literary criticism's assault on the summit of the real, the historical. Certainly, narrow personifications can partake of the limitations of the "character-types," the moral semaphores I mentioned earlier. On the other hand, we can believe that an even momentarily personified Zeal needs continuing maintenance doses of caution in order not to be crazy, whereas the abstract condition of zealousness does not per se admit of any such entailment. But that is part of another matter, of the contention between fictions and paradigms for power over moral understanding.

Longer poetic fictions pose harder problems. In Kafka's splendid parable called "The Truth about Sancho Panza" it is outrageously suggested that the don is Sancho's own fiction. This is certainly a very nice revenge taken by the spirit of prose romance against the hosts of the novel which had driven it underground, as it were, so that like the Celtic "little people" it lay hidden and protected in minority—Frankenstein, Alice in Wonderland, Andersen's little mermaid—(save in America) throughout the nineteenth century. Cervantes's great book inaugurates the novel by saying implicitly even to *The Faerie Queene,* "You're nothing but a pack of delusions of metaphors." And it does so by means of a character, a *character,* who never quite learns this, loyally accompanied by another one who knows it from the start. Spenser is the ancestor of our major speculative poetry (and, in America, of Hawthorne and Melville), as Cervantes is of Dickens and Eliot and Balzac. Never was a maker of fictions, of "feignèd colours shading a true case," more concerned than Spenser with *history,* being unable from the outset of *The Faerie Queene* to name Calliope or Clio as his muse, and having to make up a new one out of both. (But think of the consequences for post-Petrarchan poetic fictions of a time and place wherein a figure at the end of an absolutely *aufgehoben* Beatrice-Laura-Stella-Cynthia-Astraea-Delia series, Elizabeth, is in real, historical control, capable of imprisoning the sonneteer not in the tower of her glances but in the tower of her Tower.) But think of Spenser's personages, of Britomart; or Guyon; or Artegall; or of the witch whose gormless son is smitten with the inaccessible beauty of Florimell and who, lest he become violent, makes a simulacrum for him, a golem girl inspirited with a male, Belial-like demon; or of the ogre named Lust, who comes home to the captive girls in his cave and, contemplating the feast he will make of them, falls to the floor and masturbates. Even in these remarkable figures we do not feel the presence of characters. But to talk of Mammon's House; of Isis Church; of Acrasia's bower and Mt. Acidale, is to invoke places that are as characteristically present as Prospero or Lady Macbeth. I think, in fact, that *location* in romance is a much more powerful, more—in the novelistic sense—*characteristic* trope than personification, and that places are more like novelistic or dramatic characters than persons are.[5] Certainly in the complex prose romances we all compose for ourselves every night, where one *is* seems to predominate over, indeed, even to generate, *who* is there with one and even perhaps *what* one is oneself. But the poetics of dreaming is a matter that poses vast questions of its own, and the nature of dream personages, more like those of romance and even lyric than like those of play or narrative, is too vast to be dealt with here. And yet it might be observed that the legacy of romance to the history of fictional character includes both manifest and latent residues. Various sorts of temples and labyrinths (as Angus Fletcher has characterized them) in *The Faerie Queene* are like various sorts of mothers and fathers in drama or story. But the modern forms also inherit whole genres of personage that include simulacra, doubles, shadows, animated representations such as Spenser's look- and sound-alikes and his artificial Florimell that lead to Hawthorne's brilliant reworking of such episodes in his great story "Feathertop"; the doubles of Poe, Dostoyevsky, and Borges. Not so much representations of people, they are more like representations of such representations, shadows of shadows rather than of substances. Like personages in dreams, they can be strangely placelike. And, for all their representational pathology, they raise again a central question about fictional characters.[6]

Representations of persons are, of course, tropes. But a fashionable contemporary mode of insisting on this, of decomposing character into mere written characters (or "signs"), has all of the intellectual charm and force of writing about, say, my colleague Professor X, "but he's really only a lot of proteins!" Of a famous heuristic series of responses by a great Zen master to the question "What is Buddha?," only one of them—"Made of wood and covered with gold!"—is a deconstruction prescribed specifically for a particular epistemological disease. To mistake this as an answer to all instances of the question might be to earn a rap on the head. For literary characters *are* characteristically personlike. What we must indeed remember about representations of persons is the remarkable nature and power of the preposition "of" which connects the two incommensurables.

But after all, if we were to attempt to write a Theophrastan sketch, a "Character of the Literary Character," we should have to point out one characteristic which is too easily distorted in the characterization of it by extreme literalists. I should say a word about it in conclusion, because the quality of "lifelikeness" which misunderstood notions of character insist that we address may indeed be saved for serious discourse if it is not taken too literally or reductively. Lifelikeness in a fictional character can mean the irreducibility of a trope—that is, the "depth" or "roundedness" of personages in a tale will often be a matter of the depth or roundedness of something they are said to say or to do, and, hence, of that authorial saying. This constitutive power accomplishes what descriptive detail can seldom do. Chaucer's characters in *The Canterbury Tales* are truly Shakespearean precursors because they are authors themselves: their varying modes of narration, genres of story, consciousness of audience all shape the tellers as well as the tales. The questionable regime of the Monk, the "outrider" whose modern descendant is perhaps J. F. Powers's Father Burner (in "Prince of Darkness"), reveals his own sense that he may be pushing things a bit too far by the overkill of his narrative orthodoxy. We ask ourselves of the fiction what we would of a person: does "he" *know* what he's doing, deliberately choosing to relate an absolutely square series of "tragic" stories of the fall of great and powerful people? or is the lack of imagination manifested in his choice of tale and his telling of it itself a function or cause of a life of bent vows? It is that very problematic aspect of the personage, our sense that we would have to know him much better in order to resolve the question, that constitutes the lifelikeness. Unlike the unresolved questions presented by "flat" characters (which means by bad and unpoetical writing), these are significant tropes of those rhetorical probings with which we do our own moral questioning of ourselves and others.

On the other hand, consider Chaunteclere and Pertelote, the barnyard couple in the wildly imaginative, parodic, and humanely affirmative story told by the otherwise totally self-effacing Nun's Priest. They elicit even more interpretive musing. (And thereby, we might say, possess the figurative depth into which such musing might move.) Chaucer has his own first-person narrator barely describe the Nun's Priest, and all of the depth emerging in him is displaced onto the principal characters in the story he tells. It is a tale which follows the almost open-ended narration of the Monk that has been mercifully broken off by the Knight and the Host, their patiences variously outworn. Ultimately, we have to decide whether Chaucer knew what he was doing in making the matter of the Monk so resonantly prob-lematic or, on the other hand, whether the ambiguity results from (*a*) his bungling or (*b*) the fussy ineptitude of an interpreter. (One would think that eighty-odd years of modern Chaucer criticism ought to have resolved the matter, but of course it hasn't, which probably means that Chaucer was a true poet.)

The Nun's Priest's story presents an analogous but tougher problem. The cock Chaunteclere, having dreamt of an extremely vulpine-looking appari-tion's menacing him, discusses it with his favorite wife, Pertelote. They engage in learned debate, he maintaining the prophetic power of dreams, she trying to convince him that it was all something he had eaten. After a time, Chaunteclere refuses to continue the argument:

> Now let us speke of myrthe, and stynte al this.
> Madame Pertelote, so have I blis,
> Of o thyng God hath sent me large grace,
> For whan I see the beautee of youre face,
> Ye been so scarlet reed about youre eyen,
> It maketh al my drede for to dyen;

—And at this point, he adduces a common medieval Latin tag: "For al so siker as *In principio, / Mulier est hominis confusio*" which, in a moment of tender longing, he immediately mistranslates: "Madame, the sentence of this Latyn is, / 'Womman is mannes joye and al his blis,'" whereupon he flies down from his perch and takes erotic advantage of the broad ground to tread Pertelote twenty times before prime. This amorous distraction leads him to forget his dream and become careless of the fox—who, later on, almost eats him—in a descent that might have meant his total fall. Indeed, his first turning away from the argument with his wife in a half-admiring, half-condescending forsaking of her mind for her body has double ironic force. It is the prototype either of the most plangent and lovely of modes of reconciliation or, when performed by the unimaginative wretches that most people can be, what are fashionably called today "sexist" rhetorical moves. This very shift of attention leads to his downfall. Yet this is not because Pertelote was right—and because he therefore should have gone on debating with her to learn the truth—but, indeed, because she was quite, and dangerously, wrong. Abandoning the symposium for bed was not simply turning away from good advice.

But what of the mistranslation of the Latin? Conjoining it with the orig-inal generates the paradoxical metalinguistic assertion, *"Woman's is man's undoing means that woman is man's joy and all his bliss."* This promulgates a formulation of ruin as bliss, the topos of the *felix culpa* or paradox of the fortunate fall that is perhaps being enacted in the Nun's Priest's reticently "merry" tale. (That the words *"in principio"* are left untranslated points up even more the parodic aspect of the whole story. The first two words of Genesis in the Vulgate act as a kind of frame for the story that nobody in it, telling it, or hearing it can manifestly acknowledge. Only the master-framer, Chaucer, can do so, and only latently, by such an omission.) Putting the text and the translation together causes a principle momentarily to break out, as it were, from its hiding-place in an element of practice. But this is to treat the utterance as a sign alone, unreeling as if in some banderole in the sky of a northern Renaissance painting, and to cast Chaunteclere as a mere semaphore. Chaunteclere and Pertelote are personages of character, however. We must ask even more about the quotation and its mistranslation than would be asked by traditional contextualizing scholarship, or new-critical delight in paradox propounded, or fashionable post-structuralist delight in the eruption of narrative into moments of uttered or inscribed puzzle. Whenever a palpable mistake occurs in a fiction, the author's sophistication comes into question for a moment: where is the solecism to be located? In this instance, any of the following might be the case:

a. *Chaunteclere doesn't know the meaning of the Latin,* in which case his base pride of learning goeth before his fall and, moreover, the *confusio* of truth is deep: it's not just Latin that he gets wrong, but *that* Latin, got wrong in *that* way. This would be clear dramatic irony.

b. *Chaunteclere knows the meaning of the Latin, but he knows that Pertelote doesn't.* In this case his condescension is of another order entirely, and he is implying that Pertelote, that darling little airhead, had best not know of troubled matters between the sexes, no matter how much they were generated *in principio.* (This was the view taken by slightly more sophisticated Yale undergraduates of ca. 1960—trainees in a state-of-the-art upper-middle-class unimaginativeness about relations between the sexes shared by their companions at Vassar and Connecticut College for Women.)

c. *Chaunteclere knows that, and how, he is mistranslating; Pertelote knows likewise; Chaunteclere knows that Pertelote knows; Pertelote knows that Chaunteclere knows that she knows*—in short, that intimate, domestic, mentally caressing wit is in operation, the kind of wit which plays with truisms that clutter the landscape like natural hazards, and whose existence and danger all travelers must acknowledge, but which two loving adventurers must constantly acknowledge they have escaped. This is the married phase of the conspiracies (for example, "we're not dull, sublunary lovers") constantly being invoked by Donne. Every sophisticated reader of novels would probably want to continue the rhetorical analysis of the utterance of the mistranslation in his or her own way. But this is perhaps to say that the paragraph—Dickensian, Eliotic, Jamesian, Proustian, or whatever—that might result would provide ample proof that it was a true fictional character whose depths were being probed.

In drama, as in narration heavily glossed by a narrator or observer, such problems either do not arise or are quickly solved; they may even be posed as problems the quest for whose solution becomes part of the narrative itself. To dramatize this scene from Chaucer would demand some kind of mute reaction from Pertelote; a dramatist and/or director would have to opt for something like (*a*) or (*b*) or (*c*). Not to choose (*c*) would be crude, but such, alas, are so many pious readings of great poetry. It might be observed here that the mode of dramatic monologue is interesting, in considering the generation of literary character, in another way. In its highest, Browning-esque (rather than Tennysonian, monodramatic) form, it conjures up speakers whose primary characteristic is a synecdochal problematic aspect. They exist in, and as, fragments of a large fiction. Even in the simpler of them (say, "Count Gismond," where the indeterminacy is of event and motive, or in its original companion-piece, "My Last Duchess," where the situation is more like a nasty reversal of the Chaucerian scene, with a question of who knows what and who knows what is known by whom) the problem not only generates, but may be said to *be,* the depth. Imagine, for example, the scene from Chaucer evoked only in a dramatic monologue of Chaunteclere's, a Browningesque "X to Y" in its complexity, but in a traditional rhetorical pattern which goes back, after all, to Ovid's *Heroides*. Chaucer himself—or rather, his narrator, here the Nun's Priest—cannot deal with the nuances of (*c*), and Pertelote's reaction is wisely suppressed. Although we might imagine a Boccaccian debate after the story, the questions up for contention in *The Canterbury Tales* are themselves conventionalized and less subtle than the narrative machinery framing them.

But questions of narrative—whether of the wanderings, missions, and unfoldings of romance or of the playing-out of life's dealt hands in novels— are not my province here. It is primarily with the character or essence of fictional character or personhood, with which I have been concerned. Let us take a parting glance at perhaps our most puzzling use of the modern word. Among Emerson's mysterious semantic variations on the theme of Aristotelian *ēthos* played in his essay on "Character" (1844) we hear that last sense of *character* as integral personal force or weight (for example, not as in "a man of good character" but in "someone of character," as one might say, "someone of quality"). That Emerson does not simply mean "force" or "power," but rather something more like the "potential energy" of classical physics is clear from his account of something in certain men "which begot an expectation that outran all performance. The largest part of their power was latent. This is what we call Character,—a reserved force which acts directly by presence, and without means . . . a certain undemonstrable force, a Familiar or Genius." Emerson's typical mode of expansion shifts the concept from being an essential force to a forceful essence, to a sort of *genius loci* of someone's persona or nature—ultimately, a sort of eponymous fictional character in the book of oneself. "Character is centrality," he says later on in the essay, then immediately repudiates an idea of character as central to a self, but rather glosses that centrality as being "the impossibility of being displaced or overset." In other words, what makes one the central figure in the book of one's life.

Emersonian character thus confounds again the notions of "mark," "marking," "essence," "fictional person so marked," "inner quality for which the mark is a sign," and "strength or force possessed by and or all of these." Ultimately, fictional person and distinguishing feature seem inextricably linked for him. It is as if Emersonian character were characteristic of all strongly propounded fictional characters, constituting something of their poetic nature, their fictiveness, their real originality.

12 🐾

The Philosopher's Cat:
Examples and Fictions

"Perhaps it is of more value," said Wallace Stevens, "to infuriate philosophers than to go along with them."[1] I'm not sure that I want the possible value of the following remarks to be so tested. I write as a poet who has wondered from time to time what a *via media* would be like that ran between these two alternatives, and who has indeed wandered into the no-man's-land in which such a path might somewhere lie. But in any event, the ways in which poets go along with philosophers (I mean true poets and real philosophers) may necessarily be infuriating, perhaps eventually to both. And yet the picture which Stevens implicitly invoked—of a cat-and-mouse relation between philosophers quick to anger and poets quick to bait—is nevertheless an extraordinarily domestic scene. It is played out in an eternal Tom-and-Jerry animated cartoon (in what the Hollywood age of double features in movie houses called "continuous performances") down in the pantry of our speculative life.

Poetry's views of philosophy have always been problematic. The "gentle lady, young and most fair, who gazed at me from a window, very compassionately, so far as it appeared, so that all compassion ["pietade"] seemed gathered in her"[2] was, for the Dante of *La Vita Nuova,* a kind of alleviating presence in the face of primary loss. But for subsequent generations, the gaze of philosophy could easily turn poets to stone and their work into versified doctrine. James Merrill, in an unpublished remark, avowed that "I tend to look away from Philosophy, as I would from the sight of a nude grandparent. No doubt she has played her genetic role in poem after poem, endowing this one with a fine brow and that one with contrariety, traits which they themselves, caught in their sensual music, set no store by." But one purely terminological point should be noted here. Neither Keats's simply rhetorical question in "Lamia"—"Do not all charms fly / At the mere touch of cold philosophy?"—nor Wordsworth's unimpressive outcry in "A Poet's Epitaph,"

> Philosopher! a fingering slave,
> One that would peep and botanize
> Upon his mother's grave

(which could easily be thought of as sanctifying, as well as desecrating, the spot) is at issue here. "Philosophy" simply means "natural science" in these instances: Keats is adducing Newton's reduction of the rainbow, emblem of divine covenant, to a prismatic phenomenon (a reduction hailed as a mental triumph in much eighteenth-century verse which Keats might have felt to be inimical to poetry in any case).

Poets can enlist, with varying success, what they can perhaps misread as generally antiphilosophical remarks by philosophers themselves, such as Kierkegaard's well-known aphorism "What the philosophers say about Reality is often as disappointing as a sign you see in a shop window, which reads: Pressing Done Here. If you brought your clothes in to be pressed, you would be fooled; for the sign only is for sale."[3] Or, more problematically, Wittgenstein's "I think I summed up my attitude when I said: philosophy ought really to be written only as a poetic composition" [Philosophie dürfte man eigentlich nur dichten], coupled with his quotation of Longfellow:

> In the elder days of art,
> Builders wrought with greatest care
> Each minute and unseen part,
> For the gods are everywhere

to which he added "(This could serve me as a motto)."[4] Yet this did not make him of the poets' party, because only another poet could construe the notion of finishing hidden surfaces (or, for a set designer, painting the back sides of flats) as part of the extravagance or ulteriority of poetry.

Antiphilosophical satire, written in the name of presumably broader human concerns, has frequently fixed on sterile metaphysics as the essence of pedantic hairsplitting, as the unwitting parable of fiddling while a moral Rome burns. More recently (since Kant, at any rate, and going back probably to Descartes), epistemology has borne the brunt of such ridicule even while it captured the imagination of poets, novelists, and even—from Cézanne onward—painters, any of whom might have been invoked in such attacks as conservators of the human spirit. The reformation of metaphysics into epistemology (the redirection, for exmple, of a concern for what the world *is* into a concern for what we know, and how we know the world or anything else) can be paralleled by the somewhat less glorious revision of theology into psychology. These are both reformations, even in our Western historical sense, because they internalize the space in which the world (on the one hand) or the god (on the other) can be grasped. This internalization can also be described as a sort of troping: a statement of what is is seen as a figurative way of expressing what one knows; a relation to a god is treated as a trope or figure of an internal or psychological state of believing, hoping, trusting, depending, and so forth. The subject of both epistemology and psychology is the nature of the self. But the self has many natures: Kant, Freud, and Wittgenstein were all well aware of this, and strong poems employing the word "I" designate thereby not merely different fictive persons, but different kinds of fictive selves.

But poetical stories about philosophy can be another matter. These would turn the history of thought into a romance, as in the vision of Ishmael (in Melville's *Moby-Dick*), of a whaling-boat, with a sperm whale tied to one side of it, a right whale to the other—the American mind borne along between Plato and Locke, between poetic and schematic thought. This particular unchristened whaling-boat, it might be added, could have been named *Ralph Waldo Emerson,* who allegorizes the relation of philosophical positions in a more dialectical way. He writes in *Nature,* purportedly claiming that his own experience of an American rural day precludes the need for libraries, histories, Europes, that "broad noon shall be my England of the senses and understanding; the night shall be my Germany of mystic philosophy and dreams." (The ulterior effect of this is dialectical at another level. The whole passage is about how, just as one needs a sense of noon vs. midnight in order to cope with two philosophies, one needs to be able to read Hume vs. Hegel, say, in the hieroglyphs presented to us by noon and midnight in order to grasp their true relation.)

The contemporary poet A. R. Ammons seemingly turns away from such a notion in a poem called "Gravelly Run":

no use to make any philosophies here:
   I see no
god in the holly, hear no song from
the snowbroken weeds: Hegel is not the winter
yellow in the pines: the sunlight has never
heard of trees . . .

But the way in which Ammons seeks here to reclaim gods, songs, philosophies, and consciousness generally for the natural scene—he does so by explicitly denying that they are there, that they need be put there—is by means of a powerful, but not unfamiliar, mode of American poetic irony: he denies that he sees what Emerson saw, *because* Ammons knows that he must see in the way that Emerson sees. The running water in his poem asks, if not philosophical questions, at least questions that are not trivially about philosophizing.

Finally, of course, poets can willfully or not misread philosophers' terms, examples, arguments, and even rhetorical topoi, in their own way. A notable occasion of this would be Wallace Stevens's apparent misprision of Descartes. The latter refers in his *Third Meditation* to a "first idea of the sun,"[5] purely in the sense of an unorganized perception. Stevens takes it in the grander sense of a prior trope, an original myth, a primal concept or "first idea," in "It Must Be Abstract" (*Notes Toward A Supreme Fiction,* 1.1–3). Or again, consider how any allegorizing bias of the sort toward which poetry inclines might take, out of context, Wittgenstein's remark that "the limitless of the visual fields is clearest [*am klarsten*] when we are seeing nothing in complete darkness,"[6] which sounds to a poet's ear like a parable even as it unrolls. All of these might well produce philosophical scorn, if not outright infuriation.

The Reverend Sydney Smith, passing through a noisome street across which two women were screaming at each other, and hearing his companion comment on the way such people settled their differences, remarked, "But you see, they are arguing from different premises." The two meanings of "argue" in this celebrated piece of wit are those which give point to the more obvious pun on "premises." It is in some figurative version of physical premises—topics, occasions, formal structures like what Wordsworth called the sonnet's "scanty plot of ground"—that poetry propounds its own arguments. There is yet a third sense of the word "argument," meaning a story, a narrative, a subject matter, discussed in an earlier chapter.[7] It is these—Emerson called them "meter-making arguments"—that are poetry's concern, and when the domestic quarrel between philosophy and poetry becomes public and goes out of doors, it is not just from two opposite or adjacent buildings, but from two different sorts of premises, that the two, again in two different ways, argue.

The contention is not like that of a lovers' quarrel, but seems more like a family one to the degree that both poets and philosophers have common ancestors. Empedocles, Parmenides, Xenophanes, and other pre-Socratics were poets, writing their philosophy and their science in verse.[8] One might observe, however, that the sixth-century B.C. Xenophanes, with a philosopher's sense of injured justice, bewails in a poem the fact that athletes are praised above neglected philosophers like, specifically, himself, whereas Pindar, a couple of generations later, argues from the poet's shadowy premises and contrives to praise victorious athletes in ways that redound to the greater glory and more lasting fame of the maker of such brilliant, complex, and (never admitting this) devious praise.

And yet the battle between poetry and philosophy can be seen as descending not from a family quarrel after all, but from an internal one. The war declared by the philosopher Plato upon the poet in himself has been brilliantly chronicled by Eric Havelock and glossed by Iris Murdoch and Jacques

Derrida. Plato's follower Aristotle, as if claiming some kind of victory for one side, shunned Plato's whole poetic legacy: the dramatic form of his dialogues, his parables and fictions, the very strategies by which representation and poetic substance (even in Homer himself) are discredited.[9] Aristotle retains only the useful, homely mode of exemplification, and thenceforth, philosophy would cleave to univocal examples rather than rich and dangerous parables. Over two thousand years later, John Milton, in the midst of an argument purportedly from philosophical premises about the duty of a just society to allow anything, bad or good, to be published (but not, let us remember, necessarily to survive in print), recapitulates, in *Areopagitica,* Plato's move. At first, latently, he contrives throughout the essay to elaborate the metaphor of book as human body—implying that a text lies somewhere between being a thing and a person. And then, manifestly, in a famous passage in which he condemns the "fugitive and cloistered virtue, unexercised and unbreathed, that never sallies out and seeks her adversary," he says of "our sage and serious poet Spenser" that he dares be known to think him "a better teacher than Scotus or Aquinas." By this he means not only to praise a protestant Renaissance poet over two medieval philosophers, but, in the context of intellectual and moral virtue seen as strife, to praise parable and allegory over schematic exposition, for making moral meanings clear. Personified and localized moral abstractions, sent forth into combat or erotic trial, can better represent the role of those concepts in conscious human lives than can expositions which might from time to time descend to the use of examples.

A philosophical example—what may clarify, typify, or diagram a point in some other way for the moment—is fundamentally different from the poet's art, which has to puzzle the reader as much as it has to resolve his puzzlement. An example acts like a onetime diagram on a classroom blackboard; a poetic trope is more like a systematic erasure—clear and obscure, bold and shady—of received diagrams. Sir Philip Sidney, during the youth of English literature, affirmed poetry's distance from philosophy as well as from history; and certainly Hobbes, Locke, and Hume, who provided the main course of philosophizing in English, kept their front lines firm by continually edging out of no-man's-land. Hobbes, who held imagination (even if it wasn't what Wordsworth or Shelley or Stevens or we ourselves mean by it) to be a disease of thought, could make some interesting observations about the relation of poetic genre to social structure, but these observations might as well have been (compare them, for example, to some analogous pages of Vico) amused and concerned notes on fashionable lace collars by a man who cared a good deal for the way he dressed.

In this main line of philosophy in the English language, "literary," or "poetic," philosophy has a bad sound; it conjures up evocation rather than analysis, the dilution of technical, moral, and epistemological arguments in a bath of watered-down system building, or the frivolous rejection of rigorous argument for the condemned playground of Continental Thought, whether Hegelian, phenomenological, existential, or manifestly theological. I am referring not to the narrowed gaze of logical positivism, of course, but to the very ways in which Anglo-American—broadly speaking, analytical—philosophy seeks to widen that gaze in an appropriate manner, continuing to discuss concepts by and through discussions of the language in which they live and move and have their being. From this side of the English Channel (and the Atlantic Ocean is hardly even a trout stream, philosophically speaking, compared to it), philosophy in French or German, concerned with the relation of language to death, for example, or with questions like that of the meaning of the word "meaning" in such phrases as "the meaning of life," has seemed "soft," "literary," or frivolously exhibited. Perhaps the English language has been protected from the "poetic" philosophical system building of a Hegel by having in its conceptual history the "philosophic" poetical text building of a Spenser and a Milton who, if one reads them as they invite one to, lay vast foundations for theories of consciousness.

But while the dialectic of subject and object was expanded and explored in English and American poetry after Wordsworth and Blake, and the ironies of imagining transcendence were explored in great fables and meditative lyrics, no philosophical texts in English appeared to play a reciprocal role. From the viewpoint of Hegel (let alone of Heidegger), technical procedures in epistemology and ethics and the logic of scientific discourse simply couldn't deliver the human goods (and from the viewpoint of the Oxford of Gilbert Ryle, say, there were no goods: at most they existed only in misleading invoices). The least likely candidate for such a bridging or ferrying text that might do business across the English Channel would have once seemed to be Wittgenstein's *Philosophical Investigations*. Wittgenstein's method of questioning and then questioning the meaning of his questions seems, on the surface, to be as far from a Kierkegaardian pursuit of transcendence or from the most demonically brilliant Nietzsche (in an essay like "On Truth and Falsity Considered in an Ultra-moral Sense") as could be imagined. The fact that the canonical text of the *Investigations* (as of all of Wittgenstein's writings) is in German and English on facing pages would have to be, for the modern philosopher whose concern, as always, was with the problem rather than the writing, a trivial matter.

There is indeed one way in which the poet and the analytic philosopher look at the Continental metaphysician with a very narrow parallax between them. The Continental system reads like a failed, badly written epic to the poet; to the technical, English-speaking philosopher, its concerns can seem misplaced at best. To take a grave but simple instance: "Being" can be considered as the uniquely general condition, that which precedes anything but which can be experienced only by the most highly evolved something, the late-human consciousness. Or it can be considered as a kind of linguistic mirage arising from refractive variation in the layers of philosophic discourse. "Nothing" isn't any kind of thing, but merely an awkward knot in sense which can be straightened out by saying "not anything," just the way being can be dissolved by careful and appropriate paraphrase. Even problems of human being, like that of the continuity of being a person (the child who fathered me, the person I will be in five years, the one now in between who remembers and anticipates the others—how are they *connected?*) are susceptible to this mode of dissolution by analysis.

Conversely, when our great poet writes "Of Mere Being," of the gold-feathered bird singing in the palm that stands "at the end of the mind . . . on the edge of space," it is only for the philosophers' *Sein* that the simple, reductive kind of "mere"-ness is reserved: Wallace Stevens's "Being" is mere being, pure being, sheer being, patent being. It is *just* (but not, in any way, *simply*) being. Although in both these instances the poet and the philosophical analyst are arguing (or troping) against the prior text (here, of a systematic metaphysical tradition), their very modes of acknowledging this differ widely, as do their responses to their own language, to their own modes of writing. Again, the philosopher considers such notions as that of rightness, or in-betweenness, or the quality of being properly *something* rather than something else, or the nature of my knowledge about what you know or feel. The poet reminds him that he is always *considering* the stars— that in the etymology of the word *consider* lurks the Latin *sidus* (constellation) and that there is a fable lurking in that lurking itself. (Plato is just such a fabulist or poet; in a modern poetical philosopher like Heidegger, who etymologizes words to a fault, the substance of that poetry becomes a kind of philosophical play-dough.) Generally, philosophy is unconcerned with the way in which it is written; it is the argument, the concept, the extensions or meanings of the terms, the elements of the world or of the knowledge of it to which philosophy is responsible. Its language, especially the language it has come to use to analyze its own language, must be transparent. The philosopher shows us how, when we really use concepts without knowing them (even in almost a biblically sexual sense), our minds are somehow being used. The poet awakens us to our words and teaches us to use words on words, that we may thereby be able to use them on, for, and with the rest of the world.

Similarly, the great poet discovers the parables at work in his very means, quite apart from those constructed with them. Thus Milton, in *Paradise Lost,* book 2, represents Satan's encounter with his daughter-lover Sin and their indescribable offspring, Death. The account moves into a kind of allegorical description and narration unique to that episode in the poem, which not only echoes Spenser's earlier account of the monster Error in the middle of her dark wood, not only parodies the fable of the birth of Athena from Zeus's forehead and hideously transforms the Holy Trinity (Sin speaks of living among "The Gods who live at ease, where I shall Reign / At thy right hand voluptuous, as beseems / Thy daughter and thy darling, without end,"[10] heavily echoing the Creed); beyond this, it contracts, reduces, limits the wide imaginative range of the poem's other rhetorical devices. For this is not only Satan's story but a satanic mode of storytelling, a reductive allegorizing about the most hideous of literal forms—death—which we in fact know only by the synecdoche of corpses and much, much hearsay. But this local allegorizing makes us ask: Why this way of talking/writing? Why now, why here? Serious philosophizing suggests that such questions are never to be asked about its way of writing itself, at any point or in general (save, perhaps, as guides to rewriting, in order to make a point more clear, correct a mistake, consider a neglected case, or whatever).

The way in which philosophers write, then, has not traditionally been part of philosophy itself, whether concerned with systems or problems; and the texts of previous philosophers have been treated as the structures of systems or the repositories of problems. The late Leo Strauss was particularly interested in political philosophy and taught his students to be able to give to a philosophical text at least the same degree of attention—to rhetoric (irony and latent fable in particular), to form, and to the analysis of a more than merely philosophizing self underlying the voice of the argument—that an ordinary New Critical commentator might afford some minor seventeenth-century English erotic lyric. A literary theorist like Paul de Man, systematically trained in a Continental phenomenological tradition, will analyze the transformations of an authorial presence like that of Rousseau or Nietzsche (and even, in a recent tour de force, of so unpoetical an essayist as John Locke) in their writings. But even this "deconstruction" of philosophical texts as literary ones must necessarily dissolve all of philosophy's objects of wonder into the tropes and fables of a vast, ongoing, Western epic cycle, whose forms are Certainty, Death, Consciousness, the World, and whose individual lays are those of Other Minds, the Romance of Subject and Object, the Land of Meaning, and so forth.

Examples, then, are very different from fictions of other sorts, partly in that they are utensils forged or selected for their expository function, and partly because, as a consequence, they are undetermined. This is to say that only one or another element in the example plays a crucial analogical or demonstrative role, while other elements, which are present to complete some kind of formalized picture or story, might have been chosen by the toss of a coin. But let me get down, at once, to examples.

The philosopher's cat of my title does not exist. I want to return to this extremely problematic statement a bit later on and ask what asserting it might mean to a poet and a philosopher. But first, to that particular cat: it appears as it were in a prominent place, at the opening of the introduction to a remarkable and ambitious work of contemporary philosophy, Derek Parfit's *Reasons and Persons*. It is, of course, an exemplary cat. Here it is: "Like my cat, I often simply do what I want to do. I am not then using an ability that only persons have. . . . We know that there are reasons for acting, and that some reasons are better or stronger than others"[11]—and this last sentence leads toward the heart of his concerns in this book. As a reader, I was moved by the opening sentence. It seemed obvious that the particularity of Parfit's own cat was happily exemplary of unreasoned volition, of impulse manifesting itself with such delightful smoothness that desire seems to flow immediately into action. Perhaps even a kind of rebuke to thought, but, says Parfit, a rebuke which our humanity will not accept. (Whether cats are persons—nonhuman persons—or not is a matter for the ground rules of discourse, and I am following those rules that seem to have been drawn up by Parfit himself.) I was irrelevantly moved, not just by the cat but by its minute and personal particularity: the philosopher's cat, always there, whether nearby while he was writing philosophy or not. I may have thought of that great bit of poetic feline particularity in Christopher Smart's *Jubilate Agno*—that moment when, in a long catalogue of observations about his cat Jeoffry, the poet says, "For he can catch the cork and toss it again." *The* cork, not just "a cork," a present fact rather than a rhetorical instance (as in "For he can catch things, for example, a cork, and throw them again").

But like any serious reader of exposition, I left the philosopher's prefatory example far behind as I moved into the dense fabric of his argument. I returned to it when, in conversation with a common friend, I learned that Parfit indeed has (and had) no cat. Knowing this, one might reread the sentence in question ("Like my cat, I often simply do what I want to do") and question it in turn. One can easily and deliberately mistake, I suppose, Parfit's word "simply." I should say that cats I have known do what they want to do more complicatedly, after all—if unreasonably by our and the philosopher's criteria, then at least complicated by some sort of feline reasonableness, even though to know cats is to suppose that *le chat a ses raisons que la raison ne connaît pas*. In any event, one's own cat is always a less simple creature, with less simple ways of doing, than an exemplary cat. And here my fanciful misprision of the philosopher's "simply" leads to the serious problem. Parfit has no cat. It is not only that if he had, and if he'd really been talking about what he could rightly call "my cat," that "simply" simply would not do. (Perhaps, had he used the adverb so common in some other philosophers' writing, "just," one would have been left only with the central problem of the fib about the cat's actuality.) In any event, we must ask what his writing has thereby contracted for. Fiction? Why? And, if so, how far are we to go into, and even *with,* the fiction? Does he mean to say, "Like my fictional cat"—(or even, very differently, "Like a fictional 'my cat'")—

"my fictional 'I' often simply (!!!!) does what it wants to"? Is there something contingent, then, about the simplicity, the doing, the wanting? No wrong is done to felinity by taking a cat as an example of something. But is there something about a (fictional) "my" (exemplary) "cat" that may be wrong?[12]

But to ask these questions, clearly, is to have missed a point and possibly to be silly or a little crazy. Surely this is "only an example." Holding a philosopher responsible for the language (what some would wrongly, I think, call the style, or poetic nuances) of an example may not be philosophical. Philosophers often criticize each other's examples for being inapt, or misleading, or for just not exemplifying what they purport to. But taking a philosopher's writing at its word is something that poetry might want to do, even as poetry holds nature itself responsible for what it makes in its various physical languages. Even random events, says the poet, have been inscribed in the book of life and are to be read as the traces of authorial will, for which the poet's own willing language is some kind of figure. Chance, broods Robert Frost in a great sonnet, behaves likes some kind of dark designer—not like Fate or Fortune at all—in the matter of the smallest signs. A genre of contemporary poetry, in fact, consists in the interpretive reading of an error, a mistake thrown up by the manufactures of industrial technology or the language they generate, as if it were a functional sign (one thinks of the locus classicus of this device, in Elizabeth Bishop's "The Man Moth," which takes a typographical error for "Mammoth" at its word and realizes the creature, with remarkable, and metaphorically huge, effect). I know that the matter of getting it wrong (some "it" or other) is a bad way into a consideration of philosophical language, which is so concerned to get whatever "it" it is right. It would appear to be philosophically right to shun examples which are too full of meaning, which entail other analogies, which begin to smack of fictions. And yet again, this is a discursive wrong which poetry seeks, by getting the rules wrong, to set, in another way, right.

But let us consider for a while a famous and influential example, an example of what its philosophical employer called "the commonest matters, those which we believe to be the most distinctly comprehended, to wit, the bodies which we touch and see . . . one body in particular." This is Descartes, in his *Second Meditation*. And the particular example has something in common both with a poetical fiction—for such is often the nature of the objects of meditation in seventeenth-century literature—and with the later philosopher's cat:

> Let us take for example this piece of wax which has just been taken out of the hive; it has not yet lost the sweetness of the honey it contained; it still retains something of the scent of the flowers from which it has been abstracted. Its

colour, shape and size are apparent; it is hard, cold, and tangible, and if you strike it it will give back some sort of sound. Indeed, it has all the characteristics by which a body can be known as distinctly as possible. But now, as I speak, a flame is brought near to it: its lingering savour is dispelled, the scent vanishes, its colour changes, its shape is transformed, its size increases, it turns liquid, it becomes hot, almost too hot to touch, and though you may knock on it, it will give back no sound. Is it the same wax?[13]

And with this and other questions Descartes is led for several pages further into his quest for self-knowledge, for certainty—it may be remembered—about his thinking rather than about material objects themselves. Later in the meditation, he reduces even the waxness of his exemplary piece of wax to its bodyness, and we begian to realize that the wax had, all along, also presented a splendid instance of mutability of form. The disarming "Let us take, for example, this piece of wax . . ." seems to suggest that the wax was lying there on the philosopher's table; but it also seems to be taken from another place, no less easily reachable from one's chair: a case of prepared examples.

Descartes was no poet; even at the dawn of his—and thereby of modern—philosophizing he shed the realm of fiction, the matter of night, before going to work. (And this despite the temptation of reading this meditation as spiritual autobiography or even as romantic crisis poem, to which some academic sectarians today might succumb.) But at school and perhaps for some years later, Descartes had apparently loved poetry, and a great passage from the fifteenth book of Ovid's *Metamorphoses* could not have escaped him. It is part of a speech of Pythagoras, outlining his theory of metempsychosis, or the transmigration of souls; to some degree, it seems also to provide a mythological rationale for Ovid's own central trope of metamorphoses, of changes wrought on beings and things, and thereby for his whole poem. Pythagoras observes (15.165–72) that all things are constantly changing, that nothing really dies, that the spirit wanders now here, now there—from animals to humans and back—but never dies. And (in Rolfe Humphries' translation),

> As the pliant wax
> Is stamped with new designs, and is no longer
> What once it was, but changes form, and still
> Is pliant wax, so do I teach that spirit
> Is evermore the same, though passing always
> To ever-changing bodies.

> [utque novis facilis signatur cera figuris
> nec manet ut fuerat nec formam servet eandem,
> sed tamen ipsa eadem est, animam si semper eandem
> esse, sed in varias doceo migrare figuras][14]

On November 10, 1619 (according to his seventeenth-century biographer, Baillet), in the last of a sequence of three dreams, Descartes saw on his table a dictionary and a book called *Corpus Poetarum,* the works of the poets, which, on being opened, yielded the line "Quod vitae sectabor itae?" (What path shall I take in life?). Then an unknown person gave him a poem beginning, "est et non" (yes and no). But even in the dream, he was interpreting it, the dictionary being the corpus of human knowledge, the body of poetry uniting for him philosophy and wisdom, and the est et non being glossed by him as the yes and no of Pythagoras, or truth and falsehood in human knowledge. This night of dreams, he claimed, marked the turning point in his life, sending him on the road to what would give philosophizing (but not writing, I think—Montaigne had done just that before him) a new meaning. I am not concerned here with the possibility that the Ovidian Pythagoras left its imprint on the canonical one in his dream, but rather that the exemplary, reached-for-at-the-moment piece of notional wax was leading a double life as thing and as what the literary scholars call a topos, or imaginative commonplace. Not very common, perhaps (certainly not like the notion that the world is all a theater, or a play); but certainly, given St. Augustine's use of the same (that is, I believe, Ovid's) wax in an interestingly analogous situation, something rather on the way to becoming one. In "On the Immortality of the Soul," chapter 5, entitled "Mind Is Not Changed So That It Ceases to Be Mind," discussing something "said of a subject according to such a change as makes the name change entirely," he introduces the notion that

> If, for example, wax somehow changes from a white to a black color, it remains, nonetheless, wax. It is also the same if it changes to a round form from a square, or from soft to hard, or from warm to cold. All these changes are within the subject, and wax is the subject. And wax remains no more and no less wax, even though these qualities are changed. Therefore, a change of those qualities can occur in the subject, while the subject itself, in regard to its essence and its name, is not changed.[15]

The Augustinian wax, like the Ovidian and the Cartesian, is a topos or commonplace of sameness-under-apparent-change, although the differing purposes to which the paradigm is put by the three very different writers is a fascinating matter for a current sort of writing about writing about writing. Certainly, Descartes explores his knowledge of and about the wax in a very poetic sort of quest, and in the course of writing a very special sort of spiritual autobiography. This might make it all the more tempting for those current sorts of writing to deconstruct: the truth is—and is such—that you can't tell it, but that's not your fault, but rather the fault of all telling. I am not, however, concerned with such matters here. It is the "*prenons, par example . . . ,*" the fictional narrative of reaching for the clear and present bit of substance, whose rhetorical action is at issue. The figurative "taking" of exemplification, of "taking X as Y," is an act of appropriating, and using, of a very different sort from poetry's mis-taking and misusing. And yet the fiction of taking as example, Oh, I don't know, anything that's here at hand rather than some text or problem that has become text, lying in one of the old books we must make ourselves free of . . . has itself become a textualized convention. Poetry, as aware of the existence and presence of rhetorical topoi as it is of present places—scenes, landscapes, rooms, peopled or not—usually puts in the foreground its awareness of the paradigm in order to work through it. Philosophy will often pretend that there is no topos and will be infuriated at the irrelevance and perhaps the mischievousness of calling attention to it in the first place.

Descartes used the poetic figure of the wax to think with (in a radically philosophical way). The more he did so, and the more he allowed the fiction of the wax as something literally at hand to help him in his quest for belief in and beyond himself, the more like a poet he was writing. Avoiding the earlier text of the wax story told before him had deeply to do with the new kind of imaginative writing he was inventing. And yet philosophers after him, coping with his problems (not, like successive generations of poets, with the voices and the fictions of their precursors), would adopt this exemplary strategy in a totally antipoetic way. Thus arose the epistemologists' cliché—the table at which one is writing suddenly being reached for as an example. Logicians, mostly following Lewis Carroll, have for over a century filled propositional paradigms with comical names and predicates, as if thereby to call attention to the formal nature of their writing. But the philosopher's fib about his cat (or about his noncat) is a different matter from Descartes's lack of acknowledgment of the prior text, and it is adduced only in passing, in any case. The philosopher will get off the hook—the poetic hook—for even an unnecessary fiction by saying, implicitly, "so to speak." For the poet, the phrase must always be "as it were."[16] Our uneasiness, as readers and thinkers, at the kinds of situations, "data" as moral philosophers call them, specifically as they are embodied in examples, is one that we usually suppress, even as Coleridge said we suspend our disbelief in confronting fictions. There is a kind of implicit agreement, which philosophers themselves discuss with varying degrees of satisfactoriness, that schematic situations, logical and moral instances, have to disregard so much of what makes particular stories human, that it would be frivolous and irrelevant for a reader to object "And yet . . . and yet . . . and yet . . . ," even when convinced *by* the specific argument in question, *about* its outcome.

It is not with our actions, so much as with our judgments, statements about, and even beliefs about statements about, actions that technical moral philosophy has concerned itself. But we are often secretly chafing against being put in this position or that one—being this A who promises, that B who maintains, that C who would be mistaken if he said that X was good in itself. The existentialist protest against this philosophizing is that it all dissolves into ineffective language whenever we act—even when we act "on" it—and that instead of analyzing the nature of or the meaning of the words we use to describe the good, or the right, or the just, or the better or worse things to do, we thrust into the position of the "A" or "B," the "Smith" or "Jones," a more fully articulated person. (A waiter in a restaurant, for instance, or ourselves as we would be conceived with at least the imaginative plausibility of a novel or autobiographical story.) It is of such an exemplary moral agent that a French or German writer might then discuss what was the authentic or the phony thing, under those elaborate circumstances (namely, *everything*), to do. One way to characterize this protest, although one that philosophers on either side of the English Channel might consider "literary" or "frivolous," would be to say that life is not exemplary, or, at any rate, not exemplary in the traditional or analytically philosophical way.

Stanley Cavell is a philosopher whose writing embodies, rather than merely entails, an intense and vigorous rhetorical analysis of kinds of examples both epistemologists and moral philosophers use in their analyses and arguments. But this is not, then, to criticize philosophical writing from the point of view of "style." His own writing is full of fables and parables and of examples drawn from art and the rest of life which are themselves often unavowedly parabolic. In discussing the seemingly (to the unphilosophical) bloodless matter of our criteria for calling a thing what we do, he invokes the philosopher's old friend, the nearest chair, and continues with Wittgenstein's treatment of whether anything we sit on, we use chairwise, really is a chair thereby, etc. But Cavell's example of something that we might or might perhaps not want to think of as something sat in is in fact a little terrifying: perhaps someone

> doesn't bend when he "sits" on it: it is nothing so much as a plank stood on end, about the height and width of an average human being, tipped and braced back slightly from the vertical, into which there are fitted at right angles two pegs, which, you discover, are to go under the armpits, and a saddle peg in the middle to "sit" on.[17]

This seems a chair from a world of Kafka or Beckett, just as the body to place in it evokes the painted figures of Francis Bacon. To sit on it would be torture; and yet certain kinds of demands made upon clarity of certain kinds can be torture. And the whole question of how epistemological doubt can relate to, can embody or engage, matters of faith and terror usually ("better") left to existential writing is implicitly raised in the example, which is also an exemplary instance of exemplifying.

Such writing continually makes connections—sometimes in poetic whispers behind the scenes of its philosophical argument—which we want to feel we know, yet which cannot be argued for in the way we would want. Yet Cavell does this out of sophistication rather than mental innocence. His scenarios, instances, little stories, cases are informed with the kind of attention that living with novels, playing music, thinking about painting, and so forth instill and demand. His pages on dolls, statues, and our perceptions and knowledge of human presence are all memorable. Any good philosopher's examples are apt and effective; those of a stylist can be witty and allusive. Cavell's examples—especially when they are calling into question the nature and ground of other examples, and the rhetoric of exemplifying itself—are resonant.

One of the ways by which the poetic imagination can assert itself against the reductions of the exemplary—can best take examples at their word—and against the example-making-and-giving faculty of philosophers is by mis-taking them, forcibly misinterpreting them or misusing them, in order to take them back for some other kind of truth. A fine instance of this, albeit loaded to begin with by the fact that, in it, a true artist is being pitted against a cliché of philosophical writing, is from Virginia Woolf's *To the Lighthouse*. Lily Briscoe, the painter, is thinking of Professor Ramsay, the philosopher:

> "Oh, but," said Lily, "think of his work!"
> Whenever she "thought of his work" she always saw clearly before her a large kitchen table. It was Adnrew's doing. She asked him what his father's books were about. "Subject and object and the nature of reality," Andrew had said. And when she said Heavens, she had no notion what that meant. "Think of a kitchen table then," he told her, "when you're not there."
> So now she always saw, when she thought of Mr. Ramsay's work, a scrubbed kitchen table. It lodged now in the fork of a pear tree, for they had reached the orchard. And with a painful effort of concentration, she focused her mind, not upon the silver-bossed bark of the tree, or upon its fish-shaped leaves, but upon a phantom kitchen table, one of those scrubbed board tables, grained and knotted, whose virtue seems to have been laid bare by years of muscular integrity, which stuck there, its four legs in air. Naturally, if one's days were passed in this seeing of angular essences, this reducing of lovely evenings, with all their flamingo clouds and blue and silver to a white deal four-legged table (and it was a mark of the finest minds so to do), naturally one could not be judged like an ordinary person.

But of course, Lily is no ordinary person either. By turning the exemplary kitchen table upside down, she inspires it with the breath of the kind of life that physical objects lead. The kitchen table's thingness is more immediate, its material presence more accessible, now that it lies, "its four legs in the air," stuck in the fork of a tree that blossoms with its own observed particularity, its bark, its leaves carefully noted. Like Descartes's wax, the canonical table-at-which-the-philosopher-is-writing is something toward which he reaches for exemplification, as the nearest thing at hand (to stand, perhaps for something "at world," as it were). And like Descartes's wax, it unavowedly proclaims the originality of human reasoning, its independence from books and texts and a whole library of intellectual agendas, by purporting to be merely handy. And yet like Descartes's wax it is literary after all, pieces of furniture being of the tribe of Socrates' *klinē*, or couch, in the famous discussion (*Republic* 10.597a–598d) of representation, the locus classicus of the view that pictures of ordinary objects like couches suffer from a triple compounding of the felony of unreality even good, hard, palpable couches themselves are prone to. And ultimately, like Descartes's wax, it is reductive, and in its very exemplariness, a far better candidate than Plato's picture for forming an analogue of what is distant from the real.

A poet, propounder of parables rather than reacher for examples, must applaud the exuberance of Lily Briscoe's Herculean wrestling with the dullard giant of example. Upside down in the air, it loses its hold on the actuality of the table that it has been made, as example, to imprison in its jail of careless writing. The kitchen table as a complex trope of Professor Ramsay's "work" is, finally, a metaexample, an example, or at least an instance of the exemplary, which is somehow bound to give it more imaginative substance. (This is perhaps because, in order to exemplify the process of giving an example of something, you have to tell a story. Of course, I don't mean this in any trivial, self-descriptive way—any particular example, say x, of something to be exemplified, say A, is always an instance of, and possibly an example of, exemplifying; an instance of something is probably always an instance of instancing.) A philosopher—or indeed, an ordinary expositor—says, "Take, for example . . . ," and Lily Briscoe, or any other poet, might in fact, by mistaking it, take it back. But take it back for what? (it was, after all, taken *for* example, for use by the reductive engines of exemplification in the first place). Well, for another kind of talk: that is, another kind of extraordinariness in language, for metaphor (or, in the broadest sense, trope). The very phrases by which we ordinarily introduce examples can be made to shed their ordinariness, e.g. "*exempli gratia,*" abbreviated "e.g.," meaning "for the sake of example." Not, as far as poetic language is concerned, for the sake of fact, no matter how much attention Descartes lavishes upon the sensible properties of the wax. And not for the sake of fiction, either—the condition into which Lily Briscoe upends the philosophical table—but for some other service. We might momentarily differentiate between what may be going on when we say "for example," "for instance," or "say," on the one hand, and "it's rather like . . . ," on the other. Introducing a simile, or something "by way of" analogy, is more difficult, precarious, and interesting work than giving an example, for instance, even though the analogy can be used in place of a more narrowly deployed example. As for the difference between an *example* and an *instance,* I can imagine the late J. L. Austin nicely and precisely distinguishing between them, but I'm not sure whether it would be a philosophical distinction or not. In any event, I have been using the first term to cover the second.

But the philosopher's "kitchen table when you're not there," much more than the wax or the cat, is reductive, not just of lovely evenings, but of exemplifying itself. When poetry says, "for example" the example—like the comparison, the analogy, the simile—will be turned into something else. *Turned*—the Greek-derived word for that kind of turning is "trope," although an infuriated philosopher might want tendentiously to translate the word as "twisting." Untwisted similes are devices of exposition, even though sentences such as "X is like Y" do not necessarily express matters of fact. Even in full, dull expository form, "X is like Y in that both have *a*'s in their *b*'s" can never be certainly refuted by a "No it's not." (Unless, in fact, Y doesn't have an *a* in its *b*; but in that case, it wouldn't be the apparent predication of likeness that was being denied, but the truth of "in that." One might want to add that the only verifiable predications of likeness are those of "likeness-in-that. . . ." One could still say, "Shoes are like ships in that they are both denoted by monosyllabic, plural nouns starting with the same phoneme" or even "—in that they are adjacent items on the Walrus's conversational agenda." But in that case, one still might reply, "That's not really being like.")

In any event, a poetic simile is not an expository one and will often be a figurative, or troped, simile, likening X to Y with respect to their common *a*, for instance, but perhaps suppressing any mention of an even more glaringly common *b*. Far more complex than the ironic selection of an apparently irrelevant criterion (as in, say, "I hate children. They're so short"), in the case of the poet's simile, the presentation of the comparison may lead the reader to recognize the suppression, recover the hidden material, and consider as a parable the matter of why just that suppression might have occurred. Some may guess that I have been describing a particular form of simile that we begin to find in Milton, one of the greatest instances of it being the lines in which the multitudinousness of Satan's fallen legions in *Paradise Lost*, book 1 is likened to the thickness of the autumn leaves underfoot in parts of Tuscany in which Milton had himself traveled in his youth:

> His Legions, Angel Forms, who lay intrans't
> Thick as Autumnal Leaves that strow the Brooks
> In *Vallombrosa*, where th'*Etrurian* shades
> High overarch't imbow'r . . .   [301–04]

Here the density of the leaves is the *a*, and the X of the fallen angels is likened to the Y of the fallen foliage with respect to that *a*. But even as one glosses the figure, one dredges up the literally "fallen" quality of both angels and leaves and involves the proleptic figurative sense of "fall" in the case of humanity as well. So here is our unreported *b*. One of the picturesque Italian spots is Vallombrosa, "shady valley," and the Twenty-third Psalm's "valley of the shadow of death," echoing in the naming of that place, points toward the other suppressed grounds for comparison, the *c* that is death.[18] The leaves are dead, changed but still palpable, the fallen angels now in an eternal death-in-life and life-in-death. Why not mention that explicitly? The question leads us deep into the whole of *Paradise Lost,* with its continuous method of half-burying signs that point forward in time as a figure of the major tragic pattern of not knowing what one is doing. It points as well toward specific matters of Adam and Eve eating the fruit "and knew not eating death," and to our own continual eating more generally of the fruit of life, never thinking of how we thereby consume not just what we subsist upon, but what is doing the subsisting as well.

It is not just that all sorts of other tropes are packed into Miltonic similes. It is also that, frequently as in this case, one of these entails the simile's calling attention to its own nature and function. The poet doesn't *use* a simile to explain something as an expositor might. Rather, he or she will interestingly misuse it, do something funny or wrong with it, overuse it. And then the simile can lead a new sort of life of its own.

In philosophy, the burden of whose speculative past is a library of problems, not books, paradoxes and puzzles are like headaches. They are not to be cured, of course, by decapitation, which is a means for men of action, not contemplation. Alexander the Great cut the Gordian Knot—as the propagandistic fable of heroic accomplishment has it—that no one else could untie. But for poets and philosophers both, cutting the knot was boring. The philosopher contemplated the problem of the knot, trying to figure it out, in order to know more about many things: knots themselves, the nature of knottedness and knottiness in the nature of rope and of difficulty in general, the nature of us all as tiers and untiers. For the poet, the Gordian Knot was gorgeous: it existed not as an obstacle to be removed or as an embodiment of a problem to solve, but as a given of nature, what Blake termed a "minute particular" of reality. The question was what—and in both senses of the phrase—to make of it. Poetical construing and constructing are always interpenetrating, making and knowing continually giving rise to one another. One manifestation of this can be seen in the ways in which form and structure, in poetry, conjure up meaning, not merely for the reader, but for the poet to begin with. A scheme or pattern can give rise to a poetical puzzle, which can then serve to delight the poet who propounded it and allow the reader who confronts it to admire it as puzzle even more than he or she would its solution.

The lovely nursery rhyme from the seventeenth century

I saw a peacock with a fiery tail
I saw a blazing comet drop down hail
I saw a cloud with ivy circled round
I saw a sturdy oak creep on the ground
I saw a pismire swallow up a whale
I saw a raging sea brim full of ale
I saw a Venice glass sixteen foot deep
I saw a well full of men's tears that weep
I saw their eyes all in a flame of fire
I saw a house as big as the moon and higher
I saw the sun even in the midst of night
I saw the man that saw this wondrous sight

is an outright puzzle. Unsolved, it is a series of visionary prophetic prodigies, ending with the framing, even more apparently contingent assertion: "I saw the man that saw this wondrous sight." Solved, it is a string of unremarkable reports to the banal effect that the speaker had seen a peacock, a comet with a fiery tail, a cloud dropping hail, an oak encircled with ivy (an old emblem), an ant on the ground, etc., the solution depending upon repunctuating the lines, so that the trap of rhymed closure as sentence closure is escaped. The mechanism for setting the trap is, of course, the coexistence in English verse of the sixteenth through late nineteenth centuries of direct and inverted syntax, and the mode of solving it is to rewrite all the impossible direct sentences, rhymed to enforce their syntactic and vatic authority, as banal direct ones. In poetic riddles and puzzles, one wants to hang on to what one had lost: Elizabeth, Elspeth, Betsy, and Bess, the four girls in the nursery rhyme who are all one, never desert the memory as a charming tetrad of English graces, even after they have all been demystified into the same entity designated by what are merely forms of the same name. As a philosophical example in some argument about naming and natural kinds or whatever, they would vanish as soon as they had been used—the four notional girls, the only one real one, the puzzle they produce, and all. (For me, the touching thing about the "I saw a peacock" verse is the lingering mystery that even the solution allows to remain, the statement to the effect that it was at midnight that the narrator saw "the man who saw this wondrous sight"; we must imagine, I suppose, the poet who propounded the puzzle, writing by the light of his single candle, at midnight looking up and catching a glimpse of himself in his dim Venice-glass. Without the solution, there would be no such flickering shadow of self-reference.) The philosopher Gilbert Ryle once dealt with a series of perhaps exemplary dilemmas by showing that there was something wrong about the way in which they were put. But the wrongness about the way in which things are put may be part of, or at least, very like, the poetic misuse of expository language. It is the poet in Wittgenstein querying the philosopher who can observe that "philosophers use a language that is already deformed, as though by shoes that are too tight."[19] And it is the same poet in him, I think, who observes about the puzzles that are most powerful in their puzzlingness: "The solution of philosophical problems can be compared with a gift in a fairy tale: in the magic of the castle it appears enchanted and if you look at it outside in daylight it is nothing but an ordinary bit of iron (or something of the sort)."[20]

Or consider another, shorter simile, from Friedrich Schlegel's collection of aphorisms—he calls them "fragments"—the *Athenaeums fragmente*. (Aphorists, by the way, often write aphorisms about aphorisms—I think of Karl Kraus's "An aphorism is very easy to write if you don't know how," which I am always tempted to apply these days to "a poem," but the self-referentiality is merely a matter of wit.) "A fragment," says Schlegel, "like a miniature work of art, has to be entirely isolated from the surrounding world and be complete in itself, like a hedgehog" (Ein Fragment muss gleich einem kleinen Kunstwerke von der ungebunden Welt ganz abgesundert und in sich selbst vollendet sein wie ein Igel").[21] The first of these similes, "like a miniature work of art," is somewhat sly in that a point it leads to is really that a fragment *is* a miniature work of art (although it doesn't sound as strange for Schlegel to say this as it might be to say, "A sonnet is like a short lyric poem"). But the second simile bristles with implication—a hedgehog is compact, because it has rolled itself up into a ball, protecting itself against predators. Even so is the aphorism, which, the comparison implies, might have gone on at length but, in defense against unremarkableness, consequent neglect, and perhaps more as well, has drawn itself up into compactness. But what else is true of a hedgehog? The simile has overlooked—or suppressed—the hedgehog's quills, the pointed quills which it deploys by rolling up tight. Well, what is the point of an aphorism? The one we are considering, containing just this simile with its several points of comparison reaching out in various directions—compactness, wisely self-willed contraction, many-pointedness—has itself many points to make. Are all true fragments like it in regard to this? Pointedness is itself a fascinating notion when considered rhetorically. The heavy weight of the substance of much knowledge bearing down on one sharp point must pierce the thickest of mental skins. "My point" may be the meaning of part of my remarks, their purpose, their implications for you and your discourse, their strategy of disposition, some un- or understated logical or practical inference or conclusion: behind this array of rhetorical ends, the original metaphor has for ages lain shriveled into a literal meaning of "point." A great precursor of Schlegel's aphorism is to be found—where perhaps he found it—in the Book of Proverbs (26:9): "As a thorn goeth up into the hand of a drunkard, so is a parable in the mouth of a fool." The drunk, all thumbs, will stick himself with the pointed thorns of the bush; the fool, all inane blabber, will get stuck on the point of a proverb. All of which is embodied in a meta-proverb which, like Schlegel's metafragment, buries its point about pointedness in a reanimate dead metaphor. And all of which, like Milton's simile of the dead, fallen leaves, must be taken fully at its word, must be held responsible for its own language. One cannot say of a poetic comparison, "Oh, that was just an example."

Of course, this kind of overuse, or other sort of misuse, of the devices of ordinary—or even of extraordinary—exposition is not confined to schemes and patterns like that of simile. Questions, answers, commands (as we have seen), and demonstrations, instructions, and definitions are all twisted out of shape in poetic language. The very ways in which poetry refers to itself and to its own twistings even in the act of so contriving them are central to its nature and purposes. Aphorism is in itself a shadowy realm, and I'm sure that there are many aphorisms of the greatest writers in that mode—Lichtenberg, Schopenhauer, Emerson, Nietzsche—that we would indeed want to call philosophical and not poetic. Consider Lichtenberg's "A donkey is a horse translated into Dutch." This is funny and pointed, I think, only if your native language is English or German, from the point of view of either of which Dutch looks like somewhat distorted, but recognizable, language, just as donkeyhood is the low German of horseness. The philosophical nature of such an observation arises from the joke about language and nature, nature and convention, an almost Wittgensteinian agenda of criteria and resemblances. And yet the aptness of the following example of Descartes (from the *Discourse on Method*, 2) is aphoristically successful: "And although logic indeed contains many very true and excellent precepts, these are so confounded with so many others that are either harmful or superfluous that it is as difficult to distinguish the former as it would be to conjure up a statue of Diana or Minerva from an untouched block of marble."[22] No poet could object to its being Diana or Minerva who are chosen for the role of "e.g." here, the latter as patroness of wisdom and hence of thought, the former, in her armed virginity, as the enemy of the contamination of truth by "harmful or superfluous" precepts. Compacted and versified, this could be almost Popean.

Riddle, puzzle, problem, and paradox all play roles on the stage of poetry very different from those they play in philosophy. Logical paradoxes are always tight and empty, always leading—if they are true paradoxes—to a self-contradiction, an X that can be a Y if and only if it isn't. Poetic paradoxes are not like that. They can be packed into the pattern of oxymoron, that rhetorical paradox-box so beloved of Renaissance poets. (Examples discussed in the first chapter were "thou, the master-mistress of my passion" of Shakespeare's sonnet, or "See where the victor-victim bleeds" of James Shirley's seventeenth-century song.)[23] In those cases, the apparent contradiction is always resolved by taking one or both of the apparently contradictory terms that together seem to assert [*a* and *non-a*], in another sense, whether figurative or not. The "victor-victim" in the song is not impossibly winner and loser of the same battle. He is, in fact, Ajax, victor in Trojan battle, loser in a contest of words with wily Ulysses. Moreover, he represents the unique case of possibly winning and losing the same fight to the degree that he has just killed himself in chagrin at losing (thus incidentally engaging the logical domain of recursiveness): "Upon death's purple altar now, / See where the victor-victim bleeds." The logical prison bars that close on contexts of self-referentiality are here deployed in a situation of moral significance, of stoic-Christian debates on suicide, etc.

Similarly, Shakespeare's "master-mistress" of Sonnet 20 resolves itself in several ways at once—all of the poem's conceits of androgyny, not to speak of the historical fact of boys playing women's roles in the theater, etc. on the one hand, and, on the other, the meaning of the phrase a "master mistress" as someone consummately skilled or accredited (like a "master carpenter") in the guild of mistressing. In the game of poetry, most moves will affect what is happening on several boards at once; in philosophy, each verbal move must be kept free of resonances and implications, lest they become not merely irrelevant, but entangling.

One can always ask, with Iris Murdoch, of any philosopher, "What is he afraid of?" And I suppose that one can always ask with Stanley Cavell and others who might ask it too, "Is that a philosophical question?" Just so, when a poet I know asks, "What do poets know about language that philosophers don't?" I'm half tempted to add, "Yes, and (or but) would that be knowledge?" But perhaps the question should be directed not at what each knows about language but toward the ways of knowing itself. Words and expressions that are currently called "opaque" in poetry and "transparent" in exposition may be looked at in another way: the expositor uses words like utensils or tools, which is to say very carefully, or loosely, depending upon the task. The philosopher's task usually requires a good deal of care. But the poet knows words as he or she knows people, or at least, fictions of people, and poetry is, as Richard Poirier has called it, "the work of knowing." I should not totally exclude the erotic or so-called biblical sense of the word *know* as well: aside from knowing the ancestry, families, clothing, bodies, and souls of words, poetry has long been concerned with the ways in which touching and playing with them can make them yield up an erotic nature. I think again of Viola's reply to Feste: dallying with words makes them wanton—to caress them too expertly is to expand their blush of shame into a flush of arousal. Poetry uses, so it claims, words, making their own music, to sing with. Philosophy doesn't sing—it proves, argues, explains, confesses, asks and answers questions, and questions answers. But poetry sings to the music of words in two senses: it makes its own accompaniment and it addresses its own language, even while purporting only to address its subject, or the object of its apostrophe. "The truest poetry is the most feigning," says Touchstone in *As You Like It,* in a pair of quibbles on truth and authenticity, simulation and dissimulation that could not but leave philosophy infuriated. But the line remains one of poetry's truest remarks about itself: that contrivance is essential to poetry's way of being true to itself—and ringing true, as a well-cast bell or authentic coin does—and ultimately of representing truth by fiction.

I have not been speaking of the strictly philosophical family quarrel between poetical philosophers—Kierkegaard, Nietzsche, Wittgenstein—nor of what have in the past been characterized as philosophical poets (for Santayana, Dante, Lucretius, Goethe—all systematic in their building of model worlds, all scientific for their time). For the modern kinds of philosophizing, we might cite Rilke for the German ways of writing, Frost and Stevens for the American and British. Robert Frost's oven-bird, who does not sing, like other birds, in the springtime, but rather frames questions like "what to make of a diminished thing" is a philosophizing teacher. Stevens's winter reduction of a world oversmeared with mythologies to a cold scene in which the "mind of winter" can perceive "nothing that is not there and the nothing that is" qualifies its metaphysical insistence that existence is a predicate, but only by suggesting that it is true of the world regarded in a certain initially necessary wintry light.

The poet "qualifies" the metaphysical assertion, but not to tone down its possible outrageousness. And yet the poet is vulnerable to other arrows. There is a question that the philosopher might ask the poet, but that the poet should probably ask for him: "What, then, is the poet afraid of?" Metaphors, no matter how extended they may be (and for Renaissance rhetoric, allegory was usually defined as an extended trope), have a hit-and-run quality. A poet is always guilty of leaving the scene of the crime: rather than staying around to pick up the discursive pieces, he will be off on his outrageous hippogryph or whatever. Even poetic working through is not as exacting and as continually contriving to purge itself of folly as philosophic work. Poets may very well be afraid of doing that—of having to do that— which results in the habit of hit-and-run and occasionally the disposition to guilt in just that regard. (In a particular instance it may be hard to diagnose the presence or nature of this synchronic—rather than Bloomian diachronic—poetic anxiety: Stevens's "Things seen are things as seen" may or may not specifically manifest an unwillingness to do serious epistemological work.) But in general, if there is any traffic court before which a poet might be haled, it is the sessions of sour, silent thought, of philosophy. There are certain things by way of argument that poets will not do. And their constant defense against this charge is that there are certain things by way of fiction that philosophers will not see.

J. L. Austin in a celebrated footnote to a discussion of to what degree, by pretending to do something, we are *"universally* debarred from actually doing that action itself," cites what he calls a "trick example, for exercise purposes only" (a pretend example?). He propounds the case of a man who at a party "decides, in an attempt to amuse, to pretend to behave vulgarly; the party, however, is of a type at which even to pretend to behave vulgarly is, alas, to behave vulgarly."[24] But the frivolity of the "trick" allows it, the poet would feel, to occupy a serious place, along with the instances, say, of "pretending to mime," "pretending to be playful," "pretending to dance," "pretending to tell a story" (even a shaggy-dog story being a genre of tale), etc. For the philosopher, all these would be unwelcome because of the matter of figurativeness they engaged.

Throughout these remarks I have been concentrating on the differences between the relations of poets and philosophers to the language in which they live and work. Philosophy has certainly devoted a good deal of its modern life to the examination, care, recutting, and sharpening of its linguistic tools; and the attention given to just what it might mean to say that a particular word means something has commanded a noble line of inquiry from Hobbes through Frege and beyond. Poets—and here Dante, founder of a linguistic culture as well as poet, is an exception—have not theorized about language save in nonce, local, or polemical situations and in those moments in which theorizing—like climbing, swimming, overhearing, caressing—is a human activity figuratively represented in poetic practice. Instead, poets live with their words almost as—and here Milton in *Areopagitica* comes up again—people.

Poets, like expositors, may "use" words, but those uses, or practices, are more those of love than of simple manipulations. "My language is a common prostitute that I turn into a virgin," says Karl Kraus, speaking not only to the matter of the public and the personal in a poet's language, but to that of a special sort of revisionary love. Or, again, talking for poetry and not for philosophy, Kraus says that he has "drawn from the well of language many a thought which I do not have, and which I cannot put into words." (A kind of gloss on this is Wallace Stevens's "A poet's words are of things that do not exist without the words.")[25] Revealing as the figure of the well is, though, that of the woman—who so easily becomes the Muse—is perhaps more resonant. Interestingly analogous to this is Cavell's claim that "the answer to the question 'What is art?' will in part be an answer which explains why it is we treat certain objects, or how we *can* treat certain objects, in ways normally reserved for treating persons." Poetry, with its urge to trope conceptual categories along with everything else, has no problem with treating words as objects and, by more than aesthetic extension, rather like persons. This may be at once a source of, as well as a figure for, poetic ulteriority.

For most epistemologists, the mere fact that the word *know* has what is called its biblical sense, let alone the relation of that to the cognitive senses which they employ or explore or deconstruct in various ways, is irrelevant and/or otherwise trivial. For logicians, the erotic introduction in Plato's *Cratylus* to the analysis of natural and conventional ways in which words come into meaning is likewise trivial: Plato's rhetoric is all part of that unparaphrasable material thought of as Plato's "literary form." For the poet, this use of "unparaphrasable" is more like that of the colloquial "unthinkable" than perhaps the philosopher supposes. And for the poet, the first etymologies Socrates proposes in that dialogue are those of the names of his two ephebes, a stroking gesture in a dance of seductive instruction. And for the poet, the biblical sense of *know* is as much part of nature as the heat of fire, and the cognitive sense as much a given phenomenon as the brightness thereof. The eros of subject and object was as figuratively explicit for a poet like Wordsworth as it was something that lurked darkling in German philosophy.

If philosophy begins in wonder, poetry begins in the knowing of language, in love of words for and in themselves, rather than what can be done with them, although the ways in which this is true are deeper and more complex than this half-forgotten truism might suggest. To assert, then, that the baitings and infuriations of poetical mice and philosophical cats are all about language is hardly to imply that the quarrels are not very serious ones. One can ignore totally the thematic issues which might be said to lie in the philosopher's premises alone—*is*-es and *oughts;* rights and responsibilities incurred in asserting; nothing, somethings, and everythings; what one is whoever one is; and hundreds of others—as separating poetry and philosophy, because they can only be designated in words which poets can twist right down to the issues themselves, in any case.

But I cannot conclude without one other observation. I started out by characterizing the arguments about different kinds of arguments as taking place downstairs in our father's house, as it were, of our speculative life. But that house, with its many mansions, stands strangely neglected at this moment in the history of our culture. The house of seriousness does not show up on any but the older, outmoded maps of our city. The house itself is now in a decayed neighborhood, hidden in the general suburbs of inanity. I cannot think whether it is worse today to be a real poet or a serious philosopher: Whether to have to cringe inwardly whenever any public fool in politics or other forms of show business, incapacitated by his or her life from giving real thought to anything, refers to some simple generalization as "my philosophy." Or whether to wish one were altogether elsewhere whenever any piece of incoherent exposition—wanting in knowledge and neither careful nor loving of its words, but with the jagged right-hand edge that printers justifiably call "unjustified"—is called a poem. The sense that there is some serious business that is being outraged is common to both poetry and philosophy. In addition, the increasing stupidity, falsity, and emptiness of most public discourse today are their common enemies.

There is as much philosophical imagination at work in the realm of the literal as there is poetic industry in the realm of trope. Even when each examines the structure and workings of its own language, the questions will be characteristically directed toward literal or figurative ends. Austin asks, "Are *cans* constitutionally iffy?"[26] and the poet is immediately tempted to reply, "Aren't *ifs* canny?" But the mutual exasperation manifested and generated by such an exchange would remain a family affair, and the rhetorical policeman seeking to forestall the eventuality of pots and pans being flung about risks, as always, the wrath of both parties. True poets and real philosophers alike are doomed to be commonly misidentified and generally misunderstood. And despite their quarreling, they share the lonely work of conceiving, writing, framing, and propounding, beholden to no ruler, to no mob, to no market, to no fashion. Like the theologian of the past, the poet and the philosopher both write out of noble doubt, for they can only believe, and believe in, what they write themselves. Their vocations, their callings remain models of what endures contention and survives all kinds of victory.

And yet all the while, their individual, responsible attentions to those callings will lead them in different directions, along variously straight and zigzag linguistic paths. Their very maps of those paths will scarcely look alike, and the terrain through which they move is so overgrown with everything that they would appear to diverge absolutely. I have been concerned in these pages with what goes on along only the way of poetry; but here at the end I have tried for an aerial view of their courses, with a glimpse about how roughly parallel they might turn out, when viewed from above, to be. But even this view has been sketched in the systems of the poets' mapmakers, partaking of the way of the ulterior as it tried for a moment or so to suggest where a more systematic account might lead meaning to track at once, mile after mile, candor in silence and melodious guile.

Appendix

It was in the poems reprinted below that some of the notions worked out in detail in the essays in this book first occurred to me, and I thought that it might be of some interest to present, rather than merely allude to, them. For instance, the final chapter's concern with examples and tropes probably arose from a poem of mine called "Examples," written in 1971, which deliberately misconstrued certain celebrated examples in well-known philosophical texts (among them, Russell's exemplary name that proves so metaphysically inconvenient as to require rewriting as a description; G. E. Moore's case in an informal argument that existence is not a predicate: "tame tigers exist" doesn't behave under negation like "tame tigers growl"; J. L. Austin's celebrated distinction between doing something—in this case, shooting an unassigned donkey—by accident rather than by mistake).

DESCARTES' WAX

Ah, yes, the wax: this piece just now unhived, now in my hand—
Honey-smelling yet, that honey yet flower-smelling, those flowers
(Say, they are purple clover, outgrowing the white)
Still remembering their houses of grass, whose green breathings
Themselves lead back into redolence, in eternal regress,
Stirred by the mind's winds; while in its house of silence,
This wax, tawnier than the honey, shines with a noble yellow,
Lion-color, golden as a beast from which strength is plucked,
A hardened blob: warmth will make it give, warmth of the near
    candle's glowing mind
Lump of cerebrum: my thumbnail lines it into two lobes which
    caresses will spread
Or curl
And then, and then anything
A waning of sameness: but from where—

Hoard of forms hidden in a high mountain cave? the sky's inexhaustible
  grayblue Morpheum?—
Will it take shape?

RUSSELL'S MONARCH
"The present king of France is bald";
For some years he has gone without the fiction of false hair,
Fringed with a slipped, half-glory of white, while a corollary gleam
Shines from his pate in the bright light, above a land of green,
As he stands for a moment, ivory orb and cue in either hand,
In the grand billiard-room at Monterreur,
Still suggesting some of his earlier pictures: as on the east terrace back
  at Montraison
In the clear light that spoke silently of betrayals, he stood watching,
First the light itself and then, distantly, welcoming clouds.
And he sighed for the truth.
Or as in state of some kind, with much plum-colored velvet swagged
  behind him,
The heavy, dripping sleeve of an abstract arm whose hand may be
  pointing somewhere,
Or keeping something out of sight.
But if one is mistaken about him, finds out he has crowned non-
  entity with the pinchbeck of language,
Elevating him who could not even be considered a pretender,
Then say, rather "The present king of France" is bald, is too crude
  an instance;
For the blunders by which we climb, those mistakes our handholds
Are less stark than the rocks we seek to rise above,
And these: the fullness and the curl of wigs, moving above a sea of
  shoulders,
Or reposing broodily on their wooden eggs at night—
Are our additions to what is given, our patches for what is always
  being taken away.

TAKING THE CASE OF THE DONKEYS (*Austin*)
Spare philosophers in a bright field stand shooting at donkeys
Across the cold distance of rocky ground on which they are not
Toward pasture, and the gray, earnest ones grazing there,
One of whom finally drops, hit by accident,
Another, by mistake; but both by an unrelenting intent that they
  serve not as beasts of burden,
But, winged with the Exemplary, as creatures of the mind's flight.
The philosophers may not love them—their deaths are so ridicu-
  lous!—
But that would be because the philosophers are exemplary as well;
Dropping their rifles to the misty ground, and slowly merging with
  its colors,

They amble toward the melted beasts and ride them solemnly
Out of our sight.

MOORE'S BEASTS

"Tame tigers growl"
Or not, as the case may be;
But some tame tigers who do not exist are ever silent of throat,
Just as they are never narrowed of eye.
Silence of paw is something else: I have been brushed by the passage
    of fiery fur
And heard soft padfall, like the slopping of something damp in the
    long hallway;
I have heard the rip and then the shredding of stretched canvas
As, patiently standing, one paw against the golden foliage of frame,
One of them came to know, after weeks of contemplation,
That a landscape of dim forests must, in fact, go.
An ounce of tears watered the carpet and his face.
I have heard them lying half asleep along the hard terraces, their
    guarded breathing.
But mostly these children of fear are seen and not heard,
Passing across open doors, slow huge heads turning dark corners,
Looking back down corridors as if—and what can one make of the
    silences of our beasts?—
Regretful: unhurried, but surely regretful.

$7 + 5 = 12$ (*Kant*)

I think I see why this one: two primes aimed at the all but inevitable
    composite
—The one which should, had we two subsidiary thumbs, have been
    our numberer,
A reasonable base for those airy towers untopped, paling into dis-
    tances—
But, out of some gentleness, not stepped crudely upward,
Five and seven and then their sum—as if climbing were all that
    vertical scales were for—
Instead more warmly abstract: dipping in order to rise, but barely
    whispering of that,
Nor of mystery taken and pent up in hand.
Hand in hand, their *tableau vivant* never over,
They yet bow and smile, asserting a truth radiant even in daylight,
Like what lay somewhere between the given and the found,
Always golden and unspeakably glittering down in the cellars.

Similarly, I had been meditating the allegory and moral consequences of
refrain in a pair of the sonnets-manqués of my *Powers of Thirteen* (1983).
The poem started out with a willful misprision of the great refrain line,
discussed in chapter 4, of the late Latin *Pervigilium Veneris,* "cras amet qui

nunquam amavit, quiquam amavit cras amet" (tomorrow those new to loving will love, those used to loving will love tomorrow). I was led on through
the two senses of the English word *refrain* to play on "break" and "brake,"
anticipating the etymology which, in fact, I had not thought through:

> *Cras amet qui nunquam amavit, quiquam amavit cras*
> *Moriatur*—"those who never loved before will love
> Tomorrow; those used to loving will tomorrow come
> To die"—The old refrains all come down to this: either
> Reduced to *tra-la-las,* at whose regular return
> Children look at each other and, smiling, mouth the words
> And old people nod heads in time, or, if they retain
> Meaning at all, they always end up in whispering
> *"Death"* in the deep chambers hidden in among their tones.
> That is how *Greensleeves,* her smock stained from love in the grass,
> Outlasts all the boys who had a go at her. That is
> How *nonny-nonny-no* etcetera can survive
> The next stanza, and the next, and the next, and the next.
>
> Breaking off the song of the refrain, putting the brakes
> On the way that the ever-returning chorus tends
> To run away with the whole song—well, that may well be
> Breaking away from a frightening joyride before
> The wrap-up of metal around some tree or other.
> *Yes,* you say, *but something has to get out of hand so*
> *That we can go on*: and, yes, I answer, but better
> Let it be the new material in each stanza
> That bridles at sense, reckless of disaster, and leaps
> Up into the less and less trustworthy air. The same
> Old phrase comes back anyway, waiting for what we say
> To be over and done, marking its time, the heavy
> Burden of the tune we carry, humming, to the grave.

Finally, as the ultimate precursor not only of this book but of my little
manual called *Rhyme's Reason*, I should cite this poem from a long cycle of
lyrics of loss and despair, all in the so-called "In Memoriam" stanza, many
of which were published over a decade later as part of *In Time and Place*.
The verses in question explicitly propound what is most often done implicitly. Brooding over both the topography and the archaeology of the prison
unto which the cycle of poems had doomed itself, the poem tries on various
tropes of the *abba* rhyme scheme for moral size. I should only add that
"Abba" in stanza 7 is Aramaic for "Father."

OTHERS WHO HAVE LIVED IN THIS ROOM

Why have I locked myself inside
This narrow cell of four-by-four,

Pacing the shined, reflecting floor
Instead of running free and wide?

Having lost you, I'd rather not
Be forced to find my way as well
In the broad darkness visible
Of prose's desert, vast and hot;

But in the shade of these four walls
Bounce the black ball of my despair
Off each in turn, and spurn the glare
Outside the cool, confining halls.

Why, then, if so ascetic, a
Rich game? Why must I always play
The stanza called *abba*
In books of *ars poetica*?

Avoiding hollow chime or cant,
The false narration and invalid
Wails of the modern form of ballad,
Less of a song and more a chant,

Accented crotchets, semi-brave
Measures of resonance will suit
Laying the painfully acute
Finalities beside the grave.

The daughters' measures may surprise,
The Mother Memory can amuse,
But *Abba*'s spirit must infuse
The form which will memorialize.

"Memorialize" . . . But who is dead?
The unstressed "and" of "wife and man"?
Its life was measured by the span
As by the act, a word unsaid

That sleeps with memory and John
Hollander's long-unpublished poem,
And will yet rise from its mute home
In textual sepulchre anon.

This rhyme of mirrored halves arose
Headless from the ashes of
Phoenix and his constant dove
Intestate else, as Shakespeare shows:

"So they loved as love in twain
Had the essence but in one;
Two distincts, division none:
Number thus in love was slain."

Sidney and Sandys when they gave alms
To Sion's muse, and called upon

Strophes that purled through Helicon,
Used it to paraphrase the Psalms;

Herbert of Cherbury employed
The same form to determine whether
Love could continue on forever
After mere bodies were destroyed,

Writing *"in her up-lifted face*
Her eyes which did that beauty crown
Were like two starrs that having faln down,
Look up again to find their place."

Our stanza with a great to-do
Warned the seducer to be wary
And thus (trochaically) by Carew
(Or, as the learned say, Carew):

"Stop the chafèd Bore, or play
With the Lyons paw, yet feare
From the Lovers side to teare
Th'Idoll of his soul away."

Then Marvell's Daphnis, turning down
His never-yielding Chloe's last
Frantic attempt to hold him fast
By finally rucking up her gown:

"Whilst this grief does thee disarm,
All th'Enjoyment of our Love
But the ravishment would prove
Of a Body dead while warm."

Filling these decorous and deep
Cups of rhyme, Jonson's "Elegy"
bnLay still; draining their melody,
Rossetti dreamed his sister's sleep.

Shores the Virgilian river laves
Crossed with the sounding of the bar
Out in the North Sea, heard afar
Graven in Keatsian beating waves;

Heard by the voice that filled these rooms
With sounds of mourning, cries of hope
Escaped love's fire, in a trope
Of marriage, memory and tombs

Of faith deceased, to which he fled
From touch not taken, half-recalled
Stillborn caresses that appalled
The poet, not the loving dead.

I, too, fill up this suite of rooms,
A bit worn now, with crowds of word,

Hoping that prosody's absurd
Law can reform the thoughts it dooms;

An emblem of love's best and worst:
Marriage (where hand to warm hand clings,
Inner lines, linked by rhyming rings);
Distance between the last and first),

This quatrain is born free, but then
Handcuffed to a new inner sound,
After what bliss it may have found
Returns to the first rhyme again.

—Not our bilateral symmetry,
But low reflecting high, as on
His fragile double poised, the swan:
What's past mirrored in what will be.

Notes

CHAPTER 1. TURNINGS AND FASHIONINGS

1. Abraham Fraunce, *The Arcadian Rhetorike* (London, 1588), A2v. George Putten-ham, *The Arte of English Poesie,* ed. Gladys Doidge Willcock and Alice Walker (Cambridge, 1936), calls schemes "auricular" and tropes "sensible" figures.

2. *Poetics* 21, and variously in book 3 of the *Rhetoric.* Taxonomies of trope and scheme are various, and sorting them out confusing. The best brief discussion of this problem is in Richard A. Lanham's *A Handlist of Rhetorical Terms* (Berkeley and Los Angeles, 1968), 101–03.

3. William Butler Yeats, "The Song of the Happy Shepherd" (also see below, pp. 58–59). The question of this kind of guile is at least as old as Longinus: "So we find that a figure [*schēma*] is always most effective when it conceals the very fact of its being a figure." *On the Sublime* 17.1, trans. W. Hamilton Fyfe, Loeb Edition.

4. Robert Browning, *The Ring and the Book,* 1.455–56. It is the voice of the British Public who taunts him thus.

5. If lying is defined as involving two persons (cf. Aristotle *Nicomachean Ethics* 5.11.1–6, on the impossibility of treating oneself unjustly because "the just and the unjust always involve more than one person"). But perhaps it might be simply observed that if it makes sense to speak of talking to oneself, then the possibility of lying in that speech is entailed.

6. Puttenham, *Arte of English Poesie,* 3.18. I have normalized long "s," "u," and "v." See also the discussion of fictions, lies, and excuses in Paul de Man, *Allegories of Reading* (New Haven, 1979), 281–86.

7. For Williams's remark, see *Contempo* 3.2 (July 25, 1937): 5, 8; Edward Mendelson pointed this out to me.

8. De Man, *Allegories of Reading,* p. 32, invokes some aspects of this as "the Cratylic illusion."

9. Erich Auerbach, "Figura," in *Scenes from the Drama of European Literature* (New York, 1959), 11–28.

10. Justus George Lawler, *Celestial Pantomime: Poetic Structures of Transcendence* (New Haven, 1979), 74.

11. See Stephen Cushman, *William Carlos Williams and the Meanings of Measure* (New Haven, 1985).

12. Robert Frost, "The Constant Symbol," from *The Poems of Robert Frost* (Modern Library Edition), xvi.

13. All the lines from Pope discussed here are from *An Essay on Criticism,* 345–84.

14. "In jeder ihrer Darstellungen sich selbst mit darstellen und überall zogleich Poesie und Poesie der Poesie sein." Friedrich Schlegel, *Athenaeum Fragments,* trans. Peter Firchow, in his *Friedrich Schlegel's Lucinde and the Fragments* (Minneapolis, 1971), 195.

15. Xenophon, "The Banquet," trans. Sarah Fielding (1762), in *Socratic Dialogues by Plato and Xenophon* (London, 1910, Everyman Edition), 192.

16. Lawler, *Celestial Pantomime,* 11–14.

17. Fred N. Robinson, Beowulf *and the Appositive Style* (Knoxville, 1985).

18. Lee Charles Edelman, *Transmemberment of Song: Hart Crane's Anatomies of Rhetoric and Desire* (Stanford, 1987).

CHAPTER 2. QUESTIONS OF POETRY

1. Aristotle, *Rhetoric* 3.18 is also a central text on the matter of interrogation. Susan J. Wolfson, in *The Questioning Presence* (Ithaca, 1986), 17–31, raises other theoretical issues worked out in rich detail in her reading of English romantic poems.

2. John Milton, "The Fifth Ode of Horace, Lib. I" ("Render'd almost word for word, without Rhyme according to the Latin Measure, as near as the Language will permit").

3. It might be added that the poem itself is Milton's own *ex voto* trophy, the result of a self-imposed task, like the common one, in the sixteenth and seventeenth centuries, of translating the Penitential Psalms into vernacular verse when one had recovered from an illness (e.g., Francis Bacon's versions of them).

4. James Michie, *The Odes of Horace* (New York, 1963), 106–09.

5. Nor is it only the additional senses of "shadows" as "players," actors or flatterers, which complicate the picture. See *The Sonnets,* ed. Stephen Booth (New Haven, 1977), 224–26.

6. But see the deployment of interrogations in Rossetti's sonnet "The Monochord" (*The House of Life,* 79), where the quatrain and tercets constitute questions.

7. For another poem almost entirely composed of questioning, see Stevens's "The American Sublime." George Herbert's poetic questions could easily occupy many pages of analysis. So could those of his great poetic descendant, Emily Dickinson. "What shall I do when the Summer troubles," poem number 956 in Johnson's edition of the *Complete Poems,* is all questions, but in a very different way from the Herbert sonnet. No. 191's query, "If Summer were an *Axiom* / What sorcery had *Snow?*" is astonishing, as is the end of No. 1712: "Whose Doom to whom?" No. 497 exemplifies her way of starting with questions, wandering away into not-quite-answer, and returning for more query. No. 1633 reveals the realm of *agon* in her questioning. And so forth.

8. See also the discussion (below, pp. 176–77) of Spenser's interrogative formula, "Who knows not X?"

9. William Blake, *Milton,* plate 41, 12–19.

10. Friedrich Nietzsche, *Beyond Good and Evil,* trans. Helen Zimmern, 2:2.

11. See also the questions asked in section 1 of the preface to *The Genealogy of Morals.*

12. Harold Bloom, *Wallace Stevens: The Poems of Our Climate* (Ithaca, 1977), 37–40.

13. Edward P. C. Corbett, *Classical Rhetoric for the Modern Student,* 2d ed. (New York, 1971), 488.

14. Puttenham, *Arte of English Poesie,* 211.

15. *Pirke Aboth,* 1.14.

16. Sometimes the ambiguous grammar of a question can shift its gesture from interrogation to ejaculation. Keats's opening line "How man bards gild the lapses of time" is clearly only the latter; but as David Bromwich has suggested, Hart Crane's opening words in "The Harbor-Dawn" section of *The Bridge,* "How many dawns . . . ," "frame an implicit

question that half-forms itself into an imperative instead; or rather crowds in, before the suspension and first fade-out, all the qualifications that will have to participate in an answer" (letter to the author).

17. Philostratus, *Imagines,* trans. Arthur Fairbanks, Loeb Edition, 83.

18. Early versions of this poem ended with the question answered: "It seems the dancer and the dance are one" (see Thomas Parkinson, *W. B. Yeats, The Later Poetry* [Berkeley and Los Angeles, 1971], 106–07) and a "How can we tell . . . ?" in the question. The revisions add force and complexity. De Man in his discussion of these lines in *Allegories of Reading,* 11–12, missed the grammatical ambiguity.

19. This sort of ambiguity generated by other features of "how" appear in Wallace Stevens's asking of mother earth, "How is it that your aspic nipples / For once vent honey?" "How is it that . . ." means both "Why?" and "By what means?" Eleanor Cook discusses these lines in her splendid study *Stevens' Wordplay* (Princeton, 1988).

20. Questions which return as refrains frequently shift their status from closed to open, from being rhetorical to being poetical, by virtue of the effects of repetition. At the very least a "Yes, but . . ." separates the repeated interrogations. Yeats does wonders with this device, from the more closed "What shall I do for pretty girls / Now my old bawd is dead?" to "'What then?' sang Plato's ghost, 'what then?'" See also the discussion of Herbert's refrain "Was ever grief like mine?," below. I wish that space permitted me to discuss Emily Dickinson's questioning refrain "But what of that?" in No. 301 ("I reason, Earth is short"), particularly in the light of Paul Celan's German translation of it, the fierce "ja und?" of his great version.

21. Section 6 of Whitman's *Song of Myself* is of interest here. The child's "What is the grass?" provokes the marvelous series of contingent answers which finally avows the memento mori implicit in the stuff of bodies in the "And now it seems to me the beautiful uncut hair of graves."

22. For a detailed discussion of this matter, see Etienne Gilson's essay in *Les Idées et les Lettres* (Paris, 1932), 9–38.

23. The ubi sunt catalogue in two stanzas of John Lydgate's poem with the refrain— possibly proverbial—"All staunt on chaung, like a midsomer roose," is also exemplary. See R. T. Davies, ed., *Medieval English Lyrics* (Evanston, Ill., 1964), 56–59, 191–93. For more on the ubi sunt questions see John Livingston Lowes, *Convention and Revolt in English Poetry* (Boston, 1919), 100. See also the poem by Samuel Hanagid (933–1056) translated by T. Carmi in the *Penguin Book of Hebrew Verse* (New York and London, 1981), 285.

CHAPTER 3. POETIC ANSWERS

1. Puttenham, *Arte of English Poesie,* 204–06.

2. Donald Davie touches on some aspects of rhetorical inquiry used not interrogatively but narratively, in a chain of questions from Henry IV Part II, 3.1. See his *Articulate Energy* (London, 1955), 49–52. Harry Levin's *The Question of Hamlet* (New York, 1959) is also most valuable in considering how modes of questioning combine to operate as a single trope.

3. In the heightened but ordinary speech in which we talk to ourselves, the tone of grievance often makes us ask a question in the imagined voice or tone of another, sometimes caricatured into a simper, and then answer it in the cadences of our own rage. This has become, indeed, a convention of modern dramatic dialogue.

4. Emily Dickinson's apocrises are as brilliant as Herbert's and far more logically fierce. Consider No. 180's question about the consequences of an arctic flower having wandered into a tropical Eden: "What then" Why nothing / Only, your interference therefrom!" Or 902: "Which choose they? Question Memory!" Or the catechism of No. 296.

5. Bloom, *Wallace Stevens*, 38.

6. Think, for example, of the story of Tiresias and the change of sex that enabled him to experience fucking both as a woman and a man; and of how, when asked by Zeus and Hera which sex enjoyed it more, he said, "Women," which caused Hera to fly into a rage and strike him blind. A male story.

7. I suppose that even this would be too problematic, if not actually Blakean, in that the "like fire" sets up complex associations in my example with its rhyming "desire" that hint of some dialectical relation, but let it pass.

8. The refrainlike quality of the answer here points to the kind of question-and-answer in some of Yeats's paired refrains: I think of "What of the hands on the Great Clock-face?" answered by "A moment more and it tolls midnight." "What cares Love for this and that?" is glossed appositively, rather than answered, by its following "Crown of gold or ring of swine," an appositive structure at work without interrogation in "The moon shone brightly" "A full moon in March." (*Collected Poems*, ed. Richard J. Finneran, 577–79). Also see below, pp. 134–35.

9. A. D. Nuttall, *Overheard by God* (London, 1980), 12–13. Also see Stanley Fish, *The Living Temple* (Berkeley and Los Angeles, 1978), 1–53.

10. Translation of C. E. Bennett, in Horace, *Odes and Epodes*, Loeb Edition, 35.

11. John Hollander, *The Figure of Echo* (Berkeley and Los Angeles, 1981).

12. Translated by Lee M. Capel, from Kierkegaard's *The Concept of Irony* (Bloomington, 1971), 23.

13. In Hollander, *Figure of Echo*, 113–32. This mode of echo, phrasal and often apparently unwitting, can even occur in the titles of speculative prose works. One might consider the relation of William Empson's *"Seven Types of Ambiguity"* to a precursive *"Seven Lamps of Architecture,"* or of Harold Bloom's *"The Anxiety of Influence"* to *"The Anatomy of Criticism."* Robert Nozick's *"Philosophical Explanations"* echoes Wittgenstein's title. But the *"Sense and Sensibilia"* of J. L. Austin was a hollow, antiallusive joke.

14. An amusing sidelight on Carew's poem (it was frequently parodied in the seventeenth century) is cast by Robert Herrick in "The Rosarie": "One ask'd me where the Roses grow? / I bade him not go seek; / But forthwith bade my Julia shew / A bud in either cheek" (i.e., made her blush by the very act of asking her to do so). This, unlike Carew's poem, is not about the whole convention, but only about blushing, with the conventionalized Julia as a topos herself.

15. An excellent discussion of this poem from another viewpoint is to be found in Barbara Herrnstein Smith's *Poetic Closure* (Chicago, 1968).

16. This is perhaps acknowledged in A. E. Housman's "Ask me no more, for fear I should reply."

CHAPTER 4. POETIC IMPERATIVES

1. A famous instance of an imperative and a jussive, combined so as to give the latter imperative force, is the duke of Wellington's response to the courtesan Harriette Wilson's attempt at half-friendly blackmail: "Publish and be damned!"

2. The extravagance, or hyperbolic tone, of imperatives becomes interestingly problematic in the case of, say, Donne's "Batter my heart, three-personed God," even as it goes on to try to be reasonable about why battering is in order. Prayer—poetic or institutionally liturgical—always poses problems of the figurative and the literal, and a theology may or may not specify how literal or figurative any predication of God may be, let alone questions of the deity's identity. Imperatives in devotional poetry seem less rhetorically complex than questions do. But they may engage deeper matters of belief, in the speakers' insistence on the literalness of what an unbeliever would call figurative.

3. Some other Stevensian imperatives will be considered shortly, but I would note here the way in which the little poem called "Nuances of a Theme of Williams" takes W. C. Williams's injunction to the morning star, "Shine alone in the sunrise to which you lend no part," and throws back to it its own first imperative: "Shine alone, shine nakedly. . ." (here with a sense of "shine *really* alone, not as Williams personifies you in that poem called El Hombre'"); then, turning an indicative to an imperative, it goes on, "Lend no part to any humanity that suffuses you in its own light," continuing to drive the lesson home, and concludes with a "Be not . . ." sentence.

4. Lucretius, *The Way Things Are,* trans. Rolfe Humphries (Bloomington, 1968), 20.

5. See Gordon Williams, *Figures of Thought in Roman Poetry* (New Haven, 1980), 299ff.

6. "On Incomprehensibility," in Firchow, *Schlegel's Lucinde and the Fragments,* 269.

7. See the extended discussion of this line below, pp. 148–57.

8. This question is addressed in chapter 8.

9. Other replacements of opening imperative by belated question which might be considered here include Hölderlin's "Dem Sonnengott," with its opening, "Wo bist du?" and, of course, Rilke's opening of the first Duino Elegy: "Wer, wenn ich schriee . . . ?"

10. Or indeed, the version of this in Emerson's "Terminus." Ultimately this goes back to Horace, 1.14.

11. I can't refrain from noting that the shift from "people" to "pupil" in these lines represents an assimilation of the earlier plural entity in the later singular, by means of a device Stevens often uses (cf. "Phoebus is dead, ephebe") and, more pointedly here, the moment in "Farewell to Florida" when "the moon / Is at the mast-head and the past is dead."

12. See my essay "Originality," *Raritan* 2.4, 22–44.

13. The proper logic of the optative might be, for "Let there be *a,*" to say something like, "Bound variable *X,* assume the value *A.*" The rhetoric of the conventional language of Euclidian or algebraic proof, "Let *x* equal *y*" is perhaps also of interest in this regard. The phrase "Let *x* equal . . ." has a significance only completed by a consequent, "Then *ax* equals . . . ," etc. If there are *no* consequences of letting *x* equal . . . , then there could have been no need or point for the "let *x* . . ." phrase at all.

14. Or, in Allen Tate's lovely version, "Tomorrow may loveless, may lovers tomorrow make love."

CHAPTER 5. GARLANDS OF HER OWN

1. William Wordsworth, letter to ?, November 1802.

2. I also hear an echo of Spenser's "Honey Bee / Working her formall roomes in wexen frame" (*The Shepheardes Calender,* "December," 68). "Formall roomes" and the later notion of a weaving "frame" were both resonant here for Wordsworth.

3. Robert Frost's "his handiwork on which / He spent himself, the labor of his ax" ("The Wood-Pile") seems a counterexample. But its quizzical, nonce quality and its deliberate use of the ambiguity ("labor of his ax" = his ax's effort + his own *by means of* the ax) are revisionary, not conventional. See Hannah Arendt, *The Human Condition* (New York, 1959), 9–10, 72–83, 146, 153.

4. Wallace Stevens, *Opus Posthumous* (New York, 1957), 36.

5. See my *Vision and Resonance* (New York, 1976), 181, 208–09.

6. See Henry Crabb Robinson, *Diary, Reminiscences and Correspondence* (New York and Cambridge, 1877), 2:223.

7. Dell H. Hymes, in "Phonological Aspects of Style: Some English Sonnets," in *Style in Language,* ed. Thomas A. Sebeok (Cambridge, 1960), 125–26, discusses the role of

the word "constrained" in the octave, and "let" (with its opposed senses of "allow" and "prevent") in this sonnet, as what he calls "key" words—those which are comprised of phonemes dominant in the rest of the poem and which have a central meaning. He also adds that three dominant consonants here, /s/, /n/, and /t/, come together in the word "sonnet." We might consider it a sort of hypogram that breaks through the surface. I note that J. Hillis Miller has discussed these sonnets in *The Linguistic Moment* (Princeton, 1986), 63–67, but his account is in no way like Hymes's linguistic one.

8. Marcel Proust, *Le Temps retrouvé* (Paris, 1927), 2:40. My translation; the original reads: "quand en rapprochant une qualité commune à deux sensations, il dégagera leur essence en les réunissant l'une et l'autre pour les sous-traire aux contingences du temps, dans une métaphor, et les enchaînera par le lien indestructible d'une alliance des mots.

9. Walt Whitman, "A Noiseless Patient Spider," *Leaves of Grass*, ed. Harold W. Blodgett and Scully Bradley (New York, 1965), 450. The editors note an earlier MS draft of the poem with a manifestly erotic dimension to the act of bridging.

10. An inevitable, more dialectical meditation on this figure of tension and constraint is Cyril Connolly's "In a perfect union the man and the woman are like a strung bow. Who is to say whether the string bends the bow, or the bow tightens the string? Yet male bow and female string are in harmony with each other, and their arrows can be aimed. Unstrung, the bow hangs aimless; the cord flaps idly." Palinurus (pseud.), *The Unquiet Grave* (New York, 1945), 20.

11. Horace, *Epodes* 3.30.1.

12. Dante Gabriel Rossetti, Letter to William Bell Scott, August 1871, quoted by W. M. Rossetti in a note to his edition of the *Works* (London, 1911), 651.

13. Lou Andreas-Salomé, *Freud Journal*, trans. Stanley A. Leavy (New York, 1964), 148.

14. Alan Ansen, *Disorderly Houses* (Middletown, Conn., 1962), 41–42.

15. Donald Hall, *The Dark Houses* (New York, 1958), 47.

16. I quote two more sonnets on the sonnet, each by a very minor nineteenth-century writer. The first, by a Rhymer's Club versifier named G. A. Greene, is palpably sleazy in its smarmy allegorizing. That by the American Richard Watson Gilder reads like a little anthology of the poems under discussion here, but is vastly better than the first. (Also see Swinburne's splendid roundel on "The Roundel," quoted below, pp. 132–33.)

THE SONNET

I hear the quatrains' rolling melody,
    The second answering back her sister's sounds
    Like a repeated music, that resounds
A second time with varying harmony:

Then come the tercets with full-voiced reply,
    And close the solemn strain in sacred bounds,
    While all the time one growing thought expounds
One palpitating passion's ecstasy.

Ah! could I hear thy thoughts so answer mine
    As quatrain echoes quatrain, soft and low,
    Two hearts in rhyme and time one golden glow;

If so two lives one music might entwine,
    What melody of life were mine and thine,
    Till song-like comes the ending all must know!

THE SONNET

What is a sonnet? 'Tis the pearly shell
That murmurs of the far-off murmuring
    sea;
A precious jewel carved most curiously;
It is a little picture painted well.
What is a sonnet? 'Tis the tear that fell
From a great poet's hidden ecstasy;
A two-edged sword, a star, a song,—ah
    me!
Sometimes a heavy-tolling funeral bell.
This was the flame that shook with Dante's
    breath,
The solemn organ whereon Milton played,
And the clear glass where Shakespeare's
    shadow falls:
A sea this is,—beware who ventureth!
For like a fiord the narrow floor is laid
Mid-ocean deep to the sheer mountain walls.

17. See appendix, pp. 236-39.

18. Tennyson, *Poems,* ed. Christopher Ricks (London, 1969), 574.

CHAPTER 6. NECESSARY HIEROGLYPHS

1. Sir Philip Sidney, *Defence of Poesie,* modernized text from Frank Kermode and John Hollander, eds., *The Oxford Anthology of English Literature* (New York and London, 1973), 1:639.

2. Sir Francis Bacon, *De Dignitate et Augmentis Scientiarum Libros ix* (1623), trans. Ellis, Spedding, and Heath in *Works* (1857–59), 2:13.

3. Emerson, "The Poet," in *Essays and Lectures,* Library of America Edition, 450. The contrary notion of an "argument-making meter" will be implicit in many of the essays in this book, particularly if "meter" is taken as synecdochal of scheme generally. Nietzsche on melody, in *The Birth of Tragedy* 6 ("Melody generates the poem out of itself by a continuous process"), can be extended to the figurative "melody" of formal patterns. And Nietzsche finds, for example, in strophic form "innumerable instances of the way the continuously generating melody scatters picture sparks all around, which in their variegation, their abrupt change, their mad precipitation, manifest a power quite unknown to the epic and its steady flow" (trans. Clifton Fadiman).

4. "Argument" (as "story" or "matter") is what the summaries of each book of the Geneva Bible are called, a usage followed by Milton at the head of every book of *Paradise Lost.* Sidney, in the *Defence,* speaks of "the philosopher setting down with thorny argument the bare rule," but it is clear that it is the thorniness that seems to give the noun here its modern logical sense.

5. Text from *The Poems of Sir Philip Sidney,* ed. W. A. Ringler (Oxford, 1962), 201. See also Ringler's discussion of the biographical background, 436–47.

6. The force of the breaking of the final couplet in this poem was first suggested to me by David Kalstone; see the beautiful analysis of this sonnet in his *Sidney's Poetry* (Cambridge, Mass., 1965), 117–24.

7. Stuart Curran, *Poetic Form and British Romanticism* (New York and Oxford, 1986), 55. An extreme, even canonical instance of this is the witty self-description of William Carlos Williams's "girl with one leg / over the rail of a balcony," discussed by Stephen

Cushman in his excellent *William Carlos Williams and the Meanings of Measure,* 48–50. The root meaning of the very metrical term—*enjambment*—determines the joke, here, the exemplary instance being employed in a deadpan way as if it were merely an ordinary use of the scheme. Lawler, *Celestial Pantomine,* 73–103, sees in many cases of enjambment an erotic trope.

8. Wallace Stevens, "On an Old Horn," *Collected Poems* (New York, 1955), 230.

9. Dwight L. Bolinger, *Intonation and Its Parts* (Stanford, 1986), 80.

10. Chiasm can have merely oratorical force—as a prominent ornament so brandished as to say, "See, I *care* to (or *dare* to, or *deign* to, or, regrettably, *stoop* to) use such an ornament, here, now, to you." Or it can point up a contrast or structure that is already there—like a dash (such as this one) used when a comma would do: thus the unidentified line quoted by Aristotle in the *Nicomachean Ethics* 2.6, "esthloi men gar haplōs, pantodapōs de kakoi" (goodness is simple, manifold, badness). It can even be somewhat less than decorative: in the "I call it death-in-life and life-in-death" of Yeats's "Byzantium" there seems to be no irony of reversal; the inversion, a literal and necessary one, has less force than the contrast of the two different senses of "in."

11. Chiasm (Puttenham calls it "counterchange") has been recently discussed in an article by Max Nänny, "Chiastic Structures in Literature: Some Forms and Functions," in *The Structure of Texts,* ed. Ugo Fries (Tübingen, 1987); he explores a wide range of chiasmatic patterns in prose as well as in verse, but his sense of "function" does not include my concern for the troping of the scheme itself. I cannot quite agree with his argument, for example, that the opening line of "Kubla Khan" is "an emblem of the perfect symmetry" of the pleasure-dome. Lawler's comments, *Celestial Pantomime,* 51–60, and those of W. K. Wimsatt, *The Verbal Icon* (New York, 1958), 159, 162–63, 181, are extremely fruitful.

12. Leon Lipson has wittily explored the use of chiasm for satiric negation in Marxist-Leninist rhetoric in a lecture which I hope he will soon publish.

13. Geoffrey Hartman, *The Fate of Reading* (Chicago, 1975), 339–40.

14. On the other hand, the just as typically Miltonic "So farewell Hope, and thus with Hope farewell / Fear . . ." would augment, rather than diminish, the force of Satan's resolution.

15. Alexander Pope, *The first Satire of the Second Book,* line 68. I am reminded by Ronald Paulson that in the 1738 "Epilogue to the Satires" Pope has a fictional antagonist quote this line with the mistaken rebuke that it was imitated from Horace, providing another layer of gloss on the matter of false claims.

16. Note that the line continues "[within him Hell / He brings], and round about him, nor from Hell / One step . . . etc."—the concentricity is pointed up even more by "round about him." Incidentally, I note that the great York Cycle play of *The Fall of Lucifer* has a chiasmatic line which is eerily Miltonic: "We that were beelded in blys in bale are we brent nowe."

17. Richard Poirier's reading of this poem in *Robert Frost: The Work of Knowing* (New York, 1977), 14–20, is indispensable. See also my remarks on the opening enjambment in *Vision and Resonance.*

18. See also, "Foolish Narcisse, that loves the watry shore," *FQ* 3.7.45.5.

19. It will be clear that I have left out of this discussion the way in which the figure of chiasm has been wildly allegorized, without any acknowledgment of the tropes into which the scheme is variously turned, by followers of Paul de Man.

CHAPTER 7. BREAKING INTO SONG

1. See below, pp. 69–70. Daryl Hine's version is from *Theocritus: Idylls and Epigrams* (New York, 1982). For a discussion of repetitive forms in pastoral generally, see Thomas G. Rosenmeyer, *The Green Cabinet* (Berkeley and Los Angeles, 1969), 93–95.

2. The problems of antecedence and possible self-referentiality in this fascinating line are considered by Nicholas Howe, *The Old English Catalogue Poems,* Anglistica 23 (Copenhagen, 1985), 199–200. Also see Morton Bloomfield, "Deor Revisited," in *Modes of Interpretation in Old English Literature,* ed. Brown et al. (Toronto, 1986), 277–78. The other Old English refrain is the line repeated once in "Wulf and Eadwacer."

3. *Figure of Echo,* 34–43. Also see Helen Louise Cohen, *Lyric Forms from France* (New York, 1922). The use of refrains in the *piyyut,* or liturgical song, of medieval Hebrew poetry, complex and allusive, often involve intricate patterns of acrostic and sometimes anaphora as well. But the role of refrain and other repetitive forms in liturgies generally is another matter, more closely related to such devices as carol burdens than to figurations and internalizations of choral or antiphonal voice that we find in the lyric poetry under investigation here.

4. Stevens, *Opus Posthumous,* 65.

5. But see the dense and delicate modulations of the patterns of paired refrain in Rossetti's "A Death-Parting."

6. More complex is the echoic situation in which a precursor refrain gets violently reinterpreted. A celebrated example of this is the case of Carew and Tennyson, the "Ask me no more" refrains discussed above, pp. 59–63.

7. Edmond Rostand's Cyrano de Bergerac composes, in the course of a duel, the famous ballade whose refrain, "A la fin de l'envoi je touche," invokes rhetorically what it will merely describe literally at the very end, when its poetic quality has arrived at literal banality and the addressee's death. This is effected, in part, by a change from the subjunctive—and a future implication—at the earlier occurrences to indicative at the end, although with the morphology of "je touche" unchanged.

8. This ambiguity of position might have been suggested to Stickney, a learned classical scholar, by that of the refrain in the first Theocritus idyll. But it is the allegorization of the ambiguity of before-and-after which matters here.

9. The syntactic ambiguity is threefold. (1) "It's autumn in the country that I remember." (2) "I remember that it's autumn in the (that) country." (3) "It's autumn in the country: I remember / How warm a wind," etc. Throughout most of the poem, (2) and (1) seem to combine in some way. Donald Wesling kindly pointed out to me that I had not emphasized the relations of (1) and (2) clearly enough.

10. We might schematize this repetitive pattern. R, as $R = f (r + x_1, r + x_2, r + x_3, \ldots)$, where x is the varying predicate and r the invariant material.

11. Song of Solomon 4 : 9, 10, 12; 5 : 1, 2, etc. A sister figure is a sort of muse throughout Stickney's poetry.

12. See "The Sound of the Music of Music and Sound," in *Wallace Stevens: A Celebration,* ed. Frank Doggett and Robert Buttel (Princeton, 1980), 248–50.

13. This gradual accumulation of the varying refrain lines, all ending in "[some verb] his praise," I have analyzed in *The Figure of Echo,* 37–41.

CHAPTER 8. SPENSER'S UNDERSONG

1. There may be futher allusion in the resonance of "blissful bower" early in the strophe. See my *Figure of Echo,* 83–84.

2. In conversation and in an unpublished lecture. I should acknowledge Angus Fletcher's assistance on Spenserian matters generally; I should also like to express gratitude to Harry Berger, Kenneth Gross, and Joseph Loewenstein for what they have written about *Prothalamion.* Lawrence Manley reminded me, in his beautiful essay "Spenser and the City: The Minor Poems" (*MLQ* 43, no. 3 [1984]: 223–27) that "the Orphic Poet who civilized with his song, it was said, possessed as well the power to halt the flow of rivers."

3. This matter returns in grim form with the description, at the beginning of Conrad's "Heart of Darkness," of "the interminable waterway" of the Thames, "leading to the uttermost ends of the earth," running from its own early days of tribal dark under Roman occupation, to its late days of imperial grandeur, nevertheless seeming to "lead into the heart of an immense darkness."

4. The intricate numerical structure of *Epithalamion,* the mythographic pattern, and the correspondence of the positive and negative occurrences (those with a "no" or "nor" or "Not" in them) of the refrain to the relative number of hours of dark and daylight on Spenser's midsummer wedding-day are detailed in Hieatt's *Short Time's Endless Moment* (New York, 1960). Also, see Alastair Fowler, *Spenser and the Numbers of Time* (New York, 1964), 175, on *Prothalamion.*

5. David Quint, *Origins and Originality in Renaissance Literature* (New Haven, 1983), esp. 133–66. This topos appears in poetry from Henry Vaughan's poem to the river Usk through Fernando Pessoa's heteronymic Alberto Caeiro, who rejects the conventional Tagus of Portuguese tradition for his own local little river. I think also of the river in Browning's *Pauline,* ll. 768–80, joining "its parent river with a shout," that parent probably being Shelley.

6. Francis Bacon, *The Advancement of Learning* 1.5.3.

7. John Milton, *Areopagitica,* in *Complete Poems and Selected Prose,* ed. Merritt Y. Hughes (New York, 1957), 739.

8. James Macpherson, *Fragments of Ancient Poetry,* ed. John J. Dunn (Berkeley and Los Angeles, 1966), 77.

9. Tennyson, *Poems,* ed. Ricks, 1084.

10. *F.Q.* 4.11.41. In the tenth canto (stanza 15) of the same book, a river is an inducement to the making of art. On the way to Venus's Temple, there "goodly rockes, and stones of rich assay / Cast into sundry shapes by wondrous skill . . . And underneath, the river rolling still / With murmure soft, that seem'd to serve the workmans will."

11. Vallans is indeed one of those Spenserian followers who will also echo his famous line about "tuning" his poetry to "the water's fall." See below, p. 162.

12. Indeed, a Spenserian scholar of the older school—H. S. V. Jones, in *A Spenser Handbook* ([New York, 1930], 18)—remarks of a particular stanza of *Daphnaïda,* which I consider later, that it is "suggestive of Elizabethan music with its counterpoint and undersong," no doubt believing *undersong* to be a technical musical term, which it is not. Jones can only have misunderstood Spenser's own refrain in that stanza.

13. The "greene" is hardly "for maydens meete": this sarcasm is only one of Willye's many cutting moves.

14. Samuel Taylor Coleridge, "To the Author of Poems Published Anonymously at Bristol in September 1795." I note with interest the allusively Spenserian use of "tune to"—as in tuning one's playing or singing to the fall of water—as here adapted in the opening addressing the bard "whose verse concise yet clear / Tunes to smooth melody unconquer'd sense."

15. Lines 21–25. How very problematic this interruption is may depend upon whether "wrought" is transitive or, most uncommonly, intransitive here.

16. Further Spenserian allusion in later occurrences of *undersong* and its derivatives remains interesting, and I wish I had time here to go into D. G. Rossetti's "while Love breathed in sighs and silences / Through two blent sould one rapturous undersong" (*The House of Life,* 13) and William Morris's lines from "August" on the leaves on the apple bough: "In the mute August afternoon? They trembled to some undertune / Of music in the silver air."

17. For enduringly fine discussions of Wordsworth's relation to *Prothalamion* see Geoffrey Hartman, *Wordsworth's Poetry* (New Haven, 1964), 267–68 (and, on the river Duddon

sonnets, 335–37). Edward Stein, in his forthcoming study of Wordsworthian allusion generally is very perceptive. I should note here the central trope, from Denham's *Cooper's Hill* (1642) on, of a river's bosom bearing upon it a blazon of what it reflects from its banks. This is central at the beginning of *The Prelude*, as it is in Pope's *Windsor Forest*, William Cowper's river Ouse receiving "on its bosom" the image of his now-felled poplar grove, or even Hawthorne (in the preface to *Mosses from an Old Manse:* "the slumbering river has a dream-picture in its bosom," although here, the figure is internalized from reflection ("*on* its bosom") to something more abstract and secret "in its bosom." But it is with rivery auditions, rather than visions, that I am concerned here.

18. Pamela Schirmeister has pointed out to me Henry James's metaphor of the river as inspiration, in the New York Edition preface to "The Aspern Papers":

> Nothing is so easy as improvisation, the running on and on of invention; it is sadly compromised, however, from the moment its stream breaks bound and gets into flood. Then the waters may spread indeed, gathering houses and herds and crops and cities into their arms and wrenching off, for our amusement, the whole face of the land—only violating by the same stroke our sense of the course and the channel, which is our sense of the uses of a stream and the virtue of a story. [Library of America Edition, p. 1184]

The power of the stream in flood also allegorizes what in romance James loved and feared—he continues in this passage by exemplifying improvisation by *The Arabian Nights*.

CHAPTER 9. THE FOOTING OF HIS FEET

1. Wordsworth may have perceived this set of relationships. In *The Prelude* (1850, 1.166–85) he considers the notion of taking up something left undone by Milton; later on, at 3.278–85, he invokes Milton, Chaucer, and—in an atmosphere of *Il Penseroso*— "Sweet Spenser, moving through his clouded heaven."

2. Antithetical to this is the blocking quality of "others' feet"—with a clear pun on the metrical term—in the first sonnet of Sidney's *Astrophel and Stella* (in alexandrines, incidentally): "Invention, Nature's child, fled Stepdame Study's blows; / And others' feet still seemed but strangers in my way," the implication being that when they were no longer strangers, they would no longer block his path.

3. See also "the sage / And serious doctrine of Virginity" (*Comus*, 785–86). Milton is quoted from the edition of Merritt Y. Hughes (New York, 1957). But the epithet is Spenser's own, both in "The laurell, meed of mighties conquerors / And poets sage" (*FQ* 1.1.9) and, perhaps even more significantly here, the palmer is for Guyon in book 2 "a sage and sober sire" (2.1.7.7).

4. John Guillory, *Poetic Authority* (New York, 1983), 90–93, 132–39.

5. Kenneth Gross, "Spenser and the Early Poetry of Milton," *PMLA* 98:1 (1983): 22–27.

6. These didactic examples from my *Rhyme's Reason: A Guide to English Verse* (New Haven, 1981), 11. It should be observed that couplets of poulter's measure were often printed as ballad stanzas, with lines of 6, 6, 8, and 6 syllables. For a spirited treatment of the *alexandrin* in French verse, see Jacques Roubaud, *La Vieillesse d'Alexandre* (Paris, 1978), 7–59; also see the discussion in my *Vision and Resonance*, 2d ed. (New Haven, 1985), 150–53.

7. *A Paradyse of Dayntye Devises* (1578) has two poems in alexandrines; *The Gallery of Gallant Inventions* has four (one alternating with pentameters); *England's Parnassus* (1600) has a poem beginning, "Of Nepture war was made by Æolus and his traine," in blank alexandrines and credited, interestingly enough, to "Edm. Spencer." Surrey inserted

alexandrines at M. 30, 714, and 832 of his translation of *Aeneid* 4; the last one closes Dido's lament.

8. There is an alexandrine at the first line of the lament stanza in "November." The closing of "January," by the way, was crucial for Milton, who echoed it in a most complex fashion at the end of *Lycidas*. See my *Figure of Echo*, 128n.

9. The *genius loci* invoked by Drayton in the first song of *Poly-Olbion*, 8–25, might almost be Spenser as precursor. For Donne's guarded Spenserian formal echo, see the stanza form of "The Progresse of the Soule," that strange poem which declares itself to be, at the end of its first stanza, "A worke t'outweare *Seths* pillars, bricke and stone, / And (holy writt excepted) made to yeeld to none"; also, "The Valediction: Of the Book," "The Anniversarie," "An Epithalamion Made at Lincolnes Inn." For Jonson, see *The Underwood*, 23, 25; the "Epithalamion, or a Song" (number 75) is most interesting in its evasive allusion to Spenser: the twenty-four (hourly?) stanzas, all ending in alexandrines, start out with what seems to be a conscious look at their own belatedness with respect to the midsummer date of Spenser's great precursor poem ("Though thou has past thy summer standing, stay / Awhile with us, bright sun, and help our light").

10. John Dryden, *The Conquest of Granada*, 4.2.460–62. See Conrad A. Balliet, "The History and Rhetoric of the Triplet," *PMLA* 80 (1965): 528–34.

11. This line is translated by Dryden later on as "and night, with sable shades, involves his head" (*Aeneid* 4.1199).

12. It should also be observed that Pope himself, in the *Epistle to Augustus*, could not resist a bit of "representative versification" in this triplet: "Waller was smooth; but Dryden taught to join / The varying verse, the full resounding line, / The long majestic march, and energy divine." Dryden's word had been "majestic" to characterize the alexandrine and the alexandrine just quoted seems to be central to Pope's conception of it. See also Pope's letter to Cromwell dated 11/25/1710. Pope's couplet with the fast alexandrine in the *Essay* on "swift Camilla" translates, very swiftly indeed, Virgil's four lines (5.808–11); the word "skims" seems to come from Dryden's earlier translation of the same verses.

13. The "Goe, little booke," itself a Chaucerian echo, is discussed in its imperative aspect, above, pp. 176–78. A. C. Hamilton reminds me that 144, the number of syllables in both sets of verses, was the number of cubits of the wall of the New Jerusalem (Rev. 21 : 17).

14. The poetic significance for the older Spenser of rivers and streams, of moving water as a conceptual accompaniment of various sorts to poetic utterance, is discussed above, pp. 148–57.

15. Spenser was undoubtedly working from the French, not from van der Noot's Dutch versions; in any case, that rendering of the du Bellay line, "Mengdé haer clachte oock met des waters getire," is a Dutch alexandrine, but the Marot line in question, "Maer Nimphen gent songhen daer met genuchte," is a pentameter and could not, had Spenser seen it, have suggested an alexandrine. The Petrarch passage (*Rime* 323) is simply "ma ninfe et muse a quel tenor cantando."

16. See for example Drayton's *Quest of Cynthia* (1627): "Tuning to the waters fall / The small birds sang to her"; also, *Pastorals* (1619), Eclogue 3: "And let them set to gather all / Time keeping with the waters fall"; also, George Wither, *A Satyre:* "There to my fellow Shepheards will I sing, / Tuning my *Reed* unto some dancing *Spring*"; "The Sheepheards Sunne" (probably by Anthony Munday) in *England's Helicon:* "Take hands then Nimphes and Sheepheards all, / And to those Rivers musique fall / Sing true love, and chast love begins our Festivall" (and note the alexandrine closure). I count three more instances in Drayton, and six in William Browne. We may even consider, I think, Marlowe's lines from "The Passionate Sheepheard to his Love" (also from *England's Helicon*), "Seeing the Sheepheards feed theyr flocks, / By shallow Rivers, to whose falls, / Melodious byrds sing Madrigalls," as another instance.

17. Milton's echo may be reinforced by others: the pseudo-Spenserian *Britain's Ida* (1628) by Phineas Fletcher starts out, "In *Ida's vale*, (who knows not *Ida's vale?*)." Also see Joseph Hall, *Virgidemiarum* (1597), 3.6. In any case, the scene on Acidale was a sensitive one for Milton, for he echoes one of its lines in a crucial situation (see my *Figure of Echo*, 67). All of these may be traced back to Ovid's description of Arion as master of the lyre, followed by "quod mare non novit, quae nescit Ariona tellus?" (What sea, what land knows not Arion?). The rhetorical strategy seems to demand first something about *X* and then asking, "Who knows not X?" See above, pp. 18–40.

18. Pope, "Epistle to Dr. Arbuthnot," 165–66.

CHAPTER 10. DALLYING NICELY WITH WORDS

1. Marie Borroff, *Language and the Poet* (Chicago, 1979).

2. I. A. Richards, *The Philosophy of Rhetoric* (New York, 1936), 47–66.

3. Trans. Firchow, *Friedrich Schlegel's Lucinde and the Fragments*, 50.

4. See James Nohrnberg, *The Analogy of The Faerie Queene* (Princeton, 1976), 607; also Patricia Parker, *Inescapable Romance* (Princeton, 1979), 93. A. C. Hamilton's notes to his edition of the poem (London, 1977) are full of such observations.

5. Quintilian, *Institutes* 1.5.53.

6. Wimsatt, *The Verbal Icon*, 153–66; William Harmon, "Rhyme in English Verse: History, Structures, Functions," *Studies in Philology* 84:365–93.

7. See also my remarks on this poem from a different point of view in *Vision and Resonance*, 131.

8. Joseph H. Summers, *George Herbert: His Religion and Art* (Cambridge, Mass., 1954), 138–39, discusses this poem acutely and fruitfully.

9. *Vision and Resonance*, 125.

10. Stanley Fish, *Surprised by Sin: The Reader in "Paradise Lost"* (Berkeley and Los Angeles, 1967); Davie, *Articulate Energy*.

11. E. R. Curtius, *European Literature and the Latin Middle Ages*, trans. Willard R. Trask (New York, 1953), 495–500.

12. Several discussions of this poem seem to miss the etymological trope here, although James Milroy, in *The Language of Gerard Manley Hopkins* (London, 1977), 90, is interesting on "folded," and his whole book is of great value. There is generally more interest in "especial" as designating *haeccitas*, e.g., F. R. Leavis, "Metaphysical Isolation," in the Kenyon Critics, *Gerard Manley Hopkins* (New York, 1945), 121–23; Norman H. MacKenzie, *A Reader's Guide to Gerard Manley Hopkins* (Ithaca, 1981), 107–10; and Paul Mariani, *Commentary on the Complete Poems of Gerard Manley Hopkins* (Ithaca, 1970), 128–30.

CHAPTER 11. THE POETICS OF CHARACTER

1. Martin Price, *Forms of Life* (New Haven, 1983); John Burt, "Romance, Character and the Bounds of Sense," pts. 1 and 2, *Raritan* 5.2 and 5.3.

2. For prime example, John Bayley, whose astute remarks on the concept of literary character at a Lionel Trilling Seminar at Columbia in 1984 provided the occasion for some comments of mine that led to these pages. They appeared as the title essay of his *The Order of Battle at Trafalgar* (New York, 1987), 7–18.

3. Alasdair MacIntyre, *After Virtue*, 2d ed. (Notre Dame, Ind., 1984), 27.

4. The Greek word for a "character" or "person" of a drama or Platonic dialogue is *prosōpon*, in analogous extension of the word for "face," "aspect," "expression," through a sense of "mask." In discussing what is usually translated as "character" (*ēthē*) in Aristotle's

Poetics (notably 6.24 and 15) it is very easy for the reader of an English translation to slip into misconstruing "character" as *dramatis persona*. A *persona* embodies, reveals, bears *ēthē*, but a person is not, in that sense, "a character." See also the *Rhetoric* 2.12.16. Consider also how the title of William Hazlitt's *Characters of Shakespeare's Plays* (1817–18) does not refer to dramatis personae.

5. The extension of the Theophrastan sketch in La Bruyère's *Caractères de Théophraste traduits au grec, avec les Caractères our les Moeurs de ce siècle* (1688) is certainly an instance of "characters or codes," again in the moral sense of the latter. The title of Shaftesbury's *Characteristics of Men, Manners, Opinions, Times* is likewise significant in this regard, as is *Characteristics,* the one given by Hazlitt to his aphorisms.

6. Pamela Schirmeister has explored the notion of the character of place in romance much more fully, particularly in regard to Hawthorne and James, in her recently completed Yale dissertation, "The Topology of Romance."

CHAPTER 12. THE PHILOSOPHER'S CAT

1. Wallace Stevens, "Adagia," in *Opus Posthumous,* 166.
2. Dante Alighieri, *La Vita Nuova* 36, trans. Thomas Okey, Temple Classics Edition.
3. Søren Kierkegaard, *Either/Or,* trans. David F. Swenson and Lillian Marvin Swenson (New York, 1959), 1:31.
4. Ludwig Wittgenstein, *Culture and Value,* trans. Peter Winch (Chicago, 1980), pp. 24e, 34e.
5. René Descartes, *Discourse on Method and Other Writings,* trans. Arthur Wollaston (Baltimore, 1964), 122.
6. Ludwig Wittgenstein, *Zettel* #616, trans. G. E. M. Anscombe (Berkeley and Los Angeles, 1967), p. 108e.
7. See above, p. 112.
8. But Plato, *Republic* 10.607B, maintains that the *diaphora,* or quarrel, was of ancient lineage.
9. Socrates in his famous abuse of poetry in the *Ion* (533D, E; 536A) would get nowhere in his argument without reducing the content of poetry to chanted and decorated instruction manuals, but this is barely worth observing. More interesting is the misplaced trope of the chain of magnetized iron rings: for all post-Renaissance poetry, it applies more to the possession of followers by precursors. Thus all poets are, in their way, rhapsodes of some Homer, the new text being the mode of performance.
10. John Milton, *Paradise Lost,* 2.868–70.
11. Derek Parfit, *Reasons and Persons* (Oxford, 1984), ix.
12. A crucial question would seem to be, "What was the [exemplary] cat's name?" And as far as exemplary cats are concerned, I much prefer to think about one of Schopenhauer's: "I know quite well that anyone would regard me as mad if I seriously assured him that the cat, playing just now in the yard, is still the same one that did the same jumps and tricks there three hundred years ago; but I also know that it is much more absurd to believe that the cat of today is through and through and fundamentally an entirely different one from the cat of three hundred years ago." (*The World as Will and Representation,* trans. E. F. J. Payne [New York, 1958], 2:482.] The central cat of poetic meditation, rather than of technical philosophy, is, of course, Montaigne's: "When I am playing with my cat, who knows whether she have more sport in dallying with me, than I have in gaming with hir? We entertain one another with mutuall apish tricks. If I have my houre to begin or refuse, so hath she hirs." (*Apology for Raymond de Sebonde,* in Florio's translation.) It is almost impossible to feel of this cat that she is notional.
13. Descartes, *Meditation* 2, trans. Wollaston, 113.

14. Ovid, *Metamorphoses,* trans. Rolfe Humphries (Bloomington, 1961), 370.

15. St. Augustine, "The Immortality of the Soul" 5.5, trans. Ludwig Shopp, in *Writings of St. Augustine* (New York, 1947) 2:25. The wax example may go back to Aristotle, *De Anima* 2.1.412b and 2.12.424a. I do not believe that *Metaphysics* 1035a 9–22, nor even Plato, *Theatetus,* 193b–194 are relevant, though.

16. And see Longinus, *On the Sublime* 32.3–4 on such qualifications.

17. Stanley Cavell, *The Claim of Reason* (Oxford and New York, 1979), 71.

18. An important discussion of this simile is by Geoffrey Hartman in *Beyond Formalism* (New Haven, 1970), 117–19.

19. Wittgenstein, *Culture and Value,* 41e.

20. Ibid., 11e.

21. Friedrich Schlegel, *Athenaeum Fragments, #*206. I have adapted slightly the translation of Peter Firchow in his edition, p. 189. A not impossible precursor of this aphorism, given the admiration of Goldsmith in Germany, is in *The Vicar of Wakefield,* chapter 20; George Primrose, recounting his days as an aspiring hack writer, says, "The whole learned world, I made no doubt, would rise to oppose my systems; but then I was prepared to oppose the whole learned world. Like the porcupine, I sat self-collected, with a quill pointed against every opposer"—he had just referred to his writing quill.

22. Descartes, *Discourse on Method,* 2, trans. Wollaston, 49.

23. James Shirley, "Song" from *The Contention of Ajax and Ulysses.*

24. J. L. Austin, "Pretending," in *Philosophical Papers,* ed. J. O. Urmson and G. J. Warnock (Oxford, 1961), 207 and note.

25. Wallace Stevens, *The Necessary Angel* (New York, 1965), 32.

26. Austin, *Philosophical Papers,* 163.

Index